# TEL-AVIV,
## THE FIRST CENTURY

An Israel Studies Book

*Israel Studies* is sponsored by the Ben-Gurion Research Institute for the Study of Israel and Zionism, Ben-Gurion University of the Negev, and the Schusterman Center for Israel Studies, Brandeis University.

# TEL-AVIV,
## THE FIRST CENTURY

### VISIONS, DESIGNS, ACTUALITIES

*Edited by*
*Maoz Azaryahu and S. Ilan Troen*

**INDIANA UNIVERSITY PRESS**
*Bloomington & Indianapolis*

This book is a publication of

Indiana University Press
601 North Morton Street
Bloomington, Indiana 47404-3797 USA

iupress.indiana.edu

*Telephone orders*   800-842-6796
*Fax orders*   812-855-7931

⊖ The paper used in this publication
meets the minimum requirements of the
American National Standard for Information Sciences—Permanence of Paper
for Printed Library Materials, ANSI
Z39.48–1992.

Manufactured in the United States of
America

Library of Congress Cataloging-
in-Publication Data

Tel-Aviv, the first century : visions, designs,
actualities / edited by Maoz Azaryahu and
S. Ilan Troen.
      p. cm. — (An Israel studies book)
   Includes bibliographical references and
index.
   ISBN 978-0-253-35694-9 (cloth : alk.
paper) — ISBN 978-0-253-22357-9 (pbk. :
alk. paper) 1. Tel Aviv (Israel) 2. Tel Aviv
(Israel)—History. 3. Tel Aviv (Israel)—Intellectual life. 4. Tel Aviv (Israel)—Buildings, structures, etc. 5. Cities and towns—
Israel. I. Azaryahu, Maoz. II. Troen, S.
Ilan (Selwyn Ilan), [date]
   DS110.T34T45 2012
   956.94'805—dc23
                                    2011019104

1 2 3 4 5  17 16 15 14 13 12

*for Natan Aridan*

כי יש אדם שעמלו בחכמה ובדעת ובכשרון (קהלת ב:21)

*For there is man who does his work with
wisdom, knowledge and skill*

(ECCLESIASTES 2:21)

# CONTENTS

# PREFACE

This volume has multiple origins. It began with an invitation by the editors of *Israel Studies*, Ilan Troen and Natan Aridan, to Maoz Azaryahu to prepare a special issue of the journal on the occasion of the centenary of the city. Both Azaryahu and Troen have long been interested in urban history and in Tel-Aviv in particular. Troen began his career studying the urban history of the United States and shifted the focus of his scholarship after immigrating to Israel. Azaryahu is an established cultural geographer who has researched a number of issues that repeatedly brought him back to study the city in which he lives and loves. While Azaryahu took responsibility for the special issue, he and Troen collaborated on an international symposium held at Brandeis University in March 2009 that brought together several of the authors of the special issue along with other scholars. This volume is a culling of the articles published in the special issue and of those given at the symposium and subsequently reworked for publication. During this process, the editors were ably and generously assisted by Natan Aridan, a productive and original scholar in his own right and the managing editor of the journal *Israel Studies*. It is in recognition for his contributions to the success of the project that this volume is dedicated to him.

The volume easily could have been larger. Tel-Aviv has emerged as a central topic in the study of Israel. It embodies many elements that fascinate students of Israel: Zionist ideologies; Arab-Jewish relations; ethnic issues; gender studies; literature and art; commemoration and celebration; as well as a host of social and physical problems and pathologies; issues of planning and preservation, and so on. This volume represents the richness and variety of an extraordinarily vigorous body of contemporary scholarship. We are also certain that much more is to come and thereby believe that this volume will be appreciated as a pioneering effort in sharing with colleagues and other readers what excites the imagination of those engaged in the study of Tel-Aviv and Israel.

*Maoz Azaryahu*    *Ilan Troen*
*Tel-Aviv, Israel*     *Waltham, MA, USA*

# INTRODUCTION: TEL-AVIV
# IMAGINED AND REALIZED

## S. Ilan Troen

The interest in Tel-Aviv is no longer a parochial pursuit engaging residents of a city on the eastern shores of the Mediterranean. It has become a central topic for those who wish to understand Israel itself. Since the 1930s, metropolitan Tel-Aviv has constituted at least one-third of the Yishuv, i.e., the Jewish settlement in Mandatory Palestine, and later of the State of Israel. As such, it is not only the first Hebrew city established in nearly two millennia; it became, in but one century, one of the major centers of Jewish life in all of Jewish history. As this book suggests, the impact of Tel-Aviv on the intellectual, artistic, economic, and political life of Israel is beyond simple measure. It is for this reason that this volume brings together scholars in the areas of cultural studies, art history, sociology, anthropology, women's studies, Hebrew literature, social and economic history, geography, architecture, and town planning.

Tel-Aviv is where most of the Hebrew press and book publishers are located. It is the center of art, theatre, and communications. It is the location of most of the foreign embassies in Israel. It is where Israel's stock market, banks, and most major companies are headquartered. Even the *kirya,* Israel's Pentagon, is located in Tel-Aviv, rather than Jerusalem, the country's formal capital. It is the major point of entry and exit between Israel and the rest of the world. Tel-Aviv is Israel's global city.

Despite these perhaps obvious observations, Tel-Aviv has long been a neglected topic in scholarship on Israel and by Israelis in general. This requires explanation. Students of France must be familiar with Paris, as are students of Britain with London, and so on. The lack of scholarship on Tel-Aviv, until recently, may be due to several reasons.[1] I will offer two here: the first concerns the salience of Jerusalem in the Jewish world and imagination, and the second reflects the primacy of the kibbutz as the paramount symbol of Zionist achievement.

For many, Jerusalem is the iconic city of the Jewish state. Its glorified status echoes that of other major cities of the ancient world. The Greeks, Romans, and Jews placed the centers of their national religion in the mountains at some distance from the commercial centers on the coast. This was true of Athens and Piraeus, Rome and Ostia, Jerusalem and Jaffa. Cities on the coast, on the *via maris,* were far more vulnerable than those enjoying the natural protection afforded by venues in the mountains. The sacred centers and institutions of the nation's religion were thus located in the fastness of the mountain strongholds. The coastline of the Mediterranean, however, was the natural locale of commercial and cultural interchange.

As this plays out today, Jerusalem is not at the junction of world trade routes, has no economic hinterland, and is not a significant center for industry (except for tourism and pilgrimages). The city houses government offices, educational institutions, and centers for health care. Indeed, Jerusalem is a financial drain on the national economy requiring massive transfers of capital to maintain a large population that includes many unproductive citizens. Yet, it is Israel's capital by virtue of historic and traditional symbolism centering on national cults or the cult of nationalism.

In reality, Tel-Aviv is the true capital in the spheres relevant to the creation and maintenance of modern states. That recognition is taking hold in contemporary scholarship. Moreover, particularly younger academics who have made the city their home have turned to examining where they live and recognize that Tel-Aviv is the center of national culture.

My second observation is that a good argument could be made that our attention should be fixed on another centennial, that of the kibbutz, the unique form of Zionist settlement that has played an enormous role in the creation of Israel. The year 2010 marked the centenary of the founding of the "*kvutza*" or collective agricultural colony at Degania— the mother kibbutz. Central icons of modern Israel have long privileged the kibbutz and the kibbutznik who heralded and made possible the reestablishment of the Jewish people in their ancient homeland, and who have contributed so much to its defense.

At approximately the same time when a small group of idealistic Zionist settlers, imbued with socialist ideals and Zionist ideology, established Degania at *Umm Junni* near the Jordan River and the Sea of Galilee, another relatively small group of Jewish bourgeoisie, similarly committed to Zionism, organized to create an urban colony on the sand dunes north of Jaffa. The Degania centenary is being marked in other publications and conferences but is arguably less significant than marking the establishment and history of the first intentionally Jewish city in two thousand years.

To evaluate the kibbutz at its centenary is to engage in assessing decline, determining its causes, and speculating on a future. Moreover, the reality is that relatively few Israelis actually settled on a kibbutz. The high point of the kibbutz membership relative to the country's total Jewish population was in 1946–1947 when perhaps seven percent of the Jews in Palestine lived on kibbutzim. Contrary to much of Zionist ideology, the majority of Jews came to Palestine to build and live in cities. Most were also expectant capitalists rather than committed socialists.

Although the temptation stimulated by any centennial is to engage in celebration and a positive consideration of the future, there are aspects of Tel-Aviv's past and present that are worthy subjects of critical attention. Not everything turned out as expected, a common occurrence in human affairs. Nor did those who dreamed of Tel-Aviv always have a workable dream.

The frame that we will employ in this centennial volume is expressed in the subtitle: *Visions, Designs, and Actualities.* Note that we have placed "visions" and "designs" in plural. There is no one vision or design about Tel-Aviv. Understanding the diversity of visions and experiences is necessary for evaluating what actually transpired. Labor Zionism may have had primacy but not control over the Zionist movement from the late 1930s and through the June 1967 war. Moreover, Labor Zionism was a far more powerful presence in the countryside than in urban centers where it competed with liberal and bourgeois parties. This reformulation of the city's mythology is a necessary first step in appreciating the pluralism that is inherent in the city's history.[2]

The name Tel-Aviv is Nahum Sokolov's translation into Hebrew of Herzl's *Altneuland,* the title of his utopian novel, originally written in German in 1902, which so stirred the hearts and minds of masses of

Jews. Herzl imagined a splendid modern city that was surely Haifa, then a sparsely settled town that existed only in outline opposite the bay from the more substantial ancient Akko. In Herzl's novel, nearly all the actors or heroes are readily identifiable as members of his own circle of Central European Jews. As one critic has commented, *Altneuland* "resembles a contemporary Viennese melodrama" suffused with the dreams of Hugo von Hofmannsthal's poetry and the mood of Gustav Mahler's music.[3] The novel's primary settings are the salons of Europe and of Palestine. Conversation is permeated with the social and political ideas that informed planning for the new society. Drawn from a large fund of European reform thought, these ideas were no doubt familiar and congenial to educated, urban, Jewish bourgeois readers. It is no wonder then that the fledgling city would spawn a symphony orchestra, colonies of artists and writers, dreams of an opera house on European standards, and probably more cafés per capita than could be found even in Vienna itself. Indeed it was once suggested that the seal of the city should feature the Casino, a pink-colored combination coffeehouse and gambling establishment centrally situated on the promenade alongside Tel-Aviv's shore. Instead, city leaders chose a conventional beacon on a tower intended to light the way for the hoped-for masses of immigrants whose destination was Palestine.

The actual visionary who served as mayor and spokesman for this Jewish middle-class utopia has left his name in a central area of modern Tel-Aviv: Meir Dizengoff. His vision for Tel-Aviv was a product of his life experience. He came from Odessa to set up a factory on the coast for the manufacture of glass bottles for the wine produced in the vineyards planted by Baron Rothschild. Dizengoff's initial venture failed, but as long-term mayor he remained a visionary who articulated in entrepreneurial terms what Tel-Aviv should and must become. He imagined Tel-Aviv in the context of the commercial and industrial cities that were springing up across the Western world. He intended for Tel-Aviv to be modeled on the best of them and counted among the most successful. Rather than imagining European Jews as peasants working the semi-arid Palestinian countryside, he envisioned an urban society rooted in modern capitalism.

A popular figure, Dizengoff (and his successor mayors, who shared the same ideals and political preferences) succeeded in shaping the city as a haven for Zionist immigrants who saw no contradiction between Zionism and bourgeois expectations. He argued that unless Jews could find in Palestine the same standard of living and amenities found in western European societies, the country would not be able to attract large numbers of immigrants nor retain those who came. This fundamentally capitalistic ideology shaped not only the city's economy and politics but left its mark on architecture and the physical layout of the city.

Despite this capitalist influence, thousands of pioneers, especially those who arrived after World War I, would create an alternative Tel-Aviv through the socialist vision they shared. This influx of immigrants, beginning in the 1920s, was so large that there was serious overcrowding. In the early years some had to live in tents along the beach. These pioneers had to rely on their own resources and their labor union—the Histadrut. They drew on a world of thought that was deeply infused with the moral vision and technical concepts associated with radical European planning, especially the garden city movement and municipal socialism. They consciously imitated the housing reforms of "Red Vienna," in the years after World War I and prior to the rise of Hitler, as an inspiring and explicit model for action and design.

In effect, they created settlements that were the urban equivalent of the agrarian kibbutz. Their workers' housing estates were far more successful and lasted longer than the famous co-ops built by their brethren who emigrated to Manhattan, Brooklyn, and Queens and who faced similar problems at the same time. They created vital and genuine communal housing estates in the middle of Tel-Aviv as well as what were proximate suburbs—Shchunat Borochov and Kiryat Avodah, now absorbed into Givatayim and Holon of the Tel-Aviv metropolitan region. Composed of like-minded individuals who shared the same socialist ideals, they established patterns of democratic governance and a network of social organizations and educational institutions designed to propagate and perpetuate socialist values. Modeled on the Viennese *Wohnhöfe* that bore the names of Karl Marx and Rosa Luxembourg, they featured courtyards, or *Höfe*, i.e., open space surrounded by dwellings for workers. By design, they turned their backs on the corrupt, bourgeois city while focusing the attention of the residents on shared internal space. In these compounds, they provided for libraries, kindergartens and schools, health centers, meeting halls, recreation spaces, and the like.

In this way, they hoped to nurture working-class solidarity in a discrete universe by creating the "Histadrut experience." Their objective was a total environment, a *Gesamtkultur* that would nurture and sustain collective values.

The results were modest. Congestion and privation remained common and served to nourish the imagination of Hebrew authors who often commented on a society of crowded apartment dwellers taking in boarders. The constant movement of individuals and families, *me'dira le'dira* (from apartment to apartment), as epitomized by the title of Shmuel Agnon's 1939 literary classic, captures aspects of a Tel-Aviv not envisaged by Herzl or Dizengoff.

These competing realities, drawing on contrary expectations and ideas, reflected not just political and class differences, but deep cultural ones. Indeed, the pluralism of Palestine's pioneers mirrored what they dreamed of in Europe. One can find in Tel-Aviv all the divisions so manifest in Europe between and among secular and religious, traditional and modern, conservative and radical, eastern European and western European Jews. These different immigrant groups all came with their own cultural baggage that deeply affected how they imagined and behaved in this new utopia.

The point is well made in a classic retrospective by Natan Shaham, a contemporary Israeli writer, in his remarkable novel *The Rosendorf Quartet*. Written in the 1980s, Shoham describes the experience of four musicians of different class, religious, and economic backgrounds, among other distinctions, who flee Nazi Germany in the 1930s. Committed to making beautiful music together as well as to survival, they perform expertly as a quartet. We quickly learn, however, that they differ in upbringing and in their anticipations. Ultimately, they disperse on different paths, with some deciding to make music abroad and others remaining to continue what they had started in Tel-Aviv or elsewhere in the country.

Shaham's story employs the metaphor of the quartet to symbolize the simultaneous closeness and tension between varying immigrant groups in Tel-Aviv. Stories or histories using the same motif could be written of earlier founders who came from Odessa, such as Dizengoff, Bialik, and Ahad Ha'am. It could also be used to describe those who would come after World War I and the turmoil of the breakup of the

Russian and the Austro-Hungarian Empires, and of those who followed later after the devastations of World War II, as well as the waves of immigrants who arrived in the years after independence. Indeed, this motif could apply even today, to recent arrivals from inside and beyond Israel who now intend to make Tel-Aviv their home.

Although Tel-Aviv has long been characterized as the first modern Hebrew city, it has always contained a Babel of voices. Even after a century in which Hebrew was successfully established as the ubiquitous language of the street, the academy, the theatre, the press and communications, the courts, and the stock market, there is still an extraordinary array of languages represented in Tel-Aviv—many of which could scarcely have been imagined a century ago: including Tagalog, Swahili, Thai, and Chinese. The great new Hebrew city is not only the home of Zionism's New Hebrew or New Jew; it is also the home of the Israeli speakers of Arabic, Russian, and Amharic, as well as of long-term guest workers from the Philippines, Thailand, China, east Africa, and eastern Europe. Tel-Aviv is a diverse mosaic—although perhaps not a melting pot—embedded in a revitalized Hebrew culture.

This kind of diversity has evolved and perhaps multiplied over the years. The same contrasts exhibited by the bourgeois city and the workers' housing estates of the Mandate continue to exist. Scores of modern skyscrapers and high-rise apartment buildings fill the Tel-Aviv skyline today, as well as vital bohemian quarters, and glittering tourist and high fashion sections. At the same time, one can find picturesque outdoor markets that cater to low-income people in pockets of poverty and dilapidated housing often proximate to the magnificent promenade along the Mediterranean beaches, vaguely intimidating districts for guest workers near the central bus station, and other diverse zones and neighborhoods. The brilliant façade of the city seen from a distance upon close inspection can be broken down into discrete areas that represent the contrasts of a great, modern city.

Not all worthy topics can be encompassed here. The focus will be on the formative years from the city's founding through the establishment of the State of Israel, although some essays will examine the more recent past and present. A second volume would be required for chronological balance. Within this framework we will investigate different aspects of Tel-Aviv's society, culture, and politics as we group the essays into disciplinary categories. We will also explore a variety of issues not often examined in centennial symposia. They include relations between Jews and Arabs and the presence of a host of social ills from criminality, youth gangs, prostitution, and economic malfeasance, to black marketeering, pollution, and other aspects of municipal hygiene. An idealized picture of the city is likely to be modified as we consider the unwelcome ways in which it became a normal modern metropolis. Despite utopian rhetoric, these negative phenomena have been inescapable.

We begin with Yaacov Shavit's essay, "Telling the Story of a Hebrew City." He analyzes the imaginings of the city's founders and early residents and explores their expectations within the context of the world they knew. Their frame of reference was naturally European, and this offered many possibilities. We learn that the founders and early settlers did not view themselves as establishing a great city, an appreciation that emerged decades later. Indeed, they initially thought they were founding a neighborhood or housing estate. Their visions were nevertheless framed in terms that reflected the urban world in which European Jews were either already resident or rapidly becoming so, whether in Europe or in the United States. What became common to all was an appreciation that they were involved in creating a "Hebrew" city—a novel opportunity that was powerfully attractive to early settlers.

The identity of Tel-Aviv continually evolved as the city grew and changed. This process of transformation is explored by Maoz Azaryahu in an essay that charts the city's select anniversary celebrations, "Tel-Aviv's Birthdays: Anniversary Celebrations, 1929–1959." We witness the conscious construction of a collective memory through cultural productions that become essential components in building a shared identity. These "birthdays" become markers in delineating the evolution of Tel-Aviv's urban myths.

Determining when the city began is a rich topic. Hizky Shoham is also concerned with the subject but moves the discussion into a different direction in "Tel-Aviv's Foundation Myth: A Constructive Perspective." While the earliest indications of myth-making can be ascertained in some isolated essays shortly after the first homes were built prior to World War I, Shoham finds the post-war period, particularly during the 1920s, replete with the beginnings of constructing urban myths in written texts, in public events, and especially in photographic images that are celebrated as heroic icons. Establishing dates of "firsts" through these means is not merely an exercise in historical curiosity. It reflects the attempt of the early citizens to impose meaning on what they wanted to believe they were constructing.

Yoram Bar-Gal takes us from the public sphere of civic celebrations to the portrayal of Tel-Aviv in geography textbooks written in Hebrew for the city's youth in "From 'European Oasis' to Downtown New York: The Image of Tel-Aviv in School Textbooks." These texts mirror the regnant ideologies through which Tel-Aviv's leaders and citizens understood themselves. We find that the city is validated as an artifact of a Zionist program for transforming the country. This presents a challenge to the primacy of the image of the agricultural settlements in representing a viable Jewish state.

Changing course, Tammy Razi abruptly shifts the focus to some undesirable realities that were also part of building a modern city in Zion in "Subversive Youth Cultures in Mandate Tel-Aviv." In addition to housing its visionaries, builders, and all manner of city boosters, Tel-Aviv's streets also were the setting for a variety of youth cultures, some of which Razi terms "subversive." This phenomenon was also a feature of modern urban life in the cities that Tel-Aviv's promoters admired. Razi finds that Tel-Aviv's welfare department serves as a rich resource for delineating misbehavior among a population that in other places was being celebrated as a noble generation of the new Hebrews. Indeed, such a department was modeled on agencies in European and American cities where reformers endeavored to cope with similar phenomena. Zionist society not only produced heroic pioneers on its urban and rural frontiers but gangs, hoodlums, and other miscreants who were the object of concern among a considerable number of social workers. Through their records we discover how wide Zionism's "marginal" culture was. We are left wondering whether the existence of the subculture was a "natural" phenomenon or represented a measure of opposition to Zionism itself. This is particularly so in exploring relations between Jewish and Arab youth.

We then turn to other pathologies with Anat Helman's "Dirt, Noise, and Misbehavior in the First Hebrew City: Letters of Complaint as a Historical Source." She mines another section of the city's archives, literally entitled "Complaints." Here one can find letters by individuals, companies, a variety of organizations, and even tourists. Individually and collectively they provide a rich picture of the city that is not captured in film, promotional brochures, and other celebratory material. We learn of all manner of nuisances that disturbed the municipal atmosphere— both physical and social. These complaints, on the one hand, expose the reality of living in Tel-Aviv, but also reflect the widespread expectations that Tel-Aviv would somehow approximate the ideal standard expressed in public rhetoric.

Deborah Bernstein's "South of Tel-Aviv and North of Jaffa—The Frontier Zone of 'In Between'," takes us to other troubled areas. Tel-Aviv grew out of and, in some respects, in opposition to Jaffa, a historic city that was largely Arab. While Jaffa's population was ten to thirty percent Jewish until independence in 1948, the tension between Jews and Arabs within the Tel-Aviv–Jaffa region had measurable consequences on society and politics, particularly exemplified by serious attacks against local Jewish communities as well as those neighboring on the city. The 1948 war resulted in bitter fighting between these two communities and led to the flight of most of Jaffa's Arabs. This historical and sociological study also has a contemporary ring, for even now residents of Tel-Aviv readily differentiate between the northern, more affluent and modern portion of the city and the southern periphery of older neighborhoods in Jaffa and Tel-Aviv—a frontier comprising a less prosperous zone identified with "oriental" Jaffa. Bernstein takes us inside the southern border zones. She reveals that the dialectic of the historic and modern Tel-Aviv–Jaffa is not only between Arab and Jew but between Western and Oriental Jews, particularly Yemenites in this study. Bernstein reminds us that in Tel-Aviv's marginal zones the tensions between Jews and Arabs were unresolved, and mirrored on the local level the country at large.

Nahum Karlinsky's "Jaffa and Tel-Aviv before 1948: The Underground Story" continues the exploration of the relationship between Jews and Arabs through an unusual perspective—the construction of the city's infrastructure. Like the creation of roads on the city's surface, the laying of an underground pipe network involved decisions about routes, costs, and choice of builders. In effect, how, where, and by whom underground Tel-Aviv was built is as much a mirror of Jewish–Arab relations and politics as what occurred on the surface. Since the focus in this essay is on the period of the British Mandate, the role of the country's

rulers in negotiating relations between the two parties necessarily becomes part of the analysis. Despite the widely perceived reality that the
health of the city's occupants required cooperation from all parties in
constructing a salubrious and affordable network for everyone's benefit,
national/ethnic frictions continually impeded its realization. As such,
this story is but a reflection of larger tensions that had negative consequences for the city and the country at large.

Orit Rozin concludes this section on the formative history of the city
with an essay on "Austerity Tel-Aviv: Everyday Life, Supervision, Compliance, and Respectability." She takes us into the post-independence
period to reveal yet another side of the first Hebrew city. Formerly semi-
autonomous within the British Mandate, Tel-Aviv became the leading
municipality in a sovereign Jewish state. It was no longer an enclave ruled
by foreigners. Its residents came to govern themselves in their own state.

The behavior of Tel-Aviv's citizens is a central issue. Anat Helman
reviews the effectiveness of social controls occasioned by the aftermath
of the 1948 war. For a city born out of mobilizing the public to fulfill
Zionist ends, we find unexpected tension between individual and national objectives. The data on Tel-Aviv are actually similar to that found
in other Western societies in similar circumstances. That is, times of
hardship produced both rationing and black marketeering. Discipline
was difficult to achieve when citizens and state had different needs. This
examination into the behavior of Tel-Aviv's residents becomes in effect
one of Israeli culture as a whole.

Untraditional materials are used in these essays, which represent a
breakthrough in research methodologies and topics that are radically
changing Israeli historiography. Contemporary scholarship is increasingly distant from reliance on the writings of Zionist thinkers, party
platforms, or the minutes of meetings of national institutions or other
official documents that fill Israel's many archives. Represented here is a
search to understand everyday life and actual experience through many
kinds of ordinary documentation. In this way, it indicates that modern
Israeli academic writing has advanced far beyond the reporting, analysis, or interrogation of official accounts.

The second major section in this volume is devoted to language,
literature, and art. Here cultural issues are defined and studied in more
conventional ways. We shall look at poets, authors, and literary estab-

lishments and the production of visual arts. Before doing so, we shall consider an episode that reveals how implanting Hebrew culture in the first Hebrew city was realized. Zohar Shavit's essay on "Tel-Aviv Language Police" suggests the energy if not the fury with which this lofty ideal of Zionist ideologues was imposed on a sometimes unwilling or unable public.

Shavit's story reflects the assumption that the creation of a literature in Hebrew, a hallmark of the Zionist movement, had to be accompanied by ensuring that people actually spoke the language in mundane circumstances and in their private lives. Hebrew had to dominate wherever possible. Shavit reveals the conflict on the streets and public places of Tel-Aviv where ideologically driven high school youth engaged the city's multi-lingual immigrants for whom Hebrew was often a very foreign language. The story demonstrates the enormity of effort involved in making Tel-Aviv a Hebrew city and the limitations of this achievement.

Barbara Mann further explores the tensions between the languages and literatures of European Jews and Hebrew in "*Der Eko Fun Goles:* 'The Spirit of Tel-Aviv' and the Remapping of Jewish Literary History." She begins with a Yiddish poem about Tel-Aviv that was written in Buenos Aires in 1937, thereby demonstrating that Tel-Aviv had become not merely a "local" issue but a centerpiece of the modern Jewish imagination. The reality was that the Jews who crowded into Tel-Aviv came from exile, the *goles,* and some even returned. Wherever they went, they carried their culture with them, thereby vastly complicating, even reversing, the meaning of homeland and Diaspora. Is Tel-Aviv really the *Altneuland* as imagined by Herzl and other Zionists? Mann reveals that, at this stage in the city's history, Tel-Aviv was for some an exile from what they believed to be their real homeland.

Despite the goal of producing an emancipated New Hebrew, Yiddish and other languages remained the primary métier of discourse among many adults. Yiddish certainly continued as a language of creativity even as the city and its population were insistently becoming Hebraized. The same was taking place with Russian, German, and other languages of whose literatures European Jews were intimately familiar and continued to speak and read. Tel-Aviv's cultural reality was far more complicated than the official mythology suggests.

Aminadav Dykman, in "A Poet and a City in Search of a Myth: On Shlomo Skulsky's Tel-Aviv Poems," gives further expression to the contradictions and ironies of this reality. Dykman focuses on Skulsky's 1947 collection of poems, *Let Me Sing to You, Tel-Aviv* [*Ashira lakh* Tel-Aviv]. For many immigrants the regnant ideology was so powerful that they quickly divested themselves of the exilic mentality as they attempted to become natives in their new homeland. Dykman observes that this required the newcomer to reinvent himself as well as create a suitable urban mythology. In the example of the Polish-born Skulsky this process involved employing European tropes, particularly drawn from Russian literature, to distort Tel-Aviv's past and frame its future. In this case, it meant exaggerating the saga of Tel-Aviv's growth. In essence this was the urban equivalent of traditional Zionist ideology that called for making the desert bloom.

Rachel Harris, in "Decay and Death: Urban Topoi in Literary Depictions of Tel-Aviv," examines more recent literary creations from the 1970s onwards which feature less joyful and optimistic themes. She identifies a group of authors whose stories involve prostitution, urban sprawl, isolation and anomie, and even suicide. This is, of course, the converse of ubiquitous celebratory texts that emphasize growth and expansion as the measure of success. Still, her analysis suggests achievement on another plane. Harris offers that the literature she examined indicates a normalization of the Jewish experience, for such subject matter is found throughout the literatures of the modern city. Yet, there is also something particularistic about the people and Tel-Aviv. In effect, her Tel-Aviv writers describe a world that is a hybrid of both East and West, universal and unique.

With the essay by Dalia Manor, "Art and the City: The Case of Tel-Aviv," we shift from literature to the visual arts. Manor finds that, curiously, Tel-Aviv was captured on the film of photographers who recorded its history and created its icons rather than on the canvases of its many painters who chose not to use their city as a subject for their art. Many won international acclaim by depicting Palestine's rural landscapes, historic and mystical Jerusalem and Safed, and other locales, but ignored Tel-Aviv. Rather than paint Tel-Aviv, they painted "from" Tel-Aviv. This was true of such masters as Nahum Gutman and Reuven Rubin whose few works on the city have won exaggerated significance within the totality of their artistic production.

In the 1970s a shift occurred, perhaps under the influence of American Pop Art and European "Nouveau Realism," with the commonplace of the city emerging as a significant theme. In decidedly unromantic images, pollution, the crowded life of the streets, and city lights and shadows contributed to a discrete Tel-Aviv style that suggests that Tel-Aviv is a non-idealized product of Zionism. It is the mundane and secular qualities that attracted these artists rather than the alleged spirituality of Jerusalem or romanticized landscapes. This new style allowed artists to comment on a host of issues and ills confronting Israeli society, including its relations with Arabs and its alternative lifestyles—the city as it actually appeared, rather than viewed through the prism of Zionist ideology. Photographers, and increasingly filmmakers, since the 1930s were the primary documenters of the city.

The third and final section of the volume illuminates the visual presence of Tel-Aviv through its architecture and planning. We begin with Volker Welter's "The 1925 Master Plan for Tel-Aviv by Patrick Geddes." Zionists had a deep interest in detailed physical and social planning. This was most famously reflected in Herzl's own widely read *Altneuland,* a utopian novel replete with details on how Zion would look and be managed. Herzl's vision relied on the social theories and planning concepts of his time. When the officials of the World Zionist Organization began to appreciate that Tel-Aviv would likely grow out of its status as a modest suburb to Jaffa, they naturally turned to one of the preeminent planners of the period, Patrick Geddes, a world-famous Scottish sociologist and garden-city advocate. Indeed, it was particularly the garden-city idea that attracted Zionists who were familiar with it through the original novel or its German or Yiddish translations. Geddes supplied what they sought in a regional plan—the reconstruction of both town and country for modern use, a conception at the core of Zionist thought and praxis.

In many ways the Geddes plan did not work as intended. He attempted to knit together Jewish Tel-Aviv with the predominantly Arab Jaffa, since objective planning considerations informed his imagination not the political realities on the ground. Moreover, he viewed cities as organisms that would respect history, not destroy it. As such, he maintained, Tel-Aviv ought to be built with consideration to its relationship with Jaffa. In applying this concept of respect for the past and natural, organic growth, he imported extensively from his previous designs in Scotland and India. However attractive these plans appeared on paper, the citizens of Tel-Aviv would in fact turn their back on this portion of the Geddes plan. Moreover, citizens of contemporary Tel-Aviv would come to rue other portions as inappropriate to a metropolis on the Mediterranean coast. The Geddes plan is yet another instance of the distance between grand intentions and historic reality.

Part of that reality was the eventual neglect and even demolition of historic buildings as Tel-Aviv developed and adopted contemporary fashions. For many this represents the destruction of their city's history. Over the last generation nostalgia for the past has come to compete with forces presented as supporting progress. Respect for history and embracing the future have long competed in Israel, as in other modern societies. Citizens of Tel-Aviv, like their counterparts elsewhere, have organized significant and somewhat successful movements for the preservation of buildings and landmarks and gentrification of decaying neighborhoods. In "Preserving Urban Heritage: From Old Jaffa to Modern Tel-Aviv," Nurit Alfasi and Roy Fabian describe such initiatives.

The Tel-Aviv experience may be distinguished from foreign examples in that Israeli preservationists have not formed civic groups nor are they supported directly or indirectly by the political establishment. They began as a loose association of individuals committed to the same cause and only recently achieved recognized municipal standing. The authors call them "ideological developers" who have entered into the debate over the city's physical make up without any thought of formalizing their association. Perhaps this tentativeness reflects both the occasional power and the fragility of preservation in a city whose residents still seek to embrace the future. Through this lens, we observe how Zionism remains characteristically ready to yield the recent past as it searches for the new and modern.

Tensions between municipal authorities and individual residents are found in other areas. Carolin Aronis, in "Balconies of Tel-Aviv: Cultural History and Urban Politics," presents the collision of the private and public spheres over balconies, a distinctive feature of this Mediterranean city. Particularly in hot climates, balconies provide openness and ventilation. They have other liminal characteristics such as engendering communications between the privacy of the home and the street. As circumstances change, residents often enclose these balconies to expand their apartments. Viewing the balcony as an "urban artifact" and using the methodology of analyzing material culture, the author reviews a vast literature found in archives as well as exhibits and interviews to examine the interactions between residents and municipal officials. The result is a window into architectural styles and social practices since the city's beginnings as well as the changing needs of the citizenry. Interspersed are observations on how technological innovations such as air conditioning and telephones affected the visual appearance of the city.

Historically, the open space of the balcony was largely closed in the 1970s and 1980s, only to be partially and grudgingly reopened at present. In this process various urban myths have been challenged and changed. Through this evolution we learn much about lifestyles, the objectives of architects and builders, and the control and defiance relationship between authorities and residents. We again witness the breach between ideology and praxis. Tel-Aviv is at once a city intended to cater to individuals within an ideological structure that also privileges public needs and appearances. This tension is certainly not unique in modern societies. Still, the power of Zionism as a collective ideology enhances the possibility for conflict with individual needs.

The final essay in this section on architecture and planning returns us to the very beginning of the volume. Tel-Aviv may have been intended as a Jewish settlement separated from Jaffa, but complete severance rarely occurred, and there were very strong counter-movements. Particularly after the War of Independence, Tel-Aviv had the opportunity and practical need to reassess its relationship to Jaffa. Alona Nitzan-Shiftan examines the controversies over how some kind of rejoining of the two cities might be accomplished in "The Architecture of the Hyphen: The Urban Unification of Jaffa and Tel-Aviv as National Metaphor."

She begins her essay with an examination of the attempt to reunite Jerusalem's Jewish and Arab sections after the Six-Day War of June 1967 and returns to the Jerusalem experience at crucial parts of her essay. This is a significant analytical technique since Tel-Aviv–Jaffa was only one of the locales where Jews and Arabs had lived both in proximity and in the same political jurisdiction only to be separated during the pre-state conflict and subsequently forced to redefine relationships after Israel won independence and control. This complicated political story forms the background for Nitzan-Shiftan's deft exposition of the evolution of and controversies over architectural plans that gave expression to this hyphenated relationship. The author richly illustrates this essay with architectural drawings and photographs to enable the reader to visualize more concretely what Tel-Aviv became and what it did not become.

The volume closes with an essay by co-editor Maoz Azaryahu. "Afterword: Tel-Aviv between Province and Metropolis" poses the question: Is Tel-Aviv but a modest, more or less provincial city that recently sprang up on the Mediterranean littoral, or has something of wider significance been created not merely from the perspective of Jewish history, but in contemporary global terms? An enduring characteristic of those who live in and visit this remarkable city is an awareness of the tension between its reality and what it could be. As Tel-Aviv enters its second century, agreement on the specific nature of the city's significance remains unresolved.

## NOTES

1. Noteworthy among the new writings in English is Joachim Schlör, *Tel-Aviv: From Dream to City* (London, 1999).

2. A full discussion of the bourgeois versus the proletarian views of Tel-Aviv is found in S. Ilan Troen, *Imagining Zion: Dreams, Designs, and Realities in a Century of Jewish Settlement* (New Haven, CT, 2003), 85–111.

3. Amos Elon, *Herzl* (New York, 1975), 348.

# PART ONE

# Historical Issues

# ONE

# Telling the Story of a Hebrew City

*Yaacov Shavit*

### Tel-Aviv Did Not Want to Be a City

Tel-Aviv did not want to be a city. In fact, it was afraid to be a city. The fear arose from the anti-urban trend and the negative image of the city—"the dark city"—in the nineteenth century, as well as the Zionist concern that the city would attract most of the new immigrants and would compete with the agricultural settlements for resources. Only in the 1930s did Tel-Aviv realize that it was becoming a city after all.

What it really meant to be was a suburb, or a modern small town, but certainly not something on the order of the average European city. Even today, Tel-Aviv, with 390,000 residents, is certainly not a large city.

### Why Is Its Hundredth Anniversary Noteworthy?

From the perspective of the world outside Europe, there is nothing special about the founding of Tel-Aviv one hundred years ago. During the nineteenth century, outside the continent, and especially in the United States, many cities were established, and not as a result of government initiative. Within Europe, however, the situation was different; the only new city in the last 200 years is Odessa, which was founded by the Czarist government at the end of the eighteenth century.[1] Within Eretz-Israel the situation was also different. Tel-Aviv is the only new city since Ramle was established in 717 BCE by the Umayyad caliph Sulayman ibn Abd al-Malik. It is the first so-called "Jewish city" since King Herod built Caesarea in 20–10 BCE and Tiberias was founded by King Herod Antipas in 22–17 BCE. Thus Tel-Aviv was the first city founded in Eretz-Israel in 1,200 years, and it was the first Jewish city founded there in some 2,000 years.

## What Does Tel-Aviv Have in Common with Other Cities?

Although cities have much in common, each has its own history, character, and image. What does Tel-Aviv, with its brief history, have in common with other cities, and what makes it unique? Its uniqueness lies in its being the first city established by Jews for Jews, and more so, it was the first opportunity in general for Jews to found a city and to shape its character.

Meir Dizengoff, the head of the neighborhood committee and later the city's first mayor, declared in 1921,

> We are conducting the most important experiment in the entire period of our exile. We want to prove how we will behave in a new, modern city, that will be totally Jewish, that we will light by ourselves, guard by ourselves, improve by ourselves, and keep clean and wholesome [by ourselves].

He referred to a city in the urban-physical sense, as well as to the character of urban life.

The history of Tel-Aviv offers a unique opportunity to see how Jews built a city, what kind of city they wanted to build, and what kind of city grew from under their hands. If Tel-Aviv did not want to be a city, how does this statement fit with the declarations and texts that, already in the first decade of its existence, and certainly after that, seemed to predict the development of the Ahuzat Bayit neighborhood into a city?

These declarations were just rhetoric. A pamphlet dated 31 July 1906 raised the idea of establishing a Jewish neighborhood outside Jaffa. Its author, Akiva Arieh Weiss, who was the most important promoter of the neighborhood, wrote that it would be "the first Hebrew city" and that it would eventually become "Eretz-Israel's New York." He did not mean New York as a model for a city, but its role as the port of entry for immigrants. Weiss described this "modern" city:

> In this city we will build the streets [so they have] roads and sidewalks [and] electric lights. Every house will have water from wells that will flow through pipes as in every modern European city, and also sewerage pipes will be installed for the health of the city and its residents.

Weiss's vision still lacks many of the elements of a modern city, and certainly of a metropolis. S. Y. Agnon wrote in his novel *Tmol Shilshom* (Only Yesterday), "Sixty houses aren't sixty cities, but we who do not aim too high, even smallness is great for us."[2] The widespread use of the word "city" (*stadt*) should not mislead us; Tel-Aviv had no intention of becoming New York, Odessa, Vienna, or Berlin.

Other urban visions were expressed. The writer A. A. Kabak, for example, wrote in 1914 that Tel-Aviv would become a large city in which "a rich culture will flourish, large shops [will have] splendid display windows, electric streetcars will pass by with a clatter, locomotives will shriek, [and] factory smokestacks will blast." Meir Dizengoff, the first mayor, predicted in 1924 that Tel-Aviv would become a metropolis and a great Jewish cultural, commercial, industrial, and political center. However, as some of the city's first residents stated,

> In truth, no one foresaw the coming of Tel-Aviv, . . . when we drove the first stake in Kerem Jebali ["vineyard"—the first 85.5 dunams that were purchased by the first residents of *Ahuzat Bayit*] we never dreamed that our little neighborhood would grow into a big city and that the city would become the heart of the country, and if someone had predicted generations ago that within twenty-five years a big city would be built on the sandy desert north of Jaffa, [and] that [it] would have more than 100,000 residents, he would have been considered a dreamer.

In short, "Tel-Aviv was not built according to a predetermined plan, because its founders did not foresee its future."

Even architect Patrick Geddes, in his 1926 outline plan for part of Tel-Aviv believed that Tel-Aviv would be "northern Jaffa." His plan referred to a small town on just 3,000 dunams (750 acres), with small houses (residential buildings no more than three stories high), and commercial buildings, in commercial areas, of no more than four stories, as well as public parks and private gardens. This was a plan for a city of 100,000. Yet ten years after his plan Tel-Aviv numbered 150,000 inhabitants.[3]

The character of the city was not shaped in accordance with a vision or preconceived plan. Agnon wrote ironically about the first days of Tel-Aviv that naïve people who believed that their plans and their will had made Tel-Aviv were in error; the city had developed in a totally different manner from what they wanted, and that was God's doing. In secular language, the city was shaped by the life force—that is, various forces that determined the rate of urban growth and the nature of that growth. Agnon wrote that Tel-Aviv became "the complete opposite of what the founders of Tel-Aviv wanted to make of Tel-Aviv."[4] Instead of becoming an autonomous and modern suburb, it became first a town and then a city, which was not the result of a vision or a plan.

It is true that various groups had a variety of models in mind for a city,[5] but these models had only a slight influence on the course of Tel-Aviv's development, at least in its first forty years. This is true not only in relation to its physical-urban character but also in relation to its social-urban and cultural-urban character.

### "City Of Jews," "Jewish City," "Hebrew City," "European City in the Orient"?

Tel-Aviv was a combination of all of these. It was undoubtedly a "city of Jews." In 1909, the year that the Ahuzat Bayit neighborhood was established, more than a million Jews lived in New York (540,000 on less than one square mile),[6] 300,000 in Warsaw, and 150,000 in Odessa. Several cities not only had a demographic concentration of Jews but also a vibrant Jewish life. Numerous cities in Europe and in the New World had larger Jewish populations than Tel-Aviv during the British Mandate, and after. In some places, there were more Jews than in all of the Yishuv.

Jews have been portrayed as a quintessentially urban population who played an important role in the urban nineteenth-century revolution.[7] However, Tel-Aviv was both a city of Jews and a Jewish city because all the residents within the municipal boundaries, until 1949, were Jews, and because only Tel-Aviv was a city established by Jews as a Jewish enterprise. It was a city whose urban character was shaped by Jews, a city that was run by Jews, and a city whose public space was controlled by Jews. Therefore, the urban challenge to its residents and its image-shapers was all encompassing. What shaped the character of Tel-Aviv was that at least some of the important decisions that determined the development of the urban space and of the urban society were under the control of the city's residents and its leaders. It was the first and only place where Jews not only settled in a city, contributed to its growth, were an active element in it, were influenced by it, and at the same time established autonomous Jewish life, it was also a city in which they were the sole factor in its establishment, the sole moving force behind its development, and almost the sole shapers of its character.

Without the vision of the "Hebrew city," without the desire to establish a modern Hebrew city, and without the ability to oversee urban processes at least partially, Tel-Aviv would have been just another city of immigrants and refugees, like all other cities.

However, urban visions do not portray the real city, but rather how the builders of Tel-Aviv and its residents imagined the ideal city. In fact, the city grew from the bottom up, and not all its layers developed according to preconceived ideas or in accordance with plans on paper, but rather as the result of a mostly uncontrolled dynamic.

## The Life Force That Spurred the Urban Growth of Tel-Aviv

The main impetus for the establishment of the small Jewish neighborhoods that were built outside Jaffa starting in 1887 consisted of two factors: one was severe overcrowding in Jaffa, resulting from three kinds of increase: the urban growth of Arab Jaffa, an increase in the Jewish population of Jaffa as a result of internal migration (within the Yishuv), and Jewish immigration from outside the country. The second factor was the desire of some of Jaffa's Jews to improve their housing conditions. In this respect, there was no difference between moving outside the walls of Jaffa and moving outside the walls of Jerusalem's Old City, starting in the 1860s. Jaffa had ceased to be a bridge to Jerusalem and had become a favored destination. After 1909, and especially after World War I, Tel-Aviv became the favored destination of Jews from other cities in the Yishuv, and especially of many of the immigrants.

Dr. Arthur Ruppin, head of the Palestine office of the World Zionist Organization established in 1908, explained that

> In no other place did they see the same degree of independent communal management, under a leadership that [the residents] themselves elected. In no other place was there such a feeling of total security; in no other place was it possible to educate the children to the same degree with the same Jewish-national spirit; in no other place was there such a complete revival of the Hebrew language as here.

Alter Druyanov, Tel-Aviv's first official historian, had a different explanation:

> With the increase in immigration, Tel-Aviv's growth was proportionally greater than that of the other Jewish settlements in the land. [Living in] Diaspora conditions for eons made the Jew an urban and metropolitan creature. When he started becoming uprooted from the Diaspora and immigrated to Eretz-Israel, and even if that was not only because he was pushed out of there, but also because an ideology caused him to come, he was nearly powerless to part with his urban nature, and the slightest obstacle led him primarily not to the village but to the city . . . and when the immigrant found Tel-Aviv, an "almost city" that was better run than the previous one, he went there.[8]

Several years later, one of the local activists explained the preference for urban life:

> The immigrants were attracted to Tel-Aviv only because they found in it all the comforts they were used to in Europe: electric light, water, a little cleanliness, cinema, opera, theater, and also more or less advanced schools, . . . busy streets, full restaurants, cafes open until 2 AM, singing, music, and dancing.

All three were correct. The Second and Third Aliya waves of Jewish immigration to Eretz-Israel included many non-pioneering immigrants who were in search of housing, employment, and a living, which only an urban setting could provide. For many of the pioneering immigrants, Tel-Aviv was not only a way station, but also a permanent place, because its development provided employment. Without Tel-Aviv, these opportunities would not have existed. That is why, despite the absence of objective elementary conditions, already in the first decade of Tel-Aviv's history the internal forces of a city were created, and the desire to create a suburb of Jaffa, a suburb that would have a grid of streets and sidewalks, running water in the houses, and electricity, led to its becoming an autonomous town, and then a city.

Just as New York was "the Promised City," so too was Tel-Aviv, especially starting in 1924—when the United States imposed severe restrictions on immigration to its shores, and Poland imposed economic pressure (Grabski decrees) on its Jews. Many of the immigrants did not identify with the pioneering ethos, did not want to settle in agricultural settlements, and preferred to manage on their own, to work in the trades they had had prior to immigration, and to live the kind of life to which they were accustomed.

Tel-Aviv was dependent on Jaffa for many years, and even in 1945 34,000 Jews resided in Jaffa. However, the physical distance from Jaffa, the autonomous government, and the control of the urban space turned Tel-Aviv into an independent urban entity and a destination that attracted immigrants. Moreover, the agricultural and semi-urban settlements could not absorb the waves of immigration, and it was Tel-Aviv that offered housing and employment opportunities.

The Jewish population of Tel-Aviv (and Jaffa) during the British Mandate numbered between thirty to forty percent of the entire Yishuv, and in 1939 it reached thirty-nine percent. In 1950 it dropped to twenty-eight percent, and in 1952—the peak of mass immigration—to twenty-three percent. The growth was rapid. Between 1931 and 1936, the city grew by a phenomenal 215 percent, from 46,000 to 145,000; and between 1936 and 1939 it grew by another fifty-two percent, from about 154,000 residents to 220,000. It is not surprising that David Ben-Gurion wrote at the height of this rapid growth that Tel-Aviv was turning the Yishuv into a city-state (polis) rather than a city within a state (a city with the proper proportion of inhabitants in relation to the general population).

Tel-Aviv's population grew faster than that of many of the cities in the countries of immigration in the New World, even though it was not built by a central government, it received almost no financial support from the WZO or from the government, and it received only indirect aid from the Mandate government. Thus the motivating force, its life force, was immigration; immigrants' private capital (which Dizengoff estimated in 1934 at thirty million lira at the time, mostly private investment and privately held); private and public enterprise; municipal local taxes; and the activity of various agents of growth and change. Moreover, the entire complex of advanced municipal services—including education, health, and infrastructure—was all funded by the city's residents, and under their management.

Much of the city's character was determined by the nature of the capital that reached the city. There was no investment of foreign capital, no investment by big Jewish capitalists; all the investments were by people with limited capital, which enabled them to build homes that were not splendid, and certainly not monumental, and some rental properties, small workshops, and businesses.

## Was Tel-Aviv a "Modern European City"?

Upon seeing The Hague, the capital of The Netherlands, Theodor Herzl wrote in his diary on 30 September 1898, "Will is what causes cities to rise. If I point to any spot and say 'Here there will be a city!' a city will rise there."[9] Herzl believed that in the modern era human beings could harness technology to conquer nature and to build a city from scratch. When Herzl described the exemplary city he did not describe a new city, but rather Haifa, a historic city that was changing into a modern port city, had neighborhoods surrounded by greenery with single-family homes of one or two stories, and industrial plants. Yet in another context, in discussing the possibility of Jewish settlement in el-Arish, Herzl wrote, "I believed that in founding a city one should follow as much as possible in the footsteps of ancient settlement . . . a city means layer upon layer of experience . . ."[10]

In both cases, Herzl's portrayal of a modern Jewish city was influenced by utopian models of cities, and especially by the renewal of various European cities (for example, Vienna).[11] The image of the new city was shaped by his desire to keep the new Jewish, Eretz-Israel city from taking on the character of an Eastern European *shtetl*, an Oriental-Levantine city, or a large European city with all its problems. Thus Tel-Aviv was born in "opposition" not only to Jaffa, but also to the residential neighborhoods of Jews in the cities and towns of Eastern Europe. The founders and leaders of Tel-Aviv hoped to achieve this through urban planning and through various attempts to oversee and direct the development of both the physical-urban space and the urban lifestyle. They defined the city they desired by invoking the term "Hebrew city" or "the first Hebrew city," terms that simply referred to a city whose population uses Hebrew exclusively. Thus Tel-Aviv was simultaneously "Jewish," "modern," and "European." It was perceived as a manifestation of the idea of "Hebrew national and cultural revival."

However, even in this matter, the city was the creation of those who chose to live there, without any direction or intervention from above.

Its residents and the municipal leaders had the responsibility of making it a well-run city in all respects and for ensuring that it would remain so, even though they did not have the legal means to impose laws and regulations in many important areas that determine the character of a city. However, because Tel-Aviv was a "free cultural" market, the municipality and various "cultural agents" could not regulate the character of its residents, the patterns of urban growth, the purchase of land, the founding of new neighborhoods, or the investment in construction, commerce, trade, and industry. They also could not regulate—though they would have liked to—the nature of the "urban cultural market" and the character of the urban lifestyle. The inevitable result was social and economic stratification, and ethnic and cultural heterogeneity.

Tel-Aviv was, and remains, a city like all other cities. It arose and developed because most of the Jewish immigrants wanted to live in a city and because Tel-Aviv gave them housing, employment opportunities, a standard of living, and services, which agricultural settlements were unable to do. Without Tel-Aviv as an urban, commercial, industrial, public, and cultural center, the Yishuv would not have had a center.

Despite what some people believe, no guiding policy caused the poor population—most but not all of Mizrahi extraction—to be concentrated in the Jewish neighborhoods of Jaffa or in the south of the city. Many members of that population chose to live within the municipal boundaries of Jaffa, which though providing lower-level services, had lower taxes, cheaper housing, and a non-traditional character compared with Tel-Aviv. The city could not control differences in income and housing conditions.

* * *

Tel-Aviv was a Hebrew city because it was the center of Hebrew culture (which does not mean urban culture or urban lifestyle). The term "Hebrew culture" refers to the fact that the dominant language, at least in the public space, in public institutions and in the education system, was Hebrew. Moreover, all the cultural assets—including newspapers, literature, theater, and films—were available in Hebrew.

The most important fact was that Tel-Aviv was the center of Hebrew creativity and of creativity in Hebrew, where most of the writers, theater people, translators, and artists lived and worked, and where most of their audiences lived. It was the center of new Jewish creative output.

The question as to what Hebrew creativity means, what gives it Hebrew content, is debatable, but Tel-Aviv had the full range of Hebrew creativity and creativity in Hebrew, and not only parts of it (such as literary centers like those that existed for a while in Odessa, Warsaw, or Berlin). Therefore, without Tel-Aviv, Hebrew culture would not have been able to grow and develop and become the dominant culture in the Yishuv and in the state.

At the same time, Tel-Aviv's public space and "cultural market" were free to act with almost no religious or ideological restrictions. As a result, the city also became the center of the imported, generally Western, culture, both high and low, and various attempts to censor those imports failed. This combination of Hebrew culture and culture in Hebrew with modern "universal" culture that was primarily European, of high culture and the culture of leisure and entertainment, of private cultural events (many of them initiated by the city) and public events, made Tel-Aviv what it was and what it is today.

## NOTES

This article is based on the first two volumes of Yaacov Shavit and Gideon Biger, *The History of Tel-Aviv* (Tel-Aviv, 2001, 2007) and on Yaacov Shavit, *Tel-Aviv: Naissance d'une ville 1909–1936* (Paris, 2004).

1. Patricia Herlihy, *Odessa: A History, 1794–1914* (Cambridge, MA, 1986).
2. S. Y. Agnon, *Only Yesterday* (Tel-Aviv, 2000), 409 [Hebrew].
3. Nathan Mavon, *City of Concept: Planning Tel-Aviv* (Tel-Aviv, 2009) [Hebrew].
4. Agnon, *Only Yesterday*, 464.
5. S. Ilan Troen, "Establishing a Zionist Metropolis: Alternative Approaches to Building Tel-Aviv," *Journal of Urban History* 18.1 (1991): 66–101.
6. Moses Rischin, *The Promised City: New York's Jews 1870–1917* (Cambridge, MA, 1997).
7. Ezra Mendelshon, ed., *People of the City: Jews and the Urban Challenge, Studies in Contemporary Jewry* XV (Jerusalem, 1999).
8. Alter Druyanov, *Sefer Tel-Aviv* (Tel-Aviv, 1936), 204 [Hebrew].
9. Theodor Herzl, *The Jewish Cause/Diary Chapters* (Jerusalem, 1997), 550 [Hebrew].
10. Ibid., vol. 3 (2001), 128.
11. Carl E. Schorske, "The Ringstrasse, Its Critics, and the Birth of Urban Modernism," in *Fin-de-Siècle Vienna: Politics and Culture* (New York, 1992), 24–115.

# TWO

# Tel-Aviv's Birthdays: Anniversary Celebrations, 1929–1959

*Maoz Azaryahu*

On 2 May 1929, for the first time in its history, Tel-Aviv celebrated the anniversary of its founding in 1909. In 1934 it commemorated its silver jubilee, and in 1959 its golden jubilee. As civic celebrations, anniversaries commemorate significant events in the history of a nation, a political regime, a religion, an institution, or culture in general. Unlike national holidays that celebrate the founding of states and regimes, the anniversaries of the founding of cities are not celebrated annually, but rather in association with outstanding years. Jubilees, centennials, and bi-centennials are common, though not an obligatory norm.

As with a birthday, a city anniversary commemorates the beginning of the city and provides a calendric framework for the celebration of historical continuity that culminates in the present. Potentially shrouded with pathos and notions of destiny, the celebration of a city anniversary is saturated by the rhetoric of commitment to the city, pride in its history, and optimism about its future. Anniversary celebrations are not spontaneous. They are officially sponsored cultural productions. Promoted and produced by local elites, birthday parties of cities evince specific political priorities, ideological agendas, economic interests, and cultural conventions that underlie the form and content of the commemorative fabric and festive texture of the anniversary celebration.

This essay explores three successive anniversary celebrations of Tel-Aviv as an aspect of the cultural and political history of the city. The underlying premise is that an anniversary celebration is a cultural production of the city that accords with ideas about the city and its history prevailing among local political and cultural elites. The three anniversaries examined here were celebrated in the "first Hebrew city" phase of the cultural history of Tel-Aviv; accordingly, their major theme was Tel-Aviv as a Zionist success story. The historical analysis of three successive anniversaries affords an opportunity to discern continuities in the form of ceremonial patterns and recurrent themes that belonged to the ideational makeup of the city. It also highlights period-specific concerns and political contingencies that underlay particular anniversary celebrations.

## 1929—The Twentieth Anniversary

In a letter he wrote a few days after Passover 5689 (late April–early May 1929), Haim Nahman Bialik reported:

> The festivals were full of much noise and ado, perhaps a little too much. Pessach is becoming a vessel filled with quite a few celebrations that together fill our world to capacity.[1]

For the Yishuv, Passover of that year was a chain of commemorative festivals. First was Passover, the tradition-laden paradigmatic festival of Jewish memory. On the third day, Sunday, a mass event held in Petah-Tikva marked the silver jubilee of the Second Aliya. Produced by the central committee of the Histadrut, this anniversary was a celebration of the Zionist labor movement. Wednesday, May 1, was the last day of Passover. A public event at *Beit Ha'am* in Tel-Aviv attracted some 4,000 people. Leaders of the Labor movement, among them David Ben-Gurion and Eliezer Kaplan, addressed the assembled audience.

The day after Passover, Thursday, May 2 (22 Nissan), Tel-Aviv celebrated the twentieth anniversary in a series of festive events.[2] "Tel-Aviv Day" was extensively reported in the Hebrew press. The entire city was decorated with flags. The celebration consisted of three successive events. The opening event took place at the central hall of the Exhibition and Fair of Palestine and the Near East in the area of the future central bus station. Attended by the founders of the city, members of the municipal council, dignitaries of the Yishuv, representatives of Zionist organizations and of Jewish agricultural settlements, and the British governor of the district, the event consisted of a series of speeches by Mayor Meir

Fig. 2.1. Public announcement: Tel-Aviv's twentieth-anniversary celebration, 2 May 1929.

Dizengoff and guests who praised and complimented the first Hebrew city.[3] As a symbolic gesture, the mayor gave the first child born in Tel-Aviv a special certificate proclaiming him "the first natural citizen of the city of Tel-Aviv."[4]

The opening ceremony concluded by sunset. Thereafter a parade of Tel-Aviv's children and the founders, followed by the police orchestra, marched from the fairgrounds to the municipality building lit with a crown on its top. While arriving at the municipality building, the children filled the street, whereas the founders stood on the balcony facing Bialik St. After a short speech by Dizengoff and the singing of *Hatikva,* the crowd dispersed. The last leg was the jubilee ball at the exhibition hall. Dizengoff shared his reminiscences of Tel-Aviv's early years with the audience. The artistic part of the evening included music, dance, and actor Rafael Klachkin reciting Tel-Aviv poems by Zalman Shneur and Yehuda Karni.

Anniversary commemorations of a city's founding celebrate not only the beginning as a privileged moment in history, but also the thread of historical continuity that connects the past with the present. Designated "Tel-Aviv Day," the anniversary celebration sanctified the founding of Tel-Aviv as an extraordinary event that, beyond its obvious significance for the city, also had extraordinary significance in Zionist history: "This festival we celebrate today is neither the founders' only, nor of this city alone: it is a celebration for all of us, for the entire Hebrew Yishuv in the land, for Zionism, and for the movement of national revival in Israel."[5]

According to standard Zionist interpretation, the founding of Tel-Aviv was of a city created *ex nihilo* from the sand dunes, a heroic act suffused with redemptive meanings. Dizengoff reiterated conventional notions about the vision that directed the founders of the city:

> [. . .] On this day we started to fulfill a daring dream to build on sands of wilderness, on desolate seashore, an eternal edifice, a shelter for the spirit and vigor of the Jew, the first Hebrew city in the time of our new revival and redemption.[6]

A commemoration of beginning, the celebration of Tel-Aviv's twentieth anniversary was also the beginning of a new tradition that culminated in the 2009 centennial celebration. Accordingly, the decisions made in preparation for the twentieth anniversary were of special significance since they entailed some issues of principle that, when determined, potentially provided the "launching pad" for a new tradition. One issue was the shared sense that an anniversary celebration of the founding of Tel-Aviv was an appropriate and viable cultural option; another was scheduling the anniversary, which also entailed dating the beginning of Tel-Aviv; and yet another was the shaping of the festive texture of the celebration and the various themes that permeated the anniversary.

The appropriateness of celebrating the anniversary of Tel-Aviv's founding was self-evident. It seems plausible to assume that the models for emulation were St. Petersburg and Odessa, which celebrated their bicentennial and centennial in 1903 and 1894, respectively. Dizengoff— mayor, producer, and master of ceremonies of the celebration—was probably acquainted with these Russian anniversary celebrations, and for him, as for others who immigrated from the Russian Empire to the Land of Israel, an anniversary celebration of the founding of the city was a proper, even warranted, option.[7]

Despite their appeal and significance, anniversary celebrations of the founding of a city are an optional rather than obligatory norm. Moshe Glickson, the editor of *Ha'aretz*, commented that celebrating Tel-Aviv's twentieth anniversary was indeed "unusual."[8] Tel-Aviv celebrated a vicennial, a rather uncommon anniversary in connection with a com-memoration of the founding of cities. Moreover, by 1929 Tel-Aviv was not only a young, but also a small city of 40,000 residents.[9]

The official twentieth-anniversary preparations began in December 1928, in accordance with the understanding that Tel-Aviv was founded in 1909. A different issue was defining the founding event to be com-memorated and distinguished by an anniversary celebration. Dizengoff addressed this issue in *Ha'aretz,* noting that no one could "safely say" on which day of 1909 Tel-Aviv was born.[10] He enumerated different pos-sibilities: the day of the contract between the founders and the Anglo-Palestine Bank; the day the first plot was bought; and the day the corner stone of the first building was laid.

Dizengoff noted, "The idea to found a Hebrew city was not born in one day." The implication was that no one particular day could be singled out unequivocally as the day on which Tel-Aviv was founded. The an-niversary celebration took place on May 2 (22 Nissan)—a day after the second holiday of Passover, which coincided with May 1, the traditional workers' holiday. Notably, Tel-Aviv Day was celebrated two days after 20 Nissan in 1909 when the lottery for the plots of land was conducted, an event that later came to be considered as the founding of Tel-Aviv.[11] This event was captured in a photo that became an iconic representation of the moment when the city "began."

Dizengoff did not mention this event as Tel-Aviv's founding event. Moreover, according to his explanation, the relevant issue in regard to scheduling the anniversary celebration was that this was the day that followed Passover, a festival of national remembrance. "We have established the 22 of Nissan—the day following Passover—as a holiday, as the birthday of our city, forever. Every year on this day we will render an account of our deeds." He added another commemorative dimension to the choice of day for celebrating the city's founding by noting that on 11 May 1921, Tel-Aviv was granted municipal rights in the form of a constitution, a formal liberation from the "guardianship of Jaffa" and the beginning of the city's independence.

Beyond commemorating the city's founding, a major theme of Tel-Aviv Day was the anniversary as a point of transition in the city's history. Glickson noted that the anniversary had the air of "an end of a period and a beginning of a new one, it feels both like a summary and like charting new roads for the future."[12] According to this interpretation, the anniversary both commemorated the beginning and proclaimed a new start. The issue was that at this stage of its history, Tel-Aviv was recovering from the severe economic crisis that had befallen the city in 1926–1927 and produced a tremendous sense of despair.[13] The 1929 anniversary celebration served as an occasion to proclaim a new era in the history of Tel-Aviv and to generate optimism about the city, which shortly before seemed to be a failed enterprise. The anniversary celebration, according to this view, proclaimed the first twenty years to be a "foundational phase": "In these twenty years we prepared a vast number of foundation stones, now is the time to erect the building."[14]

The notion that the city's first twenty years had been but a prolonged act of founding also made it possible to acknowledge mistakes and failures and to admit misgivings and self-doubt, while not losing sight of the larger picture—the city that emerged after all these trials and tribulations to celebrate its anniversary. Construed as a watershed between the past and the future, the anniversary provided an opportunity to look back with the modesty of hindsight and to look forward with measured optimism:

> The twenty years that we passed were years of experimenting and searching, pains of creation, difficult beginnings and crises, a sort of childhood disease. From today on we enter a new period of systematic and gradual work, knowing the roads leading to the destination we aspire to.[15]

Glickson, too, was clear about the less than perfect historic record of the city: "She knew many failures, she committed many sins . . . We should not whitewash mistakes and not cover up the sins . . ."[16] Yet beyond the professed readiness to concede errors of judgment and past blunders, the celebration of the anniversary was also a vindication of the city as a Zionist project and a refutation of the notion that became popular a few years before that Tel-Aviv was a lost cause. For Glickson, "The celebration of Tel-Aviv's twentieth anniversary is a celebration of victory." In his view, "The doomsayers were proven wrong. Tel-Aviv withstood the test."

For Dizengoff, the victory of Tel-Aviv was also the victory of the middle class that vindicated his view, that capitalist principles should guide the Zionist enterprise. For him, Tel-Aviv embodied a vision, which the historian Ilan Troen succinctly terms the vision of the "bourgeois city."[17] Promoting commerce and industry as the economic foundations of the city, Dizengoff rejected socialist principles, raised the banner of free enterprise, and firmly believed in private capital, in contrast to national capital, as the appropriate instrument for building up the land:

> We pride ourselves in this city of ours, which has been entirely built with Hebrew hands, Jewish capital and Jewish will, with no distinctions of class. Tel-Aviv was founded by the initiative of private citizens . . . The up-building of our land and its revival will not be the result of the class system.[18]

*Davar,* the organ of the Histadrut [Labor Federation], offered a different perspective. The anniversary editorial noted that the doubts regarding Tel-Aviv and its prospects did not disappear even after the city's new prosperity.[19] Whereas Dizengoff emphasized the middle class and free enterprise as the pillars of Tel-Aviv's success, from the perspective of labor Zionism, beyond trade and industry, Jewish workers and municipal independence were the two crucial factors that would decide the fate of the city. The mass rally in Tel-Aviv on 1 May demonstrated the power of Labor as a political power in the city and as an ideological alternative to the bourgeois city.

For Dizengoff, Tel-Aviv Day served as a platform to propagate his vision of and views about the city he headed. The vision of Tel-Aviv as an aspiring center of international trade was evinced in the decision to associate the anniversary celebration with the fourth Exhibition and Fair of Palestine and the Near East that opened at the beginning of April in Tel-Aviv.[20] As Dizengoff explained,

> The time of the exhibition coincides with the twentieth anniversary of the city of Tel-Aviv, which is a permanent demonstration and a living exhibition of everything that Jewish pioneers can accomplish when they enjoy freedom of action while building the national home in their homeland.[21]

This was to become a tradition, as Dizengoff asserted in his opening speech of the anniversary celebration: "The exhibition and the fair will be held annually and our city will be a trading city that connects the east and the west."[22]

The link between the fair and the anniversary celebration was also demonstrated through ceremonial geography. The ceremonial structure of the celebration consisted of three successive parts: the opening ceremony at the fairground, a parade to City Hall, and the ball at the fairground. The parade that converged at City Hall emphasized its symbolic prominence as both a building and an institution. The fairground provided space to accommodate the many invited guests. Beyond practical considerations, the fairground was also a statement about the vision of Tel-Aviv as an aspiring center of trade for Palestine and the Near East.

The different themes of the anniversary celebration were presented in speeches and newspaper articles and were embedded into the ceremonial texture of the celebration. As a living testimony to their heroic endeavor, the founders of the city were distinguished guests of honor in the public events. The children of Tel-Aviv who took part in the parade to City Hall represented the future of the city. The staged meeting between the founders and the children at City Hall at the end of the parade was a gesture of much symbolic resonance: it signified in ritual form the obligation of future generations to the vision that underlay the founding of the city.

Significantly, the representative of Tel-Aviv's youth at the opening ceremony was the first boy born in the city in 1910. Celebrated as 'the first natural citizen of Tel-Aviv', the first-born child was emblematic of the success of Tel-Aviv: for the natural citizens born and raised in the city, Tel-Aviv was a hometown in the same way as the Land of Israel was the homeland of the *sabra,* the native-born Jews of Palestine, and later Israel.

Unlike monuments, ceremonies are ephemeral. Their preservation is confined to personal memories of those who shared the experience, but personal memories, unless recorded in writing or in other media, are also of limited duration. The Hebrew newspapers recorded the public events and official speeches for future generations, but their public resonance was nil the day after they were printed. The municipality distributed a commemorative pin, which was small and of limited relevance once the celebration was over except for future collectors of Tel-Aviv paraphernalia. Notably, the municipality initiated no major architectural project to integrate the memory of the anniversary into the architectural fabric of the city.

One exception was the anthology edited by Aharon Vardi. This literary monument was an anthology of a variety of references to Tel-Aviv and a comprehensive collection of speeches and reports about Tel-Aviv. Published at the end of 1928, the book-like monument, *The City of Wonders*,[23] recorded the city's first twenty years. The designation "city of wonders" was common in this period. It represented the enthusiasm shared by many a commentator for Tel-Aviv by virtue of its being ". . . one of the wondrous creations that our people created in this generation of the reviving Land of Israel."[24]

Notwithstanding Vardi's anthology, one lasting effect of the 1929 anniversary celebration was that as a first of its kind, it set a precedent. It not only rendered an anniversary celebration a viable option, it also paved the way for the tradition of anniversary celebrations.

## 1934—The Silver Jubilee

On 12 January 1934, Tel-Aviv was formally accorded city status. Since its twentieth anniversary, it had transformed from a middle-size town to a large city of 100,000 residents and some 6,000 buildings. Following the immigration of German Jews, the city experienced a construction boom that affected the shape of the city and its character.[25] New streets, buildings, coffee shops, factories, and cars lent the city the appearance of a bustling metropolis.[26] Understood in terms of tradition rather than innovation, the idea to celebrate the twenty-fifth anniversary was raised on the municipal agenda in October 1933. According to the first draft of a program for the coming celebration, "All the festivities should take on the symbolic character of national revival in the homeland and demonstrate the economic and cultural accomplishments of the first Hebrew city."[27] The proposal also linked the festivities to the Levant Fair, ". . . which is an organic part of the Tel-Avivan creation." In its first meeting, the jubilee commission set up by the municipality decided to conduct the anniversary celebration in conjunction with the Levant Fair.[28] In March 1934 the municipal council pronounced that the celebrations would coincide with the fair and ". . . in the form of a big demonstration of the accomplishments of The First Hebrew City with Mr. M. Meir Dizengoff at its head."[29]

Following the precedent set in 1929, the anniversary celebration was linked to the fair, which in 1932 was renamed Levant Fair. In 1934 the international fair was expanded and relocated to the new fairground in the north of Tel-Aviv, at the mouth of the Yarkon River. Notably, Mayor Dizengoff was also in charge of the fair in accordance with his vision of Tel-Aviv as an international trade center. Glickson elaborated on the connection between the fair and the jubilee, "The Exhibition is a fine framework for the silver jubilee, a superb center for the celebrations. The exhibition and the Levant Fair are evidence of the power of creation and the future of Tel-Aviv . . ."[30] With twenty-nine states represented and twelve national pavilions, the Levant Fair was also meant to assert the place of Tel-Aviv as "a center and key for the economic development of the Near East." For Dizengoff, the fair was the ". . . crowning glory of Tel-Aviv's activity and in it the entire wonderful symphony of will, faith and creation are reflected."[31]

Notwithstanding the message it entailed about the vision of Tel-Aviv as an aspiring international center of trade, the decision to associate the anniversary celebration with the fair was at the expense of the commemorative function of the anniversary. In 1934 the anniversary celebration opened on 1 May. However, according to the Hebrew calendar that year, it coincided with 16 Iyar, a date that had no historical significance in connection with the founding of Tel-Aviv. A by-product of this dating was that the anniversary celebration coincided with the festival of *Lag Ba'omer*.

The twenty-fifth anniversary celebration was larger and lasted longer than the twentieth anniversary celebration. Dizengoff consulted some of the prominent citizens of the city regarding the upcoming anniversary celebrations.[32] Bialik opined that the celebrations should be limited to

three days and concluded at *Lag Ba'omer*. He also favored issuing a commemorative medal and called for "the beginning of a new project," such
as a public garden.

On 26 April the Levant Fair was opened. Mayor Dizengoff and the
High Commissioner gave speeches. The mayor referred to the fair as
"Tel-Aviv's silver jubilee fair"; he also noted that the fair was "the most
prominent demonstration of the city's achievements."[33] Although not all
national pavilions were opened, during the first five days some 100,000
visitors attended the fair.[34] On Sunday evening, 1 May, the opening ceremony of the city's silver jubilee took place at the fair's amphitheater.
Yehuda Karni's "Hymn to Tel-Aviv" was sung for the first and last time
in public. On stage were the founders, members of the municipal council, and representatives of thirty-five Jewish communities from abroad.
In the opening speech, Dizengoff reiterated that Tel-Aviv was the "center
of national aspirations and the national creation of the entire Israeli nation."[35] The High Commissioner did not attend the ceremony in person,
but in the speech read on his behalf he congratulated "the wonderful
city" on its silver jubilee.

The repertoire and the duration of Tel-Aviv's silver jubilee out-
performed previous public festivals in the city, while the Levant Fair
added international flair. Many of the public events under the rubric
"today in the fair" took place: sport competitions, *Lag Ba'omer* bonfires,
and a theatrical show—"Tel-Aviv: a daughter city in Israel." Written by
Avigdor Hameiri and based on the original minutes of the founders'
deliberations, the "Americaniada"—an allusion to the popular Purim
*adloyada*—re-created a meeting of the founders, played by leading actors
of the Habimah Theater.[36] Notably, the show exuded a sense of nostalgia
for bygone times.

The ceremonial repertoire of the silver jubilee also included elements
that were first introduced at the twentieth-anniversary celebration.
Prominent among these was the parade of Tel-Aviv's children to City
Hall and the reception there by the mayor and the founders.[37] In accordance with the emphasis on the symbolic significance of the first-born
children of Tel-Aviv, which also figured prominently in the twentieth-
anniversary celebration, each pupil received a picture of the first son and
first grandson of Tel-Aviv with Bialik's poem commemorating the birth
of Tel-Aviv's first grandchild.

Fig. 2.2. Public announcement: opening ceremony of
Dizengoff Street, 3 May 1934.

The founders were assigned a prominent role in the ceremonial texture of the twentieth-anniversary celebration. As both a founder and
acting mayor, Dizengoff served in 1929 as the master of ceremonies;
however, in 1934 he was elevated to a special symbolic status that reso-
nated with his title "the city's father." In March 1934, the city council
resolved that the anniversary celebration would be "in the form of a big
demonstration of the accomplishments of *The First Hebrew City* with
Mr. Dizengoff at its head."[38] A special honor was bestowed on him on 3

May, naming after him a newly built thoroughfare—*Rehov Dizengoff*—
designed to connect the city center with the fairgrounds in the north.[39]
Notably, the new project requested by Bialik was neither a public garden
nor a museum nor a monument to the founding of the city, but a commemoration of the mayor.

Following the precedent set when the city celebrated its twentieth
anniversary in 1929, the primary theme of the silver jubilee of 1934 was
Tel-Aviv as a special achievement of the Jewish people and of national
revival. Unlike 1929, in 1934 Tel-Aviv was not "under probation": its me-
teoric development in the early 1930s indicated that the city was resilient
and progress was what lay ahead. Unlike 1929, the denunciation of the
city as a legitimate Zionist endeavor was only on the margin of the public
discourse of the city. In his speech at the opening ceremony, Dizengoff
denounced contemporary anti-Semitic propaganda and maintained
that Jews, members of an allegedly "defective race," could be productive and that Tel-Aviv was the proof that all that was needed was will
and faith.

The silver jubilee of Tel-Aviv was a celebration of triumph. Yet the
obligatory rhetoric of praises and compliments was to an extent marred
by concerns about the city losing its "civilized" character and becoming
unruly as the result of its unprecedented rapid growth. Such concerns
had been voiced by prominent public figures alarmed by what they perceived as the cultural and moral decay of the city. Notably, Bialik warned
that Tel-Aviv was facing the danger of becoming "a levantine city, like
other coastal cities. . . ."[40] In his diagnosis, "Our Tel-Aviv is sick."[41]

Tel-Aviv's silver jubilee provided an opportunity to address the concerns about the alleged vices and flaws of the city. Commenting on the
anniversary celebration, the editor of *Hapoel Hatzair,* the ideological organ of Zionist Labor, warned, "It may be a large and wonderful city, very
noisy, perhaps with a shiny façade, pseudo-European, yet socially and
culturally hollow and corrupt from within."[42] In his speech at the opening ceremony, Dizengoff maintained that the future mission of those
committed to the city was to mold its cultural character. In a testament-
like appeal he challenged the future leaders of the city:

> You, who will be entrusted with the fate of our city after me, watch over its
> cultural character; not houses, streets and gardens constitute a town but

the qualities of its residents; the language, the love of work and creation; equality, freedom, the belief in our power and the will to live a life of dignity and self-reliance. Uphold our national ideals, since the existence of our city is dependent on them.[43]

The Hebrew press reported on the events included in the festive program and printed the highlights of the speeches by dignitaries, which created a sense of popular support for the city and its mayor. The notion of a common cause between leaders and residents alike predominated.

Criticism was mainly limited to the alleged failures of the city to ful-. fill the ideals projected onto it rather than to the festive program devised by the municipal authorities. One exception was a critical evaluation of the celebration in *Davar* two weeks later. The venue suggested ulterior political motives, though these were not spelled out in the article. In an emphatic tone, the author stated, "No. The city did not celebrate. The city elders celebrated themselves."[44] The paper also claimed that the decision to relocate the festivities to the fairground in the north of the city had the effect of the celebration not having been felt in the city itself: "The city remained mundane and dust-covered as always." The author further argued that the celebration was provincial, like a fire-brigade celebrating the tenth anniversary of its first pump.

The reception for the representatives of the Jewish Diaspora on the last evening of festivities concluded the anniversary celebration with a statement about Tel-Aviv as a "center of the Israeli nation." The fair lasted longer, a mixture of pleasure and business opportunities that cemented Tel-Aviv's reputation as a center of international trade. Unlike 1929, the municipality promoted the publication of a book on Tel-Aviv. Edited by Alter Druyanov, *Sefer Tel-Aviv* was meant to be a textual monument. When the book was published it was also a commemorative token to Dizengoff who died in September 1936.

In September 1938 mayor Israel Rokach (Dizengoff's successor) announced that, "It is not the right time to conduct celebrations in Tel-Aviv."[45] The issue was the city's forthcoming thirtieth anniversary the following year. Though laconic, the reason was clear: British mandatory Palestine was still in a state of emergency following the Arab uprising that began in April of 1936, Jews were severely persecuted in Germany and Poland, and the clouds of an international conflict were gathering in Europe. Rokach, unlike his predecessor, was less appreciative of the festive dimension of municipal life. Dizengoff lived up to his title as the city's father; Rokach was mainly busy with running the city in a time of acute crisis.

Belatedly, the founders and veteran citizens of Tel-Aviv gathered in February 1940 to mark the anniversary and decided to publish an anthology of essays, reports, memories, and photos of Tel-Aviv in its first thirty years. However, this downsized project never materialized.

### 1959—The Golden Jubilee

In his introduction to an anthology published on the occasion of Tel-Aviv's golden jubilee in 1959, Mayor Haim Levanon asserted that contemporary Tel-Aviv was proof that the project conceived by those who envisioned building a "mother city in Israel" had been crowned with success.[46] Like earlier anniversaries, the golden jubilee was dedicated to celebrating the triumph of the first Hebrew city as a modern city. At this stage of its history, defining Tel-Aviv as such was more a statement about history than a declaration of allegiance to the Zionist vision underlying its founding.

However, Tel-Aviv's anniversary celebrations in 1959 were overshadowed by Israel's tenth anniversary, which had been lavishly celebrated all over the country the year before. Moreover, the approaching municipal elections cast a long shadow on the festivities.

Like former anniversary celebrations, Tel-Aviv's golden jubilee was closely linked to the fair. Unlike the former anniversary celebrations, the festive events that commemorated the founding of Tel-Aviv preceded the fair. Tel-Aviv's golden jubilee in 1959 consisted of two components that lay five months apart. The first was scheduled for March 1959 and included a sequence of commemorative and festive events. The second was the jubilee exhibition at the newly built fairground beyond the Yarkon River that was opened on 19 August 1959. Significantly, the scheduling of ceremonial events was devoid of any commemorative meaning in regard to the founding of the city. In his address at the exhibition's opening ceremony, Levanon pointed out that the opening ceremony fell on 15 Av, ". . . which in our tradition is regarded as a day of festivities."[47]

The mayor proclaimed the opening of the festive events at a special meeting of the municipal council on 10 March. On the following day Tel-Aviv's schools marked the anniversary, and members of the municipal council made a pilgrimage to Dizengoff's gravesite at the Trumpledor Cemetery. In a festive event held in the evening, the twenty-two surviving founders were given memorial pins. The culmination of the festive sequence was a grand event at the culture hall, with President Yitzhak Ben-Zvi as the guest of honor, who, in his address, recalled the early days of Tel-Aviv.

In his speech at the opening ceremony of the jubilee exhibition, Levanon explained that the municipality preferred not to "waste" money on ephemeral events, "which leave nothing but deficit behind."[48] Echoing Bialik's suggestion in 1934, he explained: "We thought it appropriate to celebrate our jubilee by launching cultural and economic projects that have a permanent value." The project he referred to was Tel-Aviv's new fairground. Beyond planting a garden and a jubilee grove, the centerpiece of the jubilee was the historical exhibition at the new fairground.

According to the mayor, the jubilee exhibition realized Diznegoff's vision.[49] The idea was to revive the Levant Fair by building a new exhibition center. The new fairground was to serve international exhibitions and to host future Levant Fairs, the first of which was to be held in 1961. The opening of the jubilee exhibition was also the inauguration of Tel-Aviv's exhibition center.[50] The main attraction of the jubilee exhibition was the 1,200 square meter municipality pavilion. According to those in charge, the theme of the exhibition was "Tel-Aviv from sand dunes to the economic and cultural center of the Yishuv and the state."[51] The inauguration ceremony was held on 19 August 1959. Minister of the Interior Israel Ben-Yehuda, representing the government, congratulated the assembled 3,000 invited guests: "Those who follow the accomplishments of Tel-Aviv's fifty years stand before a miracle that only the effort of pioneers could realize."[52]

According to the first program from December 1957, the exhibition was intended ". . . to reflect the development of the city from her founding through its jubilee and plans for the future."[53] The advisory committee was nominated by the mayor in January 1959. Its aim was to outline the program and the master plan of the exhibition in an effort "to give a constructive expression to the ideas and to visually show the dynamic development of the city, its history, patterns of life, the landscape and its future."[54] Arieh Elhanani, who had been actively involved in various Zionist exhibitions since the 1930s, was the chief designer and architect.

Among the various exhibits, the wheel of Tel-Aviv's first stagecoach evoked nostalgia for the early days of the new neighborhood. A painting depicted the contemporary metropolis in an attempt to capture the dynamic character of Tel-Aviv. The municipality's plans for the future were displayed, among them eliminating the slums, developing a park along the seashore, building a highway along the Ayalon River, and cleaning up the sea from sewage. International flavor was provided in a pavilion where thirty cities from abroad were represented by emblems and large photos.

Notwithstanding official emphasis on Tel-Aviv as a modern, even a cosmopolitan city, the most popular event of the jubilee and one that had an enduring impact on Israel's popular culture, was the show *Little Tel-Aviv*. Authored by Haim Hefer and Dan Ben-Amotz, it was performed in the fairgrounds in conjunction with the jubilee exhibition. Whereas the exhibition was an official project meant to be informative and educative, the show was privately produced. It comprised various period reconstructions of life in Tel-Aviv in its early years.[55] It offered a nostalgic view of the past as an age of innocence and boundless optimism.

Nostalgia was also the theme of Nahum Gutman's book *A Small Town with a Few People* that was also published in 1959. The combination of nostalgia for a bygone past and sense of pride regarding the modern character of the city predominated in the celebration of Tel-Aviv's golden jubilee. On the one hand there was the longing for the old Tel-Aviv, which was increasingly disappearing from the cityscape. On the other hand was a sense of pride in the new institutions that adorned the city. These included the culture hall and the pavilion for contemporary art (the Helena Rubenstein pavilion), which represented the modern side of Tel-Aviv. The day before the official jubilee ceremony *Ma'ariv* reported that a department store, the first of its kind in Israel, was about to be opened in Tel-Aviv.[56] Purportedly, this indicated that, "Tel-Aviv, celebrating its jubilee, was receiving a mark of maturity."[57]

In July 1959, only a few weeks before the opening of the jubilee exhibition and the production of *Little Tel-Aviv*, the building of the Herzliya Gymnasium (commonly known as *ha'gymnasia*) was demolished, which for many signified the erasure of history. Public anger at the demolition and the success of the *Little Tel-Aviv* show demonstrated that nostalgic attachment to the city's early history was a shared public sentiment that the official presentation at the jubilee exhibition, with its emphasis on the new and the modern, on development and progress, failed to address.

Overshadowed by the next municipal elections, the jubilee festivities served as an arena for the political struggle between the right of center General Zionists that ran the municipality, and Labor, which dominated the national government. Tel-Aviv's Workers' Council proclaimed, "Tel-Aviv's jubilee is the festival of the organized working class that constitutes fifty percent of the population of Tel-Aviv." David Ben-Gurion, prime minister and leader of Mapai, was invited to the jubilee festivities, but declined to attend. The General Zionists explained why he and his ministers avoided the festivities: "Tel-Aviv, which demonstrates the achievements of productive free enterprise and its capacity to absorb multitudes of new immigrants, destroys the legend of the 'constructive' socialism."[58] They also repeated Dizengoff's argument raised on the occasion of the city's twentieth anniversary, by which Tel-Aviv demonstrated the victory of the principle of free enterprise, and was thus a model for the state as a whole.[59] In the election, Levanon lost to Mordechai Namir of Mapai, thereby ending General Zionist political hegemony in Tel-Aviv.

Beyond party politics and election propaganda, the primary theme of the celebration was the triumph of the vision of the first Hebrew city. An article in *Ha'aretz* published on the occasion of the jubilee presented the story of Tel-Aviv as a succession of key events in the history of the development of the city as a unique Zionist creation.[60] However, according to another commentator, Tel-Aviv's success lay in its becoming an ordinary city that no longer needed self-assurances about its viability.[61] At the current stage of its history, so the commentary said, the first Hebrew city became self-evident, even obvious.

* * *

Dizengoff's speech at the opening ceremony of Tel-Aviv's silver jubilee envisioned the city celebrating its golden jubilee in 1959. Jubilees are arbitrary signposts. At the same time they also possess substantial power to mentally frame historical progression.

The three anniversaries examined here belong to the first Hebrew city phase of Tel-Aviv, when the conceptualization of the city in terms of a redemptive vision of national revival reigned supreme. As an ideational and ideological construct, the first Hebrew city coincided with the foundational phase of Tel-Aviv. It can be argued that notwithstanding official rhetoric, the golden jubilee in 1959 actually signified the end of this phase in the city's history.

Scheduling the anniversary of a city entails dating its beginning in history. However, as Keith Petersen observed, "[F]ew communities can be said to have a single date when they suddenly 'began'."[62] The celebration of the twentieth anniversary of Tel-Aviv in 1929 roughly coincided with, and therefore implicitly commemorated, the lottery of plots on 11 April 1909. However, in 1929 Dizengoff also specifically noted that no one could safely say on which date in 1909 Tel-Aviv began. When Tel-Aviv marked its silver and golden jubilees in 1934 and 1959, respectively, the ceremonial events were not scheduled according to the date of this historical event. Moreover, the issue of when the city actually began was left open. In 1939 it was specifically stated, "Indeed there are different dates that can represent the beginning of the city, but there is no definite one . . . one can choose a date for convenience."[63]

However, the notion of a birthday entails a beginning, since "the mind wants to conceive a point in either time or space that marks the beginning of all things."[64] Despite earlier reservations, Tel-Aviv was later endowed with an officially sanctioned beginning: the lottery of the plots on 20 Nissan (11 April 1909). As explained by the official *Centennial Handbook of Tel-Aviv,* the celebration was scheduled for April 2009— "One hundred years after the famous land raffle,"[65] which marked the birth of the first Hebrew city.

## NOTES

All references are in Hebrew unless otherwise stated.

1. Bialik to David Yellin, 8 May 1929, in *The Letters of Chaim Nahman Bialik,* vol. 4, ed. Fishel Lahover (Tel-Aviv, 1938), 253.

2. Anat Helman, *Urban Culture in 1920s and 1930s Tel-Aviv* (Haifa, 2007).

3. *Ha'aretz,* 3 May 1929.

4. Tel-Aviv Historical Archive (hereafter: TAHA), 4-3127b.

5. *Ha'aretz,* 2 May 1929.

6. *Ha'aretz*, 2 May, 9 April, 17 April 1929.

7. Founded in 1878, Petah Tikva marked its fiftieth anniversary by publishing a history book: *Festschrft*, ed. Yaacov Yaari-Polskin, *The Jubilee Book for the Fiftieth Anniversary of the Founding of Petah Tiqwa* (Tel-Aviv, 1929).

8. *Ha'aretz*, 2 May 1929.

9. *Davar*, 2 May 1929.

10. *Ha'aretz*, 2 May 1929.

11. Haim Feirberg "Lottery for the Plots of Ahuzat Bayit: The Creation of an Urban Myth," *Israel* 4 (2003): 83–107.

12. *Ha'aretz*, 2 May 1929.

13. Ibid.

14. Ibid.

15. Ibid.

16. Ibid.

17. S. Ilan Troen, "Tel-Aviv in the 1920s and the 1930s: Competing Ideologies in shaping the character of the Zionist Metropolis," *Proceedings of the Tenth World Congress of Jewish Studies 1989*, section B, 1: 394–397.

18. *Ha'aretz*, 3 May 1929.

19. *Davar*, 3 May 1929.

20. The official term was "The Exhibition and Levant Fair," but it was also referred to as "The Jubilee Fair," *Ha'aretz*, 8 April 1929.

21. *Ha'aretz*, 2 May 1934.

22. *Ha'aretz*, 3 May 1934.

23. Aharon Vardi, ed., *The City of Wonders: Writers and Statesmen on Tel-Aviv—for its Twentieth Anniversary* (Tel-Aviv, 1928).

24. Yoram Bar-Gal, *Homeland and Geography* (Tel-Aviv, 1993), 161.

25. Yitzhak Grinboym, "Tel-Aviv," *Yedi'ot 'Iriyat Tel-Aviv* 1932–33, 245.

26. *Ha'aretz*, 12 July 1935.

27. Letter [unsigned] to Israel Rokach, 11 October 1933, TAHA, 4-1948.

28. Yehuda Nedivi to Israel Rokach, 7 February 1934, TAHA, 4-1948.

29. *Ha'aretz*, 18 March 1934.

30. *Ha'aretz*, 28 March 1934.

31. "Tel-Aviv is twenty-five years old," TAHA, 4-1948.

32. General consultation with regard to the jubilee celebration, 27 March 1934, TAHA, 4-1984.

33. *Davar*, 27 April 1934.

34. *Davar*, 4 May 1934.

35. *Ha'aretz*, 3 May 1934.

36. "Today in the Levant Fair," advertisement, *Ha'aretz*, 3 May 1934.

37. *Ha'aretz*, 4 May 1934.

38. *Ha'aretz*, 28 March 1934.

39. *Ha'aretz*, 4 May 1934.

40. Haim Nahman Bialik, "On opening the university classes," *Spoken Lectures*, vol. 2 (Tel-Aviv, 1935), 89.

41. Bialik's farewell address before he left for Vienna to receive medical treatment, *Ha'aretz*, 3 June 1934. He did not survive his illness.

42. Yitzhak Lufban, "Tel-Aviv," *Hapoel Hatzair*, 5.29, 11 May 1934.

43. *Ha'aretz,* 3 May 1934.

44. *Davar,* 18 May 1934.

45. Rokach to A. Machner, 14 September 1938, TAHA, 4-1950.

46. Yosef Aricha, ed., *Tel-Aviv: A Historical-Literary Anthology* (Tel-Aviv, 1959), 1.

47. Mayor's opening ceremony address, 19 August 1959, TAHA, 4-3183.

48. *Ha'boker,* 18 August 1959.

49. Ibid.

50. Mayor's speech at the opening of the exhibition, 18 August 1959, TAHA, 4-3183.

51. Decision of the committee nominated by the mayor, Central Zionist Archive, A458 19.

52. *Ma'ariv,* 20 August 1959.

53. The content of the exhibition, 12 December 1957, TAHA, 4-3182.

54. Moshe Amiaz, city engineer, report on the activities of the advisory committee for the municipality's pavilion, TAHA, 4-3183.

55. Dan Ben-Amotz and Haim Hefer, "Introduction," *Little Tel-Aviv* (Tel-Aviv, 1980).

56. *Ma'ariv,* 10 March. See also *Ha'aretz,* 8 April 1959.

57. *Ma'ariv,* 27 March 1959.

58. *Ma'ariv,* 23 March 1959.

59. *Ma'ariv,* 23 August 1959.

60. *Ha'aretz,* 11 March 1959.

61. *Ha'aretz,* 13 March 1959.

62. Keith Petersen, *Historical Celebrations—A Handbook for Organizers of Diamond Jubilees, Centennials, and other Community Anniversaries* (Boise, ID, 1986).

63. Aharon Ze'ev Ben-Yishai to Eliezer Lubrani, June 13 1939, TAHA, 1027-1950.

64. Edward Said, *Beginnings: Intentions and Methods* (New York, 1975), 41.

65. *Tel-Aviv—Yafo Centennial Handbook: 1909–2009* (Tel-Aviv, 2008), 9.

# THREE

# Tel-Aviv's Foundation Myth: A Constructive Perspective

*Hizky Shoham*

## Foundation Myths

Many historical cities have invented their "sense of place" through myths of origin, which mark symbolic borders between chaos and cosmos, or nature and culture.[1] In modern cities with rapidly changing physical cityscapes, myths are used to create a sense of continuity in the form of local traditional practices, local sites of memory, shared beliefs about the city's unique "climate" (intellectual Boston, romantic Venice, effervescent Tel-Aviv, etc.), and foundation myths.[2] As in every other "mnemonic society," newcomers and the next generation are socialized into the city's collective memory by "libraries, bibliographies, folk legends, photo albums, and television archives . . . history textbooks, calendars, eulogies, guest books, tombstones, war memorials . . . pageants, commemorative parades, anniversaries, and various public exhibits of archaeological and other historical objects."[3]

In this context, my concern is the construction of the urban anniversary and its own kind of identity construction through retrospective myths of origins. Commemorating a specific moment of creation, the anniversary signifies the border between chaos and cosmos not only in time, but also in space. It symbolically differentiates the city from the chaos that preceded the city's existence and the chaos that still surrounds it. Occurring on the same calendar date, it makes a clear connection between the past moment of a city's creation and its ongoing creation in the present. On the other hand, it also demonstrates a linear narrative of continuous development from the modest beginning in the past to the massive present, emphasizing the rapid changes in urban landscape, thus evoking nostalgia. The existence of a city's active and functioning foundation myth can thus indicate the existence of a sense of place, that is, its functioning as a social site of identity construction through "mnemonic socialization" or "mnemonic tradition[s]."[4]

The various myths of Tel-Aviv are the focus of many diverse recent studies.[5] This essay deals with the gradual appearance of Tel-Aviv's foundation myth in the public sphere during the interwar years, its formative period, with 1929 and 1934 as datum-points of its twentieth and twenty-fifth anniversaries. The development of Tel-Aviv's foundation myth both reflected and created Tel-Aviv's becoming a distinct "place" with its own collective memory—which did not exist before World War I. The foundation myth, which was already crystallized in the 1930s, and has become common knowledge, includes the following basic themes:

1. There was a founding ceremony linked to the land lottery held on 11 April 1909, during the Passover holiday, which was meticulously planned by entrepreneur Akiva Arye Weiss, the first chairman of Ahuzat Bayit.

2. The founders dared to envision a huge Hebrew (another version, Jewish) city on the desolate desert sand. The urbanized entity whose growth began in the 1920s is an institutional, political, socio-economical, and cultural continuation of the suburb, or the Jewish neighborhood(s), of the late Ottoman Era. World War I was but a temporary break in this linear process.

3. The suburb was built by "Hebrew labor," by Jewish workers.

4. A somewhat surprising theme: There were many disputes and personal conflicts among the first founders, especially between Weiss and Dizengoff.

5. The myth, especially as reflected in Soskin's famous photograph, symbolizes the creation *ex nihilo* of the city "from the sands," and the self-perception of the Zionist project as a universal civilizing project of colonizing the wilderness. Implicitly, the emphasis on the sands motif constructed and fortified the sense of separation and independence of Tel-Aviv from its rival national-urban space, Jaffa.[6]

This foundation myth reflected the highly urbanized Tel-Aviv during the Mandate. However, in 1909, this myth was generally unknown or at least did not yet function as a myth. The formation of the components of this myth, their inclusion in its history, and their projection back to their alleged origins, provide a clear case study for a micro-historical examination of the invention of tradition.[7]

Although it is broadly agreed that the foundation myth was invented retroactively, its diachronic development has remained unstudied, except for some comments by Feirberg.[8] I rely on his important deconstructive study of the "land lottery" photograph, but adopt a chronological-philological method. I carefully follow the gradual construction of a new collective memory from micro-details, which were joined together to form a complete story. The narrative was gradually created through public images and accounts from the genesis period with some contributions by memory agents, who relied on more or less reliable sources, from oral stories and memories to diaries and historical documents. However, the chronological-philological study of the myth focuses not only on historical "discoveries," but also on common knowledge implicitly accepted as true. This development reveals a consistent process of growth of the myth and enrichment of details that were assumed about the city's foundation.

The myth was not invented out of the blue by talented authors with powerful imaginations, or by politicians with personal and group interests, nor was its author the protagonist, the city itself.[9] It was a story that was told, written, photographed, retold, rewritten, and reinterpreted in the city's homes, streets, newspapers, pamphlets, public events, and cafés. This essay examines mainly the written versions, or the written traces of oral versions of this story. The unexplained gaps between these sources reveal the common assumptions about the origins of Tel-Aviv, which, in the typical dynamics of folktales, differ from each other only in minor details.[10]

The focus on these common beliefs about the origin of the city engendered a methodological focus on public discourse, while the institutionalization of the anniversaries will be discussed here in passing. This essay concentrates on the retroactive determination of the city's exact genesis point in the calendar, while the other components of the myth are studied only secondarily. The study begins with the late Ottoman Era and examines the reaction to the founding of Ahuzat Bayit as a place separate from Jaffa. Then it traces the first appearances of the idea of a genesis point during the 1920s, and its chronological development into a whole foundation myth during the British era, and the myth as it is well known today.

## Was Ahuzat Bayit Ever Founded?

The history of Ahuzat Bayit may be told or written in alternative ways. The most commonly recalled version in Tel-Aviv's collective memory, and mostly employed by institutional historians, considers the neighborhood to be totally different from its predecessors, such as Neve Tzedek, Neve Shalom, and Mahane Israel.[11] Unlike these previous neighborhoods, Ahuzat Bayit necessitated preconstruction general planning; it behaved like a semi-political association that collected taxes and enforced by-laws, and was an eminently bourgeois settlement project whose establishment immediately influenced Jaffa's leisure-culture.[12] Some scholars also point to the existence of the city "as a dream" much before its actual establishment, and see its urban development as a realization of a pre-existing idea.[13]

Nevertheless, other historians prefer to write the history of Tel-Aviv only after World War I. They point to the rapid urban development of the British era, which was totally different from the rural development of the Jewish neighborhoods of Ottoman Jaffa. These authors, whose orientation is more toward the social sciences, tend to allude to "Mandate Tel-Aviv" in their publication titles.[14] Others, who wrote the history of Jaffa or Ottoman Palestine, see Ahuzat Bayit as an integral part of it, and tend to conclude its story during World War I or a little later.[15] Hanna Ram criticizes the dominant narrative, pointing to its anachronistic dimension. Ahuzat Bayit was but another failed attempt to deal with the limited accommodations in Jaffa, as were Jaffa's other novel neighborhoods.[16]

The truth lies somewhere in between, and depends on methodology and ideology. In terms of narrative, however, the dominant narrative marks, in time and space, a new beginning of the "new" city of Tel-Aviv as differentiated from the "old" Jaffa, whereas the second narrative speaks about a much more gradual process without a single point of departure (but with 1921 as a datum-point). How, then, did Ahuzat Bayit itself symbolically mark the new beginning? To what extent was the new neighborhood referred to as a different place, and since when?

If one traces the development of Ahuzat Bayit through contemporaneous sources alone, there is no doubt that there was no founding ceremony. No contemporaneous source mentioned the land lottery of 20 Nisan (11 April 1909) as a festive event. Those who did mention the lottery described it as a merely technical task. Even Weiss's retrospective memoirs, written in 1934 when the myth had already permeated the public sphere, did not describe a ceremony, symbolical act, or even festive feelings linked to the event.[17]

There was no such foundation ceremony during any other phase of the colonization process conducted "for the first time," such as the approval of the loan to Ahuzat Bayit members by JNF in October 1908, or announcement of the completion of the land transaction on 9 November. The first land lottery was not even commemorated. According to Druyanov, that event took place during the Jewish holiday of Sukkot in 5669 (1908) when forty-one lots were distributed. In fact, there were at least two lotteries.[18]

It seems that there was no commemoration of the foundation of the society on the eve of 28 Av (18 August 1906)—perhaps because the society existed before under other names.[19] Nor did anyone commemorate the beginning of the construction of the first house of Ahuzat Bayit, by Reuven and Rivka Segal, in June 1909. According to Weiss's memory, this event is described as festive—but apparently not enough to remember and commemorate the specific date.[20] Segal himself was described (in typical bourgeois rhetoric, as though he were there alone, without his wife) as a modern embodiment of the biblical Nachshon in his daring to begin construction in the desert without a guaranteed water supply. However, the real reason for the delays in the construction work was the endless debates about Hebrew labor. The Segal family was the first to begin construction because they "compromised" by using Arab labor—as most of the founding families eventually did.[21] The "pioneering" act of the Segals was thus highly controversial and far from festive.

The only known public ceremony that took place during the first stage of Ahuzat Bayit was the laying of the cornerstone of the Herzliya Gymnasia, 28 July 1909. Many years later David Smilansky recalled this historical moment as an elaborate ceremony, but at that time he defined the ceremony as "modest," and promised: "The main celebration will take place upon the completion of the construction."[22] It was never thought of as the foundation event of Tel-Aviv.

There was no public ceremony held upon the completion of the first houses in October 1909, nor the habitation of the last houses of the first group, in February 1910. One exception was a Tu Bishvat planting ceremony by Ahuzat Bayit's school children, one day before the association's first assemblage in the built neighborhood.[23] However, no one commemorated this day as the founding date of Tel-Aviv. In retrospect, it might have been ironic if the most agricultural Zionist festival would have marked Tel-Aviv's anniversary, which represented Urban Zionism.

The lack of an established foundation date was made evident by David Smilansky, who, in January 1912, reported that, "This neighborhood was built during the last 2–3 years."[24] The obvious lack of a public foundation ceremony for the neighborhood does not necessarily indicate the absence of a mythical discourse linked to the new suburb. Yosef Klausner, who visited Tel-Aviv in April 1912, not only ceaselessly celebrated the Hebrew and European character of the suburb, but also related to it as a place separate from Jaffa even in casual speech, and celebrated its administrative independence, or as he saw it, its "self-leadership." Tel-Aviv was a Jaffa neighborhood—but novel and quite different from Neve Tzedek and Neve Shalom in its European cleanliness, independent political organization, and its formal adoption of the Hebrew language. Klausner noted that, "Only three years ago this sand covered also the location on which this lovely neighborhood is now standing."[25]

Klausner, whose impressions were published in *Hashiloach* in 1912–14, may be regarded as the first mythologist of Tel-Aviv. His articles were the first known texts that made an explicit connection between Zionist ideologies (the political Zionism of the civilizing process of the Jews through Zionist colonization and the cultural Zionism of the revival of Hebrew language) and Tel-Aviv as the specific place of their supposed embodiment. This was the first text that mentioned the sands as the greater opponent of the civilizing project.

However, even for Klausner, Tel-Aviv was not an urban locale and did not have urban aspirations. There is no evidence that anyone thought about Tel-Aviv as a separate urban space, not even in the story "The Land's Puzzle" by Kabak (1912–14), the only literary text that mentioned Tel-Aviv before World War I. He described it as a peaceful bourgeois suburb blended into the pastoral sands. The one passage often quoted by literary critics and scholars as a prediction of Tel-Aviv's urban future is, in fact, part of a utopian discourse which, according to the narrative, still held no sway in the Yishuv, especially not for Tel-Aviv's bourgeois residents.[26]

It is not impossible that some of the founders of the suburb dared to dream about a mass-city that would be "Palestinian New York," as Weiss described his vision in retrospect. In his 1934 memoirs, Weiss quoted the first Ahuzat Bayit brochure, which was the most important documentary evidence of the existence of the urban vision for Tel-Aviv before World War I. However, as Ram notes, the brochure was reconstructed from Weiss's memory. Moreover, even according to his version, no more than five copies of the brochure were printed, for the members of the association's first executive committee.[27] There is the (unlikely) possibility that Weiss indeed envisioned an urban entity, "a Hebrew city," but if he did, this thought had no significant public manifestation. Many of the association's actions actually contradicted the urban vision, such as the initial prohibition of commercial activity, the closing of Herzl Street on the Sabbath, and especially the notorious location of the Herzliya Gymnasia.[28] The lack of a symbolical foundation act lends further testimony to the idea that Tel-Aviv was not initially conceived as a mass-city.

The absence of a foundation ceremony could have been the outcome of prosaic causes, such as concerns regarding Ottoman authorities or limited financial means. Historians cannot responsibly conclude anything from something that did not happen. We know for certain that there was no one single moment of symbolical foundation. This moment could have only been invented retrospectively.

The texts of Klausner, Kabak, and a few others are the exceptions. Even to the extent that Tel-Aviv was considered a unique nationalist project by its entrepreneurs or residents, others at that time who drew a picture of the Zionist project in Ottoman Palestine did not view the neighborhood as worth mentioning. That was the case not only for labor-movement-oriented writers.[29] Ya'ary-Poleskin did not write a single word on the founders of Tel-Aviv or its construction process (in describing Ruppin's deeds, for example) in his 1922 anthology *Dreamers and Warriors.* In 1926, he became Dizengoff's biographer and glorified the first Hebrew city, but in his 1922 anthology he referred to Tel-Aviv as a residential quarter of Jaffa, or as a small town, although he worked there himself and clearly recognized its nationalist character.[30]

Tel-Aviv was founded as a Jaffa neighborhood, an important and unique one, but as part of Jaffa's urban space. In terms of the construction of local Jewish identity, Jaffa was mainly contrasted with Jerusalem, as the center of "the new Yishuv." Tel-Aviv made its contributions to this image of Jaffa, but it was not more important than Neve Tzedek, for example, the Jewish intellectual center in Jaffa, or other "self-governing" colonies and urban suburbs in "the new Yishuv."[31] Whatever the limited extent of Tel-Aviv's distinctiveness with regard to Jaffa, it had not yet become a mnemonic society, a separate place of identity construction. This happened only during the Mandate.

### The Early 1920s: The First Steps

British rule in Palestine stimulated rapid development for Tel-Aviv, which lost its suburban character in favor of a typical industrial urbanizing space. Tel-Aviv gradually became recognized and experienced as an urban space different from Jaffa. This development was preceded by intense negotiation between the Tel-Aviv committee and the Mandate authorities concerning the measure of Tel-Aviv's municipal autonomy. In his first request to high commissioner Herbert Samuel, Dizengoff emphasized, "Our most urgent aspiration is to reach a [status of a] small township, like an English 'borough'."[32] A few months later, on 11 May 1921, Tel-Aviv obtained the status of "township" that implied a partial autonomy from Jaffa. Instead of the former Tel-Aviv committee, whose "sovereignty" was legitimized on a voluntary basis, Tel-Aviv was now a formal political body with some administrative autonomy and juridical authorities.

Although absolute autonomy was obtained only in 1927, when Tel-Aviv and Jaffa were declared two separate municipal authorities, talk about the first Hebrew city circulated in 1921. There were two sorts of mythical urban Zionist discourse: the political-institutional and the urban-civilizing. The former relates to the formal and informal administrative independence of Tel-Aviv municipality, which was considered not only a political achievement in itself, but also a sort of political experiment of Jews in self-government for "the first time in modern era." The latter relates to the civilizing urban project of ruling nature and creating a new society *ex nihilo,* employing the desolate sands as its ultimate symbol. During the 1920s, these two discourses were the source of two different narratives about Tel-Aviv's beginnings.

In March 1921, shortly before the declaration of Tel-Aviv as a township, the Tel-Aviv committee published the first issue of *Yedi'ot 'Iriyat*

*Tel-Aviv* (municipal bulletin). Among ongoing technical and administrative issues, the residents were also notified that

> The committee prepares and is about to publish a memorial book of the
> neighborhood Tel-Aviv. This book should have been printed a year ago,
> when the first Hebrew town on our land reached ten years, but it was
> delayed, not in our fault, and will now be fulfilled when the small neigh-
> borhood is going to become a large and autonomic town.[33]

Quite typically, the first talk about the need to write Tel-Aviv's history appears with a sense of dramatic change in the town's legal status
and self-perception.[34] This text assumed political-institutional continuity between the predicted urban entity of Tel-Aviv and the past neighborhood, and implied that the new township of Tel-Aviv should continue using the old committee. It is not surprising that the beginning of Tel-Aviv
was dated back to 1910 (according to the text, Tel-Aviv reached its first
decade a year before 1921), when the Tel-Aviv committee was established
and the Ahuzat Bayit association was disassembled.[35] The defining moment was the decision to establish a new self-governing committee for
the neighborhood. The same narrative appeared in 1922, in an article by
Dizengoff in *Ha'aretz,* which dealt with political-institutional issues, and
mentioned "12 years of Tel-Aviv's existence," referring to its administrative dimension.[36]

A different narrative appeared in the next issue of *Yedi'ot 'Iriyat Tel-
Aviv* after the formal recognition of Tel-Aviv as a township. According
to that issue,

> The dream that was dreamed by those who left Jaffa 12 years ago and went
> to set up homes in the desolated sands of Ahuzat Bayit, was ceaselessly
> formed during these years, until it now received the real and whole form
> of recognizing Tel-Aviv as a primal city in Israel. At the first time in Jew-
> ish history . . .

The text elaborated upon the basic component of the Tel-Aviv myth
so far—the city as an independent semi-political entity—and then described how the new status of the city offered expanded opportunities,
and concluded, "Tel-Aviv will rise and flourish, and will be the main
Hebrew city in all Palestine and one of the most important cultural and
industrial centers all over the East."[37]

This chronology better fits the civilizing narrative, which emphasizes the creation of a new European civilization in Asia. The defining moment was not the decision to establish a new semi-political body, but the heroic creation of a new civilization in the desert (here in this text, the desert is also a metonym for the entire East, to be civilized by Zionist Palestine). This new narrative looked back not to 1910, the institutional origin of Tel-Aviv, but rather to 1909 (twelve years before), the pioneering beginning of the construction in the middle of the sand dunes, or the creation *ex nihilo* of a new civilization in the wilderness. No single act of foundation was mentioned, but the story of "leaving Jaffa" for the "desolate sands" to construct new homes there in the "new" place, allegedly outside Jaffa, served the purpose of symbolically separating Tel-Aviv from Jaffa, as cosmos is divided from chaos.

Tel-Aviv at this stage was perceived, at least by its leaders, as the prospect of urban Zionism, despite the fact that in the summer of 1921 Tel-Aviv was but a small town with a few thousand residents at most.[38] Urban Zionism, so far a mere utopian vision, now had Tel-Aviv as its distinct and defined space-time site. Urban Zionism began its transformation from utopia to ideology.[39]

Nevertheless, at this stage, these narratives remained underdeveloped and their reverberation in public discourse was limited. The memorial book was not published, and for several reasons there was no public celebration to commemorate the new township status.[40] However, the town developed rapidly, and people told the story of the first families and their conquest of the desolated dunes. One such narrator was Ludwig Lewisohn, a Jewish-American reporter who visited Tel-Aviv in 1925. He told the story of sixty families that gathered on the sand dunes, but thought it happened only in 1919. The inaccuracy may be partly explained by the fact that the existence of the town as a town, both as an independent municipal entity (at least partially) and as an urban-Zionist project, began only after World War I.[41] This is the first written record that references the mythical number of sixty families. If there was any commemoration of the city's foundation in 1924, its fifteenth anniversary, Lewisohn could not have made such a mistake, yet no such public commemoration was held.[42] It seems that there was no consensus about 1909 as the foundation year.

This lack of a specific foundation date was also evident in two historical articles that were published by Alter Druyanov in *Yedi'ot 'Iriyat Tel-Aviv* in September 1925, only a few months after Lewisohn's article. In prosaic language, and relying on both primary sources and memories, he told the story of Ahuzat Bayit from the initiative taken in the summer of 1906 until the decision of the association's general assemblage to choose the name Tel-Aviv for the new neighborhood, on the eve of 13 Iyar (21 May 1910). The decision was presented as the climactic, most festive moment in the process. The two articles published in 1925, unlike Druyanov's 1936 narrative, recalled no other foundation occasion.[43] In 1936 he adopted the civilizing narrative, while here he followed the institutional one.

The foundation myth, between 1920 and 1926, points to a lack of consensus regarding public recognition of Tel-Aviv as a separate urban space with its own uniquely constructed identity. Following the 1921 recognition of Tel-Aviv's "township," the committee's officials immediately began referring to their community using the Hebrew word *ir,* which denotes both a large city and an average-sized town. Yet, in the 1920s, many of Tel-Aviv's residents still referred to Jaffa when speaking about "the city."[44] In a novel published in 1923, historical Tel-Aviv during World War I was referred to as a small town.[45] In the local news section in newspapers, reports about Tel-Aviv in 1920–1921 still referred to "Jaffa." Over the decade, these sections gradually referred to "Jaffa and Tel-Aviv" or vice versa, and only toward 1928–1929 were Tel-Aviv and Jaffa referred to separately.[46]

Despite the lack of a clear foundation moment, people in Tel-Aviv told stories about its founding, and the mythical number of sixty families was already spoken of (although only fifty-five houses were in fact built in the first stage of Ahuzat Bayit).[47] Memory agents like Druyanov became more active, and the interest in the beginnings of Tel-Aviv gradually penetrated public consciousness. The existence of Tel-Aviv as a mnemonic society was in the process of being created, but the issue of the exact foundation date did not seem to provoke any public interest.

## 1926–1929: The Genesis Emerges

The dramatic change occurred not through a text or a narrative, but by a visual image. In 1926, Abraham Soskin, a photographer who lived in

Tel-Aviv, published a small book titled *Tel-Aviv*. According to the brief introduction, Tel-Aviv was "first founded in 1909" by those "who settled on the desert sand dunes." One photo in the album displayed a group of people on a sand dune, with the caption: "The meeting founding Tel-Aviv 1908."[48]

According to Feirberg, this was the first appearance of evidence of a founding event for Ahuzat Bayit, though the nature of the photographed event was unclear.[49] The photo was also included in a biography of Dizengoff, published in the same year by Ya'ary-Poleskin, with the caption "Laying the cornerstone to the neighborhood Tel-Aviv," but without mentioning any date.[50] Soskin interpreted it in retrospect as the first assemblage, but not as a ceremony, and hence dated it 1908, before the actual beginning of the project, and probably even before the completion of land purchase. Unlike Soskin, Ya'ary-Poleskin further interpreted the occasion depicted in the photo as a symbolical foundation event, and was the first to imbue it with the festive aura of a genesis moment.

For several years, the photo was quickly disseminated and republished, sometimes with one of two interpretations: it was thought to record either the first meeting of the association in 1908, presenting the institutional narrative; or the laying of Tel-Aviv's cornerstone in 1909, presenting the civilizing one.[51] Meanwhile, the option of 1910 was implicitly abandoned.

In 1929, it was already clear that the city was founded in 1909 and, for the first time, Tel-Aviv celebrated its twentieth anniversary. Many commented that a literal anniversary (i.e., the Hebrew term *yovel*) should be celebrated only in the twenty-fifth or fiftieth year, and suspected that the occasion was an aspect of the notorious Tel-Aviv "enthusiasm for celebrations."[52] However, the city took the opportunity to celebrate itself and to articulate the urban-Zionist ideology. A large ceremony was held, the first founders were honored, and their group photo was taken for history's sake (though they could trace the representatives of only thirty-four families, much fewer than the mythical sixty).[53]

A festive anthology was published, collecting excerpts from almost all the known texts that mentioned Tel-Aviv, from Kabak and Klausner of the Ottoman era, to contemporary authors who praised Tel-Aviv especially for the occasion. Even the writer Y. H. Brenner, who deeply disliked bourgeois Tel-Aviv, was recruited. Soskin's photo was chosen to open the anthology, with the caption: "Laying the cornerstone of the neighborhood of Tel-Aviv," without the date.[54] The whole anthology was already marked by the mythical tone of the civilizing narrative, which now began to take over. Consider these memories by Shalom Ash:

> When I was in Palestine in 1908, I saw a pole stuck in the sands nearby Jaffa, into which a placard was stapled: Tel-Aviv. One Jew was going around the town, holding a map with the structure of a city with its streets, boulevards and gardens, and offered pieces for sale. I was offered to purchase the whole coast for no money. I said to myself: there you have Jews' businesses! Do they presume building a city on the sand?! Today there is a large city, populated with 20,000 people.[55]

In 1908, no placard or a map of a "city with its streets, boulevards and gardens" existed. However, the fictive dimension of Ash's "memory" is well integrated into the utopian characterization of the city, which allegedly informed the actual creation of the city on the sands. The repeating motif of the sands illustrated the "illogical" idea of building a city in the middle of nowhere. In his speech, Dizengoff emphasized that

> Sixty people, equipped with no money or previous experience, but with a will alone, stood up and built a small campus, and developed it into a large city despite the "lack of reason" in it—to build houses on the wandering sand and to establish a city without a previous "hinterland."[56]

The power of the human will was the utopian motive that Herzl weaved into urban Zionism, glorifying technology and human engineering. To prove the connection between utopian thought and Tel-Aviv, Dizengoff reversed the chronology of the city's geographical development from a "hinterland," a rural area, to an urban space. In his inverted narrative, the pioneers already knew that they had established a city, and the hinterland came only later. Urban Zionism continued to develop from mere utopian thought into a specific ideology connected to a specific place. Tel-Aviv, on the other hand, embraced the utopian idea as part of its self-image, as a place "where dreams come true." The civilizing narrative was taken a step further, and the foundation myth was charged with the utopian power of the will.[57]

Yet the foundation myth was missing a key component: an exact anniversary date of the founding of Tel-Aviv. In 1929, this question remained unanswered. In a special column to the press, Dizengoff admitted that

> None of us can ascertain in what day of 1909 Tel-Aviv was born. Whether on the day of the signing on the contract between the 60 founders and the APK [Anglo-Palestine company bank], or on the day of the purchase of the first lot, or maybe on the day of the laying of the cornerstone to the first house—since the idea to establish a Hebrew city was not born in one day. Nevertheless, we determined the day of 22 Nisan, *isru-hag* of Passover, to be our city's birthday. Every year from now on, we will think about our deeds related to our city on this day, and outline the path to go in the following years.[58]

The absence of a fixed foundation date thus sharpened the awareness of the social functions of the myth. The date 22 Nisan was supposed to be institutionalized as "Tel-Aviv Day," although Dizengoff declared that "we will always remember 11 May 1921, on which Tel-Aviv was granted its first constitution—the Scroll of Independence from Jaffa's custody, our charter of autonomy."[59]

Why, then, was 22 Nisan, or 2 May, chosen for the anniversary date and not 11 May, for instance? The last day of the "Levant Exhibition and Fair" was 2 May 1929.[60] The Tel-Aviv municipality wrapped together a few tourist events—Purim carnival, the Levant Fair, and the "Macabiah" ("the Jewish Olympic games") into "the spring events," in a successful attempt to create a tourist season for Tel-Aviv.[61] As Dizengoff himself declared in his opening speech at the exhibition, "The spring season— the tourism season, was chosen this year to coincide with Tel-Aviv's anniversary."[62] On the day after the anniversary *Ha'aretz* commented, "Our tourism season is over," and reported on the development of tourism in Tel-Aviv.[63]

Establishing the city's celebration at a time when many tourists were already visiting both enhanced tourism in general and added to the city's symbolic capital. Aside from their economic success, the "spring events" celebrated the ideology of urban Zionism and its contributions to the Zionist project, with Tel-Aviv at its center.[64] "Tel-Aviv Day" on 22 Nisan was thus an attempt to create a new date on the Zionist calendar, in which urban Zionism would celebrate its own festival and its own ideology, without necessarily commemorating a specific historic birthday.

The anniversary generated a great deal of discourse (in newspapers and journals) in favor of Tel-Aviv and its prospects, and urban Zionism in general. Even the labor-movement newspaper *Davar* quoted Dizengoff on the futility of the class category in nation-building, and offered its own interpretation of the merits of the first Hebrew city, employing the myth of the Hebrew labor.[65] The pro-urban *Doar Hayom* published a few festive columns: Jabotinsky inaugurated Tel-Aviv as no less than "our capital city," without irony. Itamar Ben-Avi, a veteran supporter of urban colonization, added that "2 May (or its Hebrew alternative!) will remain a great date in the history of Palestine from now on—the day of Hebrew independence."[66] From that date forward, urban Zionism would always be commemorated in the spring.

The twentieth anniversary also saw the first appearance of the land lottery in the foundation myth in some of the histories, legends, and glorifications of Tel-Aviv. David Izmujik, one of the founders, wrote:

> On the way to Nablus after the German colony, in front of Sheikh Ali's grove, there is a valley, and behind it there are sand dunes. The wind reshapes them every year. Here and there dry grape vines are thrown aside like corpses, and the dominance in the environment are lonely, distant sycamores.—This is Tel-Aviv twenty years ago, the land of Ahuzat Bayit in those days. The sixty families, the members of Ahuzat Bayit, were ingathering in small groups after the lottery was executed, each family celebrating its sandy dust that fell to be its estate, measuring and setting borders, some on the hills, some in the plain, all are happy with their share . . .[67]

The text continues with a sentimentalized glorification of the found-ers who dared to build their homes in the middle of the desert. The function of the lottery in this narrative is double: (1) to emphasize the peaceful and natural cooperation between the founders, who were happy with what they had despite the unequal way the shares were divided; and (2) to signify the first moment when the desolate desert was marked by civilization. Combining these two functions, the lottery powerfully signified the idea of colonization by private capital: everyone had private property, but the national goal united them in the manner of a commune and prevented jealousies.[68]

Although they knew that Tel-Aviv was not founded on a specific date, the search for a genesis moment was enhanced from that time onward. Yosef Eliyahu Chelouche also mentioned the lottery, as a con-sequence of a conflict between Weiss and Sapir, the representative of APK. According to Chelouche, the members could not wait to begin the construction, and hence, "in [Hebrew] 5669 (1909) the lottery was done in a festive manner."[69]

Chelouche adds nothing to the word "festive," not even the exact date or the exact manner of the lottery, let alone a bit of atmosphere. However, this festive theme conflicts with the one described by Izmujik, who tells of the alleged personal conflicts among the founders, which supposedly had no ideological or socio-political basis. The conflicts about "Hebrew labor" were absent from his story, although he personally played a major role in them as the contractor of many homes, the gymnasia, and some public works. He also recycled the myth of the city's premature urbanity and omitted the initial debates about shops.[70] Ironically, this emphasis on the personal conflicts among the founders preserves the two unified myths of Hebrew-ness and urbanity by concealing the ideological dimension of the disagreements which hindered construction.

The twentieth anniversary was also celebrated by gatherings of the founders who told stories from the early period. We have evidence of one event that was held in the Casino Café, a party in which the founders made a kind of oral *haggada,* telling of a new exodus, not from Egypt but from Jaffan-Christian Ajami, the "Germans neighborhood," and the rest of Jaffa's streets and passageways.[71]

The writer reported an undocumented story about "the first Shabbat" after the completion of the land purchase, with other stories and memories from the genesis period. Stories such as these were probably told often, and contributed details to the larger narrative of the city's beginnings. However, since the founders were alive, and some were important public figures, their versions were thought to be more reliable. Though details were added to the myth of origins, they did not cohere into a fixed narrative until the mid-1930s.

### 1934–1936: Fixation

Nothing seemed more natural than to celebrate Tel-Aviv's twenty-fifth anniversary in 1934. On 12 January Tel-Aviv was formally accorded city status, its importance to the Zionist project was acknowledged, and the year 1909 was already fixed in collective memory as the year of the city's founding. The Levant Fair attracted international attention, and now included a "jubilee pavilion" that described the twenty-five-year history of the city and another pavilion that displayed paintings of the cityscape. The fair was conducted from 26 April to 2 May; the main anniversary celebration was held on its final day and a few days after. Unlike the twentieth anniversary that was held in a closed space, the main event of the twenty-fifth anniversary was held in the new stadium with an audience of 10,000 and was broadcast on the radio. All the newspapers in Palestine published special supplements for the occasion, and many congratulatory telegrams ware received from all over the world. It was an impressive demonstration of the power of urban Zionism.[72]

Many narratives about the history of Tel-Aviv appeared around 1934, including different periodizations, stories about the beginning of the city, and even a nostalgic comic play, which was performed during the celebrations, on the naiveté of the founders who did not predict Tel-Aviv's urbanization. Dr. Matmon-Cohen of the Herzliya Gymnasia, for example, tried to convince the public that its foundation ceremony in July 1909 was in fact the foundation ceremony of the neighborhood, and did not hide his interest in integrating the school's story with that of the city's.[73]

One powerful myth that acquired more public prominence was the image of Dizengoff, "the city's father," who had led Tel-Aviv since 1910. This personal cult included the naming of a central plaza for his wife as part of the celebrations.[74] It may seem as though this particular myth would have included the institutional narrative that dated the beginning of the city to 1910, when Dizengoff took over the Tel-Aviv committee; however, even the cult of Dizengoff was absorbed into the civilizing narrative tied to the 1909 date.

The film *This is the Land* (produced in 1934 by Baruch Agadati, screened in 1935) greatly contributed to the civilizing narrative. The film integrated both staged and documentary scenes in a "docu-drama" fashion, describing the Zionist project as a universal drama of the struggle of civilization and wilderness. The civilizing story of Tel-Aviv was well assimilated into this narrative: One scene reconstructs Soskin's photo, but adds a speech by Dizengoff (who played himself, wearing a mustache), in which he declares that this is a cornerstone for a small neighborhood but that he envisions a large city. Toward the film's end, footage of the real Dizengoff in his festive speech on the twenty-fifth anniversary is shown, when he compared the daring vision with the reality that even

surpassed the dream. The connection between the foundation of the city
and its present reality was formed not by the calendar, but by the person
who was the founder (here individual, not plural), whose vision came
true. The same narrative, using that photo, was repeated in Dizengoff's
1935 election propaganda.[75]

The photo was also used as part of the "then and now" motif on the
cover of the festive double edition of *Yedi'ot 'Iriyat Tel-Aviv*, where it was
defined as "the first assemblage" in 1909[76] that penetrated deeply into the
collective memory. However, since much more was now known publicly
about the beginnings of Tel-Aviv, the determination of the celebration's
date required the following explanation:

> Despite the fact that the cornerstone of the first house was laid on the 15
> of Sivan 5669 [1909], the Tel-Aviv municipality decided, due to technical
> reasons, to move the celebrations forward and organize them during the
> days of the Levant Fair and exhibition (which will be called "the jubilee
> exhibition").[77]

Implicit here was the persistence in keeping the 2 May date chosen
in 1929 as "Tel-Aviv Day," although the Hebrew date moved from 23
Nisan in 1929 to 17 Iyar in 1934. The justification for this calendar choice
was "technical reasons": the Zionist civil religion generally preferred
the Hebrew calendar, while the Gregorian was used for everyday needs.
Chronicles and memoirs of Tel-Aviv's foundation usually mentioned
only Hebrew dates. The anniversary should have symbolically repeated
the moment of creation, and its inability to do so required justification.
The writer A. Z. Ben-Yishai assumed that the beginning of the construction should be used as the point of origin, in the best of civilizing tradition, and signified the laying of the cornerstone of the Segals' house on
15 Sivan as this genesis.

In contrast to Dizengoff's 1929 narrative, it was now clear that the
foundation event would be on a spring date. Before the celebrations,
Dizengoff wrote that the twenty-fifth anniversary "will be celebrated in
the spring of [Hebrew] 5694. Only 25 years passed since the cornerstone
to this city was laid in a desolate desert north of Jaffa."[78] Dizengoff did
not exactly say that there was a cornerstone-laying ceremony, and his
use of this expression could be a metaphor that reflected the absorption
of the institutional narrative into the civilizing one.

Several publications about Tel-Aviv from 1934 to 1936 mentioned that Tel-Aviv was, in principle, founded in the spring of 1909. A 1936 pamphlet by Ben-Yishai stated, "The corner-stone of the first house in the suburb was laid in the spring of 1909."[79] The creation of Tel-Aviv in the spring season was common knowledge, inferred retrospectively from the traditional celebration on 2 May as part of the spring events.

However, the anniversary was not yet connected to the lottery. Weiss, who began publishing his memoirs in 1934, did not mention one single moment of creation, but rather many, in his narrative; every "first event" was festive and caused spontaneous (but not organized) celebration. Weiss was probably unhappy with his marginalization by the celebration organizers, who defined him as only "one of the founders," minimizing his historical contributions. Nevertheless, he did not portray his lottery as the moment of genesis, simply because it never occurred to him.[80] Other witnesses also recalled the event as an illustration of Weiss's resourcefulness and vigor, and added a few colorful details, but did not see it as a genesis.[81]

These new facts about the city's founding, combined with the assumption that there was indeed a founding moment, can explain Druyanov's interpretation of the famous photo of the lottery that first gave Tel-Aviv its date of birth. As Feirberg comments, the historical sources of this identification are unclear. However, it is possible that Druyanov was pushed into this interpretation by three commonly known assumptions about the beginning: that (1) there was a moment of genesis, which (2) was commemorated in the photo, and (3) occurred in the spring of 1909. However, the photo did not appear to capture a cornerstone ceremony, since no building activity is seen in it. Druyanov had enough sources to find another event that may not have been described as festive, but luckily, "the camera left us this moment as an eternal memory." Although he added some atmosphere to the description of the event, he explicitly mentioned that, "they did not know that they were the first to build the first Hebrew city," depicting this event as only a retroactive foundation.[82]

It is not impossible that Druyanov's personal bias in favor of Dizengoff made him feel uncomfortable linking the founding event to his bitter old rival Weiss. This bias may have contributed to the invention of the story about the location of the lottery on Dizengoff's private estate.

The later declaration of Israel's independence in this exact location was but another historical and mythical irony.

This version was not immediately and fully accepted as the authorized (hi)story of the foundation of the city. In 1941, Ze'ev Vilnai thought that the lottery took place during Sukkot of 5669 [October 1908], and not in Passover 1909, but he also captioned the photo "Laying the foundation stone to the neighborhood—Tel-Aviv," while in the chronological list in the same publication he wrote that this was also the day of the lottery. This was based on Druyanov's 1925 articles. Repeating the narrative about the wilderness that existed before the founding of Tel-Aviv, Vilnai assumed that the cornerstone ceremony and the lottery were the same event—filling another gap that Druyanov left.[83] The commingling of the land lottery and the foundation ceremony was more or less accepted as the constitutive myth of Tel-Aviv.

For many reasons, the years from the twenty-fifth to the fiftieth anniversary were a period of relative decline in the status of Tel-Aviv as a site of national identity construction, and public interest in its myth of origins decreased accordingly. When, in the 1950s, interest was renewed, the story of the land lottery was already extant, ready for use, with the alleged backup of Druyanov's historiographical authority.[84]

The story of the myth in its formative period is a story of multiplication of details along with a unification of narrative. As long as the story was told and retold, and made use of additional sources, it presented a more coherent narrative, richer in detail. Sometimes the retelling of the story charged it with additional meanings, and sometimes previously assumed meanings created new details that filled narrative gaps. The question as to "When exactly was Tel-Aviv established?" found an authorized answer: "In the land lottery on Passover, 11 April 1909."

## Myth and Social Necessities

This partial reconstruction of the complicated process of the crystallization of the genesis myth of Tel-Aviv has been described from microdetails, which taken separately do not necessarily possess a distinguished symbolic quality. The creation of the specific coherent narrative of the land lottery, and the respective dating of the genesis, partly came about

due to prosaic necessities, such as the decision to celebrate urban Zionism during the spring season.

This process provided a rare opportunity to employ philological
tools and track the crystallization of a folktale, with its characteristic
mythical modern-urban theme—the struggle of civilization and wilderness, and the power of human will. This investigation revealed that
the story had no one creator or author. Druyanov's versions, considered
quite authoritative, were not of his own creation, except for the closing
of a few minor gaps—just like his predecessors' and successors' versions.
As an immigrant society, Tel-Aviv invented its own nativity by telling
a story of mythical colonization. The mythical power of the story thus
reveals the groundlessness of a binary opposition between nativity and
colonization.[85]

The evolution of Tel-Aviv into a separate urban space and a place of
Zionist identity construction during the interwar years created a mnemonic society with its own myths and rituals of memory. In the case
of Tel-Aviv, it was necessary to signify the border with Jaffa not only
in space but also in time, by finding a symbolic point of genesis.[86] As a
cultural form, by which the society would count its years of existence
and celebrate itself, the modern anniversary combines the linear and
cyclical: it counts years and reflects on progress, but also returns to the
same day on the calendar and reflects on the continuity of the "place."[87]
Thus the 1929 narrative that "Tel-Aviv was not founded on one day," did
not hold sway for long.

However, one must not fall into a sociological-deterministic trap
that sees the invention of tradition as a mere result of hidden social
needs.[88] It was not inevitable that this specific myth, and not another,
would become the city's primary myth. The development of the narrative as described here was extremely incidental. In addition to social
needs, it was, first and foremost, the outcome of several practical decisions as well as genuine attempts of people to understand their past.
It would not take much, for example, for the institutional narrative to
take over, since the city's political independence was also an important
component of its image. The celebration of the city's birthday could have
been on 11 May 1921, 21 May 1910, or Tu Bishvat 1910. If one of these dates
had been chosen, the constitutive myth of the city could be much (or
a little) different. Current attempts to see the myth as an unequivocal

factor that predetermined the destiny of Tel-Aviv and Jaffa are retroactive wisdom, and do not reflect the flexible, fluid, and prosaic nature of history.[89]

## NOTES

1. Mircea Eliade, *The Myth of Eternal Return, or Cosmos and History* (Princeton, 1954), 12–21; Yi-Fu Tuan, *Space and Place: The Perspective of Existence* (Minneapolis, 1977); "The City: Its Distance from Nature," *The Geographical Review* 68.1 (1978): 1–12.

2. Henry Lefebvre, *Writing on Cities* (Cambridge, 1996), 67; Eviatar Zerubavel, *Time Maps: Collective Memory and the Social Shape of the Past* (Chicago, 2003), 40–43.

3. Zerubavel, *Time Maps*, 6.

4. Compare Zerubavel, *Time Maps*, 3–5; Edward Muir, *Civic Ritual in Renaissance Venice* (Princeton, 1981), 70–74; Mona Ozouf, *Festivals and the French Revolution* (Cambridge, 1988), 166–186; William M. Johnston, *Celebrations: The Cult of Anniversaries in Europe and the United States Today* (New Brunswick, 1991); Thomas E. Forest, "Disaster Anniversary: A Social Reconstruction of Time," *Sociological Inquiry* 63.4 (1993): 444–456; Lyn Spillman, *Nation and Commemoration: Creating National Identities in the United States and Australia* (Cambridge, 1997); Jeffrey K. Olick, ed., *States of Memory: Continuities, Conflicts, and Transformations in National Retrospection* (London, 2003).

5. Mark LeVine, *Overthrowing Geography: Jaffa, Tel-Aviv, and the Struggle for Palestine 1880–1948* (Berkeley, 2005); Sharon Rotbard, *White City, Black City: Architecture and War in Tel-Aviv and Jaffa* (Tel-Aviv, 2005) [Hebrew]; Barbara E. Mann, *A Place in History: Modernism, Tel-Aviv, and the Creation of Jewish Urban Space* (Stanford, 2006); Maoz Azaryahu, *Tel-Aviv: Mythography of a City* (Syracuse, 2007).

6. For example see Nathan Dunevitz, *Tel-Aviv: Sands that Became a City* (Tel-Aviv, 1959), 14–15; Joseph Arikha, *Tel-Aviv: 60 Years* (Tel-Aviv, 1969), 12–13; Shlomo Shva, *Ho, City, Ho, Mother* (Tel-Aviv, 1974), 243–252. For scholarly accounts see: Mann, *A Place in History*, 74–76; Azaryahu, *Tel-Aviv*, 54–58; Rotbard, *White City, Black City*, 78–88 [all in Hebrew]; LeVine, *Overthrowing Geography*, 126–132.

7. Eric Hobsbawm and Terence Ranger, eds., *The Invention of Tradition* (Cambridge, 1983), 12–14.

8. Yaacov Shavit and Gideon Biger, *The History of Tel-Aviv: From Neighborhoods to City (1909–1936)* (Tel-Aviv, 2001), 69–72; Rotbard, *White City, Black City*, 83–85. Hayim Feirberg, "The Land Lottery of Ahuzat Bayit: The Creation of Urban Mythology," *Israel* 4 (2003): 87–103 [all in Hebrew].

9. Compare Shavit and Biger, *The History of Tel-Aviv*, 9–10.

10. Urban written myths can be analyzed as folktales if they have different but genetically similar versions. See Alan Dundes and Carl R. Pagter, *Urban Folklore from the Paperwork Empire* (Austin, 1975), xix (and thanks to Amit Asis!).

11. Shavit and Biger, *The History of Tel-Aviv*, 64; see Biger, "The Expansion of Tel-Aviv's Built Territories," in *Idan: The Beginnings of Tel-Aviv, 1909–1934*, ed. Mordechai Naor (Jerusalem, 1984), 47; Nurit Govrin, "Jerusalem and Tel-Aviv as Metaphors in Hebrew Literature," *Modern Hebrew Literature* 2 (1989): 43–47; Moshe

Zimmerman, *Tel-Aviv was Never Small* (Tel-Aviv, 2001), 13; Azaryahu, *Tel-Aviv,* 33. Unsurprisingly, the first to offer this narrative was Alter Druyanov, *Sefer Tel-Aviv* (Tel-Aviv, 1936), 66 [all in Hebrew].

12. Boaz Lev Tov, "'Controversial Recreation': Patterns of Leisure and Popular Culture of Jews in Palestine between 1882–1914, as Reflecting Social Transformations" (PhD diss., Tel-Aviv, 2007), 118–120 [Hebrew].

13. Shavit, "Love and Hatred to a Non-Exist City," *Moznayim* 1–2 (1984): 32 [Hebrew]. See also Joachim Schlor, *Tel-Aviv: From a Dream to City* (London, 1999).

14. Anat Helman, *Surrounded by Light and Sea: Everyday Life in Mandate Tel-Aviv* (Haifa, 2008); Deborah Bernstein, *Marginal Women: Gender and Nationalism in Mandate Tel-Aviv* (Jerusalem, 2008); Tammy Razi, *Forsaken Children: The Backyard of Mandate Tel-Aviv* (Tel-Aviv, 2009) [all in Hebrew].

15. Yossi Katz, *Private Entrepreneurship in the Jewish Settlement of Palestine during Second Aliya* (Ramat-Gan, 1989); Ruth Kark, *Jaffa: A City in Evolution 1799–1917* (Jerusalem, 1990); Ilan Shchori, *A Dream that Became a City: Tel-Aviv, Birth and Growth—the City that Gave Birth to a State* (Tel-Aviv, 1991), 67; Gur Alroey, *Immigrants: Jewish Immigration to Palestine in the Early Twentieth Century* (Jerusalem, 2004), 163 [all in Hebrew].

16. Hana Ram, "The Genesis of Tel-Aviv: Image and Reality," *Moznayim* 1–2 (1984): 70–72 [Hebrew].

17. Akiva Arye Weiss, *The Beginning of Tel-Aviv* (Tel-Aviv, 1957), 123–125 [Hebrew]; Feirberg, "The Land Lottery of Ahuzat Bayit."

18. "Materials for the History of Tel-Aviv," *YITA* (*Yedi'ot 'Iriyat Tel-Aviv*) (1.9.1925) 1; 2–3 (15.9.1925) 26–27 [Hebrew]. Listed anonymously, but the author is Druyanov.

19. Druyanov, *Sefer Tel-Aviv,* 64–65.

20. I have a few versions: 15 Sivan (below, note 57); "one of the last days of Sivan" (Weiss, *The Beginning of Tel-Aviv,* 142); "a few days after Shavuot" (Druyanov, *Sefer Tel-Aviv,* 110–111); or 10 Sivan (Naor, *Idan,* 205).

21. Y. Ya'ary-Poleskin, *Dreamers and Warriors* (Jaffa/Petah-Tikva, 1922), 93 [Hebrew]; Druyanov, "Materials for the History of Tel-Aviv," 2–3, 26. Druyanov's 1936 version omitted this part. See also Shchori, *A Dream that Became a City,* 67.

22. David Smilansky, "The Beginning," in *Tel-Aviv: A Historical-Literary Reader,* ed. Yosef Aricha (Tel-Aviv, 1969?), 45–47; Yossi Katz, ed., *A City is Born* (Tel-Aviv, 1981), 95. See also Ya'ary-Poleskin, *Dreamers and Warriors,* 93–94; Baruch Ben-Yehuda, ed., *The Story of Gymnasia "Herzliya"* (Tel-Aviv, 1970), 55 [all in Hebrew].

23. Druyanov, *Sefer Tel-Aviv,* 123–144.

24. Smilansky, *A City is Born,* 133.

25. Yosef Klausner, *A Becoming World* (Odessa, 1915), 38–46 [Hebrew].

26. See especially p. 19 in A. A. Kabak, "The Land's Puzzle," *Hashiloah* 31 (1914): 10–19, 124–135, 205–218 [Hebrew]; Govrin, "Jerusalem and Tel-Aviv," 45; and Mann, *A Place in History,* 82, n. 25.

27. Weiss, *The Beginning of Tel-Aviv,* 86. The book collected different texts that were published in different forums since 1934.

28. Ram, "The Genesis of Tel-Aviv." For a balanced discussion see Kark, *Jaffa,* 100–134; Shavit and Biger, *The History of Tel-Aviv,* 17–24; Katz, *Private Entrepreneurship,* 152–162.

29. Ehud Ben-Ezer, "The Beginning of Tel-Aviv in Literature," in Naor, *Idan*, 122–142.

30. Ya'ary-Poleskin, *Dreamers and Warriors*, 17, 93, 250–253; *M. Dizengoff: His Life and Deeds* (Tel-Aviv, 1926), 175 [Hebrew].

31. Yehoshua Kaniel, *In Transition: The Jews of Eretz-Israel in the Nineteenth Century Between Old and New and Between Settlement of the Holy Land and Zionism* (Jerusalem, 2000), 289–318, especially 298; Govrin, "Jerusalem and Tel-Aviv."

32. Ya'ary-Poleskin, *M. Dizengoff*, 137.

33. *YITA* 1 (Tel-Aviv, 1921), 11.

34. Compare Johnston, *Celebrations*.

35. In his speech on the twenty-fifth anniversary, Weiss emphasized that Ahuzat Bayit was still active and never ceased to exist. "Speech of one of the founders," *YITA*, 6–7 (1934): 300.

36. Ya'ary-Poleskin, *Dizengoff*, 140.

37. "Tel-Aviv's Constitution," *YITA* 2 (5.8.1921): 6.

38. Shchori, *A Dream that Became a City*, 399–400; Shavit and Biger, *The History of Tel-Aviv*, 7, 93.

39. On urban Zionism as a different ideology, see S. Ilan Troen, *Imagining Zion: Dreams, Designs, and Realities in a Century of Jewish Settlement* (New Haven, 2003), 85–111.

40. Shavit and Biger, *The History of Tel-Aviv*, 163.

41. Ludwig Lewisohn, "Letter from Abroad: A City unlike New-York," *Menorah Journal* 9.2 (April 1925): 167–172. 1919 is not a print mistake.

42. Azaryahu, *Tel-Aviv*, 45, confirms that the first anniversary was celebrated in 1929.

43. Druyanov, "Materials."

44. According to A. Z. Ben-Yishai's retrospective. See Aricha, *Tel-Aviv*, 153.

45. A. Reuveni, *The Last Ships: A Novel* (Warsaw, 1923), 111 [Hebrew].

46. Based on my survey of all local news sections in *Ha'aretz, Doar Hayom,* and *Davar* every March from 1920 to 1936. See Hizky Shoham, *Mordechai is Riding the Horse: Purim Celebrations in Tel-Aviv (1908–1936) and the Building of the New Nation* (Ramat-Gan, forthcoming) [Hebrew].

47. Smilansky, *A City is Born*, 102. Compare Feirberg, "The Land Lottery of Ahuzat Bayit," 106.

48. Abraham Soskin, *Tel-Aviv* (Berlin, 1926) [Hebrew/German/English] (English source).

49. Feirberg, "The Land Lottery of Ahuzat Bayit," 93, n. 33.

50. Ya'ary-Poleskin, *M. Dizengoff*, after p. 57.

51. Feirberg, "The Land Lottery of Ahuzat Bayit," 93, n. 33.

52. M. G. [Moshe Glikson], "On the Agenda," *Ha'aretz*, 2.5.1929, 1; S. Hoffien, "The Jubilee Exhibition," *Doar Hayom*, 9 April 1929, 2.

53. The photo appears in *YITA* 5, 6–7 (1934): 305.

54. Aharon Vardi, ed., *City of Miracles* (Tel-Aviv, 1929), 6.

55. Ibid., 65.

56. "Tel-Aviv's Twentieth Anniversary," *Ha'aretz*, 3 May 1929, 1 (emphasis original).

57. Azaryahu, *Tel-Aviv,* 42; Mann, *A Place in History,* 13–16; Ilan Gur-Ze'ev, "Tel-Aviv and the Utopian Tradition," *Journal of Jewish Thought and Philosophy* 2.2 (1993): 301–328.

58. M. Dizengoff, "Tel-Aviv's day," *Ha'aretz,* 2 May 1929, 2. Glikson, "On the Agenda."

59. Dizengoff, ibid.

60. "Tel-Aviv's municipality declares Thursday, 22 of Nisan (2 May 1929) as Tel-Aviv day" ("Tel-Aviv's anniversary" [public announcement by Tel-Aviv Municipality], *Ha'aretz,* 30 April 1929, 1).

61. Yossi Goldberg, "The Development of the Tourism Infrastructure in Mandatory Tel-Aviv (1917–1948)" (master's thesis, Bar-Ilan University, 2005), 223–224 [Hebrew].

62. "Mr. Dizengoff's Speech," *Doar Hayom,* 9 April 1929, 1; "The opening of the exhibition and the Fair," *Ha'aretz,* 9 April 1929, 1.

63. "On The Agenda," *Ha'aretz,* 3 May 1929, 1.

64. Goldberg, "The Development of Tourism Infrastructure," 129–152; Hizky Shoham, "'A Huge National Assemblage': Tel-Aviv as a Pilgrimage Site in Purim Celebrations (1920–1935)," *Journal of Israeli History* 28.1 (2009): 1–20.

65. "The Festival of Tel-Aviv," *Davar,* 2 May 1929; "Twenty Years to Tel-Aviv," *Davar,* 3 May 1929, 1.

66. Jabotinsky, "From My Kingdom's Nights (to the Twentieth Anniversary of the Yishuv's Capital)"; Ben-Avi, "The Day of Hebrew Independence," *Doar Hayom,* 2 May 1929.

67. Izmujik, "Moments (Memories of Tel-Aviv, to the Twentieth Year)," *Ha'aretz,* 2 May 1929.

68. Compare Feirberg, "The Land Lottery of Ahuzat Bayit," 88–91.

69. Yosef Eliyahu Chelouche, *The Story of My Life, 1870–1930* (Tel-Aviv, 2005 [1931]), 124 [Hebrew].

70. Ibid., 121–139, especially p. 134.

71. Y. L. Wahlman, "A Party with the builders of Tel-Aviv," in *The Hebrew Capital: A Special Edition of Doar Hayom for Tel-Aviv's Twenty-fifth Anniversary* (June 1934), 57 [Hebrew].

72. "The Half-Jubilee Celebrations," *YITA* 5, 6–7 (1934): 295–308.

73. Avigdor Ha-Meiri, "Tel-Aviv—A City and Daughter in Israel [the meeting of Tel-Aviv committee twenty-five years ago]," *The Hebrew Capital,* 58–59; Matmon-Cohen, Ben-Yaakov, Ben-Avi, and others, *The Hebrew Capital,* 9–17, 36–39, 50–51, 57 [all in Hebrew].

74. Azaryahu, *Tel-Aviv,* 52–54.

75. "This is the Land," Spielberg Archive VT DA330. Dizengoff's full speech in *YITA* 5, 6–7 (1934), 307–308; on Dizengoff's propaganda see Feirberg, "The Land Lottery of Ahuzat Bayit," 94.

76. *YITA* 5, 6–7 (1934).

77. Ibid., 295.

78. M. Dizengoff, "Toward Tel-Aviv's Jubilee Exhibition," *YITA* 4, 10 (July 1933), 334.

79. A. Z. Ben-Yishai, *Tel-Aviv* (Jerusalem, 1936), 1–2.

80. *YITA* 5, 6–7 (1934), 241, 300; Weiss, *The Beginning of Tel-Aviv,* 32, 123–125.

81. K. Y. Silman, "The First Days," in *The Hebrew Capital,* 8.

82. Druyanov, *Sefer Tel-Aviv,* 107–108; Feirberg, "The Land Lottery of Ahuzat Bayit," 97.

83. Ze'ev Vilnai, *Tel-Aviv Guide* (Tel-Aviv, 1987 [1941]), 11, 13. See Feirberg, "The Land Lottery of Ahuzat Bayit," n. 34.

84. Ibid., 105–107.

85. Unlike the simplistic analysis of Zali Gurevitch and Gideon Aran, "The Land of Israel: Myth and Phenomenon," *Studies in Contemporary Jewry* 10 (1994): 195–210.

86. On the fragility of these spatial borders see Bernstein, *Marginal Women;* Razi, *Forsaken Children.*

87. Zerubavel, *Time Maps,* 46–48.

88. See Hobsbawm and Ranger, "The Invention of Tradition," 307; Norbert Elias, *The Civilizing Process: The History of Manners* (New York, 1978), 221–263.

89. See Rotbard, *White City, Black City,* 78–88; Max Weber, *The Methodology of the Social Sciences* (New York, 1949), 113–163.

# FOUR

# From "European Oasis" to Downtown New York: The Image of Tel-Aviv in School Textbooks

*Yoram Bar-Gal*

In his book *Wonderful Wizard of Oz,* Frank L. Baum describes the adventures of Dorothy and her friends on their way to a place regarded as the center of the world—the Emerald City—where the most powerful ruler of the Land of Oz dwells.[1] The sight of the city, which appears before them after an exhaustive and dangerous journey to remote locations, left them in awe. The brightness of the light, the joy and splendor of the city, the magnificent houses along the paved streets, the beautiful people strolling among the shops—all engendered a feeling of respect toward the city and its great ruler. Baum uses a familiar motif taken from the biblical story of wandering in the desert on the way to the Promised Land. In his point of view, for those living in the Midwest of the United States, the Emerald City symbolizes New York and its skyline, its wealth, the aspirations and dreams it arouses among the people living in the periphery.

Ten years after this book was written the neighborhood Ahuzat Bayit was founded upon the dunes along the Mediterranean shore of what would later become the Land of Israel. Within approximately one decade, in 1918, the image of the new neighborhood (that had no more than 200 houses) was portrayed in stereotypes that recall the descriptions of the mythical Emerald City created by Frank Baum. Already, at that stage, the neighborhood was compared in a geography textbook that appeared in Kishinev to a "European Oasis in the Asian desert." In its description, the author uses the elements of sunlight, beautiful houses, and wealth in order to emphasize its unusual European-like characteristics within its Oriental location.[2]

It seems that the implied connections between the legendary Emerald City and the real Tel-Aviv have not ended. On the contrary—a century after the Emerald City was described for the first time, and at the beginning of the twenty-first century, a geography textbook in Israel has appeared using the famous stereotypes of downtown New York to represent Tel-Aviv: skyscrapers that block the horizon, in low-angled photographs from the direction of the sea, during evening hours; city lights reflected in the water. The message is conveyed from the book covers: Tel-Aviv = New York; America is here and now!

In the first years of the city, other places in the country such as Jaffa, Jerusalem, or Petah-Tikva, occupied an important place in Hebrew literature. Tel-Aviv was fortunate to have been founded during a period in which a life of vibrant cultural creativity had already began, mainly in one of the first neighborhoods, Neve Tzedek, which was founded in 1887. Neve Tzedek and Jaffa are described by authors of the time, such as Agnon and Brenner, as the antithesis of Jerusalem, mainly in regard to its secularism as opposed to tradition and religion. These portrayals of Tel-Aviv had already been ascribed to it when it was still a small neighborhood extending over sand hills before World War I.

Nurit Govrin notes that Tel-Aviv was referred to in literature as a large, open, and dynamic city even before these attributes became a reality. She states that literary works regarded Tel-Aviv differently in every period. From the founding of the city until after World War I there was a sense of amazement and pride. In the 1920s its image was that of a place in the process of growth, with a certain criticism of its urban-Diaspora style of life. In the middle of the 1930s, its image became that of a city turning into a metropolis, with a sense of sadness at the loss of the initial intimacy.[3] The amazement and pride in the city's founding and its rapid growth are linked with the wider and deeper processes of consolidating a national Jewish identity in the country. The city served as a symbol for the new Zionist enterprise.

This essay examines the images of Tel-Aviv in Hebrew geography textbooks. Such textbooks do not have the splendor, prestige, and ostensible immortality of literary works. On one hand, they purport to present the pupils with "reality as it is" in an objective manner, but on the other hand, cultural and ideological constraints dictate the selection of essential texts presented in these books. With time, a collection of textbooks provides a historical record of cultural perceptions and perspectives.

## Geography and Homeland

When nationalism flourished in Europe in the nineteenth century, states saw the need to introduce geography as a school subject. This helped to achieve the political aims of nationalism and was accompanied by the publication of atlases and national maps.[4] The bond between the pupils and their homeland was therefore one of the implicit aims of geographical curricula, as it is in schools' study programs and textbooks aimed at achieving territorial socialization.

The Zionist movement as a national movement carried the flag of territorial socialization until the establishment of the State of Israel, when it then took upon itself the task of education. The two central subjects that corresponded with territorial socialization were "homeland" (*moledet*) and "geography." The first subject included an initial familiarity with the settlement in which the pupil lived, the basic skills in reading a map, the seasons of the year, nature. The basis for this was the first study program of the Hebrew Teachers Federation in Palestine that appeared in 1903. Since there were three separate trends in Zionist education—the liberal, religious, and socialist trends—each had its own variation of the study program. After the establishment of the State and the compulsory education law, state-sponsored study programs appeared. These programs continued to be based on those established at the beginning of the twentieth century, with a division into two educational trends—State and State Religious. An important change in the content of the geography study programs took place in the late 1960s and early 1970s, when a reform in education was carried out. This program, with periodic adaptations, is still used today.[5]

How does the subject of Tel-Aviv fit into the geography study programs? The basis for every geography study program in Israel was the regional paradigm, according to which the regions of the world were taught according to school grade. A basic review of the Land of Israel and its region was initially taught in grades 5–6; a second comprehensive review was given in grade 8, and, after the reform in education, was given in grade 9. The third time the material on the Land of Israel was taught was in the upper classes of high school as part of the matriculation examinations. After the reform, the study of the Land of Israel was divided into regions, and during each year the pupils had to study one particular region.

Until the 1960s, most textbook authors were intellectuals, teachers, and educators without academic training in geography, who worked mainly in Jewish education in the Diaspora. From the 1960s onwards, the task of writing geography textbooks was taken over by university graduates in Israel. In recent decades, the Center for Educational Technology (CET) in Tel-Aviv took over this task, and produced an important set of textbooks by teams of scientific writers and advisers.[6]

### Elation

During the period of the Second Aliya (1904–1914) and even before the Hebrew literary center emerged in Neve Tzedek, a geography book on the Land of Israel appeared in Warsaw written by Yehuda Grazowski. Not a large book, it was mainly a short inventory of what existed in the country—mountains, cities, settlements, and inhabitants. The largest city in those days, Jerusalem (with about 50,000 people according to him), receives one page in which the author notes the dependence of its Jews on the *Haluka* (charity distribution), the remains of holy places, and the shortage of water. This is followed by half a page describing Jaffa. Besides noting the ancient sites, the author mentions that the city had developed greatly in recent decades: "The number of its inhabitants is about 26,000 . . . it is a city of commerce. . . . Most of its Jewish inhabitants are artisans, shopkeepers, and laborers in the settlements."[7]

During World War I the new neighborhood of Tel-Aviv experienced traumatic events, including the expulsion of its inhabitants by the Turks. Following the war, in 1918 Ottoman rule was replaced by British rule. In 1918, the hardships of recent years notwithstanding, Moshe Tzusmer wrote, "Tel-Aviv is the jewel in the crown of the new Jewish Yishuv, a European oasis in the Asian desert."[8]

Tzusmer's book, published by the Omanut Press in Frankfurt, was a finely designed textbook, and well illustrated, comparable to high-quality publications in Europe and North America in those days. The book uses the perspective of the traveling tourist who arrives at the port of Jaffa and wanders across the country. His powerful impressions of Tel-Aviv are understandable after the experience that the tourist-narrator undergoes when he lands in Jaffa:

> But come into the city, and you will know that you tread upon eastern soil. The streets are narrow and crooked, and the light of the sun hardly penetrates them . . . the markets are usually covered, full of noise and tumult, crowded and crammed.[9]

Perhaps, for the first time, in a Hebrew geography book with a long and rich text, the author presents examples that reinforce the positive images of a "slice of Europe" built by cultivated, working, and diligent Jews as an alternative to the stereotype of the decadent, non-productive native Arabs in the country. The central interest in Tzusmer's book was to transmit the "vision" of Tel-Aviv. In describing the city, he did not focus on the classical subjects typical to geography books, such as employment data. Although the book was not sponsored by any official body of the Zionist movement, it was suffused with the same characteristics of later Zionist publications such as those of the Jewish National Fund. The contrast between the local Orient and the "slice of Europe" created by the Zionist movement became a permanent feature in most geography textbooks in the Yishuv period.

After World War I, amply illustrated geography textbooks appeared in Warsaw. One such by Eliezer Metropolitansky described the Land of Israel within the regional framework of Asia as a whole, and did not devote much space to a description of the country.[10] The Arab inhabitants of the country are described as engaged in farming. Generally speaking, the "level of work and industry" in the country is very low "because the needs of the fellahin are not many." He describes Jerusalem in seven lines, and Jaffa and Tel-Aviv in only four. Jaffa is portrayed as a port and commercial city engaged in the export of grain, oil, and fruits. But ". . . the most beautiful neighborhood [in Jaffa] is Tel-Aviv where the first Jewish Gymnasia, Herzliya, is to be found." The other large cities in the country—Hebron, Haifa, Gaza—are given only one line.

A similarly concise and slightly dry description is presented in Dr. Abraham Kamenetzky's textbook for grade 6.[11] He sums up the subject in twenty lines. At first he describes Jaffa and its orchards, its location, the number of inhabitants, and its historical importance, then mentions a new neighborhood in which all the inhabitants were Jews—Ashkenazim, Sephardim, and Yemenites, who were engaged in commerce—and where the "Jewish Gymnasia" was known to be. The brevity of the text in these books does not allow for extensive descriptions of the country and its sites, as is to be found in Tzusmer's book.

In the second half of the 1920s three geography books appeared that were devoted entirely to the "Land of Israel."[12] Intended for the educated public, they were composed with a regional approach, reviewing subject after subject, and covering all the different regions of the country. Their factual style is encyclopedic in tone. Avraham Brawer's book was of major importance because of the author's prestige and his academic and public position at that time. The three books were printed by Tel-Aviv publishing houses, which indicated the rising position of Tel-Aviv as a cultural center competing with other large Hebrew centers of geography textbook publication in the Diaspora such as Warsaw or Frankfurt.

Since the late 1920s the portrayal of Tel-Aviv increasingly overtook that of Jaffa. A case in point is the ambitious book by Eliyahu Blank (1930) published by the educational network of *Tarbut* in Kishinev, in which he attempted to make a comprehensive survey of all the regions of the world in 150 pages. This was the first basic geography textbook in which pupils studied most of the continents in the world. Intended for grade-four pupils in the *Tarbut* network, a large part was devoted to the portrayal of the Land of Israel.[13] Unlike Tzusmer's book that uses a narrative form, Blank's style is dry and "scientific." The first three pages in the article on the settlements discusses, at length, Jerusalem and its neighboring cities (Bethlehem and Hebron). Tel-Aviv is described as a city

that is more beautiful than all the places in the new Jewish settlements. Its streets are straight and paved, its houses are built with good taste and pleasantly arranged, and are all surrounded by trees and flower gardens. At the street corners the signs are in Hebrew . . . On Ahad Ha'am Street stands the *Herzlia Gymnasia*—a tall, imposing building that overlooks all the other buildings around it . . . Jaffa is a port city situated on a hill near the Mediterranean shore. It has 50,000 inhabitants. There are many orchards around Jaffa where oranges are mostly grown.[14]

The descriptions of Jaffa and Tel-Aviv by Nahum Gabrieli (1934) are found in a joint chapter called "Twins."[15] He first describes Jaffa, presented as the orchard center of the country, and as a large, vibrant commercial city through which most of the sea trade passed in the Land of Israel. He then praises Jaffa as the place in which the first Hebrew school was founded, and where the Jewish community that grew and flourished before Tel-Aviv was built. Slightly exaggerated, this presentation gives credit to Jaffa's economic role. The author also mentions the city's mixed population and its visible beauty.[16]

When Gabrieli wrote this, Tel-Aviv was already twenty-five years old, and unlike the brief description of Jaffa, he spends several pages on Tel-Aviv, giving it the title of the capital city of the Jewish Yishuv. He emphasizes its new, urban character: "Tel Aviv is no longer a garden suburb today, but a large city full of movement and activity."[17] His description of the city praises its modernity and vitality as expressed in Jewish industry and work. He notes that Tel-Aviv is "a city of learning and wisdom," with many schools and publishing houses, where a "Hebrew opera house" and a Hebrew theatre were also established. However, Gabrieli's crowning description of the city is the single, clear message to every Jewish tourist who comes to see this wonder: "The Jew will say in his heart, let us see this city in which all the people are Jews, where the streets are clean and beautiful, where the rulers, leaders, and policemen are Jewish . . ."[18]

In 1934, when Tel-Aviv celebrated its silver jubilee, the city was already larger than Jaffa. The authors of geography textbooks no longer had doubts that Tel-Aviv was the jewel in the Zionist crown. They competed amongst themselves for superlatives to garland her, as though through Tel-Aviv the vitality of the Zionist enterprise could be asserted. This tendency was especially noticeable in textbooks that used the personal narrative form. A case in point was *In the Hebrew Homeland* by Baruch Avivi and Elhanan Indelman.[19] Scores of pages are devoted to describing the experiences of Nahum, who immigrated to the country with his parents. When their ship anchors in the harbor of Tel-Aviv, they burst into tears of joy. One day Nahum tells his brother Naphtali about the history of the first Jewish city, the lottery of the plots that symbolized the founding of Ahuzat Bayit. The authors emphasize the role of Mayor Meir Dizengoff, "The first builders expended much effort in building the city of Tel-Aviv, but it was Meir Dizengoff who worked hardest of all. He gave all his strength to develop the city."[20]

Geography textbooks generally present "hard" facts about the landscape, the city, and the region—the development of the built-up areas, demographic growth, and the expanding economy. However, Avivi and Indelman took another path. In many pages adorned with numerous photographs they attempted to convince the pupils that "Tel-Aviv is a wonder-city." Through the eyes of the brothers Nahum and Naphtali, the reader encounters almost every aspect of the city: a stroll through the streets, factories, Rothschild Boulevard, the shores of the Yarkon River, the eastern bazaar, and various institutions. The authors invoke the Tel-Aviv experience in their description of the city. This is perhaps the first and most detailed book that presented the Jewish urban, secular culture created in Tel-Aviv during the 1920s and 1930s. There are vivid, colorful, and impressionistic descriptions filled with a passionate love of landscape, health, and happiness.

As portrayed in the book, Tel-Aviv of the 1930s was a "city that never sleeps." The authors emphasize that the seashore was a central aspect of urban experience, where "bathing in the sea is a special delight" and "Suntanned children, impulsive and lively, dart through the gold-tinted blue waves, showering sprays of water." To make the point, they inserted a photograph of "*Sabras,* native-born children running through the sea waves, smiling and happy."[21]

After scores of pages on Tel-Aviv, the description of Jaffa is crammed into only three pages. Nahum and his friends "[P]ass through the narrow, muddy alleys, looking at the gray houses with their red roofs . . . cooks stand in the street roasting meat and frying fish. Sellers of lemonade make the glasses chime . . . camels with outstretched necks walk in a long line . . . and unpleasant smells reach Nahum's nose."

## Empowerment

As presented by some of the textbooks of the 1930s, the symbiosis between Tel-Aviv and Jaffa does not only exist in their settlement interdependence, but also at a symbolical level. The Jewish and modern Tel-Aviv is the antithesis of Arab Jaffa. The textbooks present the establishment and development of Tel-Aviv also as a function of the relations between

Jews and Arabs, and by doing so they sanction the heroic narrative of the city. Following the story about building the Ahuzat Bayit neighborhood, the construction of the Tel-Aviv port occupies an important position in these textbooks. The port symbolizes the Jewish spirit, the initiative, and the creative solutions to the Arab attempt to strangle the Yishuv by closing down Jaffa port. Therefore, between the late 1930s and 1960, the story of the Tel-Aviv port held a central place in the subject of Tel-Aviv in geography textbooks.

In his *The Land of Israel,* David Benvenisti wrote about the building of the port of Tel-Aviv in 1936 in reaction to the Arab closing of the port of Jaffa.[22] The struggle with Arab Jaffa in the Tel-Aviv narrative reaches its height in the textbooks published during the 1950s that dwell at length on the relations between the city of Tel-Aviv and Jaffa, the War of Independence, the Jewish victory, the flight of Jaffa's Arab population, and the transformation of Tel-Aviv–Jaffa into "one large metropolis."[23]

The geography textbook on the Land of Israel written for the ultra-Orthodox population of the late 1950s, does not present the city of Tel-Aviv and its way of life in a negative way. On the contrary, Elhanan Samet, author of *The Good Land,* inserts the Jewish city into the larger framework of Jewish heritage. He presents Tel-Aviv as the "largest of all the cities in the country . . . where there are thousands of shops and large trading houses in which one can get nearly everything that is possible to obtain in the country . . . the traffic in the streets is so heavy, that they can hardly hold all the cars filled with passengers passing through them." From his perspective, of much importance is religious life in Tel-Aviv, "Because of the many residents, a large number of institutions have been erected in Tel-Aviv, including the large synagogue on Allenby St. On the ground floor there are some small synagogues, and prayers never cease to be heard in them throughout the day, from dawn to the late hours of the night."[24]

The author describes the *yeshivot, kollelim,* and *talmudei torah* "scattered throughout the many streets of the city." While Samet emphasizes the richness of religious life in Tel-Aviv, a textbook from the 1980s written for the ultra-Orthodox presents a different view:

> The founders of Tel-Aviv did not build the new settlement on the basis of Torah and mitzvot . . . But today, with God's help, in spite of its general

secular character, it has about seven hundred synagogues, both large and small! Splendid educational institutions are now installed in Tel-Aviv–Jaffa: *yeshivot, kollelim, talmudei torah, heders,* and Beit Yaakov schools.[25]

From the 1960s onwards, Jaffa almost completely disappears from the new textbooks for elementary schools. Not only was the pre-1948 history of Jaffa erased, but also its present day: its Arab population, the new immigrants who settled there, urban decline, poverty, and the crime that for years characterized the area. Instead, Tel-Aviv's urban development and expansion was emphasized. Even when Jaffa was mentioned in a new textbook, it was only in connection with the founding of Ahuzat Bayit or with the flea market, a tourist attraction within the metropolitan perimeters.[26]

From the end of the 1950s and before the reform in education was carried out in 1968, a new group of textbooks were written by graduates of the Geography Department at the Hebrew University of Jerusalem. Since academic training in this period emphasized positivistic geography, the authors favored generalizations and statistical data to convey information. The quantitative map, the graph, the table, and the diagram, side by side with aerial photographs of the city, were valuable evidence for the reliability of the narrative. The new generation of authors made extensive use of these methods in order to glorify Tel-Aviv, often by comparing it to other places in the country.

This method was used by Menashe Har-El and Dov Nir, whose popular textbook intended for high schools and teacher-training colleges was published in numerous editions over a period of forty years.[27] The second part of the book deals with the regions of the country in the form of case studies. In the chapter "From the Land of Judah" the story of Jerusalem is followed separately by the story of Tel-Aviv. Although Jerusalem is located in the hills of Judea and Tel-Aviv on the coastal plain, the authors found it appropriate to juxtapose them in one chapter. In their opinion, this combination indicated the "heart" of the country:

> Jerusalem that dwells on the mountain tops, serves as the capital and the center of Torah . . . Tel-Aviv–Jaffa is located in the very hub of the coastal plain where most of the people and buildings of the State are concentrated, and that serves as the largest employment center of our country.[28]

According to the authors, Jerusalem was only a "Torah center" while the flourishing Tel-Aviv contained "most of the people and buildings of the State." After a review of the history of Jaffa and the beginnings of Tel-Aviv, they present data on the population, industry, and commerce in the city, the development of its built areas, etc. They conclude

> it serves as the melting pot for the forces of construction and creativity in the country . . . Tel-Aviv–Jaffa is like a magnet for workers, information, and funds for a varied working public . . . each finding its own place within this city, the matriarch of Israel.[29]

According to the new pedagogical approach of "research methodology" established after the 1968 education reform, pupils were required to reach theoretical conclusions through independent study. The presentation of the expansion of Tel-Aviv's built-up area given in the new textbooks reflected this pedagogy. The proposed exercises in the textbooks enhanced the power of the city in the pupil's eyes. For example, Rina Havron (1975) suggested cutting and pasting pieces of paper in different colors on a map in order to give a concrete sense of the expanding built-up area of Tel-Aviv, "The diagrams that show the expansion of the city area gave us a concrete idea of the process of its development until it became the largest city in the State of Israel."[30]

The geographical narrative of the city is the collective story of its construction. In particular, monumental buildings in a city prove its power. After having presented a photograph of the large-sized municipality building, "brand-new, twelve-storied, in front of which extends a large plaza," Havron highlights another wonder of Tel-Aviv—the Shalom Tower (opened in 1965). A photo of the tower standing in Herzl St. fills half a page, rising above the Tel-Aviv streets, embodying a sense of power. In the following exercises, the city sights are shown from the top of the tower, and the pupil is faced with "the large city extending endlessly at its foot."

Eliezer Patkin was especially prolific in the use of photographs and published a large series of textbooks. In the book on the coastal plain, the power of Tel-Aviv is evidenced by the juxtaposition of "before and after" photographs. One photo shows Herzl St. with its one-story buildings and the Herzliya Gymnasium standing like a temple at its end. In the center of the street is a group of children, on the side the first plantings, and a horse-drawn carriage stands waiting at the door of one of the houses—a scene that seems to have been taken from one of Nahum Gutman's paintings. Presented in contrast is a panoramic view of the city (apparently from the Shalom Tower), and multi-story buildings scattered as though hinting at what the future would bring.[31]

Patkin's textbook introduced the concept of the metropolitan area: a geographical concept that refers to a cohesive continuity of cities and settlements surrounding large cities. The old city center constitutes the metropolitan heart that is empowered by the cities adjoining and linked to it by the ties of economy and transport. Patkin notes that in the city of Tel-Aviv there are 335,000 inhabitants, but that in the metropolitan area of Tel-Aviv there are about a million and a quarter inhabitants.[32] While the subject is presented only briefly in his textbook, the team of writers at the Center for Educational Technology (CET) produced state-of-the-art textbooks that made this subject prominent.[33] In *Israel, Man, and Space,* the four metropolitan cities in Israel are presented, and by comparison of data, photographs, and maps, the story of the of Tel-Aviv's growing empowerment is perpetuated. The primacy of Tel-Aviv would have been marred had the authors only included the population figures for Tel-Aviv proper. When the textbook was written in 2000, Jerusalem's population was already twice that of Tel-Aviv proper, but when the metropolitan areas are included, the ratio is reversed—metropolitan Tel-Aviv is twice as large as Jerusalem. Thus the CET team was implying that Tel-Aviv=Metropolitan Center=National Center. The accompanying text—"The city that is filled with activity all day and night has earned the title of the 'city that never sleeps'"—emphasizes this point, along with the notion that Tel-Aviv is the country's economic and cultural center.[34]

In the era of globalization, referring to Tel-Aviv as a metropolis also implies its belonging to an exclusive international club—the club of world cities; the most distinguished member being New York. However, the metropolis also has its darker aspects:

> The city suffers from several problems: high population density, heavily polluted air, insufficient public transport, the emptying out of the old city center, the flight of young families, the aging population, and the creation of disadvantaged neighborhoods inhabited by the poor, the aged, and foreign workers.[35]

Nevertheless, these negative aspects of Tel-Aviv do not diminish its power, and textbook authors draw attention to a familiar landscape detail—the high buildings at the center of the metropolis. This representation is especially prominent on the cover of the CET textbook—a photo of skyscrapers along the waterfront, with sparkling lights reflected in the water, emphasizing the vertical lines. Tel-Aviv's skyline resembles that of New York.[36]

In an era of globalization most prominently associated with McDonald's, the urban landscape is imbued with characteristics linked to American cities. The authors make use of this readily recognizable cultural image, among specific aspects of popular culture such as music, literature, cinema, television, and various magazines, that strengthen and perpetuate the Americanization of Israel.[37]

What has happened to the Zionist Tel-Aviv landscape and its representation in textbooks? Descriptions of camel caravans, white buildings, and construction workers, have disappeared from the portrayal of Tel-Aviv in the 1960s and 1970s. Yet some of these images are reintroduced into the textbooks of the twenty-first century by nostalgic reference to heritage. They provide the historical dimension of the discussion of how the contemporary city emerged, with its office and residential towers, the Ayalon Highway, its hundreds of pubs and restaurants, create the image of Tel-Aviv as an "American(ized) oasis" in the heart of the Asian desert.[38]

* * *

Ever since the founding of Tel-Aviv, it has been represented in geography textbooks in a very positive light as the crowning jewel of Zionist enterprise in the country. This evaluation of the city contrasted with the socialist tendencies that predominated in Zionist ideology.[39] We might have expected that at least some of the textbooks would have expressed an attitude of reservation toward Tel-Aviv. Such a lukewarm and reserved attitude toward the city in general was discovered by Ruth Firer, who surveyed Israeli history textbooks. This attitude, however, was not found in the geography textbooks we surveyed. In the 1950s an educator and author in the kibbutz movement claimed that the subject of the city was neglected in studies of the homeland because of the kibbutz movement's ambivalent attitude toward the city as a form of Zionist settlement. But in actuality, kibbutz children were fascinated by Tel-Aviv. As the author observes,

> Many of the children long for the lights of the city and its delights. For the kibbutz children, Tel-Aviv was a special place indeed since [f]rom that place toys and good things [candy] come, and it is the place of affluence . . . [where] shop windows are filled with all good things that blind the eyes of the little villager.[40]

How can we explain the gap between the socialist values propagated by Zionist ideology before the Labor Party lost its hegemonic position in Israeli politics in 1977 and the enthusiastic representation of Tel-Aviv in the textbooks surveyed in this essay? Perhaps the answer lies in the fact that the authors of the textbooks and those who determined the study programs in geography were themselves residents of the city. Some supported and even admired rural communal settlement, but they were not willing to decry the city and its way of life. Textbook authors subscribed to the prevailing views of their time about Tel-Aviv, as described by Maoz Azaryahu.[41] For them Tel-Aviv was the center of the Land of Israel, an original creation of great social and economic power that should not be described negatively.

Academic geography in Israel was traditionally conservative, and did not tend to subscribe to socialist ideas. Therefore, those who directed study programs in geography and textbook authors who had been educated in Israel did not succumb to radical approaches, and issues pertaining to the dark side of a large city with its social and economic problems were excluded from school textbooks. Only recently, when "critical" approaches have become acceptable in geographical curricula, introducing such issues as environmental preservation, is the (now defunct) garbage dump *Hiriya* mentioned in connection with the Tel-Aviv metropolis.[42]

Except for this particular exception, the dominant line in presenting Tel-Aviv remains as it always has been—a testimony to the vitality and power of Zionism, the center of the State of Israel, the very heart of its economy, culture, and society. Moreover, Tel-Aviv is also integrated into the international scene and aspires to be a "world city." It is not surprising that the city is now repeatedly represented by its skyline, resembling that of downtown New York.

In a detailed analysis of images of Tel-Aviv since its founding, Az-aryahu shows that over the years a number of clichés have been utilized in public discourse: "the first Jewish city," "Europe in the East," "Non-Stop City," "The White City," etc.[43] In the mythographic periodization suggested by Azaryahu, the images that appeared in the textbooks from the 1920s until the mid-1980s fit in very nicely. Textbooks used in the educational system tend to preserve these local images long after they have lost their social and cultural relevance, while the introduction of new images lags behind the public discourse of the city.

A new CET textbook for the fifth grade published on the occasion of the city's centennial offers an updated iconography of Tel-Aviv.[44] Struc-tured as a lexicon of the city, it refers to popular images of "Tel-Aviv: the City of Wonders," which were popular in the 1920s and the 1930s, and the "Non-Stop City," which became the city's official slogan in 1989. Sig-nificantly, the textbook mentions the latest addition to the list of images: the "White City," which refers to the Bauhaus architecture in Tel-Aviv.

Though these enthusiastic images and representations of the "Jewish city" that also proliferated in the geography textbooks did not precisely reflect reality, they expressed a shared fantasy. The creators of Tel-Aviv and those who wrote about the city wanted to see it as an extension of Europe or as the local version of New York. Or, as Frank Baum suggested when he described the Emerald City, the dream city of riches and power in the Land of Oz—was it all but an illusion, a mirage?

## NOTES

1. Frank L. Baum, *Wonderful Wizard of Oz* (Oxford, 1997), 110–111.

2. See later detailed descriptions of Tel-Aviv referred to in the Preface.

3. Nurit Govrin, *Literary Geography: Lands and Landmarks on the Map of He-brew Literature* (Jerusalem, 1988), 65–81 [Hebrew].

4. Benedict Anderson, *Imagined Communities* (London, 1983).

5. Although the Israeli educational system is divided into two sectors—State and State Religious—geography textbooks are generally the same version, including those used in the Arab sector, which uses translations of the books originally written in Hebrew and approved by the Ministry of Education. See Yoram Bar-Gal, "Geography Teaching in Israel: A Retrospective View," *Journal of Geography* 92 (1993), 64–68.

6. The number of geography textbooks and the variety of authors has gradually decreased during the past hundred years. One reason is the uniform study program in Israel that dictates very detailed chapter headings.

7. Yehuda Grazowski, *The Land of Israel* (Warsaw, 1903) [Hebrew]. Some Hebrew textbooks on the homeland and geography appeared in Eastern Europe and were used in the Zionist educational network *Tarbut,* but were apparently also used in other places in the country before World War II. Other books were written in the country for use in schools there.

8. Moshe Tzusmer, *Geography: A First Course* (Frankfurt, 1918) [Hebrew]. According to the notes on the book cover, it was not written originally in Hebrew but was translated by Nahum Tal and Shlomo Weinstein, and edited by Haim Nahman Bialik.

9. Ibid., 191.

10. Eliezer Metropolitansky, *Asia and the Land of Israel* (Warsaw, 1921?) [Hebrew].

11. Abraham S. Kamenetzky, *An Illustrated Geography of the Land of Israel* (Warsaw, 1922?) [Hebrew].

12. Yeshayahu Peres, *Geography of the Land of Israel* (Tel-Aviv, 1926); Avraham Yaakov Brawer, *The Land: A Book about the Land of Israel* (Tel-Aviv, 1927); Israel Belkind, *The Land of Israel in Our Times* (Tel-Aviv, 1928) [all in Hebrew].

13. Eliyahu Blank, *Know the World* (Kishinev, Romania, 1930) [Hebrew]. The cultural hierarchy in the textbook reflects the Zionist–Central European perspective. Half the book is devoted to Europe, about a third to the rest of the world (Africa, Asia, and America), and one-sixth to the Land of Israel.

14. Description of Tel-Aviv, 115–117. The author explains in the preface that he compiled the description from various sources; he apparently summarized what was written in Tzusmer's book.

15. Nahum Gabrieli, *Knowing the Homeland,* vol. 1 (Tel-Aviv, 1934) [Hebrew].

16. Ibid., 47–48.

17. Ibid., 49.

18. Ibid., 50–54.

19. Baruch Avivi and Elchanan Indelman, *In the Hebrew Homeland* (Warsaw and Tel-Aviv, 1938) [Hebrew].

20. Ibid., 25.

21. Ibid., 41–42.

22. David Benvenisti, *The Land of Israel: Knowing the Land and its Regions,* vol. 1 (Jerusalem, 1956), 67–70 [Hebrew]. Benvenisti was a prolific writer of textbooks that were very popular from the 1940s to the 1970s, most of which appeared in the 1940s, and reflected the pre-state period and the following decade.

23. David Fishman, *My Homeland, Israel,* vol. 1 (Tel-Aviv, 1954), 168 [Hebrew].

24. Elhanan Samet, *The Good Land* (Jerusalem, 1961) 13–14 [Hebrew], which was still taught in the Beit Yaakov ultra-Orthodox girls school network in the 1990s. While the description of Tel-Aviv covers over sixteen pages, the description of Bnei Brak, the large ultra-Orthodox city in Israel, covers only six pages.

25. Baruch Ordentlich, *Pleasant Land: Coastal, Central, and Southern Plain* (Jerusalem, 1984) 150–151 [Hebrew].

26. Center for Educational Technology (hereafter: CET), *The Coastal, Central and Southern Plain, and the North of the Country* (Tel-Aviv, 2000), 140, 179 [Hebrew].

27. Menashe Har-El and Dov Nir, *Geography and the Land of Israel* (Tel-Aviv, 1960) [Hebrew].

28. Ibid., 253.

29. The quotations are taken from the 1965 edition, 253–260. Another contemporary textbook, also written by graduates of the Hebrew University of Jerusalem Geography Department and used for decades, was Efraim Orni and Elisha Efrat, *Geography of Israel* (Tel-Aviv, 1960) [Hebrew]. Orni and Efrat stressed the aspect of planning and development, and rarely used superlatives.

30. Rina Havron, *The Central and Southern Coastal Plain of Israel* (Tel-Aviv, 1975), 91–98 [Hebrew].

31. Eliezer Patkin, *The Sharon and Judea Coastal Plain* (Tel-Aviv, 1982), 74–75 [Hebrew].

32. Ibid., 76–77.

33. The CET in Tel-Aviv, founded in 1971 by the Rothschild Foundation, aimed at promoting education in Israel. It specializes in the development of study programs and textbooks on various subjects. About twenty years ago a team was set up to develop programs for geography and homeland studies.

34. CET, *Israel, Man, and Space* (Tel-Aviv, 2000), 157 [Hebrew].

35. Ibid., 153.

36. CET, *The Central, Southern, and Northern Coastal Plain of the Country* (Tel-Aviv, 2000) [Hebrew].

37. See Maoz Azaryahu, "McIsrael? On the 'Americanization' of Israel," *Israel Studies* 5 (2000), 41–64; Uri Ram, *The Globalization of Israel: McWorld in Tel-Aviv, Jihad in Jerusalem* (New York, 2007).

38. CET, *The Central and Southern Coastal Plain* (Tel-Aviv, 2000), 178–179 [Hebrew]. A photo of Tel-Aviv towers taken from the sea; on the opposite side, the nostalgic yellowed Nahum Gutman drawing portraying the formation of a Jewish city growing out of the sand dunes in the shadow of Jaffa.

39. Eric Cohen, *The City in Zionist Ideology* (Jerusalem, 1970).

40. Yedidiya Yoash, "How Should We Teach Kibbutz Children about the City," *Ofakim for Education and Culture* 11 (1957), 246–247 [Hebrew].

41. Maoz Azaryahu, *Tel-Aviv: The Real City* (Sde-Boker, 2005) [Hebrew].

42. CET, *The Central and Southern Coastal Plain,* 179. See also a brief reference in CET, *Israel, Man, and Space,* on economic gaps, aging population, etc., 153.

43. Azaryahu, *Tel-Aviv: The Real City.*

44. CET, *Tel-Aviv from Aleph to Tav* (Tel-Aviv, 2008), 34 [Hebrew].

# FIVE

# Subversive Youth Cultures
# in Mandate Tel-Aviv

*Tammy Razi*

In September 1934, Shoshanna Persitz, head of the Department of Education and Culture, and the new welfare department of the Tel-Aviv Municipality (hereafter TAM), forwarded an indignant letter to K. Reynolds, the chief probation officer of the mandate government:

> You know the material that we have to deal with in Tel-Aviv: children of 12 or 15 years *without any parental supervision* [original emphasis—*T.R.*], or runaways from home in opposition to sometimes unreasonable parental control, roaming about in the streets . . . eventually led by the temptation of other boys or by hunger to commit a petty theft—this is the type of boys who need guidance and supervision.[1]

Her letter was intended, as were many other correspondences between the TAM and the mandate government, to secure the government's recognition of and financial support for the numerous welfare enterprises that the TAM was engaged in.

In this case the welfare department (titled "The Department for the Treatment of the Child" until 1939) was attempting to found a home for vagrant and neglected boys in Tel-Aviv. As in many other cases, their request for financial support was denied by the government, which nonetheless expressed its deep appreciation for these initiatives and for the general zeal manifested by the municipality in establishing a modern welfare system in the city. As in most of the other instances of being denied financial support, the TAM went ahead with its plans and established an institution for vagrant children, intending to save them from the streets and to turn them into "honest, hard-working, and productive citizens."[2]

These correspondences, alongside protocols of meetings, memoranda, files, and statistical data collected by the TAM welfare department, all dedicated to the classification and treatment of vagrant children and juvenile delinquents in the city from the 1930s to the mid-1940s,[3] expose a vibrant youth subculture evolving in Tel-Aviv during these decades. This new subculture was partly concentrated in the margins of the city, mainly in the south, in the neighborhoods bordering on Jaffa, and partly in the heart of the city—in the broad boulevards, the market area, the beach, and the many amusement parlors sprinkled in the streets. As described in Persitz's letter it consisted of groups of youths, mainly boys,[4] aimlessly roaming the streets, at times seeking "easy gains,"[5] playing card games, or engaging in illegal activities ranging from breaking into the cinema through the roofs to watch films free of charge, to petty-theft and in extreme cases prostitution, mainly in the case of girls.

This article discusses the evolution of an urban youth subculture in Tel-Aviv during the British Mandate, especially during the 1930s and '40s. The main issue raised is that this new subculture was perceived as an alternative, subversive lifestyle in comparison to the hegemonic youth culture of the Jewish community, which was mostly organized and dedicated to the nation-building process. A central component of this urban subculture was the Oriental origins of many of its youths and their frequent interactions with local Arabs. This subculture was considered not only a social threat but also a national one.

## The Young New Jew

In order to fully understand the unsettling, disruptive potential of the youthful subculture that evolved in Tel-Aviv, it is first essential to turn to the central role attributed to the younger generation in the Zionist revolution. Like many contemporaneous nineteenth-century nationalist movements, from its early days the Zionist movement considered the children and youth as the emblem of the national revolution and dedicated considerable efforts and resources to preparing the younger generation for their future role.[6]

The ethos of the "New Jew," perhaps the founding ethos in Zionist thought, was thus first and foremost imagined in terms of youthfulness: the new Jew was intended to be a proud, muscular youngster, healthy in body and spirit, in contrast to the Jew of the Diaspora imagined as inherently old, unhealthy, and neurotic. The new Jew was meant to have the powers and energy of youth that were needed to enable him[7] to become a productive laborer, close to the soil, unlike the Jew of the Diaspora— alienated from nature and living on *lüfte geschafft* or immersed in endless, unproductive, religious learning.[8]

The cult of the new Jew was therefore identified primarily with the young pioneers of the Second and Third Aliya and later on with the members of the youth movements. These movements became some of the major agents of Zionist, pioneer-oriented socialization among the younger generation. For, although even at their peak during these years, only a third of the total youth population in the Yishuv, or fewer, were members of youth movements; the accepted historiographic claim is that their influence was widely felt even among children and youth who did not join these movements.[9] Their considerable influence was a result of both the symbolic power of these youth movements as embodying the establishing ethos of the Zionist revolution, as well as their close ties with the political leadership of the Yishuv.[10]

The youth culture created within these movements functioned as their main channel of influence. For, despite ideological differences among the youth movements—the socialist *Hashomer Hatzair* as opposed to civil youth groups such as *Betar* or *Maccabi*—they shared many common features expressed mainly through youth culture. All members of youth movements, including those who grew up in the city, were dedicated to the national revival and identified this revival with agricultural work and settlements; all endorsed a collectivist, anti-individualist ethos; all developed specific rituals, uniforms, songs, slang, and even body language that contained and personified the national, rurally oriented ideology.[11]

Not all historians agree on the prominence of the youth movements and their culture. Rachel Elboim-Dror argues that the over-emphasis on the role and influence of organized youth in the '30s and '40s is a result of the dominant paradigms in the history of the Yishuv. Research in this area has tended to focus on the hegemonic groups and ideology and thus to overlook youth cultures that were not necessarily associated with the labor movement, such as religious or urban youth cultures. Thus extensive concentration on the youth movements and culture is also partly due to the easily accessible, well-documented, and organized nature of their activities.[12]

Even if the research has indeed ignored a variety of youth cultures existing alongside the youth movements and their culture, as this essay also shows, it is still vital to acknowledge their symbolic importance in contemporary eyes, in order to fully grasp the perceived potential threat of these alternative youth cultures, which may have led also, in retrospect, to the fact that until recently they were largely ignored by scholars. For, in a society immersed in a nation-building process, in which the young were destined to bear on their shoulders the weight of the national revolution and to prepare for their role as new Jews through formal and informal education, youngsters were defined primarily by their commitment to Zionist ideology and praxis. Therefore, those who were not members of youth movements were defined in opposition to the norm as "non-organized youth," although they were by far the majority.[13] Thus youngsters who chose to independently form street gangs and engage in urban activities were obviously free of ideological commitment, and were perceived as no less than a "national danger."[14]

## Documenting the Margins

As Elboim-Dror notes, the accessibility of the documentation of the organized youth culture (diaries, letters, pamphlets, printed songs, newsletters, and more) facilitated the research on youth movements and their members.[15] Tracing the tracks of the youth culture of "non-organized youth," especially those situated in the margins, is a far more complicated task since apart from a single letter addressed to the city mayor by one of these youths they have left behind no written material.[16] However, since they were seen as a concrete threat to the city's development and stability, as well as a wider, national problem, the children and youth in the streets of Tel-Aviv attracted the intense attention of the welfare authorities, on both the local and national levels.

Combined with the progressive welfare-oriented ideology held by those involved in the treatment of these children, this active interest led to an immense production of written materials documenting the professional discourse regarding the children and youths of the streets. Documents reveal that clear traces can be found of an urban youth subculture existing in the social and, at times, also geographic margins of the city.

The children and youths treated by the welfare authorities in Tel-Aviv were mostly new immigrants arriving in the city with their families during the 1920s but mainly during the '30s, with the waves of immigration from Eastern and Central Europe.[17] Yet, although the majority of immigrants settling in Tel-Aviv during these decades came from Europe and many among them required the substantial support of local welfare institutions, a relatively high percentage of the children and youth treated by these institutions were of Oriental origins.[18] Among them were youngsters who had immigrated with their families from Muslim countries such as Iraq, Egypt, and Yemen during the 1920s and '30s, and some who had migrated with their families or on their own, from the centers of the old Yishuv, from cities such as Jerusalem or Tiberius.[19]

There were multiple causes for the relatively high percentages of children and youths of Oriental origins under the care of the welfare authorities: among the poor there were many large Oriental families, whose resources were scarce and prospects limited. These circumstances were the result of the ethnic and social inequality prevalent in the society of Yishuv, and especially in the urban centers. The prejudices held by those involved in the treatment of vagrant and neglected children regarding the "backward" Oriental culture of the parents and the "natural tendency" of Oriental youths for crime and violence, both reflected the Yishuv's ethnic and social inequality and deepened it, by defining poor, Oriental youngsters as necessarily "endangered youths" needing professional intervention and guidance.[20]

The children and youths treated by the local welfare authorities in Tel-Aviv, both of Ashkenazi and Oriental origins, all came from poverty-stricken families, with parents either unemployed or working in temporary, low-wage jobs such as street-peddling or house-cleaning (in the case of the mothers). Many of these families suffered also from familial instability, ranging from constant parental quarrels, to the mental breakdowns of mothers or fathers, to divorces and a relatively high percentage of deserting fathers, a phenomenon especially typical of Jewish immigrant societies.[21]

The youngsters spent long hours in the streets, mainly in search of occasional livelihood to assist their families, but also because they did not attend educational institutions—either they had dropped out of elementary school or did not continue to high school. Most of the boys who found work in the streets were shoe-shiners, delivery boys, "newspaper boys," and street-peddlers; the girls worked at stands in the market, as waitresses, but mainly as maids in private homes.[22] There were also many youngsters working in factories. However, the constant presence of hundreds of youths roaming the streets in search of an odd job or a passing amusement was perceived at the time as a dangerous menace to the social order, and the local welfare authorities made considerable efforts to take the children off the streets.

The treatment of many of these children was made possible by the impressive welfare infrastructure established by the mid-1930s in the Yishuv. This infrastructure was founded both on the national level—with the social welfare department of the National Committee, established in 1931 and headed by Henrietta Szold—and on the local level—with the modern welfare department in Tel-Aviv, established in 1933 (The Department for the Treatment of the Child), as well as the welfare departments established in other urban settlements. The operation of the welfare systems in the Jewish community was carried out mainly by volunteers in women's organizations, such as the Hebrew Women's Organization (HWO), WIZO, and "The Working Mothers' Organization."[23] The high percentage of trained social workers among the immigrants arriving during the 1920s and especially during the '30s also had a major impact on the establishment of the welfare networks in the Yishuv.[24] Apart from the welfare activities initiated and carried out by the Jewish community, the government in Palestine played a central role in the treatment of vagrant children and youths by establishing the legal system for juvenile delinquents.[25]

The treatment of these children by the local welfare authorities in Tel-Aviv consisted of individual treatment by social workers (assistance in finding "respectable" work, for example) or by health specialists (such as mental-health specialists and psychoanalysts working with the clinic for the "psycho-hygiene of the childhood," established in 1936). Additionally, many facilities and institutions were founded, such as supervised playgrounds, clubs, schools and special classes for problematic pupils (or drop-outs), frameworks for professional training of youths, as well as closed institutions for neglected children and juvenile delinquents, both in the city and elsewhere (such as *Gvat*, the village for delinquent boys established in 1939).[26]

## Gangs and Hoodlums

The immense efforts to create frameworks and institutions for the vagrant children and youths where they would be put under the close surveillance of "responsible adults" were, at least partly, a direct attempt to battle and overcome the autonomous youth subculture that had evidently developed in the streets of Tel-Aviv since the early 1930s. Thus the youths were described as "passing entire days together roaming about the streets and lazily laying about on the beach,"[27] while spending the warm summer nights "sleeping in boxes or on benches in the boulevards."[28]

They were also reported to be lingering in gangs around the amusement halls, and were especially attracted to cinema. The chief probation officer of the mandate government heard such alarming reports from the local welfare authorities regarding the children's misbehavior in the cinemas, that he declared his wish to "spend some time seeing for myself the state of affairs with regard to the children in the streets and cinemas."[29] Following his gloomy impressions, "the district commissioner . . . decided to appoint a committee to investigate and report the prevalence and type of delinquency amongst the juvenile population of Tel-Aviv."[30]

The committee and local welfare officials all stressed the dangers related to the youths' collective infatuation with the cinema. Often lacking the money needed for purchasing tickets to the cinema but unable to overcome the temptation to watch all those "damaging Hollywood films,"[31] filled with intrigue, forbidden romance, and violence, the youngsters would either pick-pocket passersby or break into the cinema through the roofs or windows.[32] Lacking also the necessary mental and emotional filters needed to separate fact from fiction, according to authorities, these youths were especially prone to internalize these films' "immoral" if not "degenerate" values and commit crimes inspired by the big screen.[33]

The dangers posed by their enchantment with films were related to yet another feature of the vagrant youths' subculture that was perceived as threatening: the joint outings of boys and girls and the sexual hazards they carried. Reports of mixed groups of boys and girls hanging around the streets together, and even of some cases of girls impregnated by members of these "street gangs,"[34] emphasized the role amusement parlors and especially the cinema played in the joint outings. Thus, for example, in the summer of 1945 an urgent appeal was sent from the TAM welfare department to the president of the council of Ramat-Gan requesting his immediate intervention in putting an end to the screenings of "special films for Arab-speakers" in the local cinema on Thursday nights. As it turned out, these films were being watched on a regular basis by girls and boys from Tel-Aviv, who visited the cinema in large, noisy groups. Apart from the fact that these were considered "primitive films" and that the parents were apparently unaware of such outings, the cinema was a perfect setting for "dangerous liaisons" between the girls and boys. The girls in particular tended to linger on near the cinema until late at night, spending time in "dubious company," a habit that inevitably led to "serious complications."[35]

Although the "sexual promiscuity" of vagrant girls attracted the extensive attention of the welfare and law-enforcing authorities, it seems that most of the "street gangs" were composed of boys alone, and their activities were described as typically boyish.[36] Thus, for example, a gang of boys was described as preying on camels at night, stealing watermelons off their backs, or mischievously tearing open sacks filled with sand.[37] At other times gangs of boys were reported as gathering on street corners or near benches in the wide boulevards, where they would often gamble with cards or other games. When not preoccupied with these dubious activities, they would be found lazing about in the "Arab cafés," sitting for hours on the stools facing the street and smoking hash with older men, or happily just loading their bellies with alcohol.[38] In even worse instances groups of boys paid visits to brothels in Jaffa which ended, at least in one reported case, with twenty or so of the boys catching a sexually transmitted disease and needing the urgent intervention of the Hadassah Medical Federation.[39]

Even when roaming the streets in groups in search of an odd job to assist their families, the boys were suspected of misbehavior, since when "trying to get some piasters by selling bootlaces and other things in the streets . . . there is a danger that their roaming the streets may lead to delinquency";[40] or as Szold explained to the chief probation officer, "The streets offer the children opportunities for banding up together and stealing so they can satisfy their hunger."[41] These descriptions imply that boys came together not only to have fun, but for practical reasons: the kind of livelihood found in the streets often demanded joint efforts and shared initiatives, skills and creative enterprises.[42]

These types of struggles, which took place during so many hours in the streets, away from the youths' over-crowded, impoverished homes, created the necessary conditions for the flourishing of an autonomous, urban youth subculture. The opportunity to spend time with one's peer group, far away from parental control or other forms of surveillance, as well as the yearning to belong and identify with other boys sharing similar fates, enabled these youngsters to create their own independent sphere. The urban setting provided both the means of livelihood and the means of enjoying cheap amusements and thrills.

The presence of these groups was the most obvious feature of the marginal subculture that had evolved in Tel-Aviv, and it was thus the most feared aspect of the subculture by the general public and the welfare and law-enforcement authorities. Groups of boys were described as "organized crime gangs,"[43] endangering the public's safety, and the "gang" leaders were depicted as charismatic psychopaths luring innocent youths into a life of sin and depravation.[44] These alarming sketches exposed typical components of urban youth subcultures as they were characterized in sociological and anthropological studies since the late 1920s: organized groups of working-class adolescents, banded together under the figure of a strong leader, their main function being the creation of an alternative peer group that bestowed a sense of identity and self-esteem to its members, through the creation of a unique language, including codes of behavior, dress, slang, and body language.[45]

These traits were seen as especially threatening because of the particular appeal and attraction they seemed to possess for boys from "good homes who come across these street gangs near the cinema and on the beach and attracted to them . . . they enter their company, feel the taste of the life they lead, and when discovering its advantages they leave their homes and studies and join these street boys."[46] Although there is no mention of "boys from good homes," of the kind that could be found in the youth movements, this type of remark may allude to the symbolic potential of the urban youth subculture becoming an alternative to the ideologically committed, organized youth culture of the Yishuv.

## Oriental Subculture

The threat posed by these groups of boys roaming the streets was intensified by their specific ethnic backgrounds and the close ties some of them seemed to be making with the local Arabs. Descriptions of the activities these youths were involved in clearly indicate that they were taking place in Oriental spheres, shared at least partly by Jews of Oriental origins and Arabs. Boys and girls from Tel-Aviv watched films for "Arab-speakers" together; the boys would laze about in the "Arab cafés," smoking hash or playing card games with the Arab men.

There is even some evidence that those boys who visited the brothels in Jaffa were of Oriental origin and interacted with local Arabs. Though the brothels were frequented by men of many different backgrounds, including soldiers serving in the region, and though the prostitutes in Jaffa were not necessarily Arab,[47] it appears that the brothels were also quite popular among the Oriental street youth of Tel-Aviv. At least in the aforementioned case of the boys who caught the sexually transmitted disease, the names mentioned are clearly Oriental. A visit to the brothels was only one type of pleasure groups of boys found in the Arab city, but it did garner a strong reaction from local residents.[48]

"Dangerous" visits to Jaffa and relationships with Arabs, especially in a sexual context, were widely discussed by the welfare and law-enforcement authorities first and foremost in regard to vagrant girls. Indeed, the most threatening activity attributed to the girls of Oriental origins treated by the welfare authorities was their connections with Arab men. Many of them were described as having different kinds of affiliations with Arabs, ranging from romantic relationships to mere sexual encounters, and even business ties, such as working as waitresses and dancers in Arab cafés in Jaffa, or in rarer cases as prostitutes in Arab-owned brothels. It was the mere contact with Arabs that sufficed to define the girls as being in great danger of moral ruin, and their connections with Arab men became one of the strongest symbols of their vagrancy and potential delinquency.[49] It was also mainly in this context that girls were described as grouping together and paying joint visits to Jaffa, whether in search of jobs or amusements.[50]

Visits to Jaffa, intimate relationships with Arabs, as well as other shared activities, were all presented as the darkest and most threatening aspect of the vagrant youth subculture. In part, these public responses reflected a wider discourse regarding the many "troubling" similarities found between Jews of Oriental origins and Arabs. The TAM welfare authorities, for example, deplored what they termed the Oriental families' tendency to intentionally reside among Arabs, since "most of the new immigrants from Europe live in the neighborhoods close to Tel-Aviv, while the new immigrants of Oriental origins [prefer to] live in the Arab neighborhoods."[51] This was seen an indication of Oriental Jews' mental and cultural affinity with Arabs and their wish to revive the social and cultural contexts they had left behind in their countries of origin.[52]

These discussions of the similarities and ties existing between Oriental Jews and Arabs and especially in relation to vagrant youth subculture expose the fact that despite the Arab revolt of 1936–1939, areas of interaction between Jews and Arabs continued to exist. Even during the 1940s, as the Jewish-Arab conflict escalated, there were frequent reports of "forbidden" ties between Oriental Jewish youths and Arabs, as well as between adults. As Deborah Bernstein clearly proves, the location on the margins of the city, where borders and identities were often blurred or transgressed, enabled a variety of encounters between Jews—whether of Oriental or Ashkenazi origins—and Arabs.[53]

It was these encounters, especially among youth groups free of any form of surveillance, that posed the deepest threat in the public imagination during the years of intensified national struggle. The discussed similarities between Oriental youths and the local Arabs, and particularly the potential for an actual merging of national identities through romantic and sexual relations between Jewish girls and Arab men, stood at the very core of the anxiety expressed by the welfare authorities and general public at the time. Long before the contested term "Arab-Jews"[54] was coined, the urban subculture of Oriental youths disclosed the perceived dangers of upsetting supposedly clear-cut national identities and boundaries.

## A Subversive Subculture?

Urban youth subcultures were of course not unique to Tel-Aviv in the 1930s and '40s. Their general features, as well as the discourse regarding their potential threat to the social order, are surprisingly similar to those found in historical studies of urban working class youths in the late nineteenth century and first decades of the twentieth century. These studies usually discuss the flourishing of urban youth subcultures in the context of the shift from agrarian to industrial society. The new possibilities of livelihood in the cities and the potential for the relative economic independence of youngsters, alongside the thriving of cheap urban amusements and thrills, created the context for autonomous youth subcultures. The slackening of control in the private sphere and the disruption of traditional power dynamics, alongside the bourgeois fear of social unrest among the working classes, were translated into increasing public anxiety concerning working-class youths and the prevalence of juvenile delinquency among them.[55]

Many studies in the criminology and sociology of twentieth-century youth gangs have argued that these urban subcultures were intentionally opposed to the existing social order and therefore functioned as conscious subversive forces. While in the 1950s the stress was on the delinquent, anti-social nature of working-class street gangs, and the framework was that of social deviance, such as in the studies of criminologist Albert Cohen, later sociological studies discussed youth subculture as one form of expression of a variety of ethnic and gender identities, among other counter-cultures.[56]

The phenomenon of the vagrant youth subculture in Mandate Tel-Aviv possesses several specific traits that do not necessarily fit these general historical or sociological motifs. Thus in this case the historical context was not the transition from an agrarian to an industrial society, although the municipal authorities themselves tended to explain the high percentages of vagrant Oriental children as the result of their sudden shift from a traditional, Oriental society to a modern, Westernized one. As the mayor of Tel-Aviv explained, "Especially for the oriental child hitherto brought up in the seclusion of home and religious school, the sudden influence of modern European customs is bound to have a confusing effect."[57]

If modern European society was more an imagined reality in Palestine at the time than a concrete one, these kinds of explanations showed that the experience of transition from one society to another was shared by Jews from Eastern Europe as well as of Jews from Muslim countries. It is therefore partly in this context that the urban youth subculture should be understood, although the high percentage of Oriental youths in these groups still needs to be accounted for and should be further explored.

The specific characteristics of this urban youth subculture, namely its "Oriental pastimes" and ties with local Arabs, but especially the professional discourse regarding its dangers, reveal possibly the most important aspect of this social and cultural phenomenon. While in the European historical context of urban youth groups the fear evoked was related to the social unrest and class struggle that arose with industrialization and urbanization, in the case of Mandate Tel-Aviv the context was that of a nation-building process set within a national struggle. An urban subculture of youths, many of whom came originally from Muslim countries, was thus seen as perhaps the most radically subversive challenge to the embracing of the unique combination of modern, Western identity and rural aspirations—expected first and foremost from the young.

Was this subculture indeed inherently subversive? Were the gang members intentionally rebelling against these ideological commitments and values, as urban youth subcultures are usually depicted in sociological writings? Lacking the point of view of the youths involved in the creation of this urban subculture, we are left either with the interpretations of their contemporaries who felt threatened by them or with the romantic idealization of academic couch-rebels—who would insist on reading this subculture as an intentional revolt against hegemony. Avoiding these two extremes can only be done through a continuing effort to discover traces of the life experiences of these youths and the meanings they gave to the subculture they produced.

## NOTES

1. Tel-Aviv Historical Archive (TAHA), 2116B-4.
2. TAHA, 1427-4, Hedwig Gelner's report summarizing ten years of activity of the Tel-Aviv Municipality (TAM) social welfare department, 12 September 1943.

3. This article does not deal with the children and youths who were refugees and holocaust survivors arriving in the city by the end of World War II.

4. Sometimes also mixed groups of boys and girls.

5. Used by the welfare authorities mainly to describe street-peddling. See TAHA, 1769-4, David Edelson to Hedwig Gelner, 23 November 1938.

6. On the importance of youth in national contexts, especially in the nineteenth century, see Harry Hendrick, "Constructions and Reconstructions of British Childhood," in *Youth Justice: Critical Readings* (London, 2002) 30–34; John R. Gillis, *Youth and History* (New York, 1974), 39–93. On the role of youth in the Zionist movement, see Oz Almog, *The Sabra—A Profile* (Tel-Aviv, 2001), 52–123 [Hebrew].

7. Although seemingly a gender-neutral ideal, the ethos of the new Jew was an inherently masculine ideal. For a discussion of the discourse on the Zionist revolution as a gendered revolution, intended to "cleanse" the European Jews of their supposedly effeminate characteristics, see Yaron Peleg, "Heroic Conduct: Homoeroticism and the Creation of Modern, Jewish Masculinities," *Jewish Social Studies* 13.1 (2006): 31–58.

8. On the general concept of the new Jew, see Anita Shapira, "The Myth of the New Jew," in *New Jews Old Jews* (Tel-Aviv, 1998), 155–174 [Hebrew]; on its specific youthful traits, see Almog, *The Sabra*, 124–136.

9. Anita Shapira, "A Generation in the Land [of Israel]," 122–154; Rafael Gat, "The Youth Movements of the Laboring Eretz-Israel" (PhD diss., Tel-Aviv University, 1974), 11–28 [Hebrew].

10. Gat, "The Youth Movements," 22–28; Rina Peled, *"The New Man" of the Zionist Revolution* (Tel-Aviv, 2002), 25–30 [Hebrew]. For a discussion of the conformist aspects of the youth movements because of their ties with political parties, see Jonathan Shapira, *Elite without Followers* (Tel-Aviv, 1984), 107–125 [Hebrew].

11. Gat, "The Youth Movements," 22–23, 296; Mordechai Naor, ed., *The Youth Movements, 1920–1960* (Jerusalem, 1989) [Hebrew].

12. Rachel Elboim-Dror, "'Here He Comes, From Among Us Comes the New Hebrew [Man]': On the Youth Culture of the First Aliyot," *Alpayim* 12 (1996): 104–135 [Hebrew].

13. The term "non-organized youth" was used mainly during the 1930s and 1940s to describe the youth who did not join the youth movements and organizations, and was later adopted by researchers. See Mordechai Naor, *The Youth Movements*.

14. Cited from an article by Meir Dizengoff, mayor of Tel-Aviv in *YITA (Yedi'ot 'Iriyat Tel-Aviv)*, 9, 1933. The term was used originally to criticize the contemporary distain for the city. See documents of the National Committee welfare department in which these youths are discussed as a national threat; Central Zionist Archive (CZA), J1/3495, "The National Center for the Treatment of Children and Youth," 9 March 1937; J1/2453, Henrietta Szold to Yechil Ben-Zion Katz, 1 August 1938.

15. Elboim-Dror, "Here He Comes, From Among Us Comes the New Hebrew [Man]," 105–106.

16. This letter, signed simply by "one of the kids of Tel-Aviv," requested the assistance of the mayor in helping the children forced to work instead of going to school, to find the time and resources to study; TAHA, 1770b-4, 11 December 1935. See Alma Fox-Brauner, *Benda: The True Story* (Tel-Aviv, 2003), 34–53 [Hebrew], based on the

memoirs of David Ben-David (Benda), who had spent part of his childhood and youth as a street child in Tel-Aviv in the early 1940s, giving a rare voice, if only in retrospect, to the experiences of these children.

17. On immigration to Tel-Aviv during these years, see Yaacov Shavit and Gideon Biger, *The History of Tel-Aviv,* vol. 1 (Tel-Aviv, 2001), 93–94; *The History of Tel-Aviv,* vol. 2 (Tel-Aviv, 2007), 22–23 [both in Hebrew].

18. During the 1930s and '40s, the percentage of Jewish residents of Oriental origins in the city diminished considerably because of the mass immigration from Europe, which concentrated mainly in Tel-Aviv. They constituted at most a fifth of city's total population. See Shavit and Biger, *The History of Tel-Aviv,* 1–23.

19. On the immigration from Muslim countries during the British Mandate period, see: Aviva Halamish, *A Dual Race Against Time: Zionist Immigration Policy in the 1930s* (Jerusalem, 2006), 307–312. On the migration of families and youths from the centers of the old Yishuv see Tammy Razi, *Forsaken Children: The Backyard of Mandate Tel-Aviv* (Tel-Aviv, 2009), 47–51, 121–123 [both in Hebrew].

20. See, for example, the following correspondences, all attributing negative cultural and personal traits to parents and children of Oriental origins: TAHA, 1423-4, Shoshanna Persitz to the welfare department of the community of Jaffa, 8 May 1935; 1427-4, Barkol to Rokach, 27 January 1943.

21. Razi, *Forsaken Children,* 68–94. On the situation of Jewish women deserted by their husbands during the mass immigration from Eastern Europe, see Reena Sigman Friedman, "Send My Husband Who is in New York City: Husband Desertion in the American Immigrant Community," *Jewish Social Studies* 44 (1982): 1–17.

22. David Riepen, "Street Children in Tel-Aviv in the Years 1935–1944," *Society and Welfare* 1 (1984): 36–43 [Hebrew].

23. Akiva Deutsch, "The Development of Social Work as a Profession in the Yishuv" (PhD diss., Tel-Aviv University, 1970), 55–105 [Hebrew].

24. Tova Golan, "Social Work in the Yishuv (1931–1936)" (master's thesis, Bar-Ilan University, 2002), 6–64 (Hebrew].

25. Na'ava Ela'ad and Anita Weiner, *Juvenile Probation and the History of the Treatment of Juvenile Delinquents and Neglected Children* (Tel-Aviv, 1984), 29–106 [Hebrew].

26. TAHA, 1422-4, "A Proposal for Establishing A Department for the Treatment of the Child," TAM Department of Education and Health, 1933; "On the Clinic for the Psycho-hygiene of Childhood," *YITA* 7–8, 1937–1938; "Education in the Municipal Schools," 7–9, year 11, April–June 1941; TAHA, 1768-74, Hedwig Gelner to Israel Rokach, 4 March 1939; 2116-4, David Edelson, "A report on the institution for vagrant children," 2 August 1934; CZA, 125a/134, Lubinsky to Szold, 10 January 1941.

27. TAHA, 1429-4, Edelson to Rokach, 6 November 1946.

28. TAHA, 2116b-4, Edelson report, 2 August 1934.

29. TAHA, 2116b-4, Reynolds to Persitz, 18 September 1934.

30. TAHA, 2116d-4, District commissioner of the Negev district to Rokach, 31 March 1935.

31. "The TAM and the Cinema," *YITA,* 3 December 1932.

32. TAHA, 2116c-4, Abrabanel and Visser, owners of Eden cinema to the TAM inspector in charge of vagrant children, 3 December 1934.

33. "Municipal Schools in Tel-Aviv," *YITA* 5–6, December 1939–January 1940. See also Anat Helman, "Cinema Attendance in the *Yishuv* and the Early Years of the State of Israel," in *Cinema and Memory—A Dangerous Relationship?* ed. Haim Bresheeth, Shlomo Sand, and Moshe Zimmermann (Jerusalem, 2004), 73–82 [Hebrew].

34. CZA J1/7983, *Gvat* youth village committee report, 31 December 1944.

35. TAHA, 2155a-4, Kazenelson to Krinizi, 24 July 1945.

36. On the specific discourse regarding vagrant girls and the dangers of sexual promiscuity and prostitution, see Tammy Razi, "'My Daughter is Fire, Fire': Mothers and Vagrant Daughters in Tel-Aviv in the 30's and 40's," *Iyunim Bitkumat Israel* (2009); Deborah Bernstein, *Women on the Margins: Gender and Nationalism in Mandate Tel-Aviv* (Tel-Aviv, 2008), 275–290 [both in Hebrew].

37. TAHA, 2116b-4, anonymous letter by a man who voluntarily took care of vagrant children in Jaffa and the southern neighborhoods of Tel-Aviv to commissioner of the Jaffa district, October 1934.

38. TAHA, 2116c-4, Edelson to Persitz, 23 December 1934.

39. TAHA, 2116c-4, Hiski to Persitz, 8 August 1934.

40. TAHA, 1424-4, Rokach to Walters [Australian Jewish philanthropist], 20 January 1938.

41. TAHA, 2116b-4, Henrietta Szold to the chief government probation officer, 18 June 1934.

42. For a description of these joint efforts made by the boys to find work and improvise livelihoods, see Yekhiel Ben-Zion Katz, *Vagrant Children* (Tel-Aviv, 1939) [Hebrew].

43. TAHA, 2116b-4, Education Department meeting, 29 May 1934.

44. TAHA, 5 December 1934, 2116c-4, "An invitation for a discussion on the treatment of juvenile psychopaths," to Prof. Pappenheim, Dr. Wolf, Dr. Brachiyahu, and others.

45. Frederic M. Thrasher, *The Gang* (Chicago and London, 1966); William Foote Whyte, *Street Corner Society: The Social Structure of an Italian Slum* (Chicago, 1993).

46. TAHA, 2116d-4, Edelson, 31 May 1935.

47. Bernstein, *Women on the Margins*, 184–217.

48. TAHA, 2116b-4, petition by Jewish and Arab parents, artisans and merchants requesting the intervention of the district commissioner of Jaffa, 14 August 1934.

49. TAHA, 2154c-4, Hedwig Gelner to Zeligson, 4 May 1942; Barkol to Chief Rabbinate of Jaffa-Tel-Aviv, 10 May 1943. See also Bernstein, *Women on the Margins*, 275–290.

50. TAHA, 2154a-4, Rosenbaum to Zeligson, 4 May 1942. In several cases groups of girls traveled to Haifa, where they could be found mainly in the Arab cafés and brothels. See Perlson's report on vagrant girls to the members of the city council, 31 March 1938. See also Razi, *Forsaken Children*, 251–257.

51. TAHA, 1423-4, memorandum regarding the condition of immigrants in Tel-Aviv and Jaffa, May 1936.

52. Yoav Gelber, "The Consolidation of Jewish Society in Eretz-Israel, 1936–1947," in *The History of the Jewish Community in Eretz-Israel Since 1882*, ed. Moshe Lissak (Jerusalem, 2001), 335–336 [Hebrew].

53. Deborah Bernstein, *Women on the Margins*. For a discussion of encounters between Jews and Arabs in the context of leisure and popular culture during the

late Ottoman period, see Boaz Lev Tov, "Leisure and Popular Culture Patterns of Eretz-Israeli Jews in the Years 1882–1914 as a Reflection of Social Change" (PhD diss., Tel-Aviv University, 2007).

54. Yehuda Shenhav, *The Arab-Jews: Nationalism, Religion, and Ethnicity* (Tel-Aviv, 2003) [Hebrew].

55. See John Clarke, "The Three Rs—Repression, Rescue, and Rehabilitation: Ideologies of Control for Working Class Youth," in *Youth Justice: Critical Readings*, ed. John Muncie, Gordon Hughes, and Eugene McLaughlin (London, 2002), 123–137; Kathy Peiss, "Charity Girls and City Pleasures: Historical Notes on Working-Class Sexuality, 1880–1920," in *Powers of Desire: The Politics of Sexuality*, ed. Ann Snitow, Christine Stansell, and Sharon Thompson (New York, 1983), 74–87.

56. Albert K. Cohen, *Delinquent Boys: The Culture of the Gang* (Glencoe, IL, 1955); Paul Willis, *Common Culture* (London, 1990); Johan Fornäs, "Youth Culture and Modernity," in *Youth Culture in Late Modernity*, ed. Johan Fornäs and Göran Bolin (London, 1995), 1–11.

57. TAHA, 2116a-4, Rokach to Reynolds, 16 January 1934.

# SIX

# Dirt, Noise, and Misbehavior in the First Hebrew City: Letters of Complaint as a Historical Source

*Anat Helman*

Files in the Tel-Aviv Historical Archive contain hundreds of letters of complaint dating from the Mandate era. Some, regarding a variety of issues, were filed by the Tel-Aviv Municipality (hereafter TAM) secretary under "Complaints." Many others were filed under the specific topic of the complaint. Such letters, sent to the TAM by residents, officials, firms, local organizations, and visitors, can be found in files regarding gardening and cleaning, commerce and industry, licenses and transportation, to mention but a few examples. These letters serve as useful historical sources for reconstructing the daily reality in pre-state Tel-Aviv. The complaints reveal some of the less representative facets of the first Hebrew city, unattractive elements that were rarely photographed or filmed, hardly mentioned in formal presentations of the growing city, and, of course, never used in tourist brochures or Zionist propaganda.

However, we should treat these sources—like any historical documents—with some skepticism. A letter of complaint has its own generic rules. In order to gain the reader's full attention, and to increase the chances of the complaint ever being addressed, the writers have to put their case forcefully. In other words, letters of complaint are likely to include somewhat inflated descriptions, disproportions, and exaggerations. To make their point, writers often use a tone of sarcasm, dismay, and indignation. To goad the TAM into action, writers might either plead, or, more frequently, use direct or indirect threats, for instance a threat to publish the issue of complaint in the local press, or even to address the complaint to the higher British authorities.

Letters of complaint contrast the real, daily life of Tel-Aviv, full of flaws and shortcomings, with the writers' image of what the first Hebrew city *should* be like. The following complaints—a select sample from a large corpus—represent some elements of Tel-Aviv's social reality, and provide the opportunity for discussing the writers' understandings of culture, urbanity, and Zionism.

### "The Danger of Poisonous Air"

In late 1922, Dr. Chamy, a resident of Lilenblum St. "near the Eden cinema-house," complained to Mayor Meir Dizengoff about the market in his vicinity, lately opened by the TAM. He writes that the vendors put up their "sordid stalls" from which they sell fruit, vegetables, "killed hens," fish, etc. The market opens at 4:30 in the morning, accompanied by cries and screams of peasants who bring in their wares on camels and donkeys or by cars. Fowls are being slaughtered, their blood "drying on the sands and the feathers flying in the wind." The stalls are all dirty and "swarming with flies that attack [Dr. Chamy's] house." The sea breeze from the west carries into his house "all the infected odors" of the market, further enhanced by the heat. He explains that during the previous week his family suffered from headaches due to breathing in this "bad air." The market has become a source of plague, he laments, as rats are roaming the streets. Dr. Chamy ends his letter with a request to move the market elsewhere, away from the Eden cinema, since that site draws to this street "hundreds of people" every day.[1]

The description of the market is somewhat hyperbolic, but the basic details presented are confirmed by other sources. The market in question, like other markets in Tel-Aviv, was a constant source of dirt and noise, a thriving breeding ground for rats.[2] After an outbreak of plague in 1922, and under orders from the British authorities, the Eden market actually was moved from Lilenblum St. to another location. Interestingly, not all the residents in the vicinity shared Dr. Chamy's objection to the market, and local shop owners claimed that its removal had seriously harmed the formerly thriving commerce in the neighborhood.[3] Another detail in the letter that is corroborated by other sources is Chamy's claim about Eden's wide appeal. Eden, opened in 1914, was the first cinema house in town. We do not have exact figures about cinema attendance in the 1920s, but it was reported to be a highly popular pastime in Tel-Aviv.[4]

Thirteen years after the founding of Tel-Aviv as a "garden suburb," just one year after being granted autonomous "municipality" status from the British authorities, Chamy's letter exemplifies the expectations many people had of living in a quiet, clean town. He might have used his "doctor" title to lend more strength to his arguments regarding poor sanitary conditions and their dangerous effects. Although the end of the letter hints at the general danger posed by an unhygienic market located on a busy street, his letter is nevertheless characterized by a personal, rather than a public, appeal. The flies from the market stalls attack *his* house in particular, and rather than demanding that the TAM improve sanitary conditions in the market for the well-being of all Tel-Aviv residents, Chamy requests it be moved out of his own vicinity.

Whereas Chamy's letter reflects his personal expectations, priorities, and interests, many complaint letters were written, signed, and sent to the TAM by various *groups*. Two such letters, signed by twenty-five homeowners and residents of Mohaliver St., were sent to the TAM in the winter and the summer of 1924.

In the first letter the residents complain that the TAM has not yet connected their street to Nachlat Binyamin St., thus leaving it "as a remote island, separated and used only for storing all the water streaming to it from surrounding streets." This isolation is very harmful, the residents bemoan, more so because of the presence of the Hadassah Hospital morgue on their street, "a monster for the whole vicinity." The location of the morgue on a public street, visible to all who pass by, including youths and children, desecrates the dignity of the dead, according to Jewish tradition. Furthermore, the letter continues, the purification water and the burned possessions of some of the "infected deceased" find their way into the street, especially into un-built lots, and "the air is poisoned by the various and grave diseases" from which the deceased had died. The morgue proverbially chases away potential residents from the street; people do not want to rent apartments, even for reduced rents. "Rooms and even entire flats remain vacant, due to the danger of poisonous air, the heart-tearing wailing of the deceased's relatives," as well as the street's undesirable "water-pool," a source of mosquitoes and disease.[5]

In addition to describing their subpar living conditions, the residents of Mohaliver St. also suggest that they are being discriminated against by the TAM: "We do not understand at all why the municipality had decided to turn us into the scapegoat of the entire public of Tel-Aviv!" they write. Since they pay municipal taxes like all other citizens, the residents cannot understand the municipality's "weird" treatment of them, and its reluctance to pave their roads and sidewalks. They are sure, they add, that the TAM could turn their neglected area into one of the loveliest neighborhoods of Tel-Aviv. The TAM clearly put much energy into improving Tel-Aviv, planting trees in what was two years ago just a hill of sand; therefore, the residents insist that they deserve the TAM's aid rather than its neglect.[6] In addition to the distinct problems described in the letter and concerning Mohaliver St. in particular, the text also indirectly testifies, like many other sources from the 1920s, to Tel-Aviv's characteristics as a new city: the constant flux of expansion and construction, lots still vacant without any buildings, and unpaved roads and sidewalks.[7]

The residents of Mohaliver St. employ the same tone in registering another claim of unjust discrimination, in a letter sent six months later: "Unfortunately, we seem to be destined to shout without being answered. We have already mentioned the bad health conditions that we endure, not due to any fault of our own and in spite of our attempts to clean and purify and plant trees in our area." The letter dwells on three problems: (a) every winter the street turns into an infested swamp, as rain water runs into the road and even into houses; (b) although the presence of Hadassah Hospital cannot be beneficial for local residents' health, they do not demand moving it elsewhere; they do, however, ask that the location of the hospital's morgue be changed: rather than facing the street for all to see, it should be located in one of the building's internal rooms, or those facing its back yard; and (c) "In addition to all these factors, it has been decided to allocate the flat on the street corner, facing the morgue, as a hostel for tuberculosis patients. This is surely unsuitable, neither for the sick, who are put so close to the dead, nor for the healthy people who pass by. As is customary worldwide, tuberculosis patients are placed in high, airy, isolated locations, not in crowded neighborhoods like our own, where the sand flies right into our homes. In spite of all the sympathy we have for the poor tuberculosis patients, we cannot consent to risk our own health to this contagious disease."[8]

Complaints (a) and (c) refer to actual health hazards. Malaria, carried by the anopheles mosquito, was Palestine's primary endemic disease. Although in Israel's collective memory malaria is associated in particular with the pioneering agricultural settlements, it in fact inflicted hot and humid Tel-Aviv as well.[9] Lung tuberculosis was historically associated with crowded, unsanitary urban environments, in which it spread rapidly. Moreover, it was reputed to be an especially common disease among European Jews.[10] In the 1920s scores of tuberculosis patients were treated in Tel-Aviv. Even when their number increased to a couple of hundreds in the 1930s, and even after special tuberculosis sanatoriums were indeed opened in "high and airy" locations—Safed, Jerusalem, and Mount Carmel, hundreds of patients, including some in the active and contagious stage of the disease, were still treated in Tel-Aviv, in spite of its unsuitable climate and urban density.[11]

However, complaint (b), regarding the hospital morgue, refers to a symbolic "contamination" rather than a physical one. Whereas in their first letter the residents of Mohaliver St. describe the morgue as a medical hazard, in the second letter they treat it as affecting morale rather than bodily health. They also modify their initial demand: rather than requiring the removal of the morgue from their street altogether, they now only insist that it be moved to a less visible part of the hospital. As mentioned in the first letter, the aversion toward the proximity of the morgue was related to Jewish tradition, in which dead bodies are treated as profane, and therefore require purification and should be removed from the vicinity of the living. Although Tel-Aviv was mainly populated by non-religious Jews, the residue of the traditional Jewish attitude toward death, probably mingled with universal notions of morbidity, was manifested in several letters of complaint.

Some complaints reveal a strong emotional aversion to mere visual reminders of death.[12] Nine homeowners on a street bordering the cemetery complained that people are unwilling to rent their apartments because they were horrified by the blackness of the cemetery's gate, and therefore asked to paint it in a less intimidating color.[13] Equally disturbing, it seems, was the sight of the *hevra kadisha*'s (burial society) black funeral car, and neighboring residents asked it be removed from their street. One resident wrote that his wife runs a fashion "salon," "but the ladies probably refrain from our business when they see this 'monster' of a car parked near our building." Another neighbor, a gynecologist, demanded the black car be moved from under his window, as "it scares everybody, especially pregnant women." The *hevra kadisha* wrote to the TAM that they fully understood their neighbors' discontent. They knew that one resident even left the street because he couldn't stand the sight of their black car. Moreover, in addition to complaining, neighbors often attacked them, shouting, cursing, threatening to sue them, demanding to be compensated. But, the letter explains, they needed the car to be ready for any urgent call, and all the garage owners in the area refused to rent them space—"everyone is scared of the car as if it were a real monster."[14]

Other complaints regarding death and burial were related to the issue of noise. A homeowner on the street bordering the city's cemetery, for example, complained that no one was willing to rent apartments on his street, since people were unable to endure the "heart-piercing" and penetrating wailing of bereaved women, Yemenite women in particular. Realizing that the cemetery cannot be moved away, the writer of the complaint requests at least limiting the entrance hours from nine o'clock in the morning, because at present the disturbing shouts of grief start as early as six.[15] Residents of Mazeh St., also near Hadassah Hospital, were so upset by the shouts of mourners in the morgue that they asked the district governor to interfere. The governor (who, being British, was likely unaccustomed and not necessarily sympathetic to loud yelling as an expression of grief) ordered the hospital to *forbid* any wailing over the dead. However, the order was not implemented, and the street's residents complained to the TAM and asked that the dead be carried out of the hospital through the back door, rather than the door facing their street. Or else, they threatened, they would have to address their complaint to higher authorities.[16]

### "This Nightly Mayhem"

Most of the noises mentioned in letters of complaint were associated with the living rather than the dead. Numerous descriptions of Mandate Tel-Aviv attest to it being a noisy town. Curiously, it appears that the disturbance was sometimes caused not solely by the high volume of the noise or the inconvenient hours in which it occurred; letters of complaint reveal that a "disturbance" was often defined according to the writers' *moral* judgment of the activity that caused the noise.[17]

A letter from the residents of Ha'avoda St. in 1937 exemplifies this phenomenon. In a certain house on their street, they complain, young men and women dance to the sound of band-music, played on a radio or gramophone, every Friday and Saturday nights until two o'clock and even later. These young people dance not just indoors, but also on the building's open balconies, and they often affront their neighbors. "Also the voices of laughter, and jokes, and obscene jests, are all loudly heard and disrupt our peace of mind and body, which is a question of life and health for people who work all week long." Some of the residents on the street are sick people, for whom the noise and shouting pose a real threat, and children and babies too are awakened in the middle of the night. "Every now and then we have asked them to close the windows and the doors, to sing and dance more quietly, but then they always spitefully increase the noise, answer back rudely, and promise to start dancing during week nights too, in addition to the weekend." On New Year's Eve, add the writers, more than twenty cheeky couples danced in their habitual manner until two o'clock, and the "strange" shouting and laughing of these young men and women were so loud, that they had awakened the whole street. The complaint ends with the hope that the TAM will punish these people, thus stopping their malicious conduct.[18]

The disturbance described in this complaint is first and foremost a technical one, namely the loud noise, consistently preventing the neighbors from sleeping on the weekends.[19] Noise was considered especially unhealthy for sick people, whose nerves were weak. Like tuberculosis, weak nerves and mental illness were regarded as more common among Jews than among non-Jews; indeed, complaints about noise often mentioned weak nerves as a convincing reason for demanding quiet.[20] Yet the wording of the letter also discloses that the writers were not merely disturbed by the volume of the late-night noise and its unpleasant consequences, but probably disapproved of the behavior of the people who caused the noise. Whereas they themselves were hard-working people, their letters implied, the carefree men and women who danced at night were flaunting a licentious, brazen attitude, which their neighbors found alien and distasteful, in addition to its annoying audibility. It should be noted that ballroom dancing, unlike "folk" group dancing, was often associated with a Western, decadent, hedonistic, middle-class lifestyle.[21] The dancers are thus described as malicious, rude, and cheeky; their shouts are "strange" and their jests "rude." A moral objection was not the direct reason for the neighbors' basic complaint, but it seems to have intensified their grievance.

Of course some complaints about noise were devoid of negative moral judgment: even activities that were considered positive could be experienced as disturbing when conducted in the wrong place or at the wrong time.[22] However, moral, ideological, and political disagreement could add a sharper edge to a complaint. This is apparent in a letter sent in early 1935 by sixty-three homeowners in the Geulah neighborhood, regarding the youth club located in a couple of sheds in their neighborhood. This was the club of the socialist youth movement, "The Federation of Working and Studying Youth," affiliated with the General Hebrew Workers organization, the Histadrut. According to the complaining neighbors, "this club rests neither at day nor at night." During the day, it runs a school for workers' children, who are noisy, and the kitchen that supplies them with food is dirty. In neighborhoods with a school, the writers contend, residents at least are rid of the noise by night; but in Geulah they are not as fortunate: from afternoon to night, sometimes as late as two or three o'clock in the morning, youths from the "working circles" gather in the club, where they "sing, and dance, and make an awful racket, not allowing us—who work hard all day long—to rest and sleep and regain our strength." In addition to babies, who need their long night's repose, the neighborhood includes "weak people," who cannot "endure this nightly mayhem, and their nerves have been so wrecked that they have become nervously ill, and if the neighborhood will not be freed from these shoutings and rackets, their nerve illness might turn into a chronic condition." The residents of the neighborhood have lost their patience, and demand the TAM move the youth club to an unpopulated location.[23]

Thus runs the first part of the letter of complaint. Once again, the noise is described as disrupting the sleep of hard-working people and aggravating poor nerves, which seems to have been a common condition among Tel-Aviv residents. The second part of the letter contains an indignant comparison between the residents' expectations when they first settled in the neighborhood, and the grim reality created by the disruptive youth club. When they first bought their lots in the neighborhood, they continue, they had been promised that a municipal park would be built there. "All our lives we yearned for some peace and quiet in Eretz-Israel, after the hardships and torments we went through in the Diaspora [gola]." Is Tel-Aviv a lawless city, they ask, in which they have to risk their own lives, as well as the lives of their wives and children, with neither sleep nor rest possible, neither by day nor at night, even in their own homes? "Do we really have to be degraded into this state, just because the club belongs to the 'elite' of 'social justice', those attempting to change the world by bringing about the Kingdom of Karl Marx? Does this have any morality or humanity in it? Are the captains of our municipality so weak, so enslaved to our Socialists, that in order to fulfill their wishes they deem it just to sacrifice hundreds of families in our neighborhood and turn them into sick invalids?"[24]

This exaggerated rhetoric (risked lives, sacrificed residents) is a common feature in the complaint genre. More ingenious is the use of the well-known Zionist narrative about settling in Eretz-Israel as an act of deliverance from Diaspora trials. Whereas the gola is a place of inevitable "hardships and torments," Zionism promised to provide the settlers in Eretz-Israel with some peace and quiet.[25] According to the letter, the writers' initial Zionist hope was sadly shattered by the noisy youth club and by the inaction of a "weak" municipality.

The second section of the letter reveals that in addition to the volume of the noise and its inconvenient hours, the letter's writers—middle-class homeowners—also opposed the source of the noise—namely the club of "The Federation of Working and Studying Youth"—on an ideological level. The sarcastic reference to the youth club as attempting to bring about "the Kingdom of Karl Marx" is clearly unsympathetic. Political orientation, in Tel-Aviv as in the whole Yishuv, probably followed the main internal divisions among Zionists,[26] yet class rivalry was not entirely absent. In Tel-Aviv, a city where demographic growth was faster than physical expansion, class conflict was particularly manifest in the field of accommodation, as homeowners and renters often disagreed about taxes, rates, and rights.

The TAM was blamed by each side for favoring and supporting the other, and therefore ruling unjustly.[27] Tel-Aviv was known for its middle-class political orientation, economy, and culture, but in the meantime, especially during the 1930s, the Socialist faction gained increasing power within Zionist institutions and its ideology won a dominant status in Yishuv society.[28] Since the TAM was run in 1935 by middle-class factions (as in most years), the homeowners who wrote this letter seem particularly dismayed and disappointed, thus their provocative accusation of the municipality's "weakness" and its "enslavement" to "our Socialists."

The threat of being overpowered by the Socialists and their pervading influence was well reflected in the 1930s publications of the Tel-Aviv Association of Homeowners and Property Holders. Zionists who have property to invest in, claimed the association, are actually those who build the Yishuv and enrich it, but in return they are hated and discriminated against. When they resided in the Diaspora, property owners were urged to immigrate and bring their wealth to Eretz-Israel, but once they did so and built houses in the Hebrew city, they became surrounded by hostility. The "poisoned atmosphere" is so pervasive, that even homeowners accept the false anti-capitalist accusations and behave timidly, as if they were truly guilty.[29] The Socialist hegemony was apparently so omnipresent in the Yishuv, that when rallying its forces even this urban middle-class anti-socialist association adopted left-wing rhetoric and wrote to its members: "Homeowners—Unite!!!"[30]

The third and last part of the 1935 letter, sent by the Geulah neighborhood homeowners, moves from a tone of complaint, to a determined and threatening one. The writers declare that they have run out of patience and that if the municipality does not comply and deliver them from their plight, then they must address their grievances to "the proper governmental authorities, even as far as the High Commissioner." They demand that the local park be built immediately, as was promised when they bought their lots in the neighborhood. If their complaint is not answered within one month, they continue, they will have to use all possible means to correct "this injustice."[31]

Addressing "higher authorities," namely British government officials, was a common final threat in complaint letters sent to the TAM during the Mandate period. Such actions could undermine Tel-Aviv's status as an autonomous Jewish municipality, and were therefore considered an extreme step. Since Tel-Aviv's relative autonomy was regarded by Zionists as a test for Jewish self-rule, internal undermining of this autonomy was frowned upon by the general public and almost considered an act of national betrayal.

The threat to bypass the TAM's authority was not an empty threat. During the few years (1926–1928) when the Socialist faction ran the TAM, the Association of Homeowners appealed to the British court against the results of the local municipal elections, which brought into power a coalition lead by the Socialist faction. This act was rebuked not just by the injured Socialist faction and its followers, but also by the middle-class factions and associations of the city. Even after Meir Dizengoff and the middle-class factions returned to power following the next municipal elections, the Association of Homeowners sometimes contacted the British authorities if it disagreed with the TAM's policy.[32] It is unsurprising, then, that Deputy Mayor Israel Rokach took the threat seriously and hurried to reply to the letter of complaint, promising that the youth club sheds would be removed as soon as the TAM began construction of the planned park.[33]

These two letters of complaint, one sent in 1937 by residents of Ha'avoda St., the other sent in 1935 by Geulah homeowners, overlap in some ways. Both refer to disturbing noises, particularly at night. Both were written by older people, breadwinners and family men, regarding the behavior of youths, teenagers, or children. Both stress the need for rest after hard days of work. Both mention weak-nerved residents as those in special need of quiet. Furthermore, both letters disclose moral or ideological disdain of the activity that caused the disruptive noise: whereas the residents of Ha'avoda St. objected to the frivolity of the carefree young dancers, the homeowners in the Geulah neighborhood disapproved of the nest of socialist activity in their midst.

### "A Blot on the Fair Name of Tel-Aviv"

If the definition of "noise" was often influenced by moral judgment and personal viewpoints, then the question of "misbehavior" was certainly defined according to complaint writers' subjective norms and expectations.

In 1936, shortly after the outbreak of the Arab revolt, four neighbors from the same building complained to the TAM in broken Hebrew about the conduct of a fifth neighbor. "In the last few weeks we are horrified every single night from the shouting and yelling heard under our windows. We have learned that it is a fifteen-year-old girl, tortured by her father because she is supposedly going out with boyfriends. The noise of beating reaches us even up to the third floor [of the building]. Sometimes our heart almost breaks because we cannot help this poor little girl." The writers turned to the father "many times," asking him to cease his lurid behavior and stop torturing his daughter. However, "We have been answered by rudeness and threats, rejected because he claims we have no business interfering in his family affairs. We have explained to him that if he continues with his rude behavior, we will report him to the police, but he despises us and just curses us in Judeo-Spanish, Ladino. The girl's body is actually decorated with black stripes. Her face is pale and her body pathetically weak." The dismayed neighbors relate that the girl works twelve hours a day in her father's private printing business, and then is "paid" with a beating when she comes home. They end their letter with a plea to the TAM's "conscience": if it does not compel him to stop his horrid behavior, they will have to turn to the police. They hope that the TAM addresses the issue quickly, "and thus calm our nerves, which are strained as it is due to the situation in the land [i.e., the Arab revolt—A.H.]."[34]

Whereas the letter seems to be yet another complaint about a disturbing noise, it is quite clear that the writers' indignation is aimed first and foremost at what they viewed as unacceptable parental conduct. Obviously, their viewpoint clashed with that of their neighbor's: not only did the father have his own ideas about how to raise his daughter, he also regarded the issue as his private affair. His neighbors, on the other hand, felt that it was their duty to interfere and stop the beatings. It is clear from the wording of the letter that the writers were truly agitated by the proximity of violence that they regarded as morally reprehensible, and believed they were acting in the best interest of the daughter.

In response, the TAM secretary asked the district policeman in charge of crime to address the complaint, and the latter soon sent him a reassuring report. The police had looked into the case, he wrote, and the educated girl "was extremely surprised when she heard the allegations, as if her father was treating her cruelly. She has never complained to anyone about any such treatment by her father, since no such cruelty has ever existed. The neighbors' letter was probably written due to their strained nerves, as they themselves mention in their letter."[35]

The two letters thus provide two contradicting versions of the story.[36] Perhaps the girl denied the facts about her father's violence, as victims of abuse often do. Then again, perhaps the neighbors, on edge because of the violence of the Arab revolt, let their imaginations run wild. The police were obviously convinced by the educated, well-spoken girl. As previously mentioned, weak nerves were often used in complaint letters sent to the TAM, but in this specific case they provided the authorities with an alternative explanation of events. Moreover, unlike the policeman's report, and probably unlike the "educated" girl's convincing narrative, the letter of complaint was written in broken Hebrew. When faced with contradicting versions of the same story, form, rather than substance, and style, rather than facts, might sometimes be more persuasive.

The previously described letters of complaint all arose within the domestic sphere, but many letters of complaint dealt with misbehavior in the public sphere. Thus the owners of a local hotel write to the mayor in late 1938 about cafés and hotels on Allenby St., which are lately turning "into places of misdemeanor and are continually being used as clubs for drunken British soldiers and constables who like to walk about the streets, after getting drunk in the above cafés, and frighten all passersby." These soldiers sometimes enter the neighborhood's cafés and hotels, "threatening with their rifles." The writers complain that their beautiful neighborhood is being affected, since "no decent person" is nowadays willing to enter its cafés.[37] The misbehavior of British policemen and soldiers, in particular when under the influence of alcohol, had been a recurring topic in letters of complaint since the early 1920s.[38] In addition to some basic cultural differences between the British and Jewish populations (regarding the consumption of alcohol, for instance), hostility was probably inflamed on both sides by wider political tensions.[39] However, as the TAM's authority did not extend to British policemen and soldiers, there was little it could do, and the residents had to fend for themselves. As hinted in the letter, one solution was to avoid those areas most frequented by the British forces, and move to cafés located elsewhere.[40]

If Tel-Aviv residents complained about the misbehavior of drunken British policemen and soldiers, visitors from Western countries sometimes viewed the common behavior of Tel-Aviv residents as extremely impolite, or even downright rude.[41] Such were the impressions of a Canadian tourist who visited the city in 1933, during the days of the Fifth Aliya and its noticeable German component:

> I and other Americans, ardent life-long Zionists, went last February to Palestine to see and study the life of the newly rebuilt Jewish homeland, with the view of settling there, and like all newcomers there we spent most of our time in Tel-Aviv, the all-Jewish City, which is supposed to serve as a model for the future Eretz-Israel when it is hoped to be that in fact as well as in name. And having observed from close range the unethical methods and sharp "business" practices carried on in daily life between the old settlers themselves and particularly the shocking treatment meted out to the Tourists who spent time and money with the sole purpose of visiting their brothers in their new home, to participate in their joy and happiness, and worst of all, the callous inhuman dealings with our sorely tried, hunted and persecuted German Jews who barely escaped with their lives from Hitler's hand with hardly any means left for subsistence, and of such people these heartless Tel-Aviv egoists have taken advantage and mercilessly plundered their last few pounds, squeezing out their last piasters....
>
> Starting from the moment new arrivals set their feet upon the soil of the holy land, they are being preyed on and beset by hordes of Vultures, those taxi-men, baggage transferers, the hotels, those with private rooms for rent, and to a lesser degree, the restaurants; the lack of common courtesy displayed by the general public, which is so unusual for people coming from civilized countries like America and British countries; those real estate agents, continually walking Herzl Street with canes in their hands, stopping and approaching anyone looking like a stranger, offering to sell him the Moon "Old Mines" if you will only do them a favor and believe them, knowingly misleading you in a trap of unsound investment. Those things only react on their own personal hurt as it drives away the tourist industry, aside of the much greater loss involved, of placing a blot on the fair name of that beautiful first Jewish City of Tel-Aviv.[42]

True to the genre, the letter of complaint depicts daily life in Tel-Aviv in strong language: the tourists are "ardent Zionists" and the German newcomers are "sorely tried, hunted and persecuted," while the older settlers are "heartless egoists" and "vultures," whose behavior is described as "sharp," "unethical," "shocking," "callous," "inhuman," and "merciless." Indeed, like Western visitors, tourists, and officials, new immigrants from Germany were often shocked by local business ethics and manners, differing sharply from their own standards. The complex encounter of the German newcomers with the majority of eastern Europeans in Tel-Aviv and in other Zionist settlements has been described and analyzed in previous research.[43]

The letter conveys the sharp contrast between the standards held by "people coming from civilized countries" and the daily conduct in Tel-Aviv, located in the Levant and populated mainly by eastern European Jews. It also portrays the Canadian Zionist writer's initial high expectations of Tel-Aviv, a supposed model for future Jewish self-rule in Palestine. The real Tel-Aviv, as he found out, was not quite identical to the city portrayed in Zionist propaganda.[44] This gap between his lofty expectations and what he actually encountered in his visit seems to have surprised and disappointed the writer, who originally addressed his letter to the editor of *Ha'aretz*. Yet, rather than publishing the letter in the newspaper, the editor forwarded it to the TAM. The latter received quite a few letters of complaint from Zionist tourists, though most of them—unlike the quoted letter—usually singled out specific flaws within an otherwise positive impression of the city.[45]

Some of the harshest complaints received by the TAM during the Mandate, which are catalogued in the file concerning urban receptions, were sent by comparatively longtime residents of Tel-Aviv. Unlike public events, which were open to all, reception parties, held by the TAM for distinguished guests who visited the city, were exclusive events. The list of those invited to these formal parties hence became a kind of local "list of honor." An invitation to these events was considered an acknowledgment of the invitee's importance and worth; conversely, those who were not invited accused the TAM of neglect and disrespect. Individuals, companies, unions, and organizations protested about not being invited to certain receptions, citing their obvious relevance to the occasion and their undoubted contribution to the city.[46] In 1932 an exhausted Dizengoff remarked that "no party has ever gone by without some complaints and protests," and wondered whether all those who expected to be invited could ever be satisfied.[47]

Among the letters of complaint regarding urban receptions, those sent by uninvited individuals are usually more bitter and dramatic than those sent by collectivities such as companies or organizations. Often the complaint is written as if it protested the neglect of an entire sector, but this device does not disguise the personal insult suffered by the writer.

Since the offended writers of these letters were often highly educated and talented people, they could make the best of the genre's devices. Some used exaggeration, as exemplified by a letter that equates not inviting the proper guests to urban receptions with "a strange custom originating from the conditions of Czarist Russia," a symbol of despotism.[48] Others used sarcasm, as in the letter which thanks the TAM very much for inviting the writer and his wife; unfortunately, the writer continues, there was no room left for them, and they would rather have maintained their dignity by not being invited at all.[49] Still others expressed indignation, as in the case where one letter-writer notes that his wife is not invited to receptions, while other distinguished guests are invited with their wives; this "contradicts the most elementary rules of politeness and places me in a ridiculous position toward people of European culture."[50]

The young painter, writer, and illustrator Nahum Gutman was very assertive and direct about the matter. In 1937 he writes to the TAM secretary that he should be invited to municipal formal events not merely as the son of one of the city's founders (the Hebrew and Yiddish writer Simhah Alter Gutmann, known as S. Ben-Zion). He should be invited, explains Gutmann, in his own right, being the only painter who grew up from childhood in Tel-Aviv and who later made an impact on the city's art. He also contributes (as a decorator and a designer) to the urban Purim celebrations and the city's theater, he adds, and the children's books that he wrote and illustrated serve as "our classics." If the city wants to count among its sons not just bankers, merchants, and consuls, but also some artists, "then I thought that I, personally, have a place amongst them." After all this self-praise, and in order "not to become tiresome and humorless," Gutmann ends his letter with a friendly salute.[51]

Five years earlier, the Hebrew writer Yitzhak Dov Berkowitz was enraged when not invited to the opening reception of the Maccabia (an international Jewish Olympics), although a colleague who lives in the very same building *was* invited to the event. All of Berkowitz's talent as a writer was poured into his letter of complaint, addressed to Dizengoff. He states that not inviting him to the reception "was a sign of the utmost stupidity, rudeness, and ignorance, the behavior of uncultured impolite peasants who have risen to power." Berkowitz adds that he is not protecting his own honor, "as I regard it a very doubtful honor to be honored by the people of the municipality," but then mentions that he was one of the first Hebrew writers in New York who ever published papers on the topics of Eretz-Israel and Tel-Aviv. Whereas in New York, where he had lived for eight years, writers were respected by the Jewish public, in Tel-Aviv, the Hebrew city, writers are treated shamefully.[52] It was neither the first nor the only time in which the TAM was blamed for neglecting its artists,[53] but Berkowitz's letter of complaint was particularly aggressive, and might have easily been read by the mayor as a personal attack. The Association of Hebrew Writers therefore hurried to send Dizengoff a letter of apology expressing their high regard for the mayor and requested him to treat Berkowitz's strong expressions merely as "a slip of the pen in a time of anger."[54]

There is ample proof that Berkowitz was capable of writing less aggressive letters, since the archive contains another complaint, which he sent to the TAM only three months later. This letter, addressed to Deputy Mayor Rokach, concerns the lack of house numbers on his street, where he has been living for the past year and a half. Well written as expected, the letter rebukes the TAM for its neglect, employs irony and sarcasm, and even compares Tel-Aviv to Sholem Aleichem's fictional sordid Jewish town, Kasrilevke (Berkowitz was Sholem Aleichem's son-in-law and the translator of his works from Yiddish to Hebrew).[55] Yet this letter, concerning a public, urban issue, is much more moderate, calm, and humorous, than the letter Berkowitz wrote when he felt personally offended. Perhaps he assumed that after experiencing the full extent of his rhetorical wrath, the TAM would now take him seriously; and perhaps he was right: Rokach ordered the department in charge to install house numbers in Berkowitz's street "this very week."[56] Then again, a personal blow to one's pride might be more insulting than collective neglect, and therefore might evoke a sharper response.

Complaints regarding invitations to municipal receptions are particularly revealing. Precisely because they do *not* deal with urban issues of purely physical consequences, such as public health or violence, but rather with the petty issue of pride, these letters disclose the subjectivity of complaints and their tendency to exaggerate, characteristics that are apparent in many other letters of complaint as well. The demanding tone of many letters sheds light on yet another general trait of these letters: the writers' assumption that they *deserve* to be obliged. Although most complaints were not written by dignitaries and members of the urban elite, but rather by "ordinary" residents, the tone of entitlement is a recurring feature in many letters.

What gave the residents of Tel-Aviv this feeling of entitlement? Writing on the economic culture of the Yishuv, Hagit Lavsky notes that even capitalist immigrants were not thinking only about maximizing their profits, but were also driven by a national motivation: Eretz-Israel was not the most profitable option, and therefore investing one's capital in this developing country expressed a kind of "national-capitalism." The holders of capital (mostly small capital) who chose to settle in Eretz-Israel were hence characterized by another un-capitalistic trait: rather than being self-reliant, they demanded to be aided by Zionist institutions in the name of the national cause and as a reward for the economic sacrifice that they had made when opting for Eretz-Israel.[57] In Tel-Aviv, populated mainly by lower-middle-class Zionists, this "national-capitalism" may have been translated into the expectation that they would be helped by the autonomous municipality. Residents seemed to have regarded the mere fact that they lived and worked in the first Hebrew city as ample proof of their Zionist dedication and sacrifice, and therefore believed that they were fully entitled to demand the TAM's compliance.

Residents often threatened to pass their disregarded grievances to higher, British authorities, thus undermining the TAM's fragile status, and thus placing their own interests, or the interests of the specific sector to which they belonged, before the municipal-national goals (at least in theory). The Yishuv era is popularly and nostalgically depicted as an era of self-sacrifice and voluntary giving, especially when compared with the "demanding" citizenship in the state of Israel. Whereas Israelis tended to ask what the state could do for them, the members of the founding generation supposedly asked only what they could do for their national home. However, the entitled tone of so many complaint letters from the Mandate era may help to explain this supposed contradiction. It indicates that even before the founding of the state, at least in Tel-Aviv, some residents felt that their choice to settle in the land, even in its largest and richest city rather than in a pioneering peripheral settlement, should be properly acknowledged and rewarded.

Yet letters of complaint were also sent by non-residents, by Zionist visitors and tourists. Since Tel-Aviv was considered a Zionist showcase, its success was regarded as a Zionist concern, not just a local urban affair. Letters of complaint testify not only to Tel-Aviv's shortcomings, but also to the high expectations and ambitious aspirations invested in the city. Their writers cared enough—not just for their own well-being, but also for the overall quality of the city—to take the trouble to write complaints. Even if the urban ideals and lofty goals were never fully achieved, still forty percent of the Jews who immigrated to Palestine during the Mandate period chose to settle in the first Hebrew city, in spite of its dirt and its noise, its impolite public, and its pompous elites.[58]

## NOTES

1. Tel-Aviv Historical Archive (hereafter TAHA), 2-63b, letter from November 1922—Apart from two exceptions (see notes 37 and 42), all the quoted documents from TAHA are translated from Hebrew.

2. TAHA, 2-62a, sanitary reports, August 1921; 4/2484, letters, 1927; 4/2489, October 1933.

3. TAHA, 2-2b, letters, 1923; 2/33a, 1924.

4. *Hayishuv,* 6 August 1926.

5. TAHA, 2-66b, letter, 1924.

6. Ibid.

7. *Yedi'ot 'Iriyat Tel-Aviv,* 7 (1933), 245; John Gibbons, *The Road to Nazareth* (London, 1936), 82.

8. TAHA, 3-62a, letter, 1924.

9. TAHA, 3-60b, Medical report, 1926. See Naomi Shepherd, *Ploughing Sand: British Rule in Palestine 1917–1948* (New Brunswick, 1999), 132–137; Alon Tal, *Pollution in a Promised Land: An Environmental History of Israel* (Berkeley, Los Angeles, and London, 2002), 59–60.

10. See p. 428 in Mordecai Birkhiyahu, "Public Hygiene and Medicine," *Eretz-Israel's Yearbook* (Tel-Aviv, 1923), 424–429 [Hebrew]. See also Joseph Rakower, "Tuberculosis among Jews," in *Ethnic Groups of America, Vol. I—The Jews,* ed. Ailon Shiloa and Ida Cohen Selavan (Springfield, IL, 1973), 237–247.

11. TAHA, 3-60b, medical report on diseases in Tel-Aviv, 1926; 4-1376, letter, June 1932; 4-3954, memorandum, January 1938.

12. On changing attitudes to death see Philippe Aries, *The Hour of Our Death* (New York, 1981).

13. TAHA, 4-3807, letter, July 1930.

14. TAHA, 4-3807, letters, June 1937.

15. TAHA, 4-3807, letter, June 1926.

16. TAHA, 4-1397, letter, 1932.

17. Anat Helman, *Urban Culture in 1920s and 1930s Tel-Aviv* (Haifa, 2007), 46–47 [Hebrew].

18. TAHA, 4-3642, letter, September 1937.

19. The TAM could have used an existing Ottoman law regarding noise between 10 p.m. and 6 a.m., and it also established its own municipal regulations regarding the

closing hours of cafés and other noisy institutions: 4-334c, order, July 1930; 4-2862, municipal regulations, November 1931; TAHA, 4-3021, correspondence from 1931 to 1935, 3022.

20. Birkhiyahu, "Public Hygiene," 428. Compare letter, August 1935—Petah Tikva Municipal Archive, 1–48.

21. Helman, *Urban Culture,* 153–158 [Hebrew].

22. See, for instance, TAHA, 4-3828, complaints about noise stemming from youth and sports clubs—letter, June 1930; 4-3642, letter, May 1939.

23. TAHA, 4-2684, letter, January 1935.

24. Ibid.

25. On the Zionist depiction of exile, see Yael Zerubavel, *Recovered Roots: Collective Memory and the Making of Israeli National Tradition* (Chicago and London, 1995), 17–22.

26. Dan Horowitz and Moshe Lissak, *From Yishuv to State: Palestine Jews in the Mandatory Era as a Political Community* (Tel-Aviv, 1981) [Hebrew].

27. For instance TAHA, 4-2641, correspondence, The Popular Union of Tel-Aviv Neighbors and Residents from 1934; *The Popular Union of Tel-Aviv Neighbors and Resident's Bulletin* (Tel-Aviv, 1935), 3–11.

28. Ilan Troen, "Establishing a Zionist Metropolis: Alternative Approaches to Building Tel-Aviv," *Journal of Urban History* 18.1 (1991): 10–36. Naomi Shiloach, "The 'Civilian Circles' in Tel-Aviv Municipal Elections," *Yahadut Zemanenu* 14 (2001): 127–163 [Hebrew]; Yaacov Shavit, "Why Did the Inhabitants of Tel-Aviv Not Wear a Red Riding Hood? Idealism vs. Realism in the Interperation of the Yishuv—Tel-Aviv as a Meaphor," in *Economy and Society in Mandatory Palestine 1918–1948,* ed. Avi Bareli and Nahum Karlinsky (Sde-Boker, 2003), 59–78 [Hebrew].

29. The Tel-Aviv Association of Homeowners and Property Holders, *The Program and Ways of the Tel-Aviv Association of Homeowners and Property Holders* (Tel-Aviv, 1937), 4–6 [Hebrew].

30. Akiva Ariye Weiss, "The Private Enterprise in Tel-Aviv," *General Association of Houses and Lots' Owners in Tel-Aviv* (1934), 3–6.

31. TAHA, 4-2684, letter, January 1935.

32. *Yedi'ot 'Iriyat Tel-Aviv,* 20 (1927), 2–9; TAHA, 4-2954, letter, July 1929.

33. TAHA, 4-2684, letter, January 1935. The promised park, Gan Meir, planned by Mayor Dizengoff since the early 1930s, was eventually constructed in the late 1930s and early 1940s.

34. TAHA, 4-3642, letter, June 1936.

35. Ibid.

36. Compare with another case, in which the stated "facts" in a letter of complaint were denied and refuted by the municipal gardener: TAHA, 2645b, correspondence, July 1938.

37. TAHA, 4-3642, letter November 1938 [English].

38. TAHA, 2-63c, correspondences, 1922; 2-52c, August 1923; 2-90, police order, 1924; 4/316a, December 1932; 4-3455, July 1935.

39. TAHA, 4-3642, correspondence, April–July 1939; Rachel Elboim-Dror, "British Educational Policies in Palestine," *Middle Eastern Studies* 36.2 (2000): 31–32.

40. Batia Carmiel, *Tel-Aviv's Cafés, 1920–1980* (Tel-Aviv, 2007) [Hebrew].

41. TAHA, 4-3563a, "A South African's Impressions of Palestine by Marcia Gitlin," 1933; 4-149a, report, 1938; Elizabeth Montgomery, *A Land Divided* (London, 1938), 94.

42. TAHA, 4-3540, letter January 1934 [English].

43. Yoav Gelber, *New Homeland: Immigration and Absorption of Central European Jews, 1933–1948* (Jerusalem, 1990); Guy Meron, *German Jews in Israel: Memories and Past Images* (Jerusalem, 2004); Helman, *Urban Culture*, 50–51, 216–219 [both in Hebrew].

44. For example, see Aharon Ze'ev Ben-Yishai, *Tel-Aviv* (Jerusalem, 1936); *Tel-Aviv*—The Steven Spielberg Jewish Film Archives, VT DA308.

45. TAHA, 4-3452, letters from April 1924; 2-65, July 1928; 4-3627, January 1929; 4-248b, 1929.

46. For instance TAHA, 2-56b, letters, summer 1924; 4-3202, November 1926; 4-3205, April 1932; 3207, March and April 1934; 3205, February 1938.

47. TAHA, 4-3204, letters, April 1932; 4-3202, November and December 1926; 4-3207, May 1935; 4-3206, June 1939.

48. TAHA, 4-3627, letter, March 1932.

49. TAHA, 4-3220, letter, March 1934.

50. TAHA, 4-3206, letter, May 1934.

51. TAHA, 4-3207, letter, January 1937.

52. TAHA, 4-3204, letter, March 1932.

53. *Hamachar*, Sivan Tarza (1931) 22–24; *Kalno'a*, 15 October 1932, 18; *Tesha ba'erev*, 27 October 1938, 2.

54. TAHA, 4-3204, letter, April 1932.

55. TAHA, 4-2641, letter, July 1932.

56. Ibid.

57. Hagit Lavsky, "On the Nature of the Identity of Jews as Capitalists—the Case of the Jewish Community in Mandatory Palestine," in *Interrelation between Religion and Economy*, ed. Menahem Ben-Sasson (Jerusalem, 1994), 387–399 [Hebrew].

58. This contradiction of settling in Tel-Aviv while complaining about its many faults is still apparent as the city celebrates its centennial; see Izik Shashu, "Fuck-you, Tel-Aviv," *Blazer*, January 2009, 90–92.

# SEVEN

# South of Tel-Aviv and North of Jaffa—The Frontier Zone of "In Between"

### Deborah S. Bernstein

Strange is the geography of Tel-Aviv—at a distance of 200 meters from the heart of the city, from Magen David Square, lies one of the city's main suburbs. Your eyes hardly rest for a moment from the glitter of neon and the car lights of Allenby St. and already you have dropped into the oppressive darkness of the alleys of Kerem Hatemanim.

Tel-Aviv has been portrayed as the new Hebrew city, which "rose from the sands" at the empty stretch of land north of Jaffa. Tel-Aviv was perceived and presented as a new social entity, distinct from all that preceded it: from dirty and "unhygienic" Oriental Jaffa with its narrow alleys, chaotic urban order, from the Jewish ghettoes and districts in the urban centers of central and eastern Europe, and from the early Jewish neighborhoods that branched out of Jaffa, establishing separate though adjoining neighborhoods to its north and northeast.

Tel-Aviv was seen as a new creation in many respects. It was "a European oasis in the desert of Asia,"[1] it was populated exclusively by Jews, or rather "Hebrews"—the new nationalist Jewish men and women who were no longer a minority but the totality, who founded a city with no gentiles, no deprecating eye. Tel-Aviv was the center of the nationalist project where its leaders, institutions, cultural elites, and financial centers were located. All these attributes, noted by its municipal leadership, by visitors from other parts of the Yishuv, and no less strikingly by non-Jewish visitors from abroad,[2] represented the essence of the emerging city both in terms of physical space and of social composition.

Thus, the evolution of the modern, Western, nationalist, Hebrew-speaking, well-ordered urban center would take us from the starting point of Ahuzat Bayit to Rothschild Boulevard with its wide vistas, well-designed houses, and large trees along the promenade that ran through the middle of the boulevard.[3] It would take us to Zina Dizengoff Square (*Kikar Dizengoff*), the hub of life of the city, to the cafés patronized by the cultural elite, to the Herbert Samuel promenade, and the beaches with school kids, the athletes of all ages, the young men and women swimming and sun-bathing, like Westerners. Further north we would find the Orient Fair, which opened in 1930, celebrating Tel-Aviv's status as the leader of progress and economic development in Eretz-Israel/Palestine and the Middle East in general. Thus, following the transformation of the city, we would move from the founding ground of Tel-Aviv to the north, expanding to the west along the sea front, and to the east, up to the Arab villages and orchards.

Such a northward meandering would have left out Tel-Aviv's expansion to the south. In a somewhat less organized manner, urban planning and zoning combined with spontaneous and at times chaotic growth led to the emergence of new neighborhoods to the south of Ahuzat Bayit. Heterogeneous streets, houses, cafés, workshops, and markets linked the older neighborhoods to the newer ones.

The south of Tel-Aviv attracted far less attention both at the time the city was establishing itself as the center of the Yishuv and in later scholarship. The neighborhoods in the south of Tel-Aviv and somewhat beyond its municipal boundary will be the focus of this essay. The neighborhoods to the south of Tel-Aviv and to the north of Jaffa were a mixed assortment in their municipal affiliation, the period of their founding, the extent of their planning, and the nature of their marginality. They were a chain of neighborhoods established over a number of decades to the north of Jaffa, to the south-southeast of Tel-Aviv, and marginal to both. Yet even though the zone to the south was little discussed at the time, it was integral to the national and social urban narratives, as will be shown in the following sections. Some of the neighborhoods, among them Neve Tzedek, Neve Shalom, and Kerem Hatemanim, which preceded Tel-Aviv (or rather, Ahuzat Bayit), were initiated in the late nineteenth and early twentieth centuries by the desire to move out of the heart of Jaffa.[4] Others were established during the 1920s to the south of the railroad tracks leading from east to west into Jaffa, to accommodate Jews who evacuated Jaffa after the violent clashes of 1921 and to accommodate large-scale Jewish immigration to Palestine in the mid-1920s.[5] Still later, in the 1930s, we find the unplanned squatting sections of evacuees from Jaffa after the outbreak of the Arab Rebellion and the violent hostilities that accompanied it, the best known of these areas being Shchunat Hatikva.

This zone of small and large, planned, semi-planned, and unplanned neighborhoods stretched to the south of the heart of Tel-Aviv. Though located in close proximity to Tel-Aviv proper, this southern area received little attention, in comparison to the north. It was not only located on the periphery of Tel-Aviv, but along the border between Tel-Aviv and Jaffa. Thus the overall southern zone of Tel-Aviv was both a periphery and a frontier. These two attributes are not identical, though, in many respects, they did reinforce each other. The borderline was shifting, twisting, and permeable, occasionally amended and contested. It did not block movement nor did it fully separate between the Jews to its north and Arabs to its south. Though it demarcated separation, it was also an area of contact, crossing, and mixing. Thus I later discuss a frontier area rather than a borderline, an area that manifested many of the contradictory aspects of borders—division and permeability, a focus of attention and at the same time a peripheral and marginal section of the urban entity.

The rest of this essay will examine three aspects of the frontier/peripheral zone. First, the drawing of the borderline and its contestation. Second, the characteristics of the border zone, the combined and contrasting features of separation, mixing, crossing, and apprehensive proximity. And third, the marginality of the frontier zone, both in terms of municipal services and infrastructure, and in terms of the composition of its population. To conclude, the broader impact of this zone on the urban development of Tel-Aviv will be discussed.

## The Zigzag Line

There are about 55,000 Arab residents in Jaffa and about 16,000 Jews; but the town is essentially Arab. Tel-Aviv, which adjoins Jaffa on the north, has a population of about 140,000 and is entirely Jewish. The two form geographically a single town. The majority of the Jewish residents of Jaffa live near the boundary between the two towns. This boundary is a zigzag line running for the greater part through narrow streets. There has been for many years discord between the two towns and serious disturbances have taken place on the boundary.[6]

In 1921 the first border between Tel-Aviv and Jaffa was agreed upon and Tel-Aviv was granted the status of an autonomous township. The border would be amended and contested numerous times during the following years. Two major factors affected the location of the municipal borderline. First, the border was intended to incorporate the Jewish quarters and their inhabitants within the municipal territory and authority of Tel-Aviv, and the Arab quarters and their residents within the municipal territory and authority of Jaffa. Second, the continuously expanding Jewish population led to the establishment of new quarters, which challenged the "fit" of the originally agreed-upon boundaries. The combined impact of these two factors is evident both in the zigzag boundary line and in its contestation.

As early as 1918, when the residents of Tel-Aviv were recovering from the hardship of World War I and the prospect of British rule was imminent, the communal leaders of Tel-Aviv put forward their request for separation from Jaffa. This was based on the desire for economic independence, for municipal authority to impose taxes, and for an element of sovereignty related to the overall national project. By 1921 partial separation had been obtained, and by 1934 Tel-Aviv was granted full municipal independence. While the actual boundary was amended a number of times, as will be discussed shortly, it consistently twisted and turned, indicative of the tension between the guiding principle of separation and the reality on the ground. The final twisting line that appeared in the Official Gazette prior to the 1934 municipal elections, demarcated the Tel-Aviv Municipality (hereafter TAM) from Arab villages, landowners, and the town of Jaffa to its north, east, and south. In its course, the borderline made use of an assortment of landmarks—natural vegetation such as cactus hedges, agricultural cultivation such as the citrus groves of both Jewish and Arab landowners running side by side, as well as private and public construction, homes of well-known Jewish and Arab families, roads, and railway tracks.

The zigzagged line, which left a number of new Jewish neighbor-hoods south of the TAM boundary in Jaffa's municipal zone, indicates the difficulty of tracing a clear-cut separation. A number of quotes from the Municipal Corporation Ordinance demonstrate the point. Refer-ring to the southern boundary and its route from east to west, the or-dinance reads: "Thence westward exclusive of the orange grove of Attal but following the acacia fence and cactus hedge which forms the eastern boundary of the orange grove of Hassan Eff. 'Ali Mahmud which is ex-cluded, thence northward. . . ."[7] Skipping over the zigzaging line between orange groves and cactus hedges, the Valhalla quarter,[8] and the railway station, the description of the boundary continues:

> Thence north-westward along Barnett St. to its junction with Manshiya St. excluding the house of El-Akkad as far as but excluding Zakariya's Mill. Thence in an easterly direction excluding Jaber's Mill, thence north-ward but excluding the property owned by Debbas and Homsi jointly, thence northward to the house of El-Ish where it turns westward, thence northward along the western border of the Summeil Road passing, but excluding the house of Yahya Abu Sit, thence in a westerly direction to the northern limit of the house of Haj Zuhdi 'Abdo, thence in a southerly direction following the Massudiya Road, thence in a westerly direction along the property of Amin Bey Nassif to the north-west corner of said property at the sea.[9]

The borderline of 1934, which accompanied the granting of full mu-nicipal independence to Tel-Aviv, was the result of a number of amend-ments of the 1921 border and of the rejection of possible other ones. Initially the boundary between Tel-Aviv and Jaffa ran more or less along Jaffa Road (dubbed by the Tel-Aviv press as the Tel-Aviv–Jaffa Road). Before reaching the coast, the border curved to the north to avoid includ-ing the predominantly Arab Manshiya quarter within the boundaries of Tel-Aviv. Nevertheless, Manshiya was far less distinct than might be assumed, so that the borderline in fact went through the early Jewish quarters of Neve Shalom and Kerem Hatemanim, leaving some of their Jewish inhabitants as residents of Jaffa. Throughout the 1920s the border was amended a number of times. It incorporated into the TAM terri-tory a significantly large section of Jaffa, to the south of the original borderline, tracing a zigzag line around the new Commercial Center, and moving eastward around a number of new neighborhoods, as far east as the neighborhood of Neve Sha'anan.

Despite the annexation of territory previously belonging to Jaffa, the line was no more decisive than it had been before. Many neighborhoods newly established by Jewish residents blurred the national divide and, concomitantly, often contested their affiliation with Jaffa. The TAM clung to its basic principle that all Jewish quarters should be part of the "Jewish/Hebrew" town of Tel-Aviv:

> With the rapid development and expansion of Tel-Aviv, especially in the period following 1932, the need for erecting new quarters has steadily grown and the building activity has overflowed the boundaries of the town, especially to the east and south, where new quarters were built by Jewish enterprise in uninhabited areas and deserted orange groves.
>
> These new quarters were a natural continuation of Tel-Aviv, quite distant from the town of Jaffa proper; they were built by Jews, on land bought by Jews, and were inhabited by Jews who were economically, culturally, and socially connected with Tel-Aviv. For all intents and purposes, the new quarters were regarded by their inhabitants as an integral part of Tel-Aviv.[10]

The debate concerning the partition of Palestine aroused in 1937 by the Palestine Royal Commission and the Woodhead Commission (appointed the following year to devise ways for implementing such a partition), once again raised the issue of the municipal partition between Tel-Aviv and Jaffa. Both sides presented their schemes to the Woodhead Commission. Neither of the schemes would have incorporated all Jews in Tel-Aviv and all Arabs in Jaffa. As noted by the commission, the proposal of the Jewish side "suggested . . . that the existing boundary, throughout its whole length, should be moved a considerable distance to the south. . . . The effect of adopting this boundary would be to transfer from Jaffa to Tel-Aviv not only practically all the Jewish property in Jaffa, but in addition some Arab areas . . . In terms of population it would mean transferring to Tel-Aviv not only the Jewish population of Jaffa but also a large Arab population."[11] In turn, the proposed Arab scheme, we learn from the commission's report, would have involved "a considerable increase in the Jewish population and property in Jaffa."[12] Unsurprisingly, no scheme, not even that of the Woodhead Commission itself, was implemented, and the issue continued to re-emerge, especially in times of increased national tension and violent hostilities. A line of separation was never agreed upon.

Despite the continued debate over annexation and municipal affiliation, in practice the issue was not a clear cut either/or. In fact, the Jewish quarters in the territory of the Jaffa municipality were, at the same time, closely related to the TAM, to which they had no formal affiliation. However, the TAM did have social, economic, and personal ties to the Jewish quarters, and took it upon itself to provide social services to the inhabitants. These services included public education, social welfare, and public medical care.[13] Thus, as the inhabitants argued, they were paying taxes to one municipality from which they claimed to be getting very few social services, while wishing to be annexed to the municipality on which they were dependent for many of their basic needs. The situation of the inhabitants of the Jewish quarters of Jaffa remained, in many respects, in limbo, as they were both part of Jaffa and of Tel-Aviv, and as a result, on the margins of both.

### The Frontier Zone as a Space of Mixing, Crossing, and Apprehensive Proximity

The undersigned citizens and ratepayers of the Township of Jaffa beg very humbly to ask how it is possible that a sidewalk leading from one town (Jaffa) to another (Tel-Aviv) can be blocked. Such a case can be seen on the road leading from Jaffa to Tel-Aviv (on the left), where a commercial firm: J. W. Zenftman locked the sidewalk by the erection of a wall with some advertising. . . . We like to believe that this arbitrary blockading of a sidewalk has escaped the attention of the municipalities, but we hope that our present reference will lead to a change respective to the opening of the sidewalk in question.[14]

The border zone between Tel-Aviv and Jaffa had a number of characteristics. The border itself aimed at demarcating a line of separation, on the one side Jaffa and on the other Tel-Aviv. Yet this was hardly the major characteristic of the municipal border and its surroundings. It was an area of separation but, no less so, an area of contact. It was an area of mixing in which Jews and Arabs intermingled, though to a relatively minor extent. It was, to a greater extent, an area of crossing, through which Jews traveled for various purposes into Jaffa, and Arabs from Jaffa and the villages south of Tel-Aviv to Tel-Aviv proper. Finally, the best documented characteristic of the area was the element of proximity: Jews and Arabs did not necessarily meet but were in one another's immediate orbit. As the overall relations between Jews and Arabs in Palestine fluctuated, so did the significance of the proximity, or in more concrete terms, the apprehension caused by the proximity, at least as experienced on the Jewish side. These three facets will be elaborated in the following section.

## Mixing of Jews and Arabs

There is not a great deal of evidence of Jewish–Arab mixing in the area south of Tel-Aviv, given both the differences in lifestyle and the overall drive for separation on predominantly national grounds. Nevertheless, some mixing was noted in various documents, usually in passing. Intermingling took place in living accommodations in some border areas, in cafés of the "in between zone," and in the Carmel Market, located close to the Arab quarter of Manshiya. To begin with the latter, Carmel Market, which adjoined the northern tip of Manshiya, was well planned with licensed stalls, as were the other markets of Tel-Aviv. The market attracted many Arab sellers and peddlers who thronged in nearby alleys, setting up their own stalls and avoiding municipal license fees. Interestingly, the Jewish stall owners were the ones to request that this mixing, or partial mixing, continue, when the TAM attempted to remove the Arab sellers. Their presence, claimed the licensed stall holders, attracted many buyers and kept the market busy. Thus they wrote to the Finance Committee of the TAM:

> With the establishment of the new market we sat empty handed with no daily income, as all the buyers went to other places, to the Arabs, claiming that there they could buy everything much cheaper. But afterward, when the Arab merchants came to our market as well, the income improved for the whole market, and we the signatories, the sellers of meat, fish, and poultry, as well as the sellers of freshly baked bread, are very satisfied. . . . We know full well that if the Arabs will be driven away then all commerce will come to a standstill.[15]

Though Arabs and Jews worked in close proximity at the Carmel Market, mixed dwelling was not common. This occurred mainly in the

north and east of Manshiya, with its blurred boundary with Kerem Hatemanim to the north and Neve Shalom to its east. By the end of the
Mandate period, approximately 18,000 Jews lived in Manshiya, close to
its northern and eastern boundaries.[16] Thus, for example, Ora Terri, who
emigrated with her family from Yemen in 1933 as a five-year-old girl,
wrote of her family's accommodation. On arrival the small family went
first to Kerem hatemanim to her aunt's very crowded one-room dwelling unit. After a few days they moved into their own dwelling, renting
two rooms of three in a nice large apartment in Manshiya, just a short
distance away. Relations with the Arab-Christian family who rented the
third room, writes Terri, were very congenial.[17] In addition to mixed living, the proximity led to some mixing in the semi-public/semi-private
spheres of the neighborhood, most specifically in the cafés.

We learn of the Jewish cafés on Shabazi St. (Neve Shalom) with their
regular Arab patrons, of Arab cafés in Jaffa where Jews, predominantly
men, liked to frequent, and of well-known and respectable establishments such as Café Lorentz, located close to the original borderline of
Tel-Aviv–Jaffa Road.

"Owned by Hinawi, a member of a well known landed family of Jaffa
and run by F. Nusbaum, Café Lorentz placed an advertisement in *Filas-
tin* (26.3.37) announcing the opening of its new season, with novelties
including daily live music. Lorentz was a well known café, frequented
by well-off Jewish families of Tel-Aviv, British officials brought there by
their Tel-Aviv hosts, and also, it would seem, Arab patrons. Yet, it seems,
that just behind Café Lorentz another meeting place for Jews and Arabs
was located, run by the Jewish 'Rivka, blond, Ashkenazi' and the Arab
Rashad who brought together young Jewish girls and Arab men for the
purpose of prostitution."[18] This was only one of many brothels which
were located in the frontier zone, along Jaffa–Tel-Aviv Road, in Neve
Shalom and its roundabouts.[19] Cafés were arenas of gendered contact,
among other places. Along the waterfront and the beach, in the small
streets just off the promenade, along the borderline streets and in Jaffa
itself, some mixing of Jews and Arabs clearly existed. It is impossible
to assess the scope of such mixing and the extent to which Arab men
frequented Jewish establishments and vice versa, but it did take place,
and was often referenced.

## Crossing

Crossing over from Tel-Aviv to Jaffa and vice versa was common and driven by a variety of motivations. Some crossed over to carry out their shopping. No direct evidence is given, but many indications are available. The letter quoted above signed by the Jewish market stall holders makes it amply clear that many of the inhabitants of Tel-Aviv bought their daily wares from Arab merchants and peddlers whose rates were considerably lower.[20] There appear also to have been peddlers who strolled the streets of the Jewish neighborhoods at some distance from the border zone, carrying vegetables and fruits in a donkey-driven cart.[21] Arab consumers may well have crossed over to the shopping centers of Tel-Aviv during the prosperous years of the 1930s. While there is no direct evidence of this, Jewish stores in Tel-Aviv advertised in the Arabic daily press appearing in Jaffa. One can thus assume that the shops selling women's clothing, children's toys, elegant leather bags, and alcoholic beverages, which routinely appealed to the Arabic reading public, did indeed attract a sufficient number of consumers.[22]

There also seems to have been crossing for the purposes of leisure. There was clearly attraction on both sides. Some Jewish residents of Tel-Aviv, predominantly men, enjoyed the Jaffa "eastern" cafés where the nargila passed from hand to hand.[23] Additionally, some Jewish women and young girls crossed over to Jaffa, as reported by social workers who were deeply concerned by such behavior. The girls, when questioned about their presence in Arab cafés, explained that they were singers, dancers, and "artists," and worked where they were appreciated and well paid.[24] Women crossed over to Jaffa when establishing intimate relations, a subject about which there was general silence, broken by odd comments, bits of information, sensational melodramatic write-ups, and references in later written memoirs. Men of "both sides" seemed to have enjoyed meandering in the "other's" territory. Their gaze, it appears, was especially attracted by the women in conditions that may well have seemed to both exotically alluring. Thus a British journalist who visited Tel-Aviv and Jaffa in 1936 wrote:

> Only a few years ago the desolate sands were substituted by houses and streets and only a narrow stretch of sand was left for the bathers. It was the Jews who transformed the place into a beautiful place for bathing. The

Arabs never even dreamed of this but now they frequently come to Tel-Aviv to bathe in its sea. By the way, well known Arab leaders, whose public opinion on the Jewish question is highly negative, spend their time here pleasantly, in the company of their Jewish friends. Hundreds of Arabs from among the poor come to the Tel-Aviv beach to view the bathers.[25]

Apparently, the possibility that Arabs visited the Tel-Aviv beaches for the purpose of viewing Jewish bathers was a significant concern of Tel-Aviv residents. After describing the shocking lack of modesty exhibited by both men and women at the waterfront, the journalist emphasizes in conclusion: "The blasphemy is beyond description. And all this encourages our neighbors to come in flocks to gaze at the daughters of Israel in their state of shame."[26]

In turn, Haim Gouri, Israeli poet, novelist, and journalist, recounts, in poetic terms, his own attraction to the alleys of Jaffa:

A labyrinth. Endless nameless alleys, originating in light, leading on to chilled darkness and disappearing faces. The sun makes its way west above gramophonic restaurants choked with Um-Kulthumian imploring, echoes by a comforting, Egyptian, Abdul Wahabi response. Florentine beams. Balconies with iron flowers and geranium pots. I see women through arched windows. Dark women, their mouths reddened like furnaces, silent like dream-concubines. And on, with Muslim, Isphahani blue.[27]

If one gendered aspect of "boundary crossing" was the masculine gaze, a second was the social taboo of "crossing women." Crossing by men was hardly noted in public opinion and discourse. It was the women who drew attention and aroused concern. Crossing by women was seen as an interaction, or at least a potential interaction, with men "on the other side." This threatened the stereotypical view of the feminine as symbol of collective purity and moral boundaries; when Jewish women crossed cultural borders it was seen as a challenge to the coherence of the newly devised national entity.

## Proximity and Apprehension

Gouri continues to describe his attraction to Jaffa, an attraction embedded in deep apprehension, a sense of potential threat, and an inability to forget recent bloody events:

I am going to Jaffa of the goddesses and the sharp knives, of the mad ser-
mons in the mosques. I am going to Jaffa. Don't go to Jaffa! I am going to
Jaffa, to the Sheikh al-Faruki, to "al-Jami'a al-Islamiya," to the crowded,
shouting Jaffa, to Jaffa of Haj Amin, pouring out of all its mosques, green
flags noisily flying, sworded hands, ablaze with the fire of the Ottoman
*tarbush*. I am going to Jaffa. Don't go to Jaffa! You are mad! All the shutters are closed down. To Manshiya I am going, to Ajami, to Abu-Kabir,
to the blood of Brener, to the dogs, barking at me as if mad. . . . The city
is full of dreadful and horrendous rumors. All the shutters are closed.
Black smoke, black smoke is rising to the sky. A man is fleeing to the
north, he arrives collapsing, exhausted. A cart is galloping, as if crazy,
with no driver to it.[28]

Regrettably little documentation remains concerning the routine
and even amiable relations of everyday life. It would seem that the recurring outbreaks of hostility that ended with many casualties and led many
Jews living in Jaffa to flee, were a powerful fact of life on the frontier and
colored all relations. In 1946, after numerous small and large clashes,
Zakharya Kohlani knew that the border was a place of potential danger.
Living practically on the border in the neighborhood of Neve Shalom,
he was wary of any factor that might instigate further outbursts. He
explains in his letter to the mayor of Tel-Aviv:

I have learned from neighbors that the partner to my lot of land, Mr.
Shmuel Afari, has asked for a permit from the Tel-Aviv Municipality for
the retail sale of alcoholic beverages . . . The first ground for my objection
is that because his lot is located on the border between Jaffa and Tel-Aviv,
on a major street connecting the two cities, this will cause a constant
concentration of clients from among both Arabs and Jews, and will make
the place a meeting place for the lovers of drink. Your honor certainly
knows that borders are always places most vulnerable to outbursts and
attacks, quarrels and incitement, and therefore it is the obligation of the
municipal and government authorities to do whatever they can to provide
the most effective means of ensuring the safety and peace of the public.[29]

Periods of violent outbreaks exacerbated fear of the nearby Arab
population. Residents of neighborhoods affiliated with the Jaffa municipality reiterated their demand for immediate annexation to Tel-Aviv.[30]
Residents of neighborhoods affiliated with the TAM expressed their fear
of recurring riots and called for greater involvement of the municipality in protecting its frontier quarters. Thus the public leaders of Neve

Shalom wrote in January of 1941, demanding the construction of a small police station in their neighborhood:

> Since the end of the riots about one year ago, when the [Jewish] refugees began returning to their homes in the small streets on the border of Tel-Aviv and Jaffa, Arab youngsters of 15–20 years old, have begun swarming the neighborhood. They disturb the public calm, raise their voices, fight with the youngsters of the neighborhood, enter the courtyards and intimidate their residents. And most especially, to our great disgrace, they run after the Jewish girls, so that a decent family cannot permit its daughters to go into the street even in the late afternoon, lest they be harassed by the young Arab men roaming the streets till past midnight.[31]

Such complaints, addressed both to the TAM and, in the case of the Jewish quarters of Jaffa, to the High Commissioner or the District Commissioner, were closely intertwined with the feeling of marginality and exclusion from Tel-Aviv proper. The residents of the border neighborhoods demanded recognition of the role they played during the clashes of the Arab Rebellion (1936–1939) as guardians of the frontier. They should be credited for safeguarding the Hebrew city of Tel-Aviv, they wrote: "We, the homeowners of this dilapidated quarter, which serves as a buffer to Tel-Aviv, stood day and night on duty in the Civil Guard all along the frontier with our Arab neighbors, to block them from breaking into Tel Aviv."[32]

## On the Margin—The Southern Neighborhoods and Their Inhabitants

The third characteristic of the border zone was its social and municipal marginality. The southern neighborhoods of Tel-Aviv were a mixed lot. Among them were the early pre-Tel-Aviv quarters and the relatively planned neighborhoods such as the Commercial Center and to its east Neve Sha'anan, and the squatters' quarter of Shchunat Hatikva. Nevertheless, to varying degrees, they all were on the periphery of Tel-Aviv in terms of their facilities, infrastructure, urban planning, the mixed nature of their housing, living conditions, and composition of their inhabitants.

Descriptions of the early Jewish quarters are found in a variety of firsthand sources. Though physically close to Jaffa, these areas were distinct from it in many ways. A woman named Ora Terri describes her first memories of Tel-Aviv upon her arrival from Yemen in 1933. She and her parents were met at the Jaffa port by her aunt, slowly making her way through the streets of Tel-Aviv, to her own small accommodations. Terri remembers walking down a wide and busy street with glittering lights and music—Allenby St., she would eventually learn. She hoped her aunt would stop and take them to her home, but that was not to happen. After ten minutes of walking, the aunt turned to the left, moving into a narrower and more subdued street, and then turned again into a narrow dirt alley, and then into her small dwelling, one large room with two beds and a pile of mattresses for the large family. In the short walk Terri had moved, as she understood in her later recollections, from the center of Tel-Aviv to one of its peripheries.

No doubt the southern neighborhoods were seen as peripheral to the rapidly expanding modern town-cum-city. This was stated clearly and in detail in reports sent to mandate officials by the mayor of Tel-Aviv, and later conveyed by the popular biographers of Tel-Aviv, such as Dunevitz (1959) and Arye Yodfat (1969).

Yodfat for example, wrote of the short, narrow streets, many of them unpaved, with no sidewalks, and of stores and small workshops, sometimes with no windows, so that the sun came in via the open door. These narrow streets, he explained, "were in the neighborhoods which had been established prior to the establishment of Tel-Aviv, and their structure was similar to that of the nearby Arab quarters."[33]

The sense of marginality was expressed most poignantly by the residents of the early neighborhoods themselves, who bitterly complained about their neglect by the municipal authorities and their exclusion from the development that encompassed the rest of the town. Residents of both the early Jewish quarters—of Neve Tzedek, Neve Shalom, and Kerem Hatemanim—and the Commercial Center built in the 1920s, complained of a similar lack of development. The roads were not paved nor was there an adequate drainage system to channel the strong winter rains causing floods, damage to property, injuries to children and elderly folk, and subsequently diseases and failing health. Similarly, the lack of an up-to-date sewage system, which could be found in the rest of Tel-Aviv, created extremely unsanitary and unhygienic conditions. A few examples will suffice. The chairman of the local committee of Neve Tzedek emphasized that the neighborhood had been established forty years earlier when there was no running water or sewage in the houses. The eventual addition of modern toilets led to the digging of sewage pits, which, for lack of space, tended to overflow, creating a stench that made people's lives miserable as well as causing repercussions from the lack of sanitary conditions.[34]

In a similar vein, one of the leaders of Kerem Hatemanim wrote to the high commissioner protesting the neglect by both adjoining municipalities, Tel-Aviv and Jaffa, thus emphasizing the ambiguous status of the quarter, on the margins of both. Elaborating on the severe state of rain drainage, I. M. Abraham Levi, one of the public figures of the Yemenite community, wrote:

> Year by year it happens that many barracks which have cost a lot of money are pulled away by the power of rains, the water overflows the houses and devastates the furniture so that many families are deprived of all conveniences of normal living. Little children, especially school boys, are not able to leave their homes in this season and sometimes the Municipality of Tel-Aviv is compelled to send out boats to keep up the traffic. . . .
>
> Tel-Aviv and Jaffa are already provided with Electricity while the Yemenite quarter, peopled by many hundreds of families, is still without light. In the dark nights the inhabitants dare not pass the streets because of fear to stumble against stones in the darkness . . .[35]

Finally, two years later, another letter from Kerem Hatemanim to the mayor of Tel-Aviv, Israel Rokach, drove the point home once again:

> The municipality has not spent even one penny on renovation or street paving in our quarter for at least seven years despite numerous promises. . . . Our money, tax money, the meager pennies of the needy and destitute have gone to upgrade the rich neighborhoods, the neighborhoods of the north, to develop public gardens, boulevards, fountains, wonderful schools and only we, close to the center of Tel-Aviv, have remained in exactly the same state now for 15 years. Filth and grime, overcrowding and racket, but no streets, no drainage, only taxes and taxes, trials, payments, and fines.[36]

Despite recurring appeals, there was in fact much variability among the neighborhoods, both in terms of physical features and of population. The early neighborhoods were a mix of well-designed buildings, newer housing, and dilapidated huts. Those who first built their houses in these early quarters were from better-off Jewish families in Jaffa, and their impact remained, while haphazard additions of all sorts crowded the narrow streets and gave the area a slum-like look. The neighborhoods to the south of the original Jaffa–Tel-Aviv borderline combined residential housing with commerce, crafts, workshops, and small industry. In some cases the same buildings contained workshops on their ground floor and crowded living accommodations on the upper floors. Further south, moving from the southern edge of Tel-Aviv into Jaffa, commerce gave way to industry. The relative disregard by the municipality of Jaffa over building regulations and industrial permits attracted much of Jewish industry to the northern strip of Jaffa. The whole area differed markedly from the urban conception of zoning, which at least initially, guided the development of Tel-Aviv. There were no clear distinctions between residential, commercial, and industrial areas; the Commercial Center, Helanov, Neve Sha'anan, and others were a crowded mix of all three functions.[37]

Living conditions showed similar variability, as documented from time to time by the municipal institutions. Once again, as a whole the southern neighborhoods were far more crowded and enjoyed fewer facilities than Tel-Aviv proper and its northern areas; at the same time these neighborhoods were not homogeneous. A survey of dwelling conditions in the various Jewish neighborhoods of Tel-Aviv and Jaffa over the 1930s indicated the overall high level of crowding. In 1934, all quarters showed an average of at least three people per room, varying from three per room in Shchunat Shapira (in Jaffa territory), three and one-half in the heart of Tel-Aviv, four per room in Neve Shalom, Neve Tzedek, and the Commercial Center, and five to six people per room, on average, in Kerem Hatemanim and the Jewish sections in Manshiya. Over the following few years the crowding improved in most quarters, though the average remained at approximately three people per room, still very high in European terms. The Yemenite quarter on the outskirts of Manshiya nevertheless retained its very crowded living conditions of six people per room (on average) even in 1937.

Perceptions of the inhabitants of the southern quarters often followed descriptions of the inhabitants of the peripheral neighborhoods. The people were described as coming from a different social and cultural world—primitive, uneducated, completely detached from the ongoing national project. The large wave of Jewish refugees from Jaffa and its border areas during the violent clashes of the Arab Rebellion, revealed to the whole city, according to Eliezer Perlson, head of the Welfare Authorities of the TAM, "a different world, which till then was known to only a few . . . the world of the eastern neighborhoods: Orientals, the world of the ghetto, of poverty, filth, and crowding. Thousands of children without proper care. . . . If they will not be taken care of, a grave curse will grow here which will be with us for many years: disease, poverty, and children of the streets."[38]

While the refugees might have seemed strange, foreign, and threatening to Perlson, a survey of the neighborhoods of Tel-Aviv some years earlier presents a far more complex, picture.[39] The composition of the population of the southern neighborhoods was diverse rather than stereotypically homogeneous, and also of a clearly lower socio-economic status than the neighborhoods in the center and north of Tel-Aviv.

A survey of four of the neighborhoods discussed above—Kerem Hatemanim, the Jewish neighborhoods of Jaffa (mainly located in Manshiya), Neve Tzedek and its surroundings, and the Commercial Center—leads to a number of conclusions. First of all, the names of households reveal that none of the four areas was populated totally by Jews of Middle Eastern–North African countries, and were therefore much more diverse than they appeared. Nevertheless, there is a clear disparity among the neighborhoods, such that the presence of Jews of the Middle East was very clear in the first two neighborhoods, coming close to seventy-five to eighty percent of the population, and much less so in the latter two.[40]

Likewise in these first two neighborhoods, the proportion of children aged thirteen and under was extremely high, around thirty-five percent of the population, while there were far fewer young children in the other southern neighborhoods and still fewer in Tel-Aviv proper. Households differed significantly in size. There was much more evidence of large families, such as parents, four to five children, and at times an elderly grandparent in the Yemenite quarter and in Manshiya, than in others. Nevertheless, there seems to have been a significant component of Orthodox Jewish families in some of the southern neighborhoods, as can be seen by households with six to seven children.[41]

Finally, and possibly most important, are the occupational characteristics of the different neighborhoods. In the Yemenite Quarter and in Manshiya we find many laborers, often unskilled (yet in some cases skilled), including teenagers aged fourteen and older working as laborers (and in the case of girls, as domestic cleaners), and a small percentage of white-collar workers such as clerks and teachers. Peddlers and the unemployed are found more frequently among the Jewish residents of Manshiya than in the Yemenite quarter (though they are more present in the Yemenite quarter in comparison to all other neighborhoods of Tel-Aviv). The Commercial Center, on the other hand, seems to have had a far more mixed occupational composition with a much greater proportion of skilled workers, merchants, and clerks. In all cases professionals were scarce, and were far more evident in the central quarters of Tel-Aviv.

To conclude, the neighborhoods to the south of Tel-Aviv and the north of Jaffa were indeed different from many of the central and northern neighborhoods. They were much more crowded, though many other neighborhoods were crowded as well. The labor force was predominantly blue collar, with many merchants, peddlers, and some unemployed. There was a much higher proportion of teenagers, both boys and girls, who were employed as laborers and domestic cleaners than could be found in the neighborhoods of Tel-Aviv proper. The living conditions were far poorer than to the north, as was the infrastructure of the different quarters. Still, as noted above, this was not a monolithic society, and the variations within each neighborhood and among the different neighborhoods, were both evident to the onlooker and well-documented in municipal surveys. Ultimately, these neighborhoods were perceived as marginal both from within and from without: residents of these neighborhoods saw themselves as excluded from the rest of the city, while residents of the city center saw them as peripheral, both socio-culturally and in terms of infrastructure.

* * *

The discussion of the area separating and binding Tel-Aviv and Jaffa, as well as the different quarters within it, focused on the interplay of frontier and marginality. The daily life of its residents, their self-perception, and their perception by others, were far removed from the normative myth of Tel-Aviv as representing urban national growth and consolidation. The study of this area, generally ignored by historians, makes a number of important contributions to our understanding of Tel-Aviv, both past and present, as well as to the understanding of the national narrative in general.

## The Heterogeneity of Tel-Aviv

Tel-Aviv has usually been portrayed as a homogeneous town-cum-city. Its own residents, but even more so both Jewish and non-Jewish visitors, emphasized its being a monolithically Jewish urban settlement. It was assumed that all its inhabitants were Jews, spoke Hebrew, and had shed the manners of the Jewish diaspora, walking proudly as lords of their own manor.[42] Tel-Aviv was compared to Oriental Jaffa on the one hand, and to the Jewish European diaspora on the other. These descriptions, while certainly powerful, were not the whole picture. As the above discussion shows, Tel-Aviv was in fact quite heterogeneous. Its Jewish inhabitants differed among themselves in their origin, class, language and culture, family structure, accommodation, and living conditions. The southern neighborhoods, while internally varied, differed in many respects from the central and even more so the northern sections of the city. Thus the city itself, as would be expected in an urban center, was far from monolithic. Such an understanding, I would argue, brings us closer to the actual experience of many of the people of Tel-Aviv during the Mandate period, and closer to an understanding of Tel-Aviv as an urban entity.

### THE SOUTH AND THE NORTH

The dividing line between north and south is accepted today as a central principle in the physical, social, and cultural layout of Tel-Aviv. People, especially youngsters, are identified, and/or identify themselves as "northern" (*tsfoni*) or "southern" (*dromi*). In many respects the two are seen as polar opposites. This cultural image of contemporary Tel-Aviv is not my concern here. I do want to emphasize that the roots of this deep divide lie in the early days of Tel-Aviv, in the confrontation of Ahuzat Bayit and its adjoining new neighborhoods with the early Jewish neighborhoods which preceded them. This divide, as demonstrated in this essay, was further consolidated through the pre-state, Mandate period.

## BOUNDARY CROSSING

Crossing over from Tel-Aviv to Jaffa and vice versa, as discussed above, also has greater significance in relation to Israel's nation-building project as a whole. Both national entities and national movements were in a process of formation. This entailed the construction of boundaries and their consolidation. Boundary crossing, in turn, was potentially and in practice a threat to these evolving boundaries. As noted above, this threat also took on a gendered valence, as when women crossed boundaries they challenged the existing stereotype of being symbolic "boundary guardians."

The ongoing debates over the dividing line between Tel-Aviv and Jaffa, and the continued presence of both individual Jews living in Man-shiya and in Jewish quarters within Jaffa's municipal territory, serve as intriguing evidence of the difficulty of demarcating a clear-cut divide between Jews and Arabs, each committed to its own national project. It is a synecdoche of the larger problem of establishing boundaries in the country as whole, via a peaceful process agreed upon by Jewish and Arab national movements. As the Woodhead Commission (1938), appointed to propose ways for the implementation of the Partition solution adopted by the Royal Commission of 1937, stated:

> In the past, endeavors have been made to secure a better boundary be-tween the two municipalities, but it has not been possible to reach agree-ment. The problem has now become the wider one of devising a suitable boundary, not only between the two municipalities, but also between the proposed Jewish State in which Tel-Aviv will be situated and the Arab State of which Jaffa will be a port.[43]

As is well known, such an agreement was never reached.

## NOTES

The epigraph is from Nathan Dunevitz, *Tel-Aviv: The Sands That Became a City* (Je-rusalem, 1959), 109 [Hebrew].

1. Maoz Azaryahu, *Tel-Aviv—The Real City: Historical Mythography* (Sde-Boker, 2004); Dafna Hirsch, "'We Came Here to Bring the West': The Hygienic Discourse in the Land of Israel During the British Mandate," *Zmanim* 78 (2002): 107–120 [both in Hebrew].

2. For example see John Gibbons, *The Road to Nazareth* (London, 1936); Albert Londres, *The Wandering Jew Has Arrived* (Tel-Aviv, 2008), 146–160 [Hebrew].

3. On the establishment of Ahuzat Bayit (1909) as a Western, planned garden suburb and the myths surrounding it, see Yaacov Shavit and Gideon Biger, *The History of Tel-Aviv*, vol. 1 (Tel-Aviv, 2001) [Hebrew]; Azaryahu, *Tel-Aviv—The Real City;* Barbara Mann, *A Place in History: Modernism, Tel-Aviv, and the Creation of Jewish Urban Space* (Stanford, 2006).

4. Shavit and Biger, *The History of Tel-Aviv.*

5. Of these were Chelanov A and Chelanov B, the Commercial Center, and Neve Sha'anan, and toward the end of the 1920s Florentine and Shchunat Macabbi.

6. Tel-Aviv Historical Archive (TAHA), 4-2209b, Woodhead Commission Palestine Partition Commission Report (WCPPCP), ch. v. "The Boundary of Jaffa, Including the Boundary between the Towns of Jaffa and Tel-Aviv," October 1938.

7. *Supplement 1 to the Palestine Gazette Extraordinary,* 414, 12 January; "Municipal Corporation Ordinance," 1 (1934), 81–83.

8. Established by the German Templars who settled in Palestine in the second half of the nineteenth century.

9. Ibid.

10. TAHA, 4-2209a, Rokach to High Commissioner, 7 January 1945. It expressed the position the TAM held from at least the late 1920s.

11. TAHA, 4-2209b, WCPPCP.

12. Ibid.

13. For details of the social services and the financial strain on the TAM, see ibid.; Rokach to District Sub-Commissioner, 31 January 1944, and Rokach to High Commissioner, 7 January 1945. The documents present the TAM's detailed costs per person for education, school meals, hospitalization, and public welfare, and specify the small contribution by the recipients of the services and the similarly small contribution of the Jaffa municipality.

14. TAHA, 4-3642a, 20 August 1933.

15. TAHA, 4-2488, stall holder in the Carmel Market to Finance Committee, 16 June 1927, which also specified that the stall holders selling vegetables and fruits were in more direct competition and expressed their opposition to the presence of the Arab vendors.

16. Rafael Eltzer, "The Urban Border between Tel-Aviv and Jaffa during the Mandate Years" (seminar paper, Tel-Aviv University, 1991), 73 [Hebrew].

17. Ora Terri, *With a Yemenite Step, Memories and Stories* (Tel-Aviv, n.d.), 22 [Hebrew].

18. Deborah Bernstein, "Contested Contact: Proximity and Social Control in Pre-1948 Jaffa and Tel-Aviv," in *Mixed Towns, Trapped Communities,* ed. Daniel Monterescu and Dan Rabinowitz (Ashgate, 2007), 232. TAHA, 8-887, report by Investigator of the Rabbinate in response to complaints by neighbors, 30 May 1942. On Hinawi, see Tamar Berger, *Dionysus at Dizengoff Center* (Tel-Aviv, 1998), 13–44 [Hebrew].

19. Deborah Bernstein, *Women on the Margins* (Jerusalem, 2008), 184–192 [Hebrew].

20. Ibid.

21. Haim Gouri's autobiographical novel describes his mother and her neighbor housewives buying from such a peddler, with whom they seem to be familiar from frequent contact; Haim Gouri, *The Crazy Book* (Tel-Aviv, 1972), 89–90 [Hebrew].

22. Bernstein, "Contested Contact," 224.

23. *Iton Meyuhad,* 7 February 1934, the Hebrew tabloid paper of the period.

24. Ibid. According to Eliezer Perlson, head of the Welfare Authorities of the TAM, some of the girls with whom he spoke referred to themselves as prostitutes.

25. Ledislaw Ferno (or Farago, the print is not clear), 1936. Quoted in *News of TAM,* 8 (8), 183 [Hebrew].

26. TAHA, 4-3734, Yaacov Apel to Chief Rabbinate; Chief Rabbinate to Mayor, 11 May 1933.

27. Gouri, *The Crazy Book,* 98. Um-Kultum and Abdul Wahab are famous Egyptian vocalists of the mid-twentieth century.

28. Ibid., 99–100.

29. TAHA, 4-2343, Kohlani to TAM, 30 October 1946.

30. See, for example, a letter written by the residents of the small Givat Moshe near Shchunat Shapira immediately after the outbreak of the Arab Rebellion in April 1936: "As we live in this neighborhood with Arab-owned orange groves all around us, and as the recent outburst has endangered our lives and the lives of our families . . . we ask your honor to gravely consider our demands: to immediately provide our neighborhood with electric lighting and demand of the government the most urgent annexation of our neighborhood to Tel-Aviv," TAHA, 4-2207d, Residents of Givat Moshe to Mayor of Tel-Aviv, 28 April 1936.

31. TAHA, 4-2208c, Jacob Volpert and others to TAM, 12 January 1941.

32. TAHA, 4-2208b, Committee of Neve Shalom to Jewish Agency, 16 August 1939.

33. Arye Yodfat, *The Development of Tel-Aviv During the Sixty Years of Its Existence* (Tel-Aviv, 1969), 39 [Hebrew].

34. TAHA, 4-2207c, Vilner to Dizengoff, 3 February 1931.

35. TAHA, 4-2208a, I. M. Abraham Levi to Wauchope, 24 August 1936 (originally in English). See also 4-2207b, Committee of the Quarter Neve Shalom to Jaffa District Commissioner, 29 April 1929; 4-2207c; for Commercial Center, Committee to Dizengoff, 10 May 1934.

36. TAHA, 4-2208b, Committee of Kerem Hatemanim and its Surroundings to Rokach, 10 July 1938.

37. Many sources provide descriptions of the various quarters. It will suffice for our purpose to suggest two sources: Alter Druyanov, *Sefer Tel-Aviv* (Tel-Aviv, 1936), and Shavit and Biger, *The History of Tel-Aviv.*

38. Ibid., 284.

39. The survey of 1928 conducted by the TAM (TAHA, 8-86) is the latest to give detailed information on people's age, family status, and occupation. The surname could, in most cases, indicate whether the family came from Europe or from Middle Eastern countries, though the survey did not record the country of birth.

40. The family names in Manshiya and Kerem Hatemanim in many cases seem to be Yemenite, such as Dahri, Domrani, Dorani, Danhi, and Habri, with first names identified with the Yemenite community such as Rahamim, Sa'ida, Mazal, Badra, and Hamama.

41. Thus, for example, the Zelitzki family with six children to a mother aged forty-five, or the Zilberstein family with five children to a mother aged thirty-three.

42. There are a number of such descriptions by visitors; for example, the inhabitants of Tel-Aviv made a deep impression on the French journalist Albert Londres in *The Wandering Jew Has Arrived*, 146–160.

43. WCPPCP, October 1938, ch. v. Item 73.

# EIGHT

# Jaffa and Tel-Aviv before 1948:
# The Underground Story

### *Nahum Karlinsky*

Polarized cities are not simply mirrors of larger nationalistic
ethnic conflicts, but instead can be catalysts through
which conflict is exacerbated or ameliorated.
—*Scott A. Bollens,* On Narrow Ground: Urban Policy and Ethnic
Conflict in Jerusalem and Belfast *(Albany, NY, 2000), 326.*

## Models of Urban Relations in Pre-1948 Palestine

The study of the urban history of pre-1948 Palestine has gained welcome
momentum in recent years. Traditionally, mainstream Zionist and Palestinian historiographies concentrated mainly on the rural sector, which
for both national communities symbolized a mythical attachment to the
land. Along with the heroic figures of the Arab *fellah* and the Zionist
"new Jew," this particular area of focus reveals central elements of the
core identities of the two rival communities. The deconstruction of the
old Zionist and Israeli meta-narrative on the one hand, and the effort to
show the diversity as well as the modernization processes of pre-*nakba*
Arab society on the other, have given new impetus to the study of the
country's pre-1948 urban histories.[1]

From the point of view of ethnic/national relations, one can discern
two main urban categories that existed in pre-1948 Palestine: ethnically
homogeneous cities or towns and heterogeneous ones. Significantly,
most Jews and Arabs who resided in cities or towns before 1948 dwelled
not in homogeneous urban environments but rather in heterogeneous
ones, mainly Jerusalem, Jaffa–Tel-Aviv, and Haifa, the leading urban
centers of the period (1909–1948). These urban centers, along with Ti-

berias and Safed, were the main venues of regular contact between Jews and Arabs at the time. Moreover, while most of the Arab population lived in rural areas during the period under discussion (around seventy percent in 1931 and sixty-four percent by 1946), the majority of Jews (around seventy-five percent at the end of the Mandate) lived in urban centers. Primary among them was Tel-Aviv, which by 1948 accommodated about one-third of the Yishuv (the pre-1948 Zionist community).[2]

Scholars of heterogeneous urban environments identify five main types of relational settings that exist among different ethnic/national groups that occupy one urban environment: (1) *Mixed towns and cities,* where "a certain ethnic mix in housing zones, ongoing neighborly relations, socio-economic proximity and various modes of joint sociality" exist. Culturally, the mixed town or city serves as a "shared locus of memory, affiliation and self identification."[3] (2) *Divided cities,* in which, while the ethnic/national groups live in almost total cultural, economic, and geographic separation, "Conflicts in these divided cities are addressed within accepted political frameworks. Questions of what constitutes the public good are debated, but largely within a sanctioned framework."[4] (3) *Polarized towns and cities,* in contrast, "host alternative and directly opposing cultures that are contestable. Such conflicts are 'ethnonational' wherein one group seeks autonomy or separation. In such a circumstance, a strong minority of the urban population may reject urban and societal institutions, making consensus regarding political power sharing impossible."[5] (4) *Partitioned cities* are an outcome of a polarized urban environment in which the goal of eliminating ethnic differences is pursued (Jerusalem from 1948 to 1967 and present-day Nicosia).[6] (5) *Colonial cities* are those that from their inception were built for the incoming colonial population. In the modern era, Europeans were the dominant colonial population.[7]

During the second half of the nineteenth century, the combination of European influence and prevailing traditions gave rise to two modalities of urban administration and planning in the port cities of the Ottoman Empire and Morocco. One model was "inclusive"; it created a power-sharing mechanism in which not only Muslims but also local Jews and Christians and even foreigners were included. Michael Reimer's detailed study on Alexandria and other Egyptian cities, and that of Susan Gilson Miller on Tangier, are examples. The other model, a "separation" model, aspired to establish a European urban space that would be as distinct as possible from the local *medina*. Janet Abu-Lughod's study of Rabat is probably the best example of the separation-colonial model, which was associated with other Mediterranean cities as well.[8] Up to 1948, Haifa may be seen as an important example of the "inclusive/ mixed cities" model, which however, as the conflict between Palestinian Arabs and Zionist Jews grew, came very close to be a "divided" model of urban coexistence. While scholars such as May Seikaly lament the lost hegemony of the Arabs in British Mandate Haifa, the picture that emerges from the works of Joseph Vashitz, Deborah Bernstein, Tamir Goren, and others is one of economic cooperation, social and cultural interaction, and actual and symbolic power sharing, alongside the better known national and cultural differences which were accompanied from time to time with armed clashes as well.[9]

Jerusalem, on the other hand, a "mixed city" under the Ottomans, became a "divided" city during the early British Mandate and a "polarized" city by the mid-1930s. Thus, whereas economic, social, and even political cooperation took place between the city's two main national groups at the beginning of the Mandate, by the early 1930s the continuous national tension between Zionist Jews and Palestinian Arabs in Jerusalem and in the country at large became dominant in the relations between the two national sectors in the Holy City until 1948. Concurrently, discussion of the possibility of partitioning the city became prevalent as well.[10]

Curiously, relative to the growing number of studies of Jerusalem and especially of Haifa during that period, studies of Jaffa are surprisingly few. In cautiously trying to reconstruct a historical reality based on the limited research available, one may conclude that Ottoman Jaffa was a "mixed city." Jews represented a significant and growing minority of the city's population; most of them resided among the Arab population and had daily contact with it. The construction of Jewish neighborhoods north of Jaffa from 1887 onward seems to have been closely related to the contemporaneous phenomenon of the creation of new traditional and religious Jewish neighborhoods outside the Old City of Jerusalem. Initially, these neighborhoods did not represent the creation of an independent Jewish national space separate from Jaffa. That change came only upon the establishment of Ahuzat Bayit, the embryonic Tel-Aviv, in 1909.

Under the Mandate, Jews continued to reside in Jaffa proper and in new neighborhoods established within the town limits. They sent representatives to the municipal council, their voice was heard in city hall, they continued to do business in town, and many of them maintained friendly relations with their Arab neighbors. As the national conflict in the country escalated, however, many of the Jews who resided in Jaffa chose to move to the neighboring first Hebrew city. However, thousands of Jews continued to reside in the neighborhoods of Jaffa that bordered Tel-Aviv (especially Florentin and Shapira), and in 1947 about thirty percent of Jaffa's population was Jewish. During the Mandate, as Tel-Aviv became the economic, social, and cultural center of the Yishuv, the dependence of the Jewish neighborhoods of Jaffa on municipal services supplied to them by Tel-Aviv—chiefly in education and healthcare— grew concomitantly. Thus a process of intra-urban ethnic and national division began to take place in Jaffa as in Jerusalem.[11]

## The Vision of Separation

Tel-Aviv was established as a neighborhood of Jaffa; in its first ten years and up to the British conquest of Palestine (1918), it was an integral part of the Arab city. Soon after the establishment of a civil administration in Palestine (1920), however, the British granted Tel-Aviv autonomous municipal jurisdiction as a "township" (1921). In 1934, it received the status of a "municipal corporation," which signified its complete legal separation from Jaffa. Thus Tel-Aviv began its development as part of the "mixed city" of Jaffa and grew into its own urban center. While the Ottomans had adamantly insisted that Tel-Aviv be subordinated to Jaffa, the British, in apparent accord with the terms of the Mandate, quickly helped Tel-Aviv to become legally and administratively separate from Jaffa. Defined borders and two legally recognized municipalities offi-cially divided Tel-Aviv from Jaffa. Thus my contention is that whereas during the British Mandate period Haifa fit the *divided* model and Jeru-salem the *polarized* one, the combined urban area of Jaffa and Tel-Aviv should be regarded as a *partitioned* urban zone.[12]

From its inception, Tel-Aviv envisioned its character as something distinct from various "others": distinct from the Jewish neighborhoods outside Jaffa, which represented an extension of the "Old Yishuv" (pre-Zionist Jewish community), i.e., as yet another ethnic neighborhood among the mosaic of ethnic communities of the Ottoman Empire; distinct from Jaffa itself, which epitomized the "backward" "Orient" and its Arabs; and distinct from the Jewish Diaspora. The founders of Tel-Aviv also envisioned their new neighborhood as a specifically Zionist entity. It was no coincidence that soon after its establishment Tel-Aviv adopted Hebrew, the old-new language that symbolized the revival of Jewish nationalism, as its official language. No other Jewish neighborhood that preceded Tel-Aviv had done so.

During the short five years from the establishment of Ahuzat Bayit in 1909 to the outbreak of World War I, Tel-Aviv began to evolve into an important center for the Zionist communities in the Yishuv. Leading cultural, business, and political personalities in the young Zionist movement resided in the new "Hebrew" quarter. Significantly, the first Zionist educational institution, the Herzliya Gymnasium, originally founded in Jaffa, was reestablished on the highest spot in the new neighborhood. Economically, the Zionist colonies became Tel-Aviv's hinterland, creating dynamic interrelations between the urban core and its agricultural ethnic/national periphery.[13]

Like the French quarter of Rabat and the British Empire cities, Tel-Aviv was envisioned by its founders as a Western-modernist settlement situated in a non-European environment. The story of the founders' numerous meetings and detailed preparations for the implementation of their vision of constructing a European-style quarter in Jaffa is well documented. Every aspect in the planning of the future Zionist quarter was completely based on Western (mainly European) models and concepts.

An important part of this vision, repeatedly stressed by the founders and by future leaders and inhabitants of the city throughout this period, was the city as a site of cleanliness and hygiene, especially in its air and water. Central in the implementation of this vision was the disposal of sewage from the new neighborhood and the uninterrupted supply of clean water to its residents.[14]

## The Sanitary Movement Comes to Tel-Aviv

The modern roots of the vision of the city as a site of cleanliness and sanitation date to the Sanitary Movement, which originated in England in the mid-nineteenth century. Public officials and reformers such as

Edwin Chadwick who examined with great alarm the repeated outbreaks of diseases, especially cholera epidemics, among the fast-growing
population of London and other industrial cities were convinced, after
submitting these epidemics to thorough "scientific" examination, that
their fundamental origin was "atmospheric impurities" caused by con-
taminated water and other sources of "bad smell" such as "decomposing
animal and vegetable substances, damp and filth, and close and over-
crowded dwellings."[15] "Bad air," or what it is now termed the Miasmatic
Theory of Disease, was still the dominant scientific explanation for the
causes of diseases at the time Tel-Aviv was established. Moreover, even
after the Germ Theory of Disease replaced the Miasmatic Theory as the
leading paradigm for the cause of most illnesses, bad air and bad smell
remained popular signs of a possible threat to health.[16]

Like Chadwick, Tel-Aviv's founders stressed the importance of keeping its air fresh and clean by utilizing various hygienic practices, chiefly
supplying running water that would allow regular and frequent washing
and bathing, keeping water sources and sewage safely apart, cleaning
the streets, and removing any "smelly" nuisance from city limits.[17] Thus
pure air, running water, clean streets, and personal and public hygiene
became symbolic of Tel-Aviv's modernity. The vile aroma that wafted
from the open gutters of the Old City of Jaffa, as well as from the cesspools of the newly established Jewish neighborhoods of Neve Shalom
and even Neve Tzedek (the cultural center of the New Yishuv before
1909), was a recurrent theme in the Zionist literature of the period and a
representative statement about the difference between the "old" and the
promise of the new and the modern.[18]

This vision was expressed time and again throughout the period.
In 1933, for example, Tel-Aviv Deputy Mayor Israel Rokach wrote in
the municipality's organ, *Yedi'ot 'Iriyat Tel-Aviv*, on the question of the
township's sewage and its removal:

> Tel-Aviv will not be a healthy and well-maintained city until a sewerage
> system is installed there. It is well known that the installation of a sewer-
> age system improves health conditions and reduces death rates. And the
> first condition for the resort and spa city that Tel-Aviv aspires to become is
> well-maintained sewerage [. . .]. With a structured financial plan, it would
> be possible to set Tel-Aviv on a solid sanitary basis, so that no [other city]
> will be like her in the entire Middle East.[19]

A running-water system was installed in Ahuzat Bayit as the first houses in the new Zionist quarter were being built—the first to be constructed in either Jaffa or the Jewish neighborhoods that preceded Tel-Aviv.[20] However, as in other European and American cities at the time, the growing availability of running water posed a constant challenge to Tel-Aviv's leaders: how to find a cheap and efficient way of removing the increasing quantities of wastewater that were now pouring onto the new neighborhood's soil.

The founders of Tel-Aviv aspired to adapt the models used in urban European centers to their non-European environment. Thus references to the German term *Kanalisation,* which denotes a water-carriage sewerage system that removes sewage from urban areas, appear frequently in the writings of the Sanitary Committee of the TAM (Tel-Aviv Municipality) which supervised sanitary conditions there until the outbreak of World War I. One report stated that:

> The best system for the removal of all sorts of feces is the *kanalizatziya* [a Hebraization of *Kanalisation*] system, which is operating in several cities in Europe. Through the *kanalizatziya* sewers, all feces along with wastewater are removed to a designated place where the material is processed as manure for the enhancement of the fields.[21]

Two obstacles prevented the implementation of the *Kanalisation* system before the British conquest in 1918. First, the town lacked the minimum amount of running water that was needed to make the system operative. More important, however, was the cost of installing a full-fledged sewerage system that would run under the city's streets and treat the sewage before dumping it as far as possible from city limits. Naturally, the leaders of the young Jewish neighborhood of Jaffa were well aware of this: "[*Kanalisation*] is indeed the best system but unfortunately it is beyond our means. Therefore, we will have to make do with an inferior system simply because it is cheaper."[22]

The system adopted was the one used in the other Jewish neighborhoods of Jaffa and certain quarters of Jaffa itself: the cesspool system, in which the soil functions as the sink. In that regard, Tel-Aviv did not differ from the European and American cities of that period, which used the cesspool system before they were forced to install water-carriage systems due to the growing amounts of wastewater that they had to discharge.

During the mid-nineteenth and mid-twentieth centuries cesspools were in vogue in Europe and the United States where the main health concern was the possibility for sewage to reach nearby water sources. Keeping cesspools a safe distance from water sources and preventing cesspool overflow were the main tasks in that regard.[23] The TAM established a Sanitary Committee, headed by the municipal physician that regularly supervised sanitary conditions in the rapidly developing Jewish quarter. The committee inspected homes, wrote reports, and enforced regulations pertaining to cleanliness. An essential part of its work was to check closely the sanitary conditions of the cesspools in every house in town. In addition, Tel-Aviv's bylaws stipulated clearly how these cesspools should be constructed, maintained, and cleaned.[24] Fluids were absorbed in Tel-Aviv's sandy soil; "solid residue" was cleaned out periodically by Arab workers from Jaffa or by Yemenite-Jewish laborers from nearby Jewish neighborhoods, who dumped it in either nearby fields or in the Mediterranean.[25]

Upon its inception, Tel-Aviv was considered by its inhabitants and in the contemporary literature as a "neighborhood" or a "colony"; by 1914, only five years after its establishment, it was already referred to as a "city."[26] The change in terminology reflected the demographic growth of Tel-Aviv, its population quintupling from about 300 to 1,500 during this short period.[27]

Tel-Aviv grew not only due to the increase of its own population and developed area but also because new Jewish neighborhoods in the vicinity, established after 1909, merged with and became integral parts of it. They included Nahalat Binyamin, Hevra Hadasha (concentrated along Allenby St. today), and the neighborhood built by the Anglo Palestine Company for its employees.[28] By the autumn of 1913, the Sanitary Committee sent a special report to the Tel-Aviv Executive Committee (the official name of the neighborhood's active leadership at the time) recommending that the Executive Committee "begin the process of drawing up a technical scheme for a municipal *kanalizatziya* system."[29]

### The Early Mandate Years

The establishment of civilian British rule in Palestine in the summer of 1920 brought about crucial political, economic, and organizational changes as well as an accelerated process of modernization.

It was the "township" status that the Mandate government granted Tel-Aviv in 1921 that triggered the annexation of many Jewish neighborhoods around the town, which until then had not merged with their stronger sister. However, most of the older neighborhoods, such as Neve Tzedek, Neve Shalom, and Kerem Hatemanim, were populated largely by Sephardic Jews who opposed the merger and resisted it for two years, even bringing their struggle to the courts. The controversy seems to have centered on issues of property rights, taxes, and preservation of the old neighborhoods' religious way of life. Tel-Aviv, in turn, wanted to bring Jaffa's old Jewish neighborhoods under its European, nationalist, and secular clout. Indeed, the mayor of Tel-Aviv, Meir Dizengoff, described the controversy as a collision between a "European" way of life and an "Oriental passive" one.

In the end, however, most of the old neighborhoods merged with Tel-Aviv, albeit only after Tel-Aviv made some concessions on property rights and religious observance in the public domain. Even so, some neighborhoods elected not to merge with the Hebrew city and to remain part of the "mixed" city of Jaffa. These neighborhoods, along with new ones established after the 1923 merger (most prominently, Florentine and Shapira), became an in-between site that defied the notion of total separation.

This impulse toward separation expressed itself most clearly in the township's policy to set its new border with Jaffa so that "not even one house of a non-Jew or one dunam [tenth of a hectare] of an orchard [owned in this area almost exclusively by Arabs—N.K.] will come under Tel-Aviv's rule."[30] Little is known to date about the history of Jaffa during this period, including the attitude of its leadership toward the "loss" of its Jewish neighborhoods to Tel-Aviv. Subsequent accounts by Dizengoff's successor, Israel Rokach, suggest that in the early 1920s Jaffa's leadership did not mount much opposition to the merger of its old Jewish neighborhoods with Tel-Aviv. Concurrently, as we saw, Jaffa welcomed the decision of some of the neighborhoods to remain under its municipal authority and accepted new Jewish neighborhoods that were later established inside its borders. In later years, as the national conflict between Jews and Arabs intensified, Jaffa resisted attempts to allow the Jewish neighborhoods to switch to the municipal authority of Tel-Aviv.[31]

The merger of the old Jewish neighborhoods with Tel-Aviv more than doubled the Hebrew township's population, adding 5,200 new residents to the 3,600 residents of pre-1921 Tel-Aviv.[32] The newly established border with Jaffa prevented Tel-Aviv from growing further to the south; thus it continued to grow and develop along its natural growth trajectory—northward. By the end of the Mandate, Tel-Aviv's population rose to approximately 248,000 souls, who inhabited an area that sprawled to the Yarkon River in the north and Wadi Musrara to the east.

## Water Supply and the Cesspool System

Naturally, the efficient and uninterrupted supply of running water to the growing population of Tel-Aviv was a main concern for the city's leadership. In 1948, Tel-Aviv still received its water as it had in its Ahuzat Bayit days, from wells. Until the mid-1930s, the availability of abundant and high-quality groundwater only a short distance from the surface allowed the city to meet all water demands for both domestic use and for the city's growing industries. From then on, however, population increase forced the leadership to step up the exploitation of groundwater reserves by sinking more and more wells to meet the growing demand. As a result, seawater penetrated the geological stratum of the shallow groundwater, making some wells useless. This situation and the realization that Tel-Aviv would need to develop additional water sources in the future prompted the municipal and Mandate authorities to invite an expert to formulate a comprehensive plan to supply Tel-Aviv's growing demand for water.

The expert British water engineer Howard Humphreys selected by the Colonial Office in 1936, chose the only available source of water other than existing groundwater: the Yarkon / Ras el 'Ein (Rosh ha 'ayin) springs. By the end of the nineteenth century, a detailed plan for the exploitation of the Yarkon River as a main water source for Jaffa had already been put on the table.[33] Neither that scheme nor Humphrey's was ever implemented; it was too costly relative to the alternative of keeping the existing system in operation and developing it.

The problem of saline wells during the 1930s provoked an attempt by the Tel-Aviv authorities to probe for deeper geological strata that might hold additional water. The search proved enormously successful; new and deeper wells were dug, supplying the city with more and better water than the existing wells were able to provide. By the end of the Mandate, twenty-seven wells were in operation in Tel-Aviv, closely supervised by a central control system. In addition, Tel-Aviv's water was tested regularly for bacteria, in cooperation with and under the supervision of the Mandate health authorities. Chlorination was gradually introduced; by 1948, many of Tel-Aviv's wells were chlorinated. Furthermore, safe distances between cesspools and wells were strictly observed.[34]

In contrast to Tel-Aviv, source material about Jaffa's water system is scanty. The very limited sources available make it seem that by the end of 1935 the residents of the city's Ajami quarter were getting their water from "private" suppliers. The British authorities took advantage of Humphreys's presence in the area and asked him to devise a water-supply scheme for Jaffa as well. Significantly, he planned separate water-supply systems for the two municipalities, probably in anticipation of the policy of partition that the British would adopt in the wake of the 1936 Arab "disturbances." Unfortunately, the scant source material on this issue limits our understanding of the development of Jaffa's water-supply system from 1937 to 1948.[35] However, it is clear that the TAM's preventive measures against water contamination were increasingly needed, as the development of its sewerage system lagged behind progress in water supply.

In the meantime, Tel-Aviv's cesspool system deteriorated steadily, ironically due to the fast and efficient growth of the city's running-water system itself. The phenomenon mirrored the development of sewerage systems in most Western cities during the nineteenth and mid-twentieth centuries. There, as in Tel-Aviv, the high cost of installing water-carriage sewerage relative to that of installing and maintaining running water and cesspool systems constantly placed the existing sewage-disposal system, i.e., the cesspools, under excessive strain. Concurrently, per-capita water consumption in Tel-Aviv was not only greater than other cities in Palestine, such as Jerusalem, but also many Western cities at the time. In 1934, for example, per-capita water consumption in Jerusalem—which at the time still relied heavily on communal and private rainwater cisterns—was forty-five liters a day. Corresponding figures for other cities were 164 liters in Alexandria, Egypt, 114 liters in London, 216 liters in Paris, and 230 liters per capita per day in Tel-Aviv. By 1947, the differences grew, per-capita water consumption holding steady at 114 liters per day in London and climbing to 350 in Tel-Aviv. Thus, apart from Tel-Aviv's tremendous demographic growth during this period, its water consumption in total and in per-capita terms grew even faster.[36]

Contemporary 1920s sources reveal that the TAM leaders were well aware that their town was not as clean as they had envisioned. In fact, it was squalid, as Anat Helman vividly describes.[37] The possibility of an epidemic outbreak due to drinking-water contamination was a real one that served as a constant warning for the municipal authorities to find ways to improve the city's sewerage system. The notion of Tel-Aviv as a modern city that was expected to keep its air clean and its sanitary conditions at the highest standards, like the most "progressive" cities in Europe, coupled with the real threat of an epidemic, were the two fundamental driving forces for both the city's leadership and its residents to improve Tel-Aviv's sewerage system.

## Sewerage Systems in Tel-Aviv and Jaffa up to the Peel Commission Report (1937)

In the wake of the 1923 merger with Jaffa's old Jewish neighborhoods, the growing legal and administrative separation from Jaffa, and the prospect of rapid population growth due to the Mandate regime's favorable policy toward Jewish immigration, the leaders of Tel-Aviv decided to solicit technical schemes for the construction of a sewerage system for their township. Two such reports, a 1923 scheme from the Berlin-based firm Grove and a 1924 one devised by the township engineer, Uriel Avigdor, were reviewed. The sanitary engineer of the governmental Health Department rejected the Grove scheme as inapplicable to local conditions and too expensive. Concurrently, the Mandate authorities invited the drainage engineer of Alexandria to examine Avigdor's scheme. While the visiting expert had some reservations about the plan, he regarded it as a blueprint for the construction of a water-carriage sewerage system in Tel-Aviv. As for Jaffa, the Avigdor scheme seems to have instigated some initial cooperation between the neighboring towns in the construction of Tel-Aviv's main sewer, which was planned to cross Jaffa territory. Tellingly, the Alexandria drainage engineer saw this as an important outcome of the plan. The inter-municipal cooperation that it proposed, he said, "would tend to encourage the establishment of amicable relations of great value to the two communities." However, the Avigdor scheme was not implemented, most probably due to the costs involved.[38] Hence, new houses and even entire new neighborhoods were constructed with cesspools, which remained the chief method for removing sewage from the fast-growing Hebrew city.

By the end of the 1920s, the explosive growth of Tel-Aviv's population—which was expected to continue to increase at a similar rate—threatened to overburden the cesspool system. Conditions were especially acute in the southern (and older) parts of the city, where the soil could hardly absorb more wastewater. This time, the municipal leaders turned to the British authorities and solicited their assistance in constructing a sewerage system for Tel-Aviv. Two closely interconnected factors prompted this appeal. First, since the cost of installing a complete sewerage system was beyond Tel-Aviv's means, the TAM needed a substantial loan to finance the project. However, in keeping with their overall policy not to burden taxpayers with expenses incurred in the colonies, the British supervised the finances of Palestine, including municipal finances, very closely.[39] Thus Tel-Aviv had to turn to the Mandate authorities if it wanted the loan to be approved. Second, the British numbered the construction of sewerage systems among the large "public works" that had to be approved according to their unique highly bureaucratic colonial procedures. This part of the story follows.

## Crown Agents and the Consulting Engineers

Tel-Aviv's financial constraints brought a third player, the British government and its colonial administration, into the story of the bi-national sewerage systems of these neighboring cities in Palestine. The British colonial system defined major infrastructure projects (railroads, ports, water systems, roads, etc.) as "public works." Large public works in crown colonies—and in administrative terms Palestine was ruled like a crown colony—were not authorized or administered by the local colonial authorities but, rather, by a special institution in London called the "Crown Agents for the Colonies."

Little was known about this peculiar institution until David Sunderland's recent comprehensive two-volume study about it. As their title suggests, the Crown Agents were the commercial and financial representatives of the crown colonies in the Empire's metropolis. However, as Sunderland clearly shows, in addition to their benevolent mission to help develop the colonies, the Crown Agents had the important objective of assuring that the colonies would not burden the British budget and that, instead, the mother country would profit from the colonies as much as possible.

By authorizing the Crown Agents to take charge of large and lucrative public works, the Empire supervised and kept a check on the tendency of local colonial administrations to prioritize the well-being of local populations. The agents contracted out the planning and performance of these public works to a closely knit circle of "consulting engineers." Both the Crown Agents and the consultants whom they hired received a hefty fee for each contract, which raised their interest in long-term, expensive projects.[40]

In 1926, John and David Watson, of Consulting Engineers, were hired to devise detailed proposals for the construction of sewerage systems for Jerusalem, Haifa, Jaffa, and Tel-Aviv. Their reports on Jerusalem and Haifa are beyond the scope of this paper. They attest, however, to a broader policy that the British government envisioned regarding the development of infrastructure in Palestine. In 1927, a year after they visited Palestine, the Watsons submitted their proposal, which found it better to construct a single unified sewerage system for both Tel-Aviv and Jaffa and hence suggested that a main sewer for both municipalities should run through Salame Road, topographically the lowest-level road between the two municipalities. Thus the Salame Road sewer was supposed to drain most of Tel-Aviv, which in those days did not extend north of Bograshov St. As for Jaffa, the consulting engineers suggested that both the commercial area (around Bustros St. up to the Old City) and the northern neighborhood of Manshiya should be reticulated to the Salame Road sewer. The southern Ajami quarter was not supposed to be drained by the common sewer; its residents would continue to rely on the existing cesspool system. A common outlet at the end of Salameh Road in the swamp area (the Bassa) would discharge the bi-national sewage into the Mediterranean. Provisions were also made for the future development of Tel-Aviv in the direction of the Yarkon River, but the main concern in the report was the more densely populated area.[41]

## Cooperation amid Separation

From its inception, Tel-Aviv attempted to distance itself from Jaffa both physically and symbolically. Now, due to their common topography, rate of modernization, and an imposing authority, it found itself having to merge its liquid waste with that of its "other."

The full story of the relationship between Tel-Aviv and Jaffa has yet to be told. The inter-municipal cooperation in the decade between 1926 and the Arab Revolt of 1936 is but one facet of this story that requires further research. A major obstacle to telling it is the fact that the Jaffa archives disappeared during the 1948 war. The limited sources at our disposal tell a complicated tale of both tension and cooperation between the two cities on issues related to the sewerage system. This impression is compatible with the findings of other studies about relations between Jaffa and Tel-Aviv, notably the work of Mark LeVine.[42]

By 1925, when township engineer Avigdor finished drawing up his Tel-Aviv sewerage scheme, Jaffa and Tel-Aviv had already established official contacts in regard to the implementation of the plan. Some reports hint at even broader cooperation between the municipalities, involving discussions related to town planning in both urban centers.[43] In the wake of the submission of the 1927 Watson plan, the cooperation between the two municipalities on their common sewerage system was formalized. A Joint Drainage Committee was formed, headed by the two municipalities' town engineers. The committee maintained a continuous dialogue between Jaffa and Tel-Aviv on planning, budget allocations, and performance and supervision of the plan. Both municipalities financed the construction of the Salame sewer and the Bassa outlet, dividing the financial burden commensurate with each party's share in using the system. Thus Tel-Aviv financed about 60 percent of the joint venture. The Salame sewer was constructed in the early 1930s; neighborhoods in southern Tel-Aviv and the commercial district of Jaffa were connected to it by 1936. In addition to the Salame sewer and the Bassa outfall, another sewer and its corresponding outlet were jointly devised and financed; this second sewer drained both the Tel-Aviv neighborhood of Neve Shalom and parts of the Jaffa quarter of Manshiya. Its corresponding outlet was constructed near the Feingold houses, which were situated inside Jaffa's city limits. Other neighborhoods in both towns were connected to other sewers that passed under the Arab neighborhood of Manshiya and Tel-Aviv's Ezra St.[44]

The picture of cooperation is presented in a neutral, technical, and laconic manner. This makes it difficult to determine the parties' emotional or ideological attitudes toward each other and toward the notion of cooperation. It is especially difficult to reconstruct the attitude of the Jaffa municipality toward cooperation with Tel-Aviv.[45] Despite these limitations, one can posit that even as the two municipalities cooperated continuously, some tension and mistrust colored their relations. Each municipality, for example, occasionally questioned its counterpart's willingness to contribute its fair share to the financing of the joint projects. Moreover, in accordance with common perceptions and attitudes of the period, the TAM's engineer, Ya'akov Shiffman (Ben-Sira), who succeeded Avigdor in this post in 1929, belittled the Jaffa municipality's administrative ability to carry out complex technological projects. In 1938, Tel-Aviv Mayor Rokach portrayed the Jewish neighborhoods within Jaffa city limits as captives in an urban space of "cultural, economic, and social degeneration."[46] The municipal engineer of Jaffa, John Salah, on the other hand, apparently noticing the rapid growth of Tel-Aviv, tried to secure for his city an urban space that could accommodate much larger numbers of residents than even the most optimistic growth outlooks had projected for Jaffa.[47]

Despite the tension, the two municipalities continued to cooperate where sewerage was concerned. By 1936, however, the Watson scheme remained on paper, and the joint sewerage projects addressed only a small part of both municipalities' developed area. Hence, most neighborhoods in both Jaffa and Tel-Aviv still used cesspools. According to a detailed report by Jaffa's municipal engineer in 1935, residents of the Ajami quarter used cesspools for the disposal of their sewage and those in the Old City drained their wastewater straight into the sea via masonry conduits.[48]

A major obstacle to the implementation of the Watson plan was that the British procedure for approving a loan to help finance the scheme had not run its full course. In addition, regarding Tel-Aviv, it seems that except for the southern area, for which some partial solutions were found, sanitary conditions in the other developed areas were not alarming. Consequently, both the municipality and the British authorities felt under less pressure to replace the cesspools with a full-fledged water-carriage sewerage system.

Early in 1936, the Watsons were summoned again to submit another set of plans for the construction of sewerage infrastructure in Tel-Aviv and Jaffa. About a month before the eruption of the 1936 Arab uprising Shiffman met with one of the Watson brothers. In a detailed report to Mayor Dizengoff, in which Shiffman expressed his displeasure about the consulting engineers' involvement in what he considered his autonomous professional realm, he also reported the municipality's official stance on the cooperation with Jaffa:

> I explained to Mr. Watson that based on the records of the existing cooperation, and since this cooperation is undesirable for us in both its political and its technical-financial aspect, the Municipality wishes to reserve the right to decide on the extent of said cooperation and, in any event, it should be minimized as much as possible.[49]

There is no indication that an official Tel-Aviv policy to "minimize" cooperation with Jaffa "as much as possible" played any decisive role in the Watsons' second sewerage scheme, which was submitted in early 1937, just a few months before the Palestine Royal Commission under Lord Peel (the "Peel Commission") published its report.[50] In their new 1937 schemes for both Jaffa and Tel-Aviv, however, the Watsons did elaborate on the difficulties that their survey party encountered when it tried to collect firsthand data "in the field" due to the 1936 "disturbances."

The new sewerage plans were diametrically opposed to earlier ones. If the previous report firmly supported a common sewerage system for Tel-Aviv and Jaffa, the 1937 proposal advised that two completely separate systems be constructed. The main reason for this change, according to the Watsons, was that they needed to take into consideration plans concerning "the possible construction of a harbour" in the Bassa area. It is clear, however, that they went to great lengths to ensure that the sewage of one municipality would not meet that of the other. Although there is no direct reference to the Palestine partition plan of 1937, it seems more than likely that the second Watson proposal deliberately reflected the colonial policy of the day.

According to the new scheme, the Bassa outlet, which the Watsons' 1927 scheme envisaged would drain the sewage of both cities and, consequently, induce the two municipalities to cooperate, would now be eliminated. In its stead, it was proposed that Jaffa and Tel-Aviv construct two separate sewage collectors that would carry each city's wastewater to opposing outfalls—one in the north, near Jabotinsky St., for Tel-Aviv, and the other in the south, in the Ajami quarter, for Jaffa. In addition, pumping stations along the Tel-Aviv main and at the Ajami outfall were to pump each city's sewage in the proper opposing directions. Thus the declared purpose of the Ajami pumping station was to transfer the sewage of the Salame quarter and Jaffa's commercial areas not to its natural outlet at the Bassa (based on the area's topography), but rather over the hill of Jaffa's Old City to the Ajami sea outfall.

The same reasoning guided the scheme for Tel-Aviv. Instead of letting the wastewater flow along the topographical contours of the city—i.e., the southern neighborhoods' sewage would flow under Salame Road to the Bassa and the central and northern neighborhoods to the northern part of Tel-Aviv, near the Yarkon River—the second Watson scheme sought to force all Jewish sewage to be diverted north. However, total separation was not possible because the Manshiya quarter in Jaffa and the southern neighborhoods of Tel-Aviv (especially Neve Shalom) were physically interconnected. Thus the consulting engineers wrote:

> In some places it has been found advisable to locate short lengths of the Tel-Aviv sewers within the Jaffa municipality and vice-versa, and where this has been done we have endeavoured so to arrange matters that an equivalent area of Tel-Aviv will be served by Jaffa sewers. Thus, each of the two towns would deal with some 95 percent of its own sewage, the remaining 5 percent only being disposed of by the other municipality.[51]

Naturally, the 1937 Watson plan was enormously expensive. The estimate for Tel-Aviv was approximately two-thirds of a million British pounds—more than twice the entire annual municipal budget at the time—and for Jaffa was £284,000, as against a 1936/37 municipal budget of only £56,000.[52] The commissions and fees that the Crown Agents and their consultants expected to earn were directly related to the size of the budgets of the public projects that they handled.

The TAM objected to various aspects of the second Watson plan. It argued that the plan was not compatible with the local geological reality, that it would make more sense to manufacture the infrastructure components locally, and that the project should be supervised jointly by the local municipal engineer and by a representative of the Consulting Engineers, the Watson brothers, officially called "resident engineer." These suggestions, which would have reduced the cost of the system and the money earned and spent in England, were rejected by the Crown Agents. At the same time, the TAM—which had a strained relationship with the British treasury—could not obtain a loan that would allow the second Watson plan to be implemented at all.[53]

## 1937–1948

At this point, the local British officials stationed in Palestine, who had developed a sense of local patriotism toward Tel-Aviv, came to the rescue. The local British authorities helped the TAM to obtain authorization from London to establish a fund that financed small temporary sewerage systems for those parts of the city that needed them most acutely. The principal was collected from homeowners, who were for the most part happy about the prospect of getting the cesspools out of their backyards once and for all. The main neighborhoods in which new sewerage was installed included the commercial center and parts of Neve Sha'anan, Kerem Hatemanim, and the area from Trumpeldor St. south to Ezra St. Neve Shalom's wastewater continued to be drained through the sewer that passed under the Arab quarter of Manshiya and discharged at the Feingold sea outlet. Other areas, especially between the railroad tracks in the south to Balfour St. in the center of Tel-Aviv, were connected to an outlet situated near the Hassan Bek mosque.

The commercial center and Neve Sha'anan directed their wastewater to the Salame Road sewer, which channeled it straight to the Bassa outfall. Although the second Watson scheme had recommended the elimination of this outfall, no such thing was done and Jaffa, and Tel-Aviv continued to maintain both the sewer and the outlet jointly. Thus, despite the recommendation of the second Watson plan, and very much in opposition to it, Jaffa and Tel-Aviv continued to cooperate with regard to the sewerage system that served their border neighborhoods.[54]

On the eve of World War II, only twenty-eight percent (2,200) of the approximately 8,000 houses in Tel-Aviv were reticulated to a water-carriage sewerage system. Of them, sixty-six percent (1,450) were served

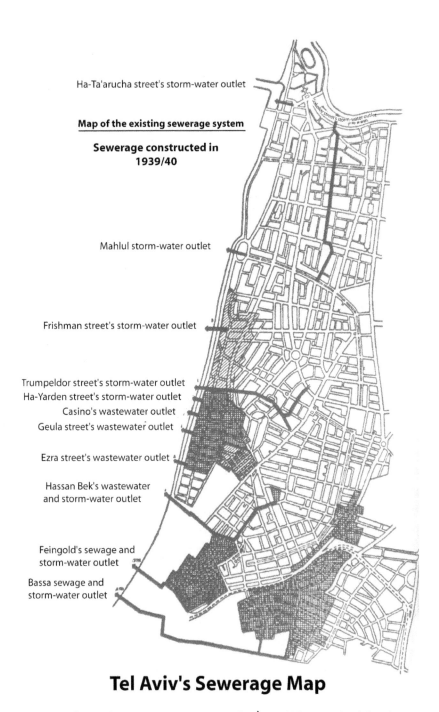

Ha-Ta'arucha street's storm-water outlet

**Map of the existing sewerage system**

**Sewerage constructed in 1939/40**

Mahlul storm-water outlet

Frishman street's storm-water outlet

Trumpeldor street's storm-water outlet
Ha-Yarden street's storm-water outlet
Casino's wastewater outlet
Geula street's wastewater outlet

Ezra street's wastewater outlet

Hassan Bek's wastewater and storm-water outlet

Feingold's sewage and storm-water outlet

Bassa sewage and storm-water outlet

# Tel Aviv's Sewerage Map

Map 8.1. Tel-Aviv drainage system in 1940. *Yediot 'Iriyat Tel-Aviv* 11 (7–9) (1940), 123.

by the sewers that passed under Jaffa's municipal area and were connected to the Bassa, the Feingold, and the Hassan Bek outfalls; only 750
houses (thirty-four percent) were connected to sewers that passed under
TAM areas.[55] The topographical structure of the two cities, the towns'
successful experience in cooperation, the moderate approach of many
leaders in Jaffa toward the Arab revolt, and pure financial considerations
obviated the total separation of the two urban entities. Thus, as World
War II loomed, six outlets discharged sewage from the Tel-Aviv–Jaffa
shore into the Mediterranean Sea, three of them in Jaffa (see Map 8.1).

During World War II, the tendency toward greater cooperation between Jews and Arabs in Palestine was also evident in relations between
Tel-Aviv and Jaffa.[56] Due to lack of funding, however, the sewerage system underwent no further development until 1945.

The breakthrough came after the war. Since the city had already
reached the Yarkon River in the north and Wadi Musrara in the east,
the TAM's main concern was the central and northern areas. This time,
in contrast to the pre-war period, the British authorities empowered
the TAM to plan and construct the sewer system on its own, albeit demanding that the new system not contradict the general outlines for
the northern part of the city in the 1937 Watson scheme. A main sewer
for the central part of the city was constructed along the shore, next to
Herbert Samuel Quay. Along with other smaller sewers and outlets, this
new collector helped to reticulate the houses in central Tel-Aviv. The
northern part was designed to be served by a different collector that ran
along Arba' ha'aratzot and Jabotinsky Streets. As in the second Watson
scheme, a sea outfall for the northern part was constructed at the end of
Jabotinsky St., giving the city's northern areas a natural drainage vent.

By the end of 1947, about 5,300 of the 8,000 houses in Tel-Aviv
(sixty-six percent) had been equipped with the proper technology that
would allow them to be reticulated to the expanded sewerage system.

Map 8.2. (*facing*) Tel-Aviv's sewerage in 1948. The darker part indicates areas in
which sewerage was constructed up to 1936; the diagonal lines signify neighborhoods
that were reticulated to the system from 1936 to 1945; and the light zigzag pattern
indicates area that were reticulated from 1945 to 1948. *Yediot 'Iriyat Tel-Aviv* 17
(10–12) (1947, 1948), 3.

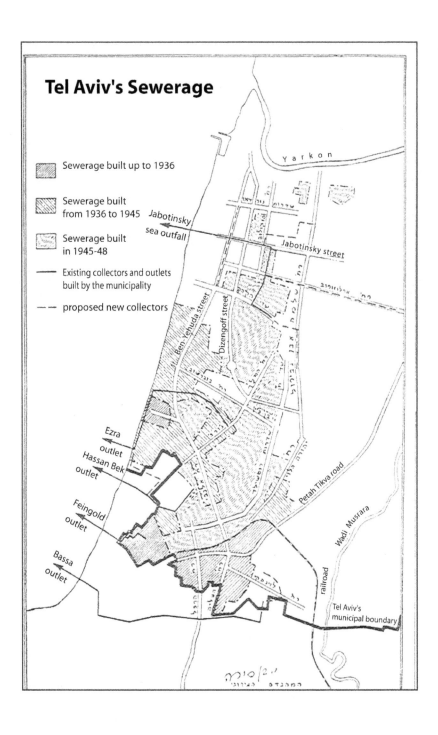

# Tel Aviv's Sewerage

Sewerage built up to 1936

Sewerage built from 1936 to 1945

Sewerage built in 1945-48

——— Existing collectors and outlets built by the municipality

– – – proposed new collectors

Yarkon

Jabotinsky sea outfall

Jabotinsky street

Ben-Yehuda street

Dizengoff street

Ezra outlet

Hassan Bek outlet

Feingold outlet

Bassa outlet

Petah Tikva road

Wadi Musrara

railroad

Tel Aviv's municipal boundary

For financial and legal reasons, however, only 3,150 houses (thirty-nine percent) actually reticulated. Of these, it may be assumed that at least the 1,750 houses that in 1939 were connected to sewers and outfalls that crossed Jaffa were still connected to them nine years later. Thus, even as 1948 dawned, about fifty-six percent of Tel-Aviv's houses that were reticulated to the city's sewerage were still attached to the city's important "other." Consequently, the cooperation with Jaffa, which persevered during World War II, continued in the years immediately following— albeit in an atmosphere that became very hostile as the events of 1948 approached.[57]

* * *

From its inception, Tel-Aviv was envisioned and built as a separate European-inspired Zionist entity. The notions of clean air, running water, and excellent sanitary conditions were an integral part of this modernist vision. However, in contrast to these aspirations and like most Western urban centers in the nineteenth and twentieth centuries, both Jaffa and Tel-Aviv used cesspools to dispose of their sewage as long as this was economically and hygienically possible. Though both Jaffa and Tel-Aviv shared the same urban-sanitation problems, in keeping with Zionist policy of the time, Tel-Aviv tried to maintain a separationist stance toward Jaffa. A third party—the British administration in London and the Mandate government—also played an important role in determining the level of cooperation between the two opposing national municipalities. More research on the pre-1948 urban Yishuv is needed before one can draw a sound conclusion as to whether the separation model offers a better solution for the achievement of peaceful coexistence in a contested urban matrix than the mixed-city model. The case discussed in this essay, however, reveals that the reality of the ethnic/national matrix in the Yishuv implies the impossibility of complete ethnic/national separation. No matter how hard it tried, Tel-Aviv could not insulate itself from its "other." Jaffa—like the Yiddish language and the Jewish Diaspora—was integral in the construction of Tel-Aviv's identity. Without it, the first Hebrew city would not have become itself.

I would like to thank the staff at the Tel-Aviv Historical Archives, its director, Ms. Ziona Raz, and its archivist, Ms. Neli Vrzrbcky, for their professional and gracious assistance in my research for this essay. I would also like to thank the graphic designer Shereen Mazzawi Srouji for her professional adaptation of the maps in this publication.

## NOTES

1. S. Ilan Troen, *Imagining Zion: Dreams, Designs, and Realities in a Century of Jewish Settlement* (New Haven, 2003), 1–159; Mark LeVine, *Overthrowing Geography: Jaffa, Tel-Aviv, and the Struggle for Palestine, 1880–1948* (Berkeley, 2005); Barbara E. Mann, *A Place in History: Modernism, Tel-Aviv, and the Creation of Jewish Urban Space* (Stanford, CA, 2006); Deborah Bernstein, *Women on the Margins: Gender and Nationalism in Mandate Tel-Aviv* (Jerusalem, 2008) [Hebrew]; May Seikaly, *Haifa: Transformation of a Palestinian Arab Society 1918–1939* (London, New York, 1995); Deborah Bernstein, *Constructing Boundaries: Jewish and Arab Workers in Mandatory Palestine* (Albany, NY, 2000); Tamir Goren, *Cooperation in the Shadow of Confrontation: Arabs and Jews in Local Government in Haifa During the British Mandate* (Ramat Gan, 2008) [Hebrew]; Yehoshua Ben-Aryeh, ed., *Jerusalem and the British Mandate* (Jerusalem, 2003) [Hebrew].

2. Jacob Metzer, *The Divided Economy of Mandatory Palestine* (Cambridge, UK, New York, 1998), 9; Yaacov Shavit and Gideon Biger, *The History of Tel-Aviv: vol. 2, From a City-State to a City in a State (1936–1952)* (Tel-Aviv, 2007), 22 [Hebrew].

3. Daniel Monterescu and Dan Rabinowitz, eds., *Mixed Towns, Trapped Communities: Historical Narratives, Spatial Dynamics, Gender Relations and Cultural Encounters in Palestinian-Israeli Towns* (Aldershot, 2007). Introduction, 3.

4. Scott A. Bollens, *On Narrow Ground: Urban Policy and Ethnic Conflict in Jerusalem and Belfast* (Albany, NY, 2000), 9.

5. Ibid., 10.

6. Ibid., 12.

7. Janet L. Abu-Lughod, *Rabat: Urban Apartheid in Morocco* (Princeton, NJ, 1980); Leonard Thompson, *A History of South Africa* (New Haven and London, 2000), 31–69; Thomas R. Metcalf, "Imperial Towns and Cities," in *The Cambridge Illustrated History of the British Empire,* ed. P. J. Marshall (Cambridge, 1996), 224–253.

8. Michael Reimer, "Urban Government and Administration in Egypt, 1805–1914," *Die Welt Des Islams: International Journal for the Study of Modern Islam* 39.3 (1999): 289–318; Susan Gilson Miller, "Watering the Garden of Tangier: Colonial Contestations in a Moroccan City," in *The Walled Arab City in Literature, Architecture and History: The Living Medina in the Maghrib,* ed. Susan Slymomovics (London, Portland, OR, 2001), 25–50; Abu-Lughod, *Rabat.*

9. Joseph Vashitz, "Social Transformations in Haifa's Arab Society: Merchants and other Entrepreneurs," in *Economy and Society in Mandatory Palestine, 1918–1948,* ed. Avi Bareli and Nahum Karlinsky (Sde-Boker, 2003), 393–438 [Hebrew]; Mahmud Yazbak, "Immigrants, Elites and Popular Organizations among the Arab Society of Haifa from the British Conquest to 1939," ibid., 367–392; Seikaly, *Haifa;* Bernstein, *Constructing Boundaries;* Goren, *Cooperation in the Shadow of Confrontation.*

10. Daniel Rubinstein, "The Jerusalem Municipality under the Ottomans, British and Jordanians," in *Jerusalem: Problems and Prospects,* ed. Joel Kraemer (New

York, 1980), 72–99; Paul A. Alsberg, "The Conflict over the Mayoralty of Jerusalem during the Mandate Period," in *Jerusalem in the Modern Period,* ed. Eli Shaltiel (Jerusalem, 1981), 302–354 [Hebrew]; Yossi Katz, *A State in the Making: Zionist Plans for the Partition of Palestine and the Establishment of a Jewish State* (Jerusalem, 2000) [Hebrew].

11.  Yosef Eliyahu Chelouche, *The Story of My Life, 1870–1930* (Tel-Aviv, 2005 [1931]) [Hebrew]; Alter Druyanov, *Sefer Tel-Aviv* (Tel-Aviv, 1936), 31–253 [Hebrew]; Shavit and Biger, *The History of Tel-Aviv: vol. 1, The Birth of a Town (1909–1936)* (Tel-Aviv, 2001), 16–192 [Hebrew]; ibid., vol. 2, 41–43, 139–146; LeVine, *Overthrowing Geography;* Bernstein, *Women on the Margins.*

12.  Arguably, the Mandate administration merely responded to a developmental path already set in motion by the founders and subsequent leadership of Tel-Aviv. Viewed from the perspective of the Mandate's municipal conduct toward Jerusalem and Haifa, it seems that the British tried to adapt their municipal policy to local conditions. Hence their support of Tel-Aviv's separation from Jaffa was not exceptional. See Nahum Karlinsky, "Partitioned, Polarized, and Divided Cities in pre-1948 Palestine." Paper given at the Annual Conference of the Association for Israel Studies, University of Toronto, 10–12 May 2010.

13.  On ventures by the "Old Yishuv" (the pre-Zionist Jewish community) into what retroactively was regarded as "new," see Israel Bartal, "Old Yishuv and New Yishuv: Image and Reality," *The Jerusalem Cathedra* 1 (1981): 215–231; Druyanov, *Sefer Tel-Aviv,* 31–253; Hanna Ram, *The Jewish Community in Jaffa: From Sephardic Community to Zionist Center* (Jerusalem, 1996) [Hebrew]; Amiram Gonen, "The Emergence of a Geographical Heartland in Israel," in *Economy and Society,* ed. Bareli and Karlinsky, 439–488.

14.  Tel-Aviv 1910 bylaws in Druyanov, *Sefer Tel-Aviv,* 158–163; Anat Helman, "Cleanliness and Squalor in Inter-war Tel-Aviv," *Urban History* 31.1 (2004): 72–99.

15.  (Edwin Chadwick), *Report to Her Majesty's Principal Secretary of State for the Home Department, from the Poor Law Commissioners on an Inquiry into the Sanitary Condition of the Labouring Population of Great Britain* (London, 1842), 369. On the Sanitary Movement, see Selwyn K. Troen, "The Diffusion of an Urban Social Science: France, England, and the United States in the Nineteenth Century," *Comparative Social Research* 9 (1986): 247–266; Joel A. Tarr, *The Search for the Ultimate Sink: Urban Pollution in Historical Perspective* (Akron, OH, 1996), 1–35; Martin V. Melosi, *The Sanitary City: Urban Infrastructure in America from Colonial Times to the Present* (Baltimore and London, 2000), 1–72.

16.  Hillel Yoffe, *A Generation of Ascenders: Memoirs, Letters and a Diary* (Jerusalem, 1971), 80–81 [Hebrew]; Melosi, *The Sanitary City,* 110–116; *Yedi'ot 'Iriyat Tel-Aviv* 4.6 (1933), 179 [Hebrew] ("Air saturated with vapors from the soil is a source of diseases").

17.  Tel-Aviv 1910 bylaws in Druyanov, *Sefer Tel-Aviv,* 158–163; Tel-Aviv Municipal Historical Archives (TAHA) 1-58.

18.  Ze'ev Smilansky, "The Jewish Community in Jaffa," *Ha'omer,* 1–2 (1907) *Ha'omer* supplement, 1–108 [Hebrew].

19.  Israel Rokach, "In Anticipation of the Construction of Sewerage and Storm-Water Drainage Systems in Tel-Aviv," *YITA* 4.4 (1933), 98.

20. In 1879, a running-water system was installed in the German Templer colony of Sarona. Nahum Karlinsky, *California Dreaming: Ideology, Society, and Technology in the Citrus Industry of Palestine, 1890–1939* (Albany, 2005), 96.

21. C. 1912–1914, TAHA, 1–58.

22. Ibid.

23. Tarr, *The Search for the Ultimate Sink*, 1–35.

24. TAHA, 1–58; Druyanov, *Sefer Tel-Aviv*, 158–163.

25. TAHA, 1–58.

26. TAHA, 1–40; 1–56a: November 1911 contract with the Municipality, in German; *Hapoel Hatzair*, 26 December 1913, in Shavit and Biger, *The History of Tel-Aviv*, vol. 1, 85.

27. Shavit and Biger, *History of Tel-Aviv*, vol. 1, 93.

28. Ibid., 83–86.

29. TAHA, 1–58.

30. Shavit and Biger, *History of Tel-Aviv*, vol. 1, 161; the discussion here is based on ibid., 159–164; Ilan Shchori, *The Dream Turned to a Metropolitan: The Birth and Growth of Tel-Aviv, the First Hebrew City in the World* (Tel-Aviv, 1990), 145–170, 193–214 [Hebrew]; and H. Katznelson, "History of Tel-Aviv's Constitution," *YITA* 12 (1942) [supplement to the 1942 *Year Book*], 13–18.

31. Israel Rokach, "Tel-Aviv's Current Issues," *YITA* 9.3–4 (1938), 55–56; Rokach, "Upon the Annexation of the Frontier Neighborhoods to Tel-Aviv," *YITA* 18 (1949), 104, 116.

32. Shavit and Biger, *History of Tel-Aviv*, vol. 1, 91–93.

33. Shmuel Avitsur, "The First Project for the Intensive Exploitation of the Yarkon Waters (The Frangija-Navon Scheme of 1893)," *Ha'aretz Museum Bulletin*, 6 (1964), 80–88.

34. TAM, Howard Humphreys & Sons, *Report upon the Water Supply of Tel-Aviv, August 1936*; David Smilansky, "A History of Tel-Aviv's Water Supply System," *YITA* 18.10–12 (1949), 131–132; see also Smilansky's detailed report, October 1948, on the history and development of Tel-Aviv's water-supply system, TAHA, 4-4490.

35. Municipal Corporation of Jaffa, John S. Salah, Municipal Engineer, *Jaffa Drainage Scheme*, 18.6.1935; J. D. and D. M. Watson, *Jaffa Sewerage*, April 1937, UKNA (UK National Archives), CO 733/341/3 248609; 2 March 1937, TAHA, 4-2529; Humphreys, *Report upon the Water-Supply of Tel-Aviv*.

36. On similar development in European and American cities, see Tarr, *The Search for the Ultimate Sink*, 1–35; Melosi, *The Sanitary City*, 1–135. On Tel-Aviv and other cities' water consumption, see David Smilansky, "What is the Water-Supply Situation in Tel-Aviv?" *Yedi'ot 'Iriyat Tel-Aviv*, 5.8–5.9 (1934), 348–349; TAHA, 4-1031.

37. Helman, "Cleanliness and Squalor in Inter-war Tel-Aviv."

38. On the Grove and Avigdor schemes, see Israel State Archives (ISA), RG 10, File 22/3, Box 1546; TAHA, 3-104a; Ya'akov Shiffman, "The Sewerage and Storm-Water Drainage in Tel-Aviv," *YITA* 5.1 (1933), 7–9, 18. Drainage of storm runoff was part of the overall drainage issue in Tel-Aviv. However, storm water did not pose the same critical health threat as the sewage; it was a problem mainly during the few heavy rainy days that occurred in the winter. In addition, storm runoff was much cheaper to deal with than sewage.

39. Nachum T. Gross, "The Economic Policy of the Mandatory Government in Palestine," *Research in Economic History,* 9 (1984), 143–185.

40. David Sunderland, *Managing the British Empire: The Crown Agents, 1833–1914* (Suffolk, UK, 2004); Sunderland, *Managing British Colonial and Post-Colonial Development: The Crown Agents, 1914–74* (Woodbridge, UK, 2007).

41. Watson, *Tel-Aviv Sewerage;* Watson, *Jaffa Sewerage;* see also related correspondence in TAHA, 4-2529; Rokach, "In Anticipation."

42. LeVine, *Overthrowing Geography.*

43. TAHA, 3-104a.

44. "Joint Drainage Works for Jaffa and Tel-Aviv: Report," (1933), TAHA, 14-274. See also files: 3-104a; 4-2512; 4-2514; 4-2532; Ya'akov Shiffman to D. M. Watson, 31 March 1936, UKNA, CO 733/341/3 248609; Rokach, "In Anticipation."

45. Jaffa's municipal archives disappeared in 1948. The author made a preliminary attempt to examine the leading Arabic-language newspaper in Jaffa, *Falastin,* in regard to the city's sewerage system. However, more research in that direction is needed.

46. Rokach, "Tel-Aviv's Current Issues," 35.

47. Salah, *Jaffa Drainage Scheme;* Watson, *Jaffa Sewerage;* Shiffman, "The First Meeting with Mr. Watson, the Sewerage Expert," 18 March 1936, TAHA, 4-2513 [Hebrew].

48. Salah, *Jaffa Drainage Scheme.*

49. Shiffman, "First Meeting with Mr. Watson."

50. The discussion that follows is based on Watson, *Tel-Aviv Sewerage,* March 1937, and Watson, *Jaffa Sewerage,* April 1937.

51. Watson, *Tel-Aviv Sewerage,* 5.

52. "Palestine's Municipal Finances," *Tel-Aviv Year Book,* 1937–1938.

53. Shiffman, "Report of the City Engineer's visit to London in Connection with the Main Drainage Scheme for Tel-Aviv," October 1939, TAHA, 4-2530; Rokach, 19 December 1937, "Tel-Aviv Main Drainage Scheme," TAHA, 4-2529. An internal Colonial Office memorandum of 10 August 1939 stated that before getting the loan "[the] municipality shall put its financial house in order." UKNA, CO 733/341/3 248609; see also other relevant correspondence and memoranda, ibid.

54. "Records of the visit to the temporary sea outlets by Messrs. S. T. Colburn, Sanitary Engineer of the Health Dept. and Y. Shiffman, City Engineer, Tel-Aviv, 11 February 1938," ISA, RG 10, 22/3/8; Se'adia Shoshani, "What Has Been Done about Sewerage in Tel-Aviv in Five Years?" *YITA* 12.5–12.6 (1942), 55–56; "Minutes of Sewerage Committee Meeting, 21 December 1938," TAHA, 4-2513.

55. Shiffman, "Explanatory Notes on the Proposed Tel-Aviv Town Center Interim Sewerage Scheme," February 1940, TAHA, 4-2530.

56. "Cooperation between the Large Municipalities [Jerusalem, Haifa, Jaffa, Tel-Aviv—N.K.] in Regard to Food Supply," *YITA* 12.1–12.2 (1941), 3; Zachary Lockman, *Comrades and Enemies: Arab and Jewish Workers in Palestine, 1906–1948* (Berkeley, 1996).

57. On the ongoing cooperation with Jaffa, see TAHA, 4-2533; ISA, RG 10, File G/182/34, Box 208; Shiffman, *The Sewerage Scheme of the City, 7 December 1945,* 4-1119/2575; see also 4-2515 (1945–1946); Se'adia Shoshani, "The Role of the Sewerage System in the Building of Tel-Aviv," *YITA* 17.10–17.12 (1947–1948), 3–4.

# NINE

# Austerity Tel-Aviv: Everyday Life, Supervision, Compliance, and Respectability

*Orit Rozin*

On 27 March 1950, the police stormed into Tiferet (glory), a popular Tel-Aviv café on fashionable Rothschild Boulevard, and inspected the patrons. Male and female officers surrounded the café at 10:30 AM on a Monday, ordering patrons to enable the search. They were supervised by the police department's economic division, called the "economic police." Women were inspected in a closed room; men remained in the general common area, and were asked to remove their jackets and shoes. The retrieved loot included twelve "black market" diamonds, fifty pence Sterling, a box of firestones for lighters, a few custom-made Chinese bracelets, and a gold bracelet (all not declared through customs), as well as two notebooks bearing "suspicious lists." All in all, 124 people and their belongings were inspected. Five suspects were held for further investigation.[1]

This event was well documented in the press. *Ha'aretz* described the reaction of the patrons. They seemed bewildered, claimed the reporter, who then stated, "It is simply frightening to enter a café for a cup of coffee, one is afraid of a sudden raid."[2] Yet the facts suggest that there were many Tel-Avivians who were not intimidated. They continued to trade on the black market, while efforts to eradicate black market activities intensified over the next few months.

In the early statehood years, Tel-Aviv was a locus of contradictions and tensions. One such tension, typical of most if not all urban locales, especially during times of economic turmoil, was between law and order and illegal economic activity. In contrast to realms of social marginality, such as prostitution and juvenile delinquency, so vividly depicted in the works of Deborah Bernstein and Tammy Razi,[3] in the case of economic activity a line between respectability and marginality cannot be easily etched. I argue that normalcy and delinquency were both present in the daily life of ordinary citizens throughout the severe months and years of austerity, during the late 1940s and early 1950s.

In major cities, symbols of political power are easily spotted on municipal buildings, police stations, and local courts; quite often, architecture plays a major tool in the presentation of power.[4] Tel-Aviv at that time lacked the requisite grandeur; yet the need of a newly established state to exert power, garner respect, and instill fear was present nonetheless. The storming of Café Tiferet by the police was a performance of power, aimed not only at catching certain felons but also at deterring Tel-Avivians from engaging in illegal economic activity.

This essay depicts everyday life in Tel-Aviv during the austerity period, and examines the tensions between an omnipresent sense of chaos created by shortages and the need of municipal and government agencies to enforce order and compliance. An ancient Mari prophecy aptly describes the reality of a city in distress: it is something akin to water underneath straw, with law represented by the straw, and avoidance symbolized by the water. After presenting a general history of the period I discuss concepts of control, enforcement, and avoidance and convey the special role played by Tel-Aviv with respect to the creation of law and order in nascent Israel.

## Austerity—A Brief History

The austerity policy in Tel-Aviv was introduced during the 1948 war (or reintroduced if we take into account the austerity enforced by the British during World War II).[5] Yishuv representatives initiated the program, although originally the municipal authorities were the ones burdened with its implementation. Municipal controllers enforced the regulations and local courts were established in order to judge offenders.[6] In April 1948, two national supervisors were appointed to register stock, control the import of foodstuffs and raw materials, and monitor supply and price control. In August, new legal means were implemented in order to tighten control over rationing and prices. The provisional Israeli government established new anti-profiteering courts (replacing the municipal ones), comprising a professional judge and two public representatives appointed by the minister of justice.[7]

In January 1949, following the first general elections, a permanent government was formed. Although the war was over, the austerity policy was not rescinded. In order to facilitate the absorption of a large number of immigrants, the government introduced a comprehensive policy of austerity that included rationing and price control of foods and other commodities; it aimed to intervene heavily in all aspects of economic life. Imposing an austerity policy on the population's daily consumption was intended to facilitate immigrant absorption without compromising basic standards of nutrition, housing, and health. The government did not intend to establish absolute equality between immigrants and non-immigrants; rather, it sought to determine a minimum level of equal access to food and, later on, to additional commodities, thereby averting demand-driven inflation that would deny immigrants the ability to support themselves.

In November 1951, as the economic situation deteriorated, foreign currency reserves dwindled and foreign banks and suppliers cut off credit; the government changed its immigration policy and, concurrently, its economic policy. These changes led, among other things, to steep price increases and a gradual ease in rationing. Thus implementation of the austerity policy coincided with the mass-immigration years, from 1948 to late 1951. Accordingly, most of our discussion focuses on these years. However, the rationing and price-control policy remained in effect (although modified and eased especially since 1952)[8] until they were officially abolished in 1959.[9]

The austerity policy was not an Israeli invention. It had been practiced in Mandatory Palestine during World War II (as well as in other countries, including the United States). As a result, the Mandatory legislator—whose statutes were largely adopted by Israeli law—left behind regulations that governed consumer behavior. Britain, too, had introduced such a policy during the war and continued to apply it during the postwar rehabilitation period.[10] In this study, the Israeli experience is compared to the British case.

During the 1948 war, there was a steep rise in food prices. After the war the new government soon formally declared an austerity policy in

April 1949. Although the public accorded the policy its general trust and cooperation, nevertheless, black-market activities continued throughout this period.[11]

In early 1950, consumer discipline slackened further, leading to the emergence of a massive black market.[12] Two of the most conspicuous factors that led to its growth were rapid expansion of the money supply and numerous mishaps in rationing.[13] The government reduced the rations that it had promised and subsequently found even this undertaking difficult to honor, resulting in distribution delays. Furthermore, the quality of the food distributed, including bread, declined steadily, and there was an extended shortage of baby food.[14]

In response to the eruption of black-market commerce, the government cracked down on the public and enforced its policy vigorously, applying a lengthy series of measures that were aimed initially at black-market dealers and later at black-market consumers. In July 1950, despite a shaky austerity regime and a series of resulting constraints, rationing and price controls were extended to clothing and footwear.[15]

During early statehood Tel-Aviv was the largest city and the center of commerce in Israel, an important base of industry and government administration, the center of culture and society, and had the highest standard of living in the country. However, the socioeconomic demographic of the local population spanned the gamut. During this period Tel-Aviv–Jaffa was home to both the poor and the rich, immigrants and veteran Israelis, Jews and Arabs, workers and the unemployed, entrepreneurs, industrialists, lawyers, and doctors.[16]

### Everyday Life in the City

#### SHORTAGES

During the initial months of the war, the Tel-Aviv Municipality (TAM) took charge of local food distribution and data regarding the stock of basic products such as sugar, flour, soap, oil, oatmeal, beans, lentils, and rice. Importers, bakers, shopkeepers, and industrialists were contacted on a regular basis and their cooperation was considered vital in order to feed the population.[17]

Not only did the general public suffer, so did the manufacturers; one of them, for example, begged the TAM to supply flour to his small pasta factory.[18] In order to save on basic supplies, TAM authorities forbade bakeries from baking buns, bagels, and cakes (fine white flour was a valued commodity). Bakers were ordered to wait twelve hours after baking bread before selling it, to reduce consumption.[19] However, in order to meet public demand, bakers continued to bake forbidden foods.[20]

From January 1950, the Ministry of Supply and Rationing had difficulty delivering the promised food rations in a timely fashion. Rations were occasionally cut back: supplies of vegetables dwindled, beef and egg rations were reduced, and in January coffee was not distributed at all. During the spring and summer there were occasional shortages of cooking oil, sugar, and bread, and in August and September, there was a severe shortage of soap.[21] In the fall and winter months of 1951, bread supplies dropped drastically in Tel-Aviv, leading to a sense of panic, which was reported in the press.[22] Vegetable supplies were also especially low in the Tel-Aviv area during that autumn.[23]

In order to improve the food supply, via the active support and financial aid of the government,[24] the TAM encouraged residents to grow vegetables in their private or communal backyards and to utilize empty lots scattered throughout the city as well.[25] The TAM urged the residents to exploit every square meter of earth and grow vegetables, in order to ease the shortages. Seeds, saplings, and even advice were promised by the TAM's gardening department.[26] Twice a year, during a few weeks in the spring and the autumn, seeds and saplings were distributed or sold for a pittance to Tel-Avivians. The small profit made in the sale was transferred to the city's Welfare Department.[27] Earth mixed with manure and boxes were distributed to those wishing to grow vegetables on their balconies or rooftops.[28] Schoolchildren were particularly encouraged to plant their own gardens; they also enjoyed receiving their distribution of seeds and saplings at a specific time and location.[29] The city nursery was so successful that even the president's wife, Rachel Yanait, submitted a request for a considerable number of vegetable seedlings.[30] Tel-Avivians also raised chickens in coops in their residential garden yards, sometimes resulting in foul odors and dirt; nevertheless, chickens were regulated and licensed by the TAM.[31]

Scarcity meant that every material or foodstuff had to be used or recycled. Stale flour was purchased by the TAM and used as glue for posting notices on billboards.[32] During Passover, potato flour was used instead of wheat.[33] Yet the scarcity of foods and materials did not result in the cessation of all public activities; public events such as parties were still organized, and the mayor maintained a modest food allocation for hosting guests and dignitaries.[34]

The TAM and state controllers struggled to impose the austerity law on the meat and poultry market, the commodities in greatest demand throughout the mid-1950s.[35] Another item in great demand was ice. During 1949, shortages of ice, especially during the sweltering summer days in Tel-Aviv, led to price inflation. Although the TAM struggled to secure production and fair distribution of ice, shortages resulted in riots and fistfights on occasion.[36] In January 1951 the Tel-Aviv municipal bulletin announced the opening of a large refrigerator factory named Amkor.[37]

By the summer of 1951, ice shortages worsened. It is interesting to note that 107,000 families in the city consumed ice, whereas 17,000 families owned electric refrigerators.[38] The issue was politicized during the 1951 general election campaign. In mid-July, two weeks prior to the elections, shortages worsened, leading the TAM to ration ice.[39] Consumers nevertheless stood in lines for hours and hours anticipating ice.[40] To ease shortages, the Chief Rabbinate issued a special permit allowing for the production of ice during Shabbat.[41] Mapai's bulletin *Hador* excoriated Mayor Rokach—who headed the increasingly popular rival party, the General Zionists—for choosing *not* to control the ice distribution problem in the city, so that the ice crisis would portray the Mapai government as incompetent, thereby boosting the General Zionist free market economy campaign, and making it more appealing to potential voters.[42] Thanks to a political campaign that successfully captured and exploited the public's dissatisfaction with the austerity plan, Rokach's party swelled from seven seats in the 1949 elections to twenty seats in the 1951 elections.[43] Even weeks after the election, long lines still appeared in Tel-Aviv.[44] At that point, Rokach, together with the government, finally appointed a joint municipal-governmental committee to find a solution to the problem of ice production and distribution.[45]

Shortages in products such as meat and poultry continued for four more years. In 1952, the government announced a new economic program, causing a steep increase in prices that also applied to controlled food. That summer, shops teemed with an array of produce; however, prohibitive prices meant that only some people were able to enjoy the relative plenty.[46]

## TIME AND SPACE

On any given weekday, housewives lined up for hours on end in front of shops.[47] As such, they lost a central perk to which a housewife was entitled: autonomy and the ability to regulate her own time for different chores.[48] A report in *Ha'aretz* describes:

> It is sufficient to pass in the hours before noon in the city streets, to see in what conditions the part of the housewife's work done outside the home—shopping—is carried out. The scene is unfamiliar to most of the population: men are confined at these times to their offices and workshops. Only a few of them have had the chance to witness this scene of many tens of women standing in line in front of a shop, as if they were waiting for charity or some allowance.[49]

Working women complained that they could not go shopping in the mornings and demanded that arrangements be made for them to have their groceries picked up in the afternoon.[50] Greengrocers told a reporter that

> If a woman wishes to obtain any kind of vegetable, she needs to spend half a day at least in shops and markets, to jeopardize her health by quarrelling over her place in line, and over half a cucumber, and only then will she be able to bring home some amount of fresh vegetables, and even this [effort] would not yield a sufficient quantity.[51]

TAM officials did their best to regulate sales. In order to prevent long lines before Rosh Hashanah in 1949, they instructed the municipal slaughterhouse to work on Mondays and Tuesdays rather than delay until Wednesdays or Thursdays, in order to avoid Friday's long lines. They also offered to ask residents with electric refrigerators to shop earlier in the week (Wednesday or Thursday), because they could preserve their food better than other residents who owned iceboxes. TAM controllers also volunteered to police the huge lines of consumers waiting to purchase meat and poultry before Shabbat and Jewish holidays, as violence was anticipated. Tel-Aviv did, however, enjoy fresh beef for the holidays—1,500 cows were imported from Turkey. Other cities had to settle for imported frozen meat.[52]

A passerby walking the streets of Tel-Aviv in those days would also on occasion witness crowds demonstrating. The residents of Salame—a former Palestinian village now housing immigrants—took to the streets to demand water and electricity, a telephone connection, and a proper road.[53] Women in Jaffa protested to demand that their sanitary conditions be improved. In the Carmel Market, women demonstrated against shortages. This demonstration was not peaceful; women were bitten and pushed by the police. In workshops and factories around the city, many workers went on thirty-minute strikes protesting the endless food shortages. Perhaps the most colorful was the hunger parade organized by the Communist party and Mapam, which passed through Brenner St. along Allenby St. and continuing to Ahad Ha'am St.[54] Street vendors were commonplace, some bearing a TAM license, others without, who sold their wares on the street or traveling door to door.[55] However, despite these day-to-day setbacks, to some degree life went on, while people struggled to make ends meet.

## AVOIDANCE: CRIME AND PUNISHMENT

Avoidance of food regulations was rampant. Ice vendors got tickets for not publicizing the price of ice, as stipulated by the law; milkmen were unwilling to submit merchandise for inspection, while others sold "forged" milk that did not meet commercial quality regulations. A butcher and a poultry monger refused to sell meat to their clients.[56] A grocer refused to sell margarine, oil, bread, and soap to his clients, probably because he wanted to sell them on the black market and make a greater profit.[57] Other shopkeepers refused to sell sardines, marmalade, butter, and fresh fish. Many offenders overcharged for the goods they were selling: noodles, flour, biscuits, eggplants and beetroot, cheese and peppers, or held on to unregistered merchandise. Still others moved merchandise from their stores to private homes (most likely for black market sales).[58]

TAM controllers were busy inspecting street vendors and shopkeepers. Offenders received tickets and were put on trial in local courts on charges of profiteering and speculation. Administrative punishments such as forcing shops to close were also used. An attempt was also made to shame offenders by publishing their names in the newspapers.[59] Defendants who stood on trial also caught the eye of the tax authorities.[60]

What began as municipal courts established to judge cases of profiteering and speculation during the 1948 war evolved into the state's judicial system.[61] Each board comprised three judges—one professional jurist and two laypeople (citizens). Whereas offenders were probably unpopular, it seems that it was difficult to persuade laypersons—who were chosen by political parties and organizations and approved by the minister of justice for precisely this purpose—to appear in court and perform their civic duty. Their reluctance to participate, among other problems that arose with the court arrangement, resulted in a judicial process that was muddled and inefficient. Members of the TAM as well as consumer organizations complained about the ineffectiveness of these courts.[62] When the black market rose in popularity, so too did the number of boards of judges.[63] Tom Segev notes that these boards often identified with and pitied the defendants, rather than expressing public outrage over breaches of regulation.[64]

In contradistinction to nostalgic images of national and social solidarity, keeping the shopkeepers and vendors in check was difficult, even during times of fierce fighting, such as during the 1948 war. A list of decisions made by the Tel-Aviv court dealing with economic offenders on 7 May 1948 reveals an unfavorable portrait of this community at war. Offenders differed in the scale and nature of their "crimes." Many committed petty crimes, such as a grocer accused of selling five eggs and fifty grams of cheese for just over the accepted price (40 IL fine), or a grocer who got caught selling one jar of Australian marmalade for a slightly inflated price (10 IL fine). However, others were caught with large quantities of smuggled goods: one grocer smuggled a box of 214 eggs into the city (15 IL fine), another seller had fifteen sacks of flour and was caught operating a non-licensed bakery, which was promptly shut down and the flour confiscated by the TAM.[65] The TAM archives reveal hundreds of similar cases.[66]

Although it seems that during the war the TAM did its best to enforce the regulations, citizens complained that not enough was done to ensure food distribution at the regulated prices. One angry citizen wrote to Mayor Rokach:

> I accuse you, the municipality and its staff . . . to whom the Tel-Aviv
> taxpayer pours several hundreds of thousands every month of having
> allowed a limited number of merchants and . . . speculators to suck the
> blood of the poorer classes. . . . I accuse your present system of *pakachim*
> [controllers] who are corrupt from head to toe and totally unreliable
> to look after the interests of the poor purchaser, for they readily close
> their eyes to every criminal act when the criminal grocer or greengrocer
> shoves a large fresh bunch of his product into their bags free of charge
> . . . In the name of justice and decency I demand that the public be
> saved . . .[67]

After the war, supplies were distributed more reasonably, prices
dropped and black-market transactions appeared to be more limited
in scope. However, the beginning of 1950 marked a clear change. As
shortages worsened, reports of the expanding black market gathered
momentum.[68] In response, Minister of Supply and Rationing Dov Joseph toughened enforcement measures. In late January, he announced
an inspection campaign against suppliers of the black market as well
as against its consumers.[69] State inspectors and police officers patrolled
the markets and the shops, boarded buses, and inspected passengers.
Even consumers' homes were searched, a strategy that elicited public
outrage.[70] Nevertheless, it was difficult to achieve compliance.

In May 1951, the mayor of Tel-Aviv admitted that the city resorted to
the black market in order to purchase needed materials for schools and
hospitals.[71] *Hador*'s leading editorial the following day accused Rokach
of sabotage: "If Tel-Aviv's municipal authority allows itself to breech
the law and even makes this practice public—why would an ordinary
citizen feel ashamed, why would a housewife refrain from doing so?" The
press did not let go of this story. Questions were raised as to whether the
TAM should be prosecuted. The *Jerusalem Post* asked whether Rokach
should not have at least directed the police to the suppliers of such materials.[72] The predicament facing the TAM was real. It was challenging
to continually equip schools and kindergartens, since in certain locations everything—including sinks, taps, pipes and gutters, foodstuffs,
and stationery—was repeatedly stolen from them.[73]

Another way of circumventing the system was by obtaining a sick
card, which meant acquiring a note from a medical doctor who had been
approved by the TAM. Tel-Aviv boasted an impressive percentage of sick

people. The number of sick residents in the city was on the rise; while Minister of Supply and Rationing Dov Joseph condemned this trend, local authorities were concerned about the health and welfare of Tel-Aviv residents. Many residents complained when the municipal doctor denied their request for additional food. Tel-Aviv's poor suffered from nutritional deficiencies yet were also inclined to sell additional rations they were awarded by their doctor's note in the black market in exchange for cash.[74] By 1952, the TAM claimed that 10 percent of Tel-Aviv residents were receiving assistance from the welfare department.[75]

### SPECIAL ATTENTION

In terms of law enforcement, special attention was awarded to urban areas in general and to Tel-Aviv in particular. The economic supervision divisions of the Ministry of Supply and Rationing and later the police department's economic police raided streets, shops, storage facilities and warehouses, markets, and celebrated cafés and restaurants.[76] It seemed as though no stone was left unturned.

Numerous items were sold regularly on the black market in Tel-Aviv and Jaffa, but perhaps most celebrated were the local restaurants and hotels known to serve meat when it was virtually unavailable else-where, without coupons (which were used to monitor sales and keep both consumers and suppliers in check).[77] Liverpool, a Tel-Aviv café, was said to function as a commodities market exchange. Vendors selling black-market commodities swarmed around the Carmel Market area, offering eggs, chicken, ducks, and geese without coupons, and fruits and vegetables above the legal price.[78] Around the Levinsky St. Market immigrants from different countries sold assorted black-market items, including preserved meat and eggs. Hard-to-get, fine-looking vegetables and fruits were sold within minutes.

Although controllers and police officers were sometimes present, they rarely intervened.[79] Tikva Weinstock, a reporter, described the Levinsky St. market as the headquarters of organized crime. She then portrayed another black-market zone: "Lilienblum [street and market—O.R.] is the new immigrant's kingdom where they stroll up and down. They offer small 'Nescafe' boxes . . . and dried plums . . . and pork liver spread. . . ."[80] Lilienblum remained a synonym for black market long after the austerity period was over, serving as a locale for illegal currency transactions until the 1980s.[81]

In October 1950, Ben-Gurion decided to exploit his personal charisma to lead the war on the black market, and established a taskforce to tackle the problem. Among other aforementioned measures, the task force targeted Carmel Market as a locus for fierce action. The same committee decided to turn some cases into show trials meant to attract the public's attention.[82] The popular magazine *Ha'olam Haze* criticized these actions, stating that the government was intimidating the public rather than persuading it and that intimidation failed to fight the black market even in the Soviet Union.[83]

### COMPLIANCE—THE BRITONS AND THE JEWS

An area where similar concerns were raised was taxation. When discussing the creation of a tax-compliant culture in early statehood years, legal historian Assaf Likhovski found that an initial willingness to pay taxes in early statehood years petered out, that the

> early idealism waned. One factor that caused this, perhaps, was the improvement in Israel's security. An additional factor leading to a decline in compliance was the government-imposed austerity measures that eroded the living standards of the population and extracted more and more money from the new citizens through a series of compulsory loans ... in reaction, Israeli taxpayers began to evade taxation en masse, ignoring the patriotic rhetoric of their politicians.[84]

The government viewed tax avoidance as a major problem. Initially it reacted to the problem through arbitrary assessment and collection methods, yet this method only exacerbated the crisis, leading to a breakdown in the relationship between the public and the administration. However, in later years it established more effective methods that reduced friction and tension with the taxpayers, gradually yielding a tax-paying culture.[85]

During the 1950s and 1960s, the Israeli tax-paying culture was often compared to that of Britain. Many of the various sources compiled by Likhovski note that there are fundamental differences between an established nation and a nascent state, between a homogeneous nation like Britain and a heterogeneous one, like Israel. Some state officials thought that the reason for mass tax avoidance was related to a hostile attitude characteristic of the Diasporic Jew.[86] However, in comparing Israeli compliance with austerity restrictions to that in Britain, there are no marked differences. Historians Ina Zweiniger-Bargielowska[87] and David Kynaston present an unfavorable portrait of British citizens. Food regulations were often ignored. Emergency legislation akin to that in Israel was breached, items were sold above the maximum price and without coupons, sales were conditioned, coupons were traded, false declarations were made, and animals were slaughtered illegally.[88]

Illicit activities were attributed to Diasporic Jews. Kynaston quotes a contemporary woman: "It's very easy to spot people who buy things without coupons. . . . They have the Jewish stamp, over decorated & doll eyed bits & pieces of fur & tucks."[89] Yet illicit activities were part of the everyday life of most Britons, just as they were part of the everyday life of most Israelis. A Briton quoted by Kynaston describes a local business community as one that is run on chicanery and trickery.

> Even persons of the utmost integrity, after six years of war, were motivated by self-preservation. It wasn't so much of "dog eat dog," rather to make sure that no opportunity of easing one's existence was missed. I doubt if a single Englishman did not avail himself of the help of the "black market."[90]

It seems that Tel-Avivians (and Israelis in general) resembled Britons more than they imagined.[91] A Tel-Aviv housewife, like her British counterpart, was more inclined to cooperate with rogue offenders than to rat on them.[92] Zweiniger-Bargielowska notes that when shortages worsened, enforcement was tightened. However, when the supply situation improved, a more relaxed attitude was adopted.[93] In Israel, by 1955, once the food supply was sufficient, some 20,000 cases scheduled for trial were dropped by the state.[94] A similar gap existed between public morale and private conduct. In Britain and in Israel the black market was condemned in public while respectable citizens continued to use it in private.[95] Yet in Israel people started to admit openly that they were shopping in the black market, including figures as celebrated as the mayor of Tel-Aviv.[96] This shift toward disclosure was a signal to the authorities (as well as to society in general) that the austerity order was on the verge of collapse.

## Discussion—Austerity and the City

In addition to an array of alleged moderate supervision and enforcement measures taken by local and governmental authorities to eradicate
black-market transactions, in October 1950 soldiers and police closed
all roads leading to Tel-Aviv. Armed patrols erected road blocks on all
pathways and fields around the city, stopping every car and pedestrian
to search and inspect. A similar "siege" was repeated in February 1952.[97]
How should the state's grandiose effort be understood? What does it
mean to conduct a self-imposed besieging of a major city, the major
societal, commercial, and cultural center?[98]

## Contemplating Theories

Likhovski employs critical theory to examine the relationship between
the state and the normalized citizen and relies on the works of critical
theorists such as Michel Foucault and Norbert Elias. The approach
he employs describes the rise of modern states (and the emergence
of non-state institutions such as mental hospitals or schools), not as
part of a progressive and liberal trajectory of growing individual lib-
erty, but rather in terms of increasing constraints on the freedom of
action of individuals. He claims that these individuals are subject to
various methods of surveillance and discipline designed to turn them
into self-policing citizens.[99] Likhovski traces efforts made by the state
to manufacture the "normalized" taxpayer. Perhaps the spectacular
display of force was also intended to facilitate the creation of a normalized citizen.

When considering the failure to impose food regulations on the
residents of Tel-Aviv, the work of de Certeau comes to mind. He rejected
some of Foucault's all-encompassing observations, and suggested an alternative. He paints a picture of urban life as dominated by freedom
from control:

> The language of power is in itself "urbanizing." But the city is left prey to
> contradictory movements that counter-balance and combine themselves
> outside the reach of panoptic power. The city becomes the dominant
> theme in political legends, but it is no longer a field of programmed and
> regulated operations. Beneath the discourses that ideologize the city, the

ruses and combinations of powers that have no readable identity prolif-
erate; without points where one can take hold of them, without rational
transparency, they are impossible to administer.[100]

## Why Tel-Aviv?

Why was Tel-Aviv targeted for enforcement? Tel-Aviv was not just another Israeli city—it was the major city, a city ruled by the "Bourgeoisie
in Democracy."[101] In addition to being the Hebrew city, its mythical
profile was related to the middle class as well as to solipsism, hedonism,
and escapism.[102] Tel-Aviv housed the major newspapers, and served
as the center of communications and newspaper coverage.[103] It epitomized the new nation, or the "new Jerusalem," as well as modernity
and progress.[104]

What de Certeau calls the "rational organization of the city"[105]
implies an amalgam of values and concepts that at their core stands
for a certain social order. History portrays cities as the birthplace of
citizenship.[106] The linkage made between the city, the middle class, and
respectability implies compliance with the law (usually legislated by
middle-class lawyers). We may also rely on Henry Near, who argued
that urban development rather than rural development was at the center
of the state's attention, after independence.[107]

Due to Tel-Aviv's mythical and societal role in the Israeli landscape,
policymakers felt that it was critical to modify the behavior of Tel-Aviv
residents—so that their actions would more closely resemble the visions
of policymakers. One could argue that in their view, an untamable Tel-
Aviv that served as the center of commerce and culture as well as the
center of black-market transactions had to be purged—in order for the
government to establish a body of proper citizens, with whom it could
correspond, relate to, rely on, and rule.

## Politics

Unlike the "normal" European bourgeoisie law, the austerity regulations
represented distributive justice rather than urban-capitalistic justice,
one that sanctifies property rights above all. In this sense, the need of
the TAM to regulate food allocation during the war is comprehensible

only in the framework of an "exceptional" time or state of emergency. Therefore, the conduct of TAM officials after the war must be examined. As shown above, during 1950 and 1951, Rokach and his General Zionists Party sent out contradictory messages; on the one hand, the mayor and his staff had to enforce the regulations; on the other hand, he and his party were fighting against those same regulations. Rokach's party won a landslide victory in the TAM elections of November 1950. Their campaign was based on targeting the inefficient austerity regime and calling for a free-market economy.[108]

## Respectability: Mask, Shame, and Guilt

On the psychological level, one could argue that the special attention Tel-Aviv received under the austerity regime was motivated by frustration and perhaps even political vengeance, pioneered by government officials who were primarily Mapai members and therefore (at least publicly) austerity supporters. The fact that lawmakers wanted to punish the rebelling TAM (ruled by their rivals) may also explain this phenomenon. However, on a larger scale, the raids on Tel-Aviv residents highlighted the need to create a body of respectable citizens. The motivation was not to cast shame on the entire population, but rather to guide it in the right direction. I doubt that the authorities were thinking of the Foucaltian self-policing normalized citizen; rather, they were hoping to create a more-or-less respectable citizenry, that would at least exhibit the semblance of proper behavior.

It is quite clear that not all enforcement measures were aimed at achieving similar goals. It seems that some actions were used to catch black-market whales[109] and others targeted ordinary citizens, including small-business owners and consumers, hoping to catch a decent number of offenders, knowing that they could not try them all in a burgeoning court system. Yet black-market dealers were not deterred. "The most interesting thing about this market," wrote one reporter about the Levinsky Market, "is that inspection authorities hardly bother the vendors. Indeed, rarely is a 'sweep' done—but when they are done, such sweeps impress more as a performance rather than an act of an honest will to fight the black market. Only a few hours after the sweep, Levinsky St. becomes 'normal' again, the street vendors return . . ."[110]

At least some of the time, enforcement agencies pretended to instill fear and reinstate order, but were actually faking it. The raid on Café Tiferet and the self-imposed siege forced on Tel-Aviv were also a kind of spectacle or show (which Foucault identifies with the weak state). One could not expect that order would be established after such operations, at least not for a prolonged period of time, considering the prevalence of scarcity. It seems that the authorities (or at least some of them) were not entirely aware of the hollowness of this spectacle and of the similarities between their actions and those of British rule which preceded them (and failed).

A journalist criticizing the act and relaying the terror of visiting a café seems exaggerated on both accounts. It is assumed that these grand raids were performed as a result of an intelligence tip, but that they were also carried out to present the actual and symbolic power of the government on a matter that was of utmost importance to it. Every state, particularly a new one that carries out emergency policies, needs to inculcate a proper image, even without real, effectual control. Concurrently, Israel was battling to control its borders against daily Palestinian infiltrations, and probably felt that it had to at least exert power over its own citizens. Thus special attention was directed at the largest and most influential city, Tel-Aviv, which seemed to be in need of taming.

Austerity actions were used to restore an image of respectability, an image of law and order vital for the continuation of normalized, regulated urban life.[111] One possible target of such actions was to retrieve formerly respectable citizens from the claws of black-market commerce. When these citizens lied about shopping in the black market, it meant they were ashamed of it—or at least they knew what they were doing was considered "wrong" in "society."[112] However, when respectable citizens openly admitted to using the black market, it meant that the whole austerity regime was on the verge of collapse, since there was neither a consensual silence[113] nor shame or guilt over breaching the regulations. Water was no longer hidden under the straw;[114] the mask of culture, compliance, and respectability, was removed.

Drawing from the concepts of deregulation presented by de Certeau and Foucault, which assume self-discipline to be an outcome of social supervision,[115] we can now evaluate the historical facts described above. Self-policing, so it seems, works only in certain settings and under certain conditions.[116] It is more effective when a citizen believes that it is worthwhile to abide by the rules. However, if or when the situation changes—namely, if people feel that they need to evade the power projected on to them, as de Certeau claimed, they will probably act differently.[117] Thus, it seems as if conditions of scarcity fashion not only new practices, but also new rules of conduct.[118]

In order to build the new nation of Israel, a center of gravity had to be established and a law-abiding citizenry needed to be created, so that local authorities and the government would have a public that could be mobilized, addressed, and recruited. Even though the public was unable or unwilling to meet the government's ultimate demands, the government pretended for a while that its efforts were bearing fruit, hoping that reinstating the "mask" would eventually yield an internalized change. The display of power—as much as the display of respectability—was and probably remains a necessary building block in the creation of a new nation.

I would like to thank Prof. Assaf Likhovski, Dr. Avital Margalit, Dr. Guy Seidman, and Dr. Anat Helman for their comments on earlier drafts of this paper. Thanks are due to Prof. Yaacov Shavit and Prof. Yoram Shachar for stimulating conversations, and to Dr. Scott Uri and Dr. Tali Lev who assisted me with instructive suggestions for reading material.

## NOTES

1. *Haboker,* 28 March 1950.

2. *Ha'aretz,* 30 March 1950.

3. Deborah Bernstein, *Women on the Margins: Gender and Nationalism in Mandate Tel-Aviv* (Jerusalem, 2008); Tammy Razi, *Forsaken Children: The Backyard of Mandate Tel-Aviv* (Tel-Aviv, 2009) [both in Hebrew].

4. Billie Melman, *London, Place, People and Empire (1800–1960)* (Tel-Aviv, 2009), 41.

5. Guy Seidman, "Unexceptional for Once: Austerity and Food Rationing in Israel, 1939–1959," *Southern California Interdisciplinary Law Journal* 18.1 (2008): 96.

6. Tel-Aviv Historical Archive (hereafter TAHA), 4, 37b, 466, Rosenbluth to Rokach, 10 August 1948.

7. Moshe Naor, "Supply Regulation and Control: The Austerity Policy," in *Citizens at War: Studies on the Civilian Society during the Israeli War of Independence,* ed. Mordechai Bar-On and Meir Chazan (Jerusalem, 2006), 191–92, 198–200 [Hebrew]; Seidman, "Unexceptional for Once," 128.

8. By January 1955, only sugar, oils, rice, legumes, coffee, flour, eggs, tea, and meat were still rationed. I. Shadmi, *Ma'ariv,* 13 January. By June, meat was no longer rationed, *Zmanim,* 6 June 1955.

9. Don Patinkin, *The Israel Economy: The First Decade* (Jerusalem, 1965) [Hebrew]; Nadav Halevi and Ruth Klinov-Malul, *The Economic Development of Israel* (New York, 1968); David Horowitz, *The Israeli Economy* (Tel-Aviv, 1954) [Hebrew].

10. Nahum Gross, "The Economy of Israel," in *The First Decade: 1948–1958,* ed. Zvi Zameret and Hannah Yablonka (Jerusalem, 1997), 139–140 [Hebrew]; Ina Zweiniger-Bargielowska, *Austerity in Britain: Rationing, Controls, and Consumption, 1939–1955* (Oxford, 2000), 6; Seidman, "Unexceptional for Once," 95–130.

11. Israel State Archive (ISA), PM's Office, Institute for Research of Public Opinion. *Austerity and Economic Planning as Viewed by Israelis* (Jerusalem, 1949) [Hebrew].

12. *Ma'ariv,* 23 January 1950; Mordechai Naor, "Austerity," in *Immigrants and Transit Camps, 1948–1952,* ed. Mordechai Naor (Jerusalem, 1987) 99–100; Gross, "The Economy of Israel," 140–141 [all in Hebrew].

13. Nahum Gross, *Not by Spirit Alone: Studies in the Economic History of Palestine in the Modern Era* (Jerusalem, 2000), 333–334 [Hebrew].

14. Orit Rozin, *Duty and Love, Individualism and Collectivism in 1950s Israel* (Tel-Aviv, 2008), 34–35 [Hebrew].

15. Haim Barkai, *The Primordial Era of the Israeli Economy* (Jerusalem, 1990), 37 [Hebrew]; Orit Rozin, "The Austerity Policy and the Rule of Law: Relations between Government and Public in Fledgling Israel," *Journal of Modern Jewish Studies* 4.3. (2005): 276–278.

16. Yaacov Shavit, Gideon Biger, and Haim Feirberg, *The History of Tel-Aviv,* vol. 2 (Tel-Aviv, 2001), 95–98, 195–207, 224–225, 243–267 [Hebrew]; *Davar,* 12 October, 1, 13, 28 December; *Herut,* 22 June 1949.

17. TAHA, sec. 4, 38, 466, report regarding stock, 10 May, see Shlush to association of importers and merchants, 19 April; Suzeiv and Kantor to Shlush, 15 April 1948.

18. TAHA, 4, 37b, 466, Krenter to Rokach, 21 June 1948.

19. *YITA,* 18, 1–2, 1948–1949.

20. *YITA,* 18, 3–4, 1948–1949 (25 August 1948).

21. *Ma'ariv,* 8, 23 January, 20 February, 24 September 1950.

22. *Davar,* 30 December; *The Jerusalem Post,* 30 December; *Haboker,* 30 December; *Al Hamishmar,* 8 October 1951.

23. *Ha'aretz,* 12 October 1951.

24. TAHA, 4, 2648a, 1146, 6 March 1952; 2647d, 1145, Ministry of Agriculture, "Encouraging growing of vegetables," 20 December 1951.

25. *Haboker,* 29 October 1951; TAHA, 4, 2648a, 1146, Shoshani to Yarok, 21 June 1953.

26. TAHA, 4, 2647b, 1145, public announcement, 22 March 1948.

27. TAHA, 4, 2648a, 1146, public announcement, 40-1953, 10 March 1953; 8 April 1952; 2647d, 1145; 2647b, 1145.

28. TAHA, 4, 2648a, 1146, public announcement, 29 February 1952.

29. TAHA, 4, 2647b, 1145, public announcement, 19 May 1949. See also 2647g, 1145, Rabinowitch (a sixth-grade pupil) to Rokach.

30. TAHA, 4, 2648a, 1146, Rachel Yanait to Nedivi, 19 January 1953.

31. TAHA, 4, 2648b, 1146, Nedivi to Yerushalmi, 30 August 1953.

32. TAHA, 4, 3043, 1206, Kalir to Manager of the Supply and Rationing Ministry, 21 June 1951.

33. TAHA, 4, 3043, 1206, Tax Department to TAM secretary, 4 April 1954.

34. TAHA, 4, 3043, 1206, TAM Culture Committee to the inspector of foods, 22 June; Kalir to inspector of foods, 28 May 1951.

35. TAHA, 4, 37b, 466, list of tickets issued 22–29 November; 2–9, 3–20, 22–31 December 1948; Tel-Aviv court of profiteering, case 39/49, 1 February 1949; 38, 466, National Committee Economic Department to Perlson, 3 February 2008.

36. TAHA, 4, 37b, 466, Kalir to Oterer, 13 May 1949.

37. *YITA*, Year 20, 21 (5–6) 1950–52 (January 1951).

38. *YITA*, Year 21 (3–4) August 1951, 55–56.

39. *The Jerusalem Post*, 12 July 1951.

40. *The Jerusalem Post*, 16 July; *Haboker*, 15 July 1951.

41. *Yedi'ot Aharonot*, 19 July 1951.

42. *Hador*, 17 July, see also, *Besha'aruriyat Hakerach*, 16 July 1951.

43. Rozin, *Duty and Love*, 151–152.

44. *Al Hamishmar*, 12 August 1951.

45. *Al Hamishmar*, 23 August 1951.

46. *Davar*, 8 January 1953; Gross, *Not by Spirit Alone*, 336–340.

47. *Dvar Hapoelet*, 1 February 1951, 211, and 11 November 1949, 246.

48. Dorothy Hobson, "Housewives and the Mass Media," in *Culture, Media, Language*, ed. Stuart Hall, Dorothy Hobson, Andrew Lowe, and Paul Willis (London and Birmingham, 1986), 109.

49. *Ha'aretz*, 29 August 1950.

50. TAHA, 4, 38, 466, Shverin to Nedivi, 18 March 1948.

51. *Haboker*, 25 September 1951. *Ha'aretz* dedicated a series of reports about the lines in which housewives had to queue, 16 September; 1, 4, 8, 25 July 1949.

52. TAHA, 4, 3049, 1208, Kalir to Perri, 12 September 1949.

53. *Kol Ha'am*, 21 June 1951.

54. *Kol Ha'am*, 6 August 1953; *Ha'aretz*, 13 November; *Kol Ha'am*, 13 November; *Al Hamishmar*, 27 September; *Kol Ha'am*, 14 September 1951.

55. *Hatsofe*, 10 September; *Ma'ariv*, 26 May 1951.

56. TAHA, 4, 38, 466, Kalir to Osterer, 27 April, 6 May 1949; Nedivi to *Davar, Ha'aretz, Haboker*, 22 August 1948; 37B, 466, for additional reports.

57. TAHA, 4, 38, 466, official statement of inspector/controller Frankel, 29 March 1948.

58. TAHA, 4, 38, 466, list of tickets issued by controllers, 17–18 July; list of tickets issued by Tel-Aviv controllers 29 June–1 July 1948; 37B, 466.

59. TAHA, 4, 38, 466, Nedivi to *Davar, Ha'aretz, Haboker*, 22 August 1948.

60. TAHA, 4, 37b, 466, income tax assessor to Nedivi.

61. *YITA*, Year 21 (1–2), May–June 1951, 48; Seidman, "Unexceptional for Once," 128.

62. TAHA, 4, 37b, 466, and especially, Tel-Aviv court for speculation and profiteering to the minister of justice, 6 June; minister of justice to Rokach, 23 June 1950.

See letters on the need to recruit more judges dated 2–24 December 1951; 3043, 1206, Minutes of TAM consumer protection committee, 22 July 1951.

63. TAHA, 4, 37b, 466, TAM lawyer to Rokach, 26 October 1950.

64. Tom Segev, *1949 The First Israelis* (Jerusalem, 1984), 303 [Hebrew].

65. TAHA, 4, 38, 466, Protocol 2, 7 May 1948.

66. TAHA, 4, 38, 37b, 466.

67. TAHA, 4, 38, 466, Zedek to Rokach. See also Meir to Rokach.

68. *Ma'ariv*, 15 February 1950.

69. *Ma'ariv*, 31 January; *Ha'aretz*, 10 October 1950.

70. Mordechai Naor, "Austerity," in *Immigrants and Transit Camps, 1948–1952*, ed. Mordechai Naor (Jerusalem, 1987), 103 (97–110) [Hebrew]; *Ma'ariv*, 22 February, 2 March; *Ha'aretz*, 23, 28 February, 2 March; *Davar*, 27 February; *Haboker*, 2 March 1950; ISA, Ministry of Supply and Rationing, G207/14/8/23.

71. *Ha'aretz*, 3 May 1951.

72. *Ha'aretz*, 4 May. See also *Jerusalem Post*, 4 May. Rokach later denied his earlier statement, *Hador*, 7 May, *The Jerusalem Post*, 14 May 1951.

73. TAHA, *YITA*, Year 21 (7–8), December 1951–January 1952, 55–56.

74. TAHA, 4, 3049, 1208, "data regarding the rise in number of sick who need the assistance of the city's extra food rations," 31 July; municipal economics and statistics department (MESD) to Rokach, 31 July; MESD to Perri, 12 September; Kalir to Perri, 27 September; Goldberg to Rokach, 7 October 1949. See more citizens' letters in the above-mentioned file, Kalir to Rokach, 19 April 1950. Sick rations were not distributed on occasions when shortages worsened, *Al Hamishmar*, 30 November 1951; Dov Joseph, *Yona Vacherev* (Ramat Gan, 1975), 235 [Hebrew]; MESD to Perri, 12 September 1949.

75. *Haboker*, 26 June 1952.

76. TAHA, 4, 3049, 1208, Rokach to Kaplan, 30 November; ISA, Ministry of Supply and Rationing, G207/14/8/23, Vishlitzky and Amiram report to Sefer, 16 June 1949; *Ma'ariv*, 6 October 1950.

77. *Ha'aretz*, 9 and 10 October 1950; Segev, *1949 The First Israelis*, 304.

78. *Al Hamishmar*, 23 December 1953; *Ma'ariv*, 25 May 1952.

79. *Ma'ariv*, 17 May 1952.

80. *Ma'ariv*, 25 May 1952.

81. Docks, ports, and large industrial areas where food traffic was heavy were the most infected with black-market transactions in Britain. See Zweiniger-Bargielowska, *Austerity in Britain,* 160.

82. ISA, P714/19, Dov Joseph, Minutes of Consultation with the Histadrut about the war on the black market, 1 October; Minutes of meeting of the war on the black-market task force (MATE), 29 September 1950; *Ma'ariv*, 29 May 1952.

83. *Ha'olam Haze*, 12 October 1950, 6.

84. Assaf Likhovski, "Training in Citizenship: Tax Compliance and Modernity," *Law and Social Inquiry* 32.3 (2007): 672 (665–700).

85. Ibid., 680–682.

86. Ibid., 685.

87. Zweiniger-Bargielowska, *Austerity in Britain,*151–153.

88. Ibid., 151–155; Rozin, "The Austerity Policy and the Rule of Law," 273–290.

89. David Kynaston, *Austerity Britain 1945–1951* (London, 2007), 111.

90. Ibid., 112.

91. The behavior of Britons during World War II was considered exemplary, *Ha'aretz,* 9 October 1950.

92. *Ma'ariv,* 9 August 1950; Zweiniger-Bargielowska, *Austerity in Britain,* 157. Crime rates, however, differed. See Shavit, Biger, and Feirberg, *The History of Tel-Aviv,* 232–233.

93. Zweiniger-Bargielowska, *Austerity in Britain,* 156.

94. *Ha'aretz,* 3 January 1955.

95. Zweiniger-Bargielowska, 159; Segev, *1949 The First Israelis,* 302; ISA, P714/19, Minutes of a Consultation with the Histadrut about the war on the black market, 1 October; *Ha'olam Haze,* 5 October 1950, 29 October 1951.

96. Rozin, *Duty and Love,* 50.

97. *Haboker,* 5 October 1950, 14 February 1952, 6 November 1951.

98. Shavit, Biger, and Feirberg, *The History of Tel-Aviv,* 17; S. Ilan Troen, *Imagining Zion: Dreams, Designs, and Realities in a Century of Jewish Settlement* (New Haven, 2003) 94, 96.

99. Likhovski, "Training in Citizenship," 667–668; Michel Foucault, "Governmentality," in *The Foucault Effect: Studies in Governmentality,* ed. Graham Burchell, Colin Gordon, and Peer Miller (Chicago, 1991); Michel Foucault, *Madness and Civilization: A History of Insanity in the Age of Reason* (London, 2001).

100. Michel de Certeau, *The Practice of Everyday Life* (Berkeley and Los Angeles, 1984), 95, 48–49. See also, Henri Lefebvre, *Everyday Life in the Modern World* (New Brunswick, 1994), 73. Foucault assumes that power invokes resistance; however, it is but a partial, weak, and fragmentary resistance. Michel Foucault, *The History of Sexuality,* vol. 1, trans. Gabriel Ash (Tel-Aviv, 1996), 66–67 [Hebrew].

101. Troen, *Imagining Zion,* 100 (the slogan used by former mayor Dizengoff).

102. Ibid.; Anat Helman, *Urban Culture in 1920s and 1930s Tel-Aviv* (Haifa, 2007), 24; Maoz Azaryahu, *Tel-Aviv—The Real City* (Sde-Boker, 1995), 338–339 [all in Hebrew].

103. Shavit, Biger, and Feirberg, *The History of Tel-Aviv,* 266.

104. Helman, *Urban Culture in 1920s and 1930s Tel-Aviv,* 173–209; Azaryhahu, *Tel-Aviv—The Real City,* 258–259, 227. Compare with Melman, *London, Place, People and Empire,* 301.

105. de Certeau, *The Practice of Everyday Life,* 94.

106. John Allan, Doreen Massey, and Steve Pile, ed., *City Worlds* (London, 1998), 1; James Holston and Arjun Appandurai, "Cities and Citizenship," in *Cities and Citizenship,* ed. James Holston (Durham, NC, 1999), 3.

107. Henry Near, *The Kibbutz Movement—A History* (Jerusalem, 2008), 428–429 [Hebrew].

108. *Haboker,* 10 November 1950.

109. Rozin, "The Austerity Policy and the Rule of Law," 283; ISA, P714/19, Minutes of Consultation with the Histadrut about the war on the black market, 1 October; MATE Minutes, 29 September 1950.

110. *Ha'aretz,* 21 May 1951.

111. de Certeau, *The Practice of Everyday Life,* 94.

112. *Hapoel Hatzair* 45 (27–28), 25.

113. Eviatar Zerubavel, *The Elephant in the Room: Silence and Denial in Everyday Life* (Oxford, 2006), 50–52.

114. Benjamin R. Foster, "Water Under the Straw: Peace in Mesopotamia," in *War and Peace in the Ancient World,* ed. Kurt A. Raaflaub (Malden, MA, 2007), 67.

115. Sara Mills, *Michel Foucault* (Tel-Aviv, 2005), 57, 65 [Hebrew]; Michel Foucault, *Discipline and Punishment: The Birth of the Prison* (New York, 1995).

116. Foucault, *Discipline and Punishment.*

117. de Certeau, *The Practice of Everyday Life,* xiv.

118. Rozin, "The Austerity Policy and the Rule of Law," 287.

# PART TWO

# Language, Literature, and Art

# TEN

# Tel-Aviv Language Police

## Zohar Shavit

Tel-Aviv . . . Herzl St. boys and girls were pouring out of *Gymnasia Herzliya* at the end of the school day. Just then, two famous Yiddishists who were traveling around the country found themselves in front of the school. The greater of the two said to his companion: "The Zionists boast that Hebrew has become second nature to the children of Eretz-Israel. Now you'll see that their boast is nothing but lies. I'll tweak a child's ear and I'm sure he won't yell '*Imma!*' [Mother!] in Hebrew, but rather '*Mamme!*' in Yiddish." He did as he said he would: he walked up behind a child and tweaked his ear, and the child immediately turned and yelled at him in Hebrew, "*Hamor!*" [What an ass!]. The famous Yiddishist turned to his companion and said, "I'm afraid they're right . . ."

This anecdote, adduced by Alter Druyanov,[1] reflects the great pride of the Jewish Yishuv in Tel-Aviv's children, whose Hebrew was natural and native. Speaking Hebrew became one of the symbols of the city of Tel-Aviv and was a point of pride for its leaders. The creation of Tel-Aviv as a Hebrew city symbolized its uniqueness and the great promise it held. The city's leaders, teachers, and writers, as well as other public figures, joined in the constant struggle to maintain the city's Hebrew character.

The Hebraization project, established to create a common language and culture for Jews who had immigrated to Eretz-Israel in order to build their national homeland, was seen as the emblem of the Zionist endeavor. It was believed that only a common Hebrew culture would make the transformation of a variety of groups with different languages, symbol systems, and cultural codes into a national society with a shared value system.

In February 1914, a few months before the outbreak of World War I, the "Language War" ended with the victory of the Hebrew camp. *Ezra* (Help), a German-Jewish philanthropic organization that established and fostered educational institutions in Eretz-Israel, agreed that Hebrew would be the language of instruction in physics and mathematics in the Technikum (later called the Technion), and that all the teachers and professors who did not have a command of the language would have to learn it within four years. In 1925, when the Hebrew University was established in Jerusalem, nearly all the courses were taught in Hebrew. During the British Mandate, Hebrew became established as the main spoken language of the Jews of Eretz-Israel.

In 1922, the Mandate authorities decreed that English, Arabic, and Hebrew would be the official languages, and that all governmental orders, official announcements, and official forms must be in Arabic and Hebrew. Joseph Klausner, in a front-page article in the daily *Ha'aretz,* had good reason to refer to the high commissioner's order as "a historic event" and "the bill of rights of our national language."[2]

The Yishuv witnessed a surge of publications in Hebrew. Especially notable was a wide range of literature and newspapers. Cultural entrepreneurs and cultural agents made great efforts to introduce the Hebrew language into all spheres of life and to disseminate Hebrew culture. To this end they enlisted every possible verbal and non-verbal text. Starting in 1936, the programs of *Kol Yerushalayim* (the Voice of Jerusalem), the Eretz-Israel radio station, were also recruited for the promotion of Hebrew language and culture.

The Hebrew revival project bore fruit and came to be nationally recognized as a success story, perhaps one of the greatest achievements of the Zionist movement.

### Hebrew and Other Languages

Despite recognizing that the Hebraization project was a success story, I contend that the project did not come to full fruition in many parts of the private sphere or in certain parts of the public sphere, even before the large waves of immigration of the Fourth and Fifth Aliya, and especially after. If not for the unrelenting, sometimes even violent, campaign that took place mostly in the first Hebrew city, the Hebrew language would not have triumphed over other languages—mainly Yiddish—and would not have become the national language of the Yishuv or the official language of the State of Israel.

A considerable part of the first generation of immigrants to the country, and some of the second generation, continued to live a bilingual life in the private sphere and in parts of the public sphere; Hebrew served only some of their needs. Even the shining knight of the Hebrew language, the poet and translator Abraham Shlonsky, peppered his letters in the 1920s with Russian words written in Cyrillic letters (rather than in Hebrew transliteration).[3] H. N. Bialik, national poet and glorious symbol of the revival of the Hebrew language, is said to have preferred to speak Yiddish in intimate situations. His conversations with Simon Rawidowicz contain many words in Yiddish, especially when Bialik was emotional—either angry or contemptuous: "*Vos vill er der kakker* [and he repeated this epithet about ten times]? *Vos veys er? Vos hot er gelernt?*" ("What does that *kakker* want? What does he know? What has he learned?").[4]

The older generation remained loyal to its mother tongue out of convenience, nostalgia, a partial clinging to the "old" culture, lack of a sufficient knowledge of Hebrew, or sometimes even a total lack of knowledge of Hebrew. Many families continued to speak their mother tongue or spoke a mixture of their mother tongue and Hebrew, and this multilingualism was very common.

In the pamphlet "*Gdudenu*" (Our Battalions), the founders of the Hebrew Language Defense League (hereafter HLDL) described the state of the language in the first Hebrew city:

> In the streets of Tel-Aviv you hear talking and singing in a variety of foreign languages. You might even think you were not in Eretz-Israel, but in the Diaspora. The situation has reached such a state that newspapers in jargon [Yiddish] have started appearing in Jerusalem, the capital; many announcements in the streets are spoken in jargon; at meetings, speeches are made in various languages; all we need is for foreign-language schools to open and then we will have a second Diaspora here.[5]

In an interview granted to Shimon Shor[6] in 1997, the elderly Aharon Hoter-Yishai (formerly Chotoretzky) still lamented the linguistic situation in Tel-Aviv in 1923, when the HLDL was established, and particularly the meager presence of Hebrew in the public sphere: ". . . the state of Hebrew was deplorable, really deplorable. Letters from municipal [hereafter TAM] institutions were written in other languages, not Hebrew. All the signs on shops [and] cafés were in other languages. Yiddish, Polish, English."[7]

## Tel-Aviv Fights for Hebrew

Against this background one can understand the emotional address by Mayor Meir Dizengoff to the citizens of Tel-Aviv, and particularly to the immigrants who had recently arrived, pleading with them to help preserve the Hebrew character of the city:

> Because Tel-Aviv is not just a Levantine city with a hodgepodge of peoples and languages, but rather a cultured Hebrew city with only one language, the language of the Tanakh, and all the other foreign languages that have been brought from alien countries must make way for this language. . . . Because if every new immigrant brings his former language with him, what will become of us? We will create here a Tower of Babel and not a Hebrew homeland. Preserve the Hebrew spirit of this city, which is our pride and the pride of the entire Jewish people! Forsake your foreign idols and be Hebrew in your speech, in your names, in your signs, and throughout your daily lives.[8]

From Tel-Aviv's earliest days, and especially since the 1920s, the city's leaders and various public bodies acted out of concern for the Hebrew character of the city. Their actions to make Hebrew its dominant language included public relations efforts. In a letter to Tel-Aviv's culture committee, Haim Bograshov (later Haim Boger), the principal of the Herzliya Gymnasia (the first Hebrew school in the world), described these efforts as "propaganda for disseminating the Hebrew language in Tel-Aviv."[9] This process consisted of a never-ending struggle to make Hebrew the sole language of communication of both Jewish and non-Jewish groups, an attempt to impose Hebrew on people addressing the TAM, and an attempt to fight groups that conducted their activities, even partially, in languages other than Hebrew and to use various sanctions against them.

Some of Tel-Aviv's residents, including some anonymous figures, took part in the struggle to protect Hebrew. Thus, for example, A. Benayahu of 39A Eliezer Ben-Yehuda St., wrote to the city's culture committee complaining about a shopkeeper who "hung on his store a *sign on which the Hebrew inscription is at the bottom* [emphasis in the original], below the English inscription."[10] Three days later Mayor Israel Rokach wrote to Mr. Max Cohen of the candy shop on Allenby St. asking him to change his sign.

> We take the liberty of drawing his honor's attention to the bad impression on the public made by the defamation of the Hebrew language and we are certain that his honor will take into consideration the feelings of the public and will give the Hebrew language a more respectable place on his sign.[11]

## The Hebrew Language Defense League's Struggle for Hebrew in Tel-Aviv

Most of the activities for establishing the dominance of Hebrew were initiated by the HLDL,[12] however, which saw its role as "... defending Hebrew and making it totally dominant in our daily lives."[13] The HLDL was established in 1923 by a group of Herzliya Gymnasia students with the help of their teachers, especially Bograshov. Later, they were joined by students of the Levinsky Women Teachers' Seminary, students from the High School of Commerce, a group of workers and clerks, and dozens of young people from Tel-Aviv. According to a study by Shimon Shor, in its founding year the HLDL had 175 members, among them seventy-five students in the upper grades of the Gymnasium, forty workers, thirty students from the Levinsky Seminary, fifteen clerks, and fifteen students of the High School of Commerce.[14]

The HLDL initiated a series of public events. For example, three years after the death of Eliezer Ben-Yehuda, "the reviver of the language," they wanted "to decorate passersby on the streets of Tel-Aviv with 'Ben-Yehuda' ribbons" and also asked the city "to kindly decide to open a street named after Ben-Yehuda."[15] They also set up a teachers' department that taught Hebrew at no charge, initiated the establishment of a group of librarians that helped libraries of *Histadrut Ha'ovdim Ha'ivrim* (the Union of Hebrew Workers) and Barzilai Library, and built a reading tent on the seashore. In December 1924, the HLDL also organized the Hebrew Book Exhibition[16] and evenings of popular opera.[17] Members went out into the streets and handed out flyers promoting

Hebrew (Hoter-Yishai, in his old age, called them "stickers"): "A schism of languages—a schism of hearts," "One language—one soul," "Hebrew [person], speak Hebrew!"

Most of these activities initiated by the HLDL went far beyond public events and included snooping, which Haim Arlozoroff angrily referred to as "the language secret police."[18] His anger was sparked by a letter sent to him by the HLDL Jerusalem Branch, signed by M. Ish-Shalom and M. Carmeli.[19] They complained about Arlozoroff's use of letterhead paper on which his address appeared only in English and also about the fact that he was corresponding with Zionist institutions in English.

Arlozoroff argued that the HLDL had no right to interfere in what he considered a private matter. However, the HLDL believed that the correspondence of the head of the political department of the Jewish Agency was always a public matter and never "a personal and private matter."[20] In a subsequent letter they compared the use of the language by public figures to questions relating to Hebrew labor and purchase of foreign products:

> And just as we think that Ferdman's hiring of foreign laborers *in his own orchard* [emphasis in the original] is not a private matter, and just as buying foreign products is not a private matter, and so on, so is it not a private matter when someone, and even more so when someone who is our political representative, shows contempt for Hebrew, even in his personal letters.[21]

When the HLDL learned that A. Lerner, a member of the city council, had participated in a meeting of the Association of Polish Immigrants "that was run in a foreign language" and "had given a speech in a foreign language," they hastened to write a letter of complaint, which, however, did not get a sympathetic hearing from the TAM. The response was that "Tel-Aviv Municipality cannot oversee the doings and activities of a member of the city council outside the municipality and in matters that are not connected to it."[22]

The issue of the relations between the private sphere and the public sphere was on the HLDL's agenda from its inception. It obviously had a very broad understanding of the boundaries of the public sphere, as is clear from letters it sent to several public figures. It did not hesitate to interfere in the education of the children of Dr. Pochovsky, a member of the TAM council, who sent them to a non-Hebrew-speaking school. It is unclear from the correspondence which school it was, but most probably it was the Alliance School. The HLDL argued that it was "a school that attacks our language and culture and undermines the foundations of our school system throughout the country," and therefore demanded that he send his children to a Hebrew-language school.[23]

> The fact that a man like him, one of the builders of the new Yishuv, sends his children to a school that is not one of ours, for whatever reasons, and thus forgets his obligation toward the nation—this fact requires not just one league of "defenders" but rather a whole public of "defenders." ... According to him, "educating one's children is the parents' business." We are very, very surprised by this statement. As a doctor, his honor undoubtedly knows that if a well-known person comes down with a disease known to be contagious and for whatever reason is not willing to cure it, the public has the full right to force that person to submit to its orders, because the individual's illness endangers everyone and is a threat to their lives.[24]

Even Meir Dizengoff was not immune. When the younger HLDL members found out that a letter from his firm was printed on "English letterhead paper without a single Hebrew letter" (though the letter itself was written in Hebrew), they quickly demanded that the matter be set right.[25] TAM secretary Yehuda Nedivi responded a week later, "Since the letter itself is written in Hebrew, one should not make an issue of [something] that certainly does not show anyone's intention to be contemptuous of our national language."[26] In addition to acting as the "language secret police," the HLDL set up a squad that walked through the streets of Tel-Aviv correcting all the mistakes on signs and putting up Hebrew signs to replace the non-Hebrew ones.

Besides sanctions, help was offered to those willing to adapt to Hebrew. For example, *Yedi'ot Tel-Aviv* proposed Hebrew names for businesses; for a shop selling various types of sewing items it proposed the name *"Caftor Vaferach"* ("knop and flower"); for a restaurant it proposed *"Bete'avon"* ("bon appetit"); for a messenger service it suggested *"Naphtali"* (after one of the Twelve Tribes of Israel, whose emblem was a hind let loose), and for a vegetarian restaurant they proposed *"Yechi"* ("let them live").[27]

The posters on billboards of the TAM, in addition to the HLDL manifestos, suggest that some of the interactions of daily life were not carried out in Hebrew. The HLDL endeavored to change that and demanded of "the Hebrew public" that they communicate in Hebrew. Of the merchants they demanded, "Reply to your customers only in Hebrew! Keep your accounts only in Hebrew! Conduct every transaction and every sale only in Hebrew!" Of the customers they demanded, "Ask your questions only in Hebrew, and if they do not understand you, harden your heart [and] explain once or twice until you get what you need!"[28]

The HLDL demanded that when using public transportation—in those days few people owned private cars—passengers force the drivers to speak Hebrew. They were asked to insist that Hebrew be the language of communication with the drivers and to comment publicly if they caught drivers conversing with other passengers in any language other than Hebrew:

> Hebrew person, when you enter the coach and the car speak to the driver only in Hebrew! Do not answer the driver if he speaks any other language! If you hear the drivers talking or calling out in a foreign language while you are entering or getting out of the coach or the car, do not remain silent; address them and point out their wrongdoing.[29]

They also demanded that the TAM Council, "when drawing up contracts with the automobile offices, demand assurances that they will forbid the drivers of their automobiles to continue showing contempt for the Hebrew language."[30]

In 1928, the HLDL complained that

> In the casino on Tel-Aviv's shore, owned by Tel-Aviv Municipality, a play was presented in a foreign language (German). We view this as a grave insult not only to ourselves, who are young and zealous, but also to all the citizens of Tel-Aviv, the first Hebrew city.[31]

Nahum Greenblatt, who had rented the casino, immediately responded and wrote to top TAM officials:

> I hereby wish to express my sincere regret over this unintentional error. I assure you that from now on, as long as the casino is in my hands, such an event will never happen again. Please forgive me for the above.[32]

In 1930, the HLDL protested against the screening of a Yiddish-language film, *Die Yiddishe Mamme* (The Jewish Mother) to be screened at the Mugrabi Opera Cinema, after the owners of the Eden and Ophir cinemas had committed themselves not to show films in Yiddish on condition that all the other cinemas act accordingly. In a letter to Deputy Mayor Rokach, the HLDL claimed that "already in the early days of the Tel-Aviv Committee, a tradition was established that jargon would not be used in public in Tel-Aviv without permission. When the city gave the cinema as a concession, there was a special clause in the lease regarding the prohibition of renting the hall for plays in jargon."[33]

On the basis of this lease, the HLDL demanded that the owners of the Mugrabi Opera Cinema not screen the film. Nevertheless, the film was shown on 27 September, under the protection of the British Police. A riot broke out in the hall, and following the intervention of Deputy Mayor Rokach, a repeat screening was forbidden.[34]

## Violent Struggle

The struggle for the Hebrew language was characterized by a very passionate, almost obsessive devotion to the goal, and often involved violence. In 1914, when Chaim Zhitlowsky was invited to give a lecture in Yiddish in a Jaffa café about "the future of the Jewish people," *Herzliya Gymnasia* students arrived with their principal, Dr. Bograshov, at the house where Zhitlowsky was staying and tried to persuade him not to lecture in Yiddish. When they failed to do so, Bograshov tore his collar, in a kind of *kria* (a ceremony of rending associated with Jewish mourning), and the students waiting outside tore their shirts and shouted to Zhitlowsky, "Over our dead bodies" (literally, "You will be treading on our bodies"), in an attempt to keep him from leaving for the lecture. In the *Book of the Second Aliya*, Mary Yatziv[35] writes that the house where Zhitlowsky was staying was stoned and gunshots were heard. Two weeks before, a stink bomb was thrown when Abraham Goldfaden's operetta *Shulamis* was presented in Yiddish.

In their attempts to prevent lectures and plays in Yiddish from taking place, the HLDL did not hesitate to use force. They threatened the owners of theaters that they would cause damage wherever non-Hebrew events took place. They regularly bought tickets to plays and disrupted them, caused an electrical short in a theater, and threw stink bombs.[36] Hoter-Yishai described their methods in the struggle against the use of foreign languages on shop signs—they offered to share the cost of changing the signs to Hebrew. After the owner of one café objected, Hoter-Yishai smashed his large display window.[37]

On the eve of Simchat Torah (7 October 1928), HLDL members tried to disrupt a reception in honor of Jacob Zerubavel that *Poalei Zion Smol* (the Zionist-Marxist party) wanted to hold in a club in Tel-Aviv. Members of the *Betar* youth movement and HLDL members marched through the streets and then tried to break into the club; when they encountered resistance, they threw bricks and stones and ran off. This rampage generated a storm of controversy, led to the establishment of a committee of inquiry, and was denounced by the TAM council.

Jewish newspapers in the United States claimed that children were expelled from *Herzliya Gymnasia* as part of the battle against Yiddish. Thus, for example, it was reported that the children of the printer of *Das Yiddishe Arbeiter* (The Jewish Worker) were suspended from the school until their father would commit himself to not publishing pamphlets in Yiddish.[38] Dr. Matmon-Cohen reportedly urged eight-year-olds "to battle Yiddish to the last drop of their blood" and also reportedly expelled a girl from school who replied that she was in favor of both Hebrew and Yiddish. Similarly, it was reported that Yiddishists were dismissed from their places of work.[39] However, it is not clear whether these events actually took place, or whether they were simply unsubstantiated rumors resulting from internal battles between the Zionists and the Yiddishists in the United States.

## The City Officials' Struggle for Hebrew

It is apparent from correspondence in the TAM Archive that the city used to return letters addressed to it that were not written in Hebrew. In an internal memo, Nedivi wrote, "Please do not accept official letters written in any language other than Hebrew."[40] High-ranking officials spent time sending back the non-Hebrew letters, adding a letter signed by the mayor or his deputy or the TAM secretary.

The accompanying laconic letters generally took the following form:

To:

Re: His honor's invoices of January 1, 1926, written in a foreign language

Dear Sir,

Enclosed we are returning the abovementioned invoices together with [his] letter. We believe that his honor is aware of the fact that the language of our municipality is Hebrew, and therefore we would be pleased if he wrote to us only in that language.

Respectfully,

D. Bloch

Deputy Mayor of Tel-Aviv[41]

Only rarely was a brief explanation given. A letter in German was returned to Mr. Nathan Coronel with the excuse that "we do not have anyone in our office who can translate this into Hebrew";[42] Mr. Eliezer Axelrod was told that his letter was returned "because it is not possible for us to conduct correspondence in a foreign language";[43] Mr. Bloomstein, of a book shop on Allenby St., who had apparently sent an invoice to the city, received a warning letter: "Invoices and letters in languages other than Hebrew will be returned in future to his honor."[44]

Mr. Weintraub of the Bar Kochba Café received the following explanation: "We think that his honor knows that the language of our municipality is Hebrew and therefore we will be pleased if he will write to us only in that language."[45] To Shlomo Feingold they wrote, "I see it as my duty to bring to his honor's attention the distressing fact that his honor finds it necessary to conduct all his written transactions with his municipality in a foreign language, even though he knows that the official language of the municipality, and especially with regard to its citizen-residents, is Hebrew."[46]

In later years, the style of the letters became even more laconic and less polite. Unlike the first letters, which politely stated, "Therefore we ask him to write to us only in the above language and we will not delay reading his request,"[47] subsequent letters stated, "Enclosed we are returning his honor's letter written in a foreign language. Please write to us in Hebrew."[48] Letters to public institutions had a reproachful tone. Thus, for example, a letter to the Zionist leadership signed by Bloch, deputy mayor of Tel-Aviv, stated, "We regret that we need to remind you that the language of Tel-Aviv Municipality is *Hebrew* [emphasis in the original] and that you must write to us only in that language."[49] Usually, the language in which the letter had been written was referred to as a "foreign language";[50] the few exceptions concerned letters written in German, Arabic, or Russian.[51]

Occasionally the recipients responded positively, as in the apologetic letter of Shlomo Feingold (which he signed "Yeffe Zahav"): "I applaud with thanks his comment, which is both polite and courteous. I assure him in the most serious and positive manner that from this day on I will correspond with his honorable office only in the language of the prophets."[52] Ms. Gertrude Samuel, too, sent Dizengoff an apologetic letter in which she explained why the invitation to the exhibition she had organized at Mrs. Rokach's home was in English, and not in Hebrew: "I am sorry for this sad error of mine and I strongly feel a need to explain this matter to your honor and to promise that it will definitely not happen again."[53]

In a letter to the hotel owner Mrs. Frieda Moskowitz, Bloch rejected her request to continue keeping the guest book at her hotel in English. She argued that at the age of fifty she could not learn to write Hebrew and that she had neither the time nor the ability to do so.[54] Bloch demanded that the hotel guest book (which apparently was open to police inspection) "be written in Hebrew." He explained that, "One must not require the municipal officials and policemen to know foreign languages used by perhaps a tiny minority of the city's population."[55]

Dizengoff severely reproached Moshe Gopenko, the principal of the Shulamit School of Music, because a change in the evening program was announced in Russian: "First of all, you all need to know that the Shulamit Music School is a Hebrew school and that during official performances no one is permitted to speak to the audience from the stage in a foreign language." Dizengoff added, "I heard that several teachers permit themselves to teach in the Russian language. I am informing his honor that this must be stopped and that every teacher must adapt to our language. His honor must make it clear that the language of instruction is Hebrew."[56]

The HLDL was on the lookout for every infraction, both major and minor, and spoke out whenever, in its view, the honor of the Hebrew language was besmirched. It protested that the inscriptions on the trucks that cleaned the city, "the wagons that spray water in the streets," did not grant Hebrew its rightful place because they "are written in English on the top and in Hebrew on the bottom."[57] On the same day it received an answer signed by Nedivi, in the name of the mayor: "Even before we received your abovementioned letter, the order was given to change the inscription on the vehicle."[58] In an internal memo, Nedivi wrote, "I saw that on the new water-spraying vehicles they had written the name of Tel-Aviv Municipality in English on top and in Hebrew on the bottom. Please inform me as to who decided this matter."[59] He explained to the HLDL that, "This inscription was made abroad and the vehicle arrived here with the inscription [already] on it."[60]

In addition to city officials and members of the HLDL, the city's residents were on the alert regarding the presence of Hebrew in the public sphere. They kept track of the "level of Hebraization," pinpointed every infraction in the public sphere, and acted determinedly to correct it. Thus, for example, Bezalel Yaffe of the Geula Company wrote an angry letter to Dr. Benzion Mossensohn, chairman of TAM's culture committee, complaining that the collector of the *varko* (*vergi* in Turkish—property tax) had not agreed to give him a receipt in Hebrew and had claimed that even the city was willing to receive receipts "written in Arabic or Turkish." Yaffe demanded that "a regulation be enacted that would require every municipal official to respect our language and its right to exist. Every transaction with the local and central government would be only in Hebrew; the municipality [would be] forbidden to pay anyone unless they presented receipts in our language."[61]

With regard to non-Jews, a directive was given in one of the internal memos to accept letters "only in one of the official languages,"[62] but even in these cases the TAM tried to impose Hebrew on the officials of the British Mandate. For example, in a letter to Dr. Rankin, the chief physician of Jaffa District, Bloch called his attention to the difficulties caused by letters in English: "We allow ourselves to bring to his honor's attention that all the letters to us from his office are not in Hebrew and that this makes our work very difficult."[63] A year later, the Health Ministry official in charge of Tel-Aviv tried to persuade Dizengoff to add an English translation to letters in Hebrew. He explained his request on technical grounds: letters arriving on Friday afternoon would not be dealt with before Monday, because of the Jews' and Christians' Sabbaths.[64] Apparently he did not receive a positive reply, because he sent a repeat request a month later.[65]

This practice of sending repeat requests continued for years. Thus, for example, a complaint was sent to the district officer of Tel-Aviv to the effect that recently "letters have been received from his honor's office only in the English language," and included the request that "it be arranged that in future we receive his letters at least with a Hebrew translation attached."[66] City officials continuously monitored the Hebrew version of the various forms used by the British Mandate. For example, a long correspondence was conducted concerning "the fractured Hebrew in form O.M. 41 with regard to extermination of pests,[67] and the officials were not satisfied until they were informed that there were new and corrected forms.[68]

## Hebrew in Tel-Aviv—Some Data

To what extent did the efforts to make Hebrew the dominant language in Tel-Aviv bear fruit? According to data of the Palestine office of the Zionist Organization, forty-three percent of Tel-Aviv's residents spoke Hebrew in 1914;[69] slightly more than the percentage of Hebrew-speakers in the general Jewish population (forty percent), which at the time numbered 85,000.[70] According to the 1916–1918 census, seventy-five percent of the young people in the new towns and villages (Tel-Aviv and the colonies), stated that their language was Hebrew.[71] In Jaffa, in Haifa, and in the rest of the country the proportion of Hebrew-speakers in the second generation was about half.[72] In the parents' generation the picture was different: slightly more than a third spoke Hebrew in Tel-Aviv; in the villages, in Jaffa, and in Haifa the proportion of Hebrew-speakers was only one-fifth.[73] The number of Hebrew-speakers continued to grow. According to a 1928 survey, sixty percent of Tel-Aviv residents could speak Hebrew.[74]

According to a memo presented to David Ben-Gurion,[75] two-thirds of the 300,000 Jewish adults (some 200,000), knew Hebrew to some degree.[76] The author of the memo was concerned about the one-third of the adult population that did not know Hebrew, and held a pessimistic vision of the future: "In the absence of a national effort, in another five years the number of residents in the country whose language is Hebrew will be a negligible minority."[77]

Ben-Gurion was concerned about the place of Hebrew in the life of the Yishuv. Several years earlier (in 1930), in a questionnaire that he asked to have administered to members of the Histadrut (*The Questionnaire for Studying the Life-style of the Workers*) he included several questions concerning the degree of Hebrew knowledge among Histadrut members:[78]

> Are there books in the house, and in which languages?
> Does he read Hebrew newspapers, non-Hebrew newspapers, and which ones? (Russian, Yiddish, German, etc., and give the names)
> Does he know Hebrew? Does his wife know Hebrew?
> The language he uses in speaking with his wife, the language he uses in speaking to his children.

In light of the surveys conducted in November 1948, six months after the declaration of the state, this concern seems unjustified. At that time, seventy-five percent of all the 700,000 Jewish residents of Israel stated that they use Hebrew as their sole or main language.[79] These data are indeed impressive, but one should view them in light of other data concerning the scope of knowledge of Hebrew. There is reason to believe that survey and census results often testify much more to the image of the language and its status than to the scope of its use and respondents' depth of knowledge. It is reasonable to believe that the respondents to the surveys, aware of the place of the Hebrew language in the national revival, were unwilling to admit a lack of knowledge of the language. Thus, for example, a rather specious picture arises from the census carried out by the British Mandate in October 1922. Of 83,794 Jews who were counted, 80,396 declared that Hebrew was their spoken language, while only 1,946 declared it was Yiddish. Not even one of the 15,065 residents of Tel-Aviv declared Yiddish to be his language (as opposed to 999 of 5,639 residents of Jerusalem and 356 of 5,087 residents of Jaffa).[80]

It seems plausible that the results of this census, carried out by a foreign government, was an expression of the desire to create an image of the Yishuv as a Hebrew entity rather than a reflection of the real situation. Roberto Bachi argues in his statistical analyses that one must read some of the census findings carefully because, according to him, they "were tainted to a great degree by inaccurate declarations that resulted from intentional political propaganda aimed at making all the Jews declare 'Hebrew' in response to the question about languages."[81]

The understanding that these censuses ought to serve the Zionist propaganda effort is clear in Ahad Ha'am's angry letter to Mordechai Ben-Hillel Hacohen, in which he reproached him for statistics published in the Russian-language Jewish journal *Razsvet* sent by Bezalel Yaffe.

> According to that, forty-three percent of all the residents speak Hebrew, and thirty-five percent speak jargon. I am surprised at our Rabbi Bezalel, who has written something incorrect that can serve as ammunition for the Hebrew-haters. Because if even in Tel-Aviv most of the residents speak other languages, and jargon is almost as dominant as Hebrew, where is the revival of Hebrew? In order to give a correct idea of the situation as it really is, one should have broken down the figures—children only, men only, women only—and then the picture would have been totally different, and everyone would have seen that almost all the children speak Hebrew, and that most of the men do.[82]

Ahad Ha'am was right. All the data indicate clearly the increase in the number of Hebrew-speaking children. Already in 1914 the percentage of children who used Hebrew as their sole or main language was 53.7 percent, as opposed to the percentage of adults, 25.6 percent.[83] In November 1948, 93.4 percent of children between the ages of two and fourteen used Hebrew as their sole language.[84] According to Bachi, from 1916 to 1918 Yiddish was spoken by about seventy percent of the parents of Ashkenazi origin and by about one-third of the second generation. In 1948, the percentage of Yiddish-speakers was still forty-seven percent.[85]

It seems that the linguistic situation in the private sphere involved the use of the mother tongue or a macaronic language (a mixture of words from several languages in a single sentence). Sometimes there was a "division of labor" of languages among the speakers: the children spoke to their parents in Hebrew, and the parents spoke to the children in other languages.

In addition to examining the division of labor between the languages in the private and the public spheres with regard to the use of Hebrew, one should also examine the gap between active and passive knowledge of the language. The ability to speak Hebrew is hardly ever a guarantee of full command of the language; not everyone who declares himself a Hebrew-speaker knows how to read and write the language. An indication of this can be found in several sources, including surveys of the extent of knowledge of the language, data regarding book loans from libraries, and the import of books to the country. The results of a survey conducted in 1947 among members of Kibbutz Beit Hashitta (founded in 1928) reveal the large gap between the ability to speak Hebrew and the ability to read and write it; ninety-five percent of the survey's participants responded that they are able to speak Hebrew, but only thirty-eight percent responded that they are also able to write it.[86]

The data about book imports show a huge demand for non-Hebrew books, a demand that even grew during the time of the Yishuv. The import of books to Eretz-Israel grew more than 2.5 times between 1923 and 1929 (from 10,000 to 25,823 books); this growth rate was greater than that of the Jewish population, and certainly of the adult Jewish population (the 1922 census counted 83,790 Jews; in 1931, 174,606 Jews were counted).[87]

An analysis of the languages of the libraries' books shows a clear preference for non-Hebrew books, despite the favoring of Hebrew books in the library's purchasing policy. This was especially true for libraries of *kibbutzim* and *moshavim*. In the libraries of Hakibbutz Hameuchad most of the budget was spent on buying Hebrew books: IL 4,794.389, in comparison to IL 335 for buying books in other languages.[88]

In Tel-Aviv, where the number of Hebrew-speakers was especially large, the number of foreign-language books in the TAM library kept growing.[89] In 1934, the library's foreign-language books outnumbered Hebrew books by many thousands, and this was the case three years later as well. In the Hakibbutz Hameuchad libraries, where it was decided to earmark nearly the entire requisition budget for Hebrew books, one-third of the books were not in Hebrew. The large number foreign-language books shows that only part of the Yishuv in the 1930s and 1940s was either able or motivated to read books in Hebrew.

A survey of Tel-Aviv's Sha'arei Zion Municipal Library in 1925–26 shows that a large number of readers, mainly students, borrowed books in Hebrew, but many continued to borrow non-Hebrew books. Thus, for example, in the month of Tishrei, readers borrowed 1,456 Hebrew books, 400 in Russian, 111 in German, 99 in English, 85 in French, and 40 in Yiddish. In Adar, they borrowed 1,306 books in Hebrew, 460 in Russian, 102 in German, 89 in English, 67 in French, and 113 in Yiddish.[90] If we take into account the fact that a large part of the books' borrowers comprised students who read only Hebrew, the proportion of adults who read Hebrew shrinks greatly. One may assume, therefore, that a large part of the public continued to read in its mother tongue or in the language of its country of origin. Even when most of the books in the library were in Hebrew, about one-tenth of the readers still read in other languages, and more than one-fifth of the readers read other languages in addition to Hebrew.

Hebrew culture and language were granted a special status and value in the construction of an autonomous Jewish national society in Eretz-Israel. Because of this great symbolic value, cultural entrepreneurs emphasized the differences between the role of Hebrew culture in the Diaspora and its role in Eretz-Israel. In the Diaspora, Jews—even Zionists and Hebrew-enthusiasts—consumed a considerable part of their culture in languages other than Hebrew. In Eretz-Israel they sought totality, exclusivity, and total dominance of Hebrew culture, both in the public sphere and in the private sphere. The official ideology demanded that one must live only in Hebrew and consume culture only in Hebrew: one must not only read Hebrew newspapers and Hebrew books and attend Hebrew theater, but also shout and steal in Hebrew. The national poet H. N. Bialik described his hopes of Hebrew in a conversation (in Yiddish) with Rawidowicz: "*Ich vill oz m'zol alles tun oif Hebraish . . . M'zol oich kakken oif Hebraish, schreien, ganeven, noifen oif Hebraish . . .*" ("I want everything to be done in Hebrew . . . One should shit in Hebrew, shout, steal, commit adultery in Hebrew.")[91]

\* \* \*

Frameworks of non-Hebrew culture were also created in Eretz-Israel, but Hebrew culture succeeded in creating the image that it was dominant in all aspects of life. It seems that one of the great achievements of the Hebraization project was the image of the naturalness, authenticity, and totality of an entire public that lived every aspect of its life in Hebrew.

My study, whose initial findings are presented here, challenges the accuracy of this image. Its power was great, but in practice it appears that the renunciation of other languages and cultures took place only at the official level, as Nissan Torov declared in 1936: "Total 'Hebrews' are, for the moment, the exception."[92] A considerable portion of immigrants were not totally cut off from their original cultures. Those cultures were imported to Eretz-Israel and existed in it alongside the official culture, but like illegitimate children, they were ignored and excluded.

To Prof. Joseph M. Klausner—with many thanks—from the bottom of my heart (literally and metaphorically) for his high level of professionalism and devoted care.

## NOTES

1. Alter Druyanov, *The Book of Jewish Humor and Folk Tales,* vol. 3 (Tel-Aviv, 1962), 165, Anecdote 2636 [Hebrew].

2. *Ha'aretz,* 10 September 1920.

3. Gnazim Institute, Archive, 11575/1, 11576/1, letters to Yitzchak Lamdan.

4. Simon Rawidowicz, *Conversations with Bialik* (Jerusalem, 1983), 76 [Hebrew].

5. Cited by Shimon Shor, *The Hebrew Language Defense League 1923–1936* (Haifa, 2000). 8 [Hebrew].

6. Ibid., 66.

7. Ibid.

8. Rechavam Ze'evi, *A City in its Advertisements 1900–1935,* vol. 2 (Tel-Aviv, 1988), 311 [Hebrew].

9. TAHA, 4a-140, Letter, 12 December 1924.

10. Ibid., Letter, 22 June 1928.

11. Ibid., Letter, 25 June 1928.

12. On the history of the HLDL, see Shimon Shor, *The Hebrew Language Defense League 1923–1936.*

13. Bialik House Archive (BHA), Letter to Chaim Arlozoroff, 8 April 1932.

14. Shor, *The Hebrew Language Defense League,* 12.

15. TAHA, 1b-3, Letter, 2 December 1925.

16. Ibid., Letter, 19 December 1924.

17. Ibid., Letter, 7 December 1924.

18. BHA, Letter, 28 March 1932.

19. BHA, Letter, 9 March 1932.

20. BHA, Letter, 8 April 1932.

21. BHA, Letter, 19 June 1932.

22. TAHA, 4a-140, Letter, 5 September 1928.

23. Lavon Institute (PLI), 2324/19, Letter, 20 November 1924.

24. PLI, 2324/18, Letter, 1 December 1924.

25. TAHA, 4a-140, Letter, 25 October 1933.

26. Ibid., Letter, 2 November 1934.

27. "Proposal for Names of Businesses," *Yedi'ot Tel-Aviv,* 5 (1934), 203 [Hebrew].

28. Ze'evi, *A City in its Advertisements,* 306.

29. Ibid., 310.

30. Ibid., Letter, 19 July 1928.

31. Ibid., Letter, 5 July 1928.

32. Ibid., Letter, 12 July 1928.

33. Ibid., Letter, 8 September 1930.

34. Arye Leyb Pilowsky, "Yiddish and Yiddish Literature in Eretz-Israel 1907–1948" (PhD diss., the Hebrew University of Jerusalem, 1980), 171–172 [Hebrew].

35. Bracha Chabas, ed., in collaboration with Eliezer Shochat, *The Book of the Second Aliya* (Tel-Aviv, 1957), 567–568 [Hebrew].

36. Ibid., 68–69.

37. Shor, *Hebrew Language Defense League,* 67.

38. Arye Leyb Pilowsky, "Yiddish and Yiddish Literature in Eretz-Israel 1907–1948," 103.

39. Ibid., 102.

40. TAHA, 1b-3, Memo, 11 November 1925.

41. TAHA, 1b-3.

42. Ibid., Letter, 3 March 1925.

43. Ibid., Letter, 18 March 1925.

44. Ibid., Letter, 4 March 1926.

45. Ibid., Letter, 6 April 1926.

46. Ibid., Letter, 7 December 1925.

47. Ibid., Letter to Max Cohen, 16 May 1926.

48. Ibid., Letter to H. Jacobowitz, 27 May 1926.

49. Ibid., Letter, 1 May 1925.

50. For example, TAHA, 1b-3, Letters to the America-Palestine Bank, 23 February; Y. Reibstein, 8 March 1925.

51. For example, TAHA, 1b-3, Letters to Y. Cohen, 18 February [Russian]; Mr. A. Tzalal, 31 March 1925 [German]; 4a-140, Joseph Batito, 28 December 1932 [Arabic].

52. TAHA, 1b-3, Letter, 19 November 1925.

53. TAHA, 4a-140, Letter, 12 December 1933.

54. TAHA, 1b-3, Letter, 24 November 1925.

55. Ibid., Letter, 1 December 1925.

56. Ibid., Letter, 9 December 1925.

57. Ibid., Letter, 10 March 1926.

58. Ibid., Letter, 10 March 1926.

59. Ibid., Memo, 4 March 1926, 2:55 PM[!].

60. Ibid., Letter, 10 February 1926.

61. Ibid., Letter, 18 May 1923.

62. Ibid., Memo to TAM secretary Yehuda Nedivi, 11 November 1925.

63. Ibid., Letter, 5 August 1924.

64. Ibid., Letter, 20 January 1925.

65. Ibid., Letter, 17 February 1925.

66. TAHA, A41-140, Letter, 24 January 1933.

67. Ibid., Letter, 25 June 1928.

68. Ibid., Letter, 29 July 1928.

69. Adami, "*Chag Ha-Ivrit*" (Celebration of Hebrew), *Haor,* 3 March 1910, 21.

70. Rafael Nir, "The State of the Hebrew Language in the Process of National Revival," in *The Construction of Hebrew Culture in the Jewish Yishuv in Eretz-Israel,* ed., Zohar Shavit (Jerusalem, 1998), 31–39 [Hebrew].

71. Roberto Bachi, "The Revival of the Hebrew Language as Seen in Statistics," *Lěšonénu*, 20 (1956), 65–82 [Hebrew].

72. Ibid.

73. Ibid., 68.

74. Shmuel Janowski, "Statistical Conversations," *Ha'aretz*, 2 June 1928.

75. Ben-Gurion Archive (BGA), SUU/394, Memo, 30 April 1936.

76. Yeudah Even Shmuel, BGA, SUU/394.

77. Ibid.

78. BGA.

79. Roberto Bachi, "The Revival of the Hebrew Language as Seen in Statistics," 65–82; "A Statistical Analysis of the Revival of Hebrew in Israel," *Scripta Hierosolymitana* 3 (1956): 179–247.

80. "Findings of the Eretz-Israel Census," *Kuntras* 126 (5 May, 1923): 3 [Hebrew].

81. Roberto Bachi, "The Revival of the Hebrew Language as Seen in Statistics," 69, n. 8.

82. Ahad Ha'am, Letter of 27 March 1912, *Letters*, vol. 4 (Jerusalem-Berlin, 1925), 267–268 [Hebrew].

83. Bachi, "The Revival of the Hebrew Language as Seen in Statistics," 72.

84. Ibid.

85. Ibid., 75.

86. Binyamin Poznanski, "On the Cultural Activity in Beit Ha'shitta," *Mibifnim* 13.1 (1948): 129 [Hebrew].

87. Roberto Bachi, "The Population of Israel"; published in the C.I.C.R.E.D series in conjunction with the Institute of Contemporary Jewry, The Hebrew University; and the Demographic Center, Prime Minister's Office (Jerusalem, 1977), 5.

88. Levi Reuven, "The Crop of Hebrew Books in Eretz-Israel in 1944–1945, in Numbers," *Yad Lakoreh* 1.3–4 (1946): 99 [Hebrew].

89. Based on the *TAM Yearbooks, 1938–1939*, 74–75; 1939–1940, 86; 1940–1941, 87; TAM Report 1938–1939, 151.

90. Data based on *Ktuvim A*, 1926, 11.

91. Rawidowicz, *Conversations with Bialik*, 43.

92. Nissan Torov, "On the Psychology of the Hebrew Reader," *Hadoar* 14.10. (1935): 167.

# ELEVEN

# Der Eko Fun Goles: "The Spirit of Tel-Aviv" and the Remapping of Jewish Literary History

*Barbara Mann*

Blessed be the glory of the Lord from his place;
also the noise of the wings of the living creatures. . . .
Then I came to the exiles at Tel-Aviv.
—*Ezekiel 3:12–15*

Tel-Aviv . . . is not Eretzyisroel . . . Tel-Aviv is *goles.*
—*Eretzyisroel in 1937, Sh. Fraylach*

I am the very spirit of Tel-Aviv,
Good morning to you! . . .
White houses under me.
Long, beautiful wide-spread streets . . .
What a difference from Jaffa.
From the narrow, stinking "streets."
Culture, culture!—
Called out from all sides.
—*Reuben Joffe, "I fly over Tel-Aviv,"*
Tel-Aviv: Poema *(Buenos Aires, 1937), 25*

In *Mayne Zibn Yor in Tel-Aviv* [My Seven Years in Tel-Aviv], a Yiddish memoir published in Buenos Aires in 1949, we find the following conversation between two new immigrants in Haifa; one of the men, newly arrived from Warsaw, is considering moving to Tel-Aviv:

I'm going to Tel-Aviv.
Why Tel-Aviv?
Because in Tel-Aviv there are *"goles-yidn"* [Jews from the Diaspora].

Well we've got some here from *goles* as well.
But there are more in Tel-Aviv and I yearn for them,
since the entire European *goles* is confined to the ghetto.[1]

There are a number of ironic reversals contained in this exchange: firstly, Tel-Aviv, the very spearhead of Zionist urban redemption, is a center not for "new Hebrews" or even "new Jews," but for plain old *goles-yidn*. Moreover, the speaker yearns to be with them, precisely because they remind him of home, of *goles*. Thus the entire dichotomy of exile v. homeland is turned upside down—Europe, not Israel, is where the heart is; and Tel-Aviv itself has become *"goles"*-ized, a new home not simply for Jews, but a specific kind of Jew, *"goles-yidn,"* Jews from home.

This ironic exchange between two immigrants in Yiddish will help frame one of the main questions arising from the literary representation of Tel-Aviv, a city whose cultural development coincided with a period of tremendous social, political, and geographic upheaval: how has the depiction of Tel-Aviv challenged, and even undermined, Jewish culture's normative dichotomy between exile and homeland? While modern Hebrew literature has historically traversed a variety of landscapes and spaces in diverse and often oppositional fashion, an essential affinity for exile is, I suggest, at the center of Tel-Aviv's identity as an urban space— an identity that was deeply informed and shaped by the city's literary representation. Perhaps not surprisingly, this connection to exile and the Diaspora found in Hebrew texts is even more pervasive in Yiddish writing about the city.

In order to both substantiate and complicate this claim, this essay offers an interpretive analysis of Reuben Joffe's *Tel-Aviv: Poema*, a book-length series of Yiddish poems published in Buenos Aires in 1937. Joffe's work has not received any critical attention and his book was neither extensively reviewed nor even advertised in the press when it originally appeared.[2] Its naïve and "boosterish" tone is out of keeping with the darker sensibility of Hebrew writing about the Yishuv in the late 1930s. Yet the volume apparently sold well in Jewish communities in Latin America.[3]

The poem seems unique, moreover, in its breadth and detail; certainly very little comparable exists in the Hebrew poetry of this period, in terms of its length and detailed focus on the social and physical geography of the city.[4] Alongside the iconic spaces found in many literary

Fig. 11.1. Book cover of
*Tel-Aviv: Poema* (1937).

depictions of Tel-Aviv such as the sea, Jaffa, the Carmel Market, Habima Theater, and Rothschild Boulevard, Joffe also includes poems devoted to the Yemenite Quarter, Brenner House, the relatively new neighborhood of the Borochov Quarter (today Givatayim), and sites along the Yarkon River such as Napoleon Hill. Joffe's *poema* teems with the business of Tel-Aviv's citizens: shopping, traveling, arguing, eating, and making their way home, to the beach, or to the synagogue on Shabbat. The *poema* is careful to point to the specifics of life in Tel-Aviv, as opposed to that of Jerusalem or what it calls "the colonies," indicating, for example, that although cinemas and theaters are closed on Friday nights, many of the Tel-Aviv's citizens gather for public lectures or communal singing.

Beyond its potential poetic value, the very existence of *Tel-Aviv: Poema* offers an opportunity for examining normative assumptions about Tel-Aviv and the newly emergent Hebrew literary culture in the Yishuv. Indeed, to the extent that our understanding of Tel-Aviv's history has been shaped by its literary depiction, uncovering Joffe's poem and its vision of the city will necessarily complicate those received, normative narratives about the city's origins. This essay constructs a series of lenses through which to read Joffe's poem: the immediate context of contemporaneous Hebrew and Yiddish writing in the Yishuv, especially writing about Tel-Aviv, and the broader domain of space and landscape; the somewhat broader context of the genre of the *poema* or long poem, especially in its Russian incarnation; the tradition of urban poetry in Yiddish literature; and finally, the site of Buenos Aires, both actual and theoretical.

The "thick description" of the *poema* that emerges also serves as a meditation on the limits and boundaries of Jewish literary space: what happens when we add the term "space" to Jewish literary history? On the most elemental level, we gain an appreciation for the specific material, geographic conditions in which different literary texts operate and to which they often refer. In this case, a Yiddish poem about Tel-Aviv, published in Buenos Aires, is found in the New York Public Library; Yiddish journals from Palestine are reviewed in the YIVO archives in New York, themselves relocated from Vilna. Furthermore, Joffe's *poema* becomes the site in which we can begin to interrogate the normative parameters of Jewish literary history. The value of his book lies ultimately in how it asks us to rethink the map of Jewish literary culture—before the war and since.[5]

### Tel-Aviv's Literary Topography: From Hebrew to Yiddish

Clearly literature bears an essential relation to the life and history of any city—one need only think of the visceral nature of Dickens's London, Joyce's Dublin, and Roth's New York to be reminded how crucial a vehicle literature is for the preservation of urban memory. From S. Y. Agnon's epic novel *Tmol Shilshom* [Just Yesterday] (1946), which recorded the city's early life through the eyes of its immigrant protagonist, Yitzhak Kummer, through the evocative and influential prose of Yaakov Shabtai, whose *Zikron Dvarim* [Past Continuous] captured the city's crumbling appeal in a later, postwar period of relative decline and disappointment, Tel-Aviv has become the *de facto* normative setting of Hebrew fiction. In a sense Tel-Aviv's relationship with literature actually predates the existence of the city itself—to the extent that Jewish utopian fiction of the late nineteenth century, culminating in Herzl's *Altneuland* (1902), anticipates some of the modernity and cosmopolitan qualities that came to characterize Tel-Aviv, especially its literary depiction.

Early writing about Tel-Aviv often exaggerated the city's scale and sophistication, describing it as a thriving cultural center when it was barely a village.[6] This gap between Tel-Aviv imagined and the actual city often emerges from the abiding memory of diasporic landscapes within Hebrew writing about the city.

The author of the Yiddish memoir cited at the beginning of this article was so tempted by the appeal of the *goles-yidn,* those Jews from home. Tel-Aviv imagined, especially in its foundational years, and perhaps to a certain extent even still, remains a city haunted by the diasporic homes of its inhabitants.

Hebrew poetic creation, in particular, found strength both in a nostalgic longing for the Diaspora's physical contours and in a valorization of exile's psychological disposition. Modern Hebrew writing might be an interesting subset of what Svetlana Boym has called "ironic nostalgia," that is, an "accept[ance] . . . of the paradoxes of exile and displacement."[7] Poets working in Tel-Aviv during its culturally formative period—the 1920s to the 1940s—were largely modernist in practice; literary modernism privileged both the location of exile and the position of the alienated poet-citizen within the city. Moreover, Hebrew poetry, as a genre, bears a special relation to the situation and trope of exile; the very conditions for poetry, for song, are inextricably linked within the Hebrew literary imagination to Exile. In the famous section from Psalms 137—"By the rivers of Babylon, we lay down and wept"—what begins as a declaration about the impossibility of poetry ("How shall we sing the Lord's song on foreign soil?") culminates in one of the most resonant and memorable series of images in the history of the lyric: "If I forget thee oh Jerusalem, may my right hand lose its cunning, if I do not remember thee, let my tongue cleave to the roof of my mouth" (Psalms 137:1–6). Memory, a necessary by-product of exile, leads to the creation of song, and song becomes the necessary container of memory.[8]

Thus the tension between the native son or daughter, returning to the ancient homeland, and the alienated *flâneur* [an aimless wanderer] possessing anonymity and critical distance, was a formative element of Tel-Aviv's urban imagination. This clash of alienation and attachment, between displacement for the sake of one's poetic sensibility and migration in the name of some transcendental cause, is captured in a couplet from Avraham Shlonsky's well-known poem cycle "In Tel-Aviv" (1927): "I, a Jew, came for no reason/ I, a Jew, returning home."[9] For Shlonsky and other poets of the *moderna,* the European metropolis remained a real and abiding presence within the physical plane of the city, and thus in their work. "In Tel-Aviv" embeds the unique details of the city's emergent public sphere—a caravan of camels, working hands, and buckets of tar, the sound of a *shofar* [ram's horn], cries of a Hebrew newspaper seller, and the boy who sells *gazoz* [soda]—within a typical *Dammerung,* a twilight setting common in European modernist poetry—the lighting of a street lamp, a passing automobile, the neighborhood café.

At the opposite end of the poetic spectrum from Shlonsky's modernist vision, we find a very different drama of the city's "miraculous" creation in Pesach Ginsburg's *Kiryat ha-chol* [Sand Metropolis] (1925),[10] a *poema* narrating the mythic origins of a city in the sands, as viewed through the eyes of a Bedouin tribe.[11] A dervish prophesizes "a great nation comes from afar/ a mighty enemy from the ends of the earth: hundreds, thousands, minions . . . ,"[12] who will populate a wondrous city, which will appear fully formed, hovering upon the sea. When the floating structure emerges from the morning mist, it has neither sails nor masts, and no human presence can be detected. Yet out of this floating set of towers come voices of disbelief and longing—"Is that you my mother, a palm-studded desert: Is that you my mother, golden sand dunes? Is that you who called to me, land of fiery heat and wilderness."[13] In addition to these come voices of nostalgia for "Andalusia, stepmother land, desired and despised,"[14] for "Yemen . . . upon whose chest I wept hot tears," and for the "Ukraine, daughter of sadness, shedding tears/ leaves over the graves of your dead sons."[15] The *poema* concludes as the Bedouin retreat into the desert:

> The Bedouin mount their camels and ride off
> To tell the city-of-palms, work-of-God,
> And the tribes of Nayot, wonders-of-God,
> Who planted an Eden in Zion.
> And a wandering fleet of souls established a city,
> Built *kuryat al ramal* on the seashore.
> And that is the City of Sand, until this day.[16]

Such depictions of a relatively barren land awaiting human intervention are typical of poetry of the Third Aliya (1919–1923); within Shlonsky's
work we can find a more proactive version than that of Ginsburg cited
above. *"Mul ha-yishimon"* [Facing the wilderness], which appeared in
*Ktuvim* in September 1929,[17] has been read as an oblique response to the
violence of that summer in the Yishuv, especially in Hebron and Jerusalem.[18] Briefly, the poem describes a drama between the formerly slum-
bering desert—personified as the "God of the Wilderness" and its native
inhabitants, as they attempt to resist the "civilizing" forces of the Jewish
workers. The land is described as a dormant, mythical space, whose rest
is disturbed by the sounds and instruments of building: shovels, hoes,
cement, tar, hands, and song—the city itself becomes "a song of cement."

In Shlonsky's poem, nature is also viewed as a hostile force, a *hamsin,* for example, threatening the existence of the city. The poem also
motivates a biblical, even mystical register, evoking the image of Jacob's
ladder when describing the movement of pails being passed from hand
to hand. These physical instruments participate in what the poem calls
the "*mered*," an ostensible revolution, perhaps, against the "natural" order, which in the poem is awakened from its slumber and provoked to a
state of revenge; or perhaps the "*mered*" is emblematic of Zionism's revolutionary character, and the desired transformation of "Diaspora Jew"
to "new Hebrew." In either case, the poem's view of nature is such that
the dunes can no longer be viewed as a kind of neutral or pastoral site;
natural space and social space are cast as mythic, even tragic, enemies,
whose meeting inevitably leads to conflict and violence.

Joffe's *poema* is notably different from both Shlonsky's pessimistic
rendering of Tel-Aviv as another stop along the modernist way, and his
exhilarating vision of the city struggling against a politically charged
natural landscape; it also has no truck with Ginsburg's redemptive, Orientalist vision of a struggle between nature and culture, between native
and interloper, and begins with the city fully formed.

Hebrew symbolist poetry of the 1930s sought to depict Tel-Aviv as
a universalized space, an arena for the age-old struggle between nature
and civilization, out of which an urban space, *ex nihilo,* is borne; this
vision of Tel-Aviv as "a city like other cities," urban fruit of Zionism's
dream of "normalcy," is the implicit core of Hebrew renderings of the
city. These literary depictions all contributed to the city's narrative of

origins, and indeed, its modernity. In contradistinction, Joffe's *poema,* with all its gritty particularity of street and marketplace, reminds the reader of the more mundane details of this landscape. Its narrator wonders not at the mythological efforts of the pioneers, but over the simple existence of a Jewish policeman (who presumably spoke Yiddish!). Furthermore, the very existence of the *poema* in Yiddish, a language of the Jewish Diaspora, undermines the ostensible "co-dependence" between Hebrew and Tel-Aviv (see below). In offering a somewhat different literal and figurative view of the city, Joffe's *poema* points to the necessarily constructed quality of the familiar Hebrew narratives.

Both temporally and spatially, the *poema* begins on the edge, between two realms—at dawn and by the narrator's bedroom window, which takes place mostly outdoors, in the city's public spaces. The situation of this opening scene suggests that the entire *poema* may indeed be a dream.[19] Or is the dream-world's fantastical state simply the best way to depict Tel-Aviv? The first-person narrator is awakened in his darkened room:

> I hear how someone knocks,
> quiet and distinct
> and wonder to myself
> who . . . disturbs my sleep?

The same knocking is heard at the window and the speaker rises angrily, opening the shutters to let the bright sun stream in:

> Someone touched my hand.
> I can't see anyone,
> I'm afraid. . . .

And then a voice is heard:

> I am the very spirit [*geist*] of Tel-Aviv,
> Good morning to you!

And so the adventure begins.

Over the course of sixteen separate poems from "Tel-Aviv Appears" to the concluding "*Der eko fun goles*" [The Echo of Exile] the reader is treated to a "tour" of Tel-Aviv's sites and sounds by, it seems, a supernatural incarnation of the city itself. Together they fly over the city viewing it largely from above.

I do not consider *Tel-Aviv: Poema* a newly discovered masterpiece. Part reportage, part travelogue, it is imaginative in parts, sentimental in others, generally engaging and informative, but except for the single zany idea of Tel-Aviv's *geist* never truly inventive on a poetic level. Nor does it contain any of the ironic friction of contemporary Hebrew verse, which made much of the implicit comparison between Tel-Aviv's relative "youth" or "infancy" and the cultural maturity and weight of the European metropolis. Part of the poem's value may be how it leads us to reexamine our normative assumptions regarding the near-synonymous relation between Tel-Aviv and Hebrew—encapsulated in the by-now clichéd phrase "the first Hebrew city."

Although this synchronicity between the city and its language may seem too entrenched to deserve comment, a few observations are in order: the name "Tel-Aviv" came from the title of Nachum Sokolov's translation of Herzl's *Altneuland*—the newness of spring will emerge from the ancient roots of an archaeological site. Yet what does it mean in fact for a city to be "Hebrew"—the phrase suggests a role for the Hebrew language over and above linguistic competency, and alludes to the broader domain of culture, and the concatenation of values associated with the Zionist project: new, forward-looking, pioneering, healthy, fresh, connected to the land. The fact that the city is described as "Hebrew" during a period in which most of its citizens spoke other languages—both at home and on the street—should lead us to critique the connection between the place and the terms of its description. This is precisely what the existence of *Tel-Aviv: Poema* asks us to do. Does Tel-Aviv look different in Yiddish? Does this difference extend beyond elements connected to individual artistic sensibility? If we compile a set of traits common to Hebrew poetry about the city in the interwar period, a kind of poetic DNA for early Tel-Aviv, how does Yiddish deviate, and how not? Broadly speaking, I suggest that Yiddish writing about Tel-Aviv, such as the author's longing for *goles-yidn,* sensitizes us to the imagined city's exilic qualities. *Tel-Aviv: Poema* seems to stretch the very geographic norms of Jewish literary production, almost *ad absurdum:* a Yiddish poem about Tel-Aviv, published in Buenos Aires.

Yael Chaver has elegantly described in her work on Yiddish prose fiction, that in the Yishuv, Yiddish writing during the interwar period was often more inclusive than contemporaneous work in Hebrew, and also more oppositional vis-à-vis the predominantly Zionist norms of the day. Yiddish prose in its Palestinian period was characterized by what Chaver calls a kind of "social heterogeneity," which allowed for a wider variety of ethnic, social, and linguistic representation.[20] Furthermore, Yiddish depictions of the public sphere during Tel-Aviv's riotous *adloyada* [carnival-like] Purim celebrations were likely to include extended observations of Moslems and Christians as they themselves observed the costumed Jewish revelers cavorting in the streets.[21] Notwithstanding the efforts of the Hebrew Language Defense League, Yiddish was often noted in early accounts of the city as a marker of intimacy and familiarity in the newly emergent public sphere. Beginning in the late 1920s, numerous Yiddish "little magazines" started to appear, and continued into the early years of the state.[22]

Poetry and fiction in these Palestinian Yiddish journals seem almost wholly taken with the Zionist tableau of working the land, individually or *batsavta* [as a group]. The landscapes depicted are largely pastoral, and the narratives follow the travails of protagonists who move from settlement to settlement, from one collective group to another. Given the largely socialist political leanings of Yiddish authors, the consistency of these themes is not surprising. (For example, one poem begins: "Red—is the clothing of my muse . . ."[23]) Perhaps writing about urban life with the exception of Jerusalem, seemed both too diasporic and bourgeois for these writers, who were already facing the stigma of writing in Yiddish, not Hebrew, ostensibly the language of national redemption. Furthermore, the outrageously anti-realist tone and supernatural underpinnings of *Tel-Aviv: Poema* went against the grain of a fictional enterprise that sought to represent a pioneering lifestyle, with the nitty-gritty vernacular details of an emergent national society.

An interesting assessment of Yiddish literary views of poetry about Tel-Aviv may be inferred from a critique of contemporaneous Hebrew literature, published in *Shatmen* in 1938. The article reviews the achievements of recent Hebrew writing in the Yishuv and finds them wanting; Hebrew literature has no tether to the traumatic reality of contemporary life and has not successfully depicted the revolutionary sea changes shaping modern experience: "something has shaken up the world—and this shaking has not been heard in modern Hebrew literature." Yosef Chaim Brenner is one of the "few who have been possessed by the deep, creative discontent of the new Jewish man [*nayem yiddishn mentsch*] in the land of Israel."[24] The reviewer cites favorably some lines from Shlonsky's *Mul ha-yishimon* [Facing the Wilderness] and Uri Zvi Greenberg's *Hagavrut ola* [Masculinity rising] (both from the 1920s), and also mentions Lamdan's "Masada" and David Shimonovitch's *Sefer ha'idilyot* [The Book of Idylls], but the article concludes with a mostly damning assessment of what Hebrew literature has not accomplished: the reviewer wonders why contemporary Hebrew literature has not yet produced a poet "who will unroll the heroic megilla of Jewish workers in the Land of Israel." "Where is the new Hebrew drama," the reviewer asks, and what of the Hebrew women poets, "Anda Pinkerfeld, Elisheva, Leah Goldberg, Bat Miriam . . . does not the scent of cafés drift from their poetry?"[25] In a single sentence, the writer condemns "women's writing" as well as the ostensible decadence and "feminized" quality of both city life and poetry about it; instead the writer calls for the great "Eretz-Israeli novel, grand stories that should reflect our fortunate and tragic existence."

This view demonstrates the normative disposition of Zionist critical thought, which viewed literature in particular, and culture more broadly, as deeply harnessed to the national project: "great" literature, the only kind worth writing, must address the "great" themes. Given the particular ideological and thematic yardstick described here for Hebrew literature, the expectations for Yiddish writing may have been even more severe. It's no wonder, then, that Tel-Aviv appears so infrequently in Yiddish writing of the period; perhaps it should not surprise us that the question of canonicity, so central in this period in Hebrew literary history, also shapes the development of critical categories for Yiddish as well.[26]

Joffe's work does seem to draw on the generic conventions of the Russian *poema* and the *feuilleton* [editorials], two related forms that rely on an impressionistic, highly subjective view of the city. While these forms may also be found in Hebrew and Yiddish writing, Russian literature provides an especially illuminating context, where the *poema*'s long history is intimately connected to the depiction of urban space.

## The *Poema* Travels from Petersburg to Tel-Aviv

What exactly is a *poema* and what examples might Yoffe have had in mind when composing such a work that seems to be *sui generis*? In the most fundamental sense, the *poema* is a hybrid form made up of both lyric and narrative components; it often contains supernatural elements, and sometimes epic and comic as well as parodic elements. Already a mixed genre, the *poema* has most expressly rubbed against the grain of generic expectations when connected to urban space. The most well-known example of the modern *poema* is Pushkin's "The Bronze Horseman: A Petersburg Tale" (1833), which describes the establishment of Petersburg. According to cultural historian Julie Buckler, "Works whose titles pair the 'Petersburg' designation with an explicitly generic term . . . often seek to confound the very categories they invoke—most notably, Pushkin's 'Tale'."[27] Buckler views the *poema* as the foundation of St. Petersburg's urban mythology, an exemplary instance of "literary eclecticism," a style that deliberately deploys a diverse assortment of canonical and non-canonical texts. This literary mode approximates the architectural eclecticism of St. Petersburg's main social and cultural thoroughfare: Nevsky Prospect.[28] Eclecticism also left its mark in Tel-Aviv, especially in the older neighborhoods surrounding Rothschild Boulevard; with its public gardens and architectural diversity, Rothschild has itself served as a kind of substitute for Nevsky Prospect in Tel-Aviv's cultural imagination.

Was Joffe trying to endow Tel-Aviv with the kind of grand history that typifies the treatment of place, especially urban space, in the Russian *poema,* in a time when the city itself was in search of a "usable past"? To answer this question, we must look briefly at Pushkin's "Bronze Horseman" (1833). Despite the enormous differences between the two works, some telling points of comparison may be drawn. Puskin's *poema,* subtitled "A Petersburg Tale," relates the story of the founding of St. Petersburg, beginning with the vision of Peter on the Neva River; it then leaps forward in time to narrate the misfortunes of the protagonist Evegeny, who suffers the loss of his fiancé when the city is flooded, and who eventually confronts—in surreal and hallucinatory fashion—the city's founder, as embodied in the statue of the bronze horseman in the city's central square. (This element of fantasy is perhaps found in Joffe's poem in the device of the "*geist.*")

Initially, the city is envisioned by its founder Peter as both a bulwark and a "window into Europe,"[29] symbolizing the tension between "Westerness" and "Russianness" that characterized Russian culture in the nineteenth century. A similar cultural tension characterizes the establishment of Tel-Aviv, a product of both "Europe" and "the Levant," of Diaspora and homeland.[30] St. Petersburg is also expressly imagined in competition with another, older Russian urban space: "Now time-worn Moscow has grown dim/ beside the youthful capital/ Just as a purple-mantled widow/ Seems pale beside a new queen."[31] This description of the city as a woman, and the comparison of the "new queen" to the ancient "widow," recalls imagery used to depict Tel-Aviv in relation to Jerusalem.

Finally, Pushkin's poem details a furious storm in which the city is flooded as its citizens look helplessly on: "The restless Neva thrashed and roared/ And like a cauldron steamed and boiled./ Then all at once, a maddened beast,/ She pounced upon the helpless city."[32] The conflict between nature and the city, in which urban space is brutally attacked, even victimized, by the forces of nature recalls the "battle" between the forces of nature and the city in Shlonsky's *Mul ha-yeshimon* [Facing the Wilderness]. The lines of what Chana Kronfeld calls "historical inter-texuality"[33] that may be drawn here create a dizzying, multi-directional network: does Shlonsky parody Pushkin, creating for Tel-Aviv a sensational drama of "Hebrew" workers conquering the sands? Does Yoffe parody Shlonsky's pretensions to write an epic poem about such a young city?[34] Or were they both trying to parody the young Natan Alterman?

Alterman seems to be the key figure in the background of Joffe's *poema*, particularly his *feuilletons*—short, humoristic essays about Tel-Aviv published during 1932–1935. Alterman sequestered the "high" from the "low"—the great odes of *Stars Outside* from the lighter lyrics of his *Shira kala* (published under the suggestive title of "*Regaim*," literally, "moments" but also (?) "throwaways"). Surely we can now also see the connections between the two bodies of work. Like the *poema*, the *feuilleton* is a hybrid, sub-canonical genre with a historical connection to urban space. Something of Joffe's poem resembles the parodic quality of Alterman's essays. Although scholarship has convincingly situated Alterman in relation to Baudelaire's Parisian *flâneur*,[35] the canonical model *par excellence* of literary modernity, Joffe's *poema* provides a kind of missing link to this other, somewhat bawdier, literary urban space—the Russian boulevard of the *feuilleton* and the *poema*, of Pushkin, Dostoevsky, and Gogol.

These three urban qualities—a tension between localness (Russian or Mediterranean) and Europe; a "youthfulness" in relation to another,

more established city; and a conflict with the natural surroundings—
recalls the work of Yuri Lotman on the mythology of Petersburg.[36] In
a semiotic analysis of Petersburg and its symbolism, Lotman raises the
distinction between concentric and eccentric cities, cites of the edge and
cities of the center. Concentric cities, according to Lotman, inevitably
represent something larger themselves, usually the state or the divinity:
the classic example is, of course, Jerusalem, though Rome and Moscow
are also mentioned. The topographic imagery of concentric cities is usually connected to a mountain or hills, while "eccentric" or edge cities are
"situated 'at the edge' of cultural space: on the seashore, at the mouth of
the river."[37] These edge cities draw not on the contrast between earth and
heaven (e.g., *Earthly Jerusalem, Heavenly Jerusalem*), but on the distinction between nature and artifice: "the city is founded as a challenge to
Nature and struggles with it."[38] So St. Petersburg struggles, again and
again, with the waters of the Neva River. Tel-Aviv, in its imagined foundations, struggles again and again against the sands, and sometimes
even with the sands' natives.

### Flying over Tel-Aviv: "You Must See Jaffa"

The aerial view in Joffe's poem bears some resemblance to the utopian,
ultra-modern vision of urban space found in Herzl's *Altneuland*—for
example, the electric train that zips around above that novel's imagined
port city of Haifa. More significantly perhaps, the *poema*'s aerial views
and focus on the physical and commercial infrastructure of the city
(transportation, municipal services, commerce, and culture) recall the
kinetic dynamism of the city as depicted in cinema of the interwar period, especially Carl Mayer's 1927 *Berlin: Symphony of a City*. Although
Mayer's film, and interwar German cinema more broadly, offered a critique of modernity that is absent from Joffe's work, the *poema* does
present the city as a collage of human activity and mechanistic devices, a
place where old meets new and the consequences are neither uniformly
positive nor predictable. Perhaps an even better cinematic comparison
may be found in films prepared by the various Jewish national institutions in the 1930s, whose scenes of Tel-Aviv's emergent public sphere featured repeated images of banks and policemen, as if to assure the viewing audience of some semblance of civic order and economic stability.

The speaker and his winged feminine companion visit a variety of settings around the city. After their initial encounter in his bedroom, the speaker is borne upon Tel-Aviv's "little wings and deposited at the corner of Allenby and Sheinkin,"[39] where they encounter a traffic accident between a scooter and a donkey-drawn wagon. Next they visit *Shuk Ha-Carmel* and the city's multiethnic, mercantile scene—the street where "both sides come together"[40] and Arabs merchants ply their goods in Yiddish: *finif for a piastre* [five for a piaster]. Just down Allenby from the *shuk* is the city's Great Synagogue (the poet certainly knew his topography). Nearby, someone has set up a gramophone and a crowd has gathered, including a mailman and a "Jewish policeman" side by side, listening to a *chazanishe shtiklech* [bits of cantorial music]. This tableau is too good to be true, depicting as it does an idyllic scene of a new Jewish municipal culture—the mailman and the cop pausing within the public sphere to appreciate some remnant of the *alteheim* [old home]: as Tel-Aviv explains, "in a Jewish state, one listens to Jewish music."[41]

However, Tel-Aviv insists the city's true essence is revealed in its *politiker*—the "statesmen" of Rothschild—who gather on benches on both sides of the boulevard to discuss matters of the day (such a scene is truly an iconic staple of many early accounts of Tel-Aviv). Their conversation revolves around the responsibility for building the Jewish state. One older man asks sarcastically:

> —Who has built the Land of Israel?
> The Zionists?
> Herzl?
> I'll tell you, this is all a godly thing/God's work
> God built it!
> He sent people here—
> He threw out the Turks
> It was all by his power . . .[42]

On the one hand, the poem has nothing but praise for Tel-Aviv's earthly creations. On the other, these merely human efforts pale in the face of the divinity, and its supernatural ambassador: the "Land of Israel" and the immediate surroundings of Tel-Aviv are truly a "godly thing." Finally, as opposed to the often ambivalent contrast between Tel-Aviv and the capitals of Europe found in Hebrew poetry of the day, this poem expressly compares Tel-Aviv to European cities and finds them equals. Moreover, while there are many grand cities in Europe, Tel-Aviv's uniqueness lies in its solitary status within the Levant; the poem rhapsodizes that "a jewel among jewels is not so noteworthy, but a jewel in a heap of stones shines."[43] This idea squares with that of another contemporaneous Yiddish source that viewed Tel-Aviv as "a speck of Europe in the middle of Asia."[44]

One extended depiction in the early part of the poem focuses on the topography of Jaffa, a city that the *geist* insists he must see. The stereotypical depiction of Jaffa squares with the Hebrew literary norms of the day: "narrow stinking narrow alleyways" filled with "dirt, / merchandise lying in the streets. . . ." Some of the Arab merchants are blind from "living unhygenically." From a café—the smell of nargillahs and "wailing music." Though possessing a kind of "ancient distinction,"[45] Jaffa is described as untouched by *yiddishe kultur,* meaning—modernity. This Orientalist ambivalence—a distaste for what is perceived as the city's current condition mixed with admiration for its ancient pedigree—typifies contemporaneous Hebrew writing about Jaffa, a city largely figured as Tel-Aviv's "other," an ancient doppelganger in need of rehabilitation.

One poem in Yoffe's book, titled "After Eating," offers another, slightly different vision of Jewish-Arab relations in the city:

> Later in the street,
> in the heart of the city
> I saw the spirit no longer.
> On the widely spaced balconies
> all the families could be seen,
> warming themselves in the sun,
> and this is how winter was in Tel-Aviv . . .
> An Arab with a sack on his back
> walking down Rambam Street,
> crying out first in Hebrew,
> then in Yiddish:
> - Old pants! Old shoes! . . .
> A little Arab girl was running around
> with flowers [*blumen*]
> - Flowers, flooow-ers!. . . . [*prachim . . . prachiiiiiiim*]

Unlike other poems in the series that target a particular landmark or historical site, this poem describes an ordinary street in the heart of the city. Jewish families rest on the balconies, a liminal space that is one of

Tel-Aviv's defining architectural features, and an important symbol of the strong link between public and private spheres.[46] Below them, an Arab—the very figure of the wandering Jew with a sack on his back—hawks *alte zachen* [old things], still a ubiquitous call in some Tel-Aviv neighborhoods. The language of the mercantile sphere is Hebrew and Yiddish—a young girl, instead of selling *alte zachen,* sells flowers.

This idyllic scene offers some of the ethnic and linguistic capaciousness that characterizes Yiddish literature of the Yishuv. We may also distinguish the older Arab figure, who addresses his audience in the language of the *alteheim* from the younger Arab figure, the girl who speaks only Hebrew.[47] The tableau is in keeping with the notion of Yiddish as a language that is always somehow in dialogue with the lowest social classes.[48] Notably, Yoffe's poema brings us a Hebrew scene embedded in Yiddish, suggesting Yiddish's historical role in preserving certain semantic spheres of older, rabbinic terminology. Thus the view of language envisioned in this instance is almost a traditional Jewish polylingualism, where different languages play distinct functions within a single cultural and social system.

## The Echo of Exile

The last portion of the *poema* tours the areas surrounding Tel-Aviv, including Ramat Gan, Shchunat Borochov, and Har Napoleon by the Yarkon. On observing the physical and cultural achievements of Tel-Aviv's citizens, the speaker breaks into song:[49]

> *Hava neranana, hava neranana*
> Hitler is forgotten
> Jewish troubles and pain are forgotten
> Forget the bloody Jewish life

In the wake of this outburst, the poem turns to contemplate the Jewish population abroad, and lists the urban centers of Jewish life in the Diaspora: the *Grenadierstrasser* of Berlin, the East Ends of New York and London, Vienna's *Leopoldshtadt,* the *pletzel* of Paris, the cities and *shtetlach* of Poland, Rumania, and Lithuania.[50] Yoffe's book ends with an extended five-page poem *Der eko fun goles* [The Echo of Exile][51] that describes the memory of Diaspora life, in which scenes of anti-Semitic violence are rendered in gruesome detail. The hyperbolic excessiveness of these passages, and the placement of this section at the *poema*'s conclusion, serves to deflate its otherwise sunny optimism; these reminders of what Tel-Aviv's citizenry have left behind powerfully contrast and undermine the catalogue of vibrant normalcy that constitutes the rest of the poem.

It could be that the nightmarish vision of these concluding pages is what led to the book's particular cover, an expressionist cartoon-like vision by someone named Becker. The cover shows the Tel-Aviv shoreline, crowded with tombstone-like buildings that look as if they are about to topple over and be engulfed by the sea. Alternately, what is figuratively depicted as the shoreline might more literally represent a tear in the paper, or an incomplete drawing. In the cover's lower right corner, a secondary drawing confined to a circular frame depicts a household scene, turned upside down with violence, similar to the pogrom described within Joffe's poem. There is also bright red blood on the floor; this same red is repeated in the letters of the book and author's name, and in some details of the figure popping out of Tel-Aviv's buildings. Is this the figure of the poet—wide-eyed, bushy-haired, open-mouthed, and dressed in a suit and tie? His oversized thumb (!) either represents his pen or, equally likely, is a phallic symbol. In either case, he offers it to the scene before him, and it is loosely echoed by the smaller, no less grotesque, image of the boy's red fingers in the smaller picture below. His skin tone is remarkably dark (in relation to the cover as a whole); indeed, a similar sort of "self-darkening" of skin tone as a mark of nativeness characterizes Reuven Rubin series of portraits from the 1920s. This combination of unusual physical characteristics suggests an agitated, oversized persona that is out of proportion to the physical landscape. Finally, the cover's depiction of Tel-Aviv and Europe does not seem to coincide with their representation as near-polar opposites of Jewish existence, within the body of the *poema*. An editor in Buenos Aires may well have added it, with or without the author's permission.

The tension between the cover and the *poema* further heightens the confusion surrounding the book and its provenance, and the biographical obscurity of its author, whatever his name is; as far-fetched as it may sound, I suggest we imagine that Rueben Joffe himself never stepped foot in Tel-Aviv. Indeed, until there is evidence to the contrary, we cannot know for sure. If, as I have proposed, the literary depiction of Tel-Aviv produced powerful narratives of historical origins, it is conceivable (perhaps even serendipitous) that a Yiddish poet, sitting in some location distant from Tel-Aviv—be it Buenos Aires, New York, or some other "center" of Jewish life, or even in a *shtetl,* making daily trips to the local reading library—could indeed imagine himself as "transported" to contemporary Tel-Aviv, to view its sites and sounds in much the same fashion as Joffe's narrator is borne on the wings of the *poema*'s female *geist.* It is a mark of the success of Tel-Aviv's literary existence that the *poema* holds out this tantalizing possibility. At the same time, however, the very existence of this Yiddish rendering of the city points to the general instability of Tel-Aviv's literary depictions; Joffe's *poema* is a site that thus tends to compromise and undermine those very paradigms upon which it depends for legibility.

It is only at the *poema*'s conclusion that it comes to resemble, in significant ways, the gritty realism or even surrealism that characterizes modernist poetic visions of urban life. Therefore, we should ask, what other kinds of literary inspiration might a Yiddish poet in the 1930s have drawn on while contemplating a poetic treatment of the urban scene? To begin with, we can simply note that the level of urban detail in the *poema,* was perhaps more possible in Yiddish in this period, given the plethora of Yiddish writing set in the city. This seems an almost mathematical kind of calculation—there is more Yiddish writing about the city than Hebrew writing, because there are more cities where Yiddish is spoken and written. Or rather fewer cities where Hebrew is the dominant language of vernacular literary expression, and only one city—Tel-Aviv—where the connection between Hebrew and the urban object of its affection is absolutely essential, a bond which is, arguably, equally important for both the evolution of Hebrew literature and the development of the city.

We must look beyond the territorial confines of modern Hebrew literature, and ask: might this poem's "real cousin" be the New York work of Moshe Leyb Halpern? Given the wide influence of Halpern's 1919 poem cycle *In Nu York,* one might suspect inspiration, if not exactly influence. I do not pretend to claim here that we have discovered a Tel-Avivian Halpern (we already have the young Uri Zvi Greenberg for that). For one thing, Yoffe's work is distinctly, almost obsessively, local in its reference, a far cry from the largely symbolic, allegorical, role that New York plays in Halpern's work. The poems themselves are worlds apart in terms of their aesthetic temperament; however, *Tel-Aviv: Poema* shares with Halpern's *In Nu York* an appreciation for how the passage of time is experienced in the city: both poem cycles begin at daybreak and end at night. Could the violence of the *poema*'s last section—*Der eko fun galus*—be itself an echo of Halpern's *A Nacht,* with its brutal nocturnal evocation of a pogrom? Is this how Yiddish city poem cycles by Jewish immigrants in the interwar period inevitably conclude—even if they are about Tel-Aviv, the center of the new homeland? *Tel-Aviv: Poema* seems to anticipate what will only begin to permeate Hebrew later in the 1930s, that is, an awareness of the catastrophe unfolding in Europe.[52]

There are, of course, other long Yiddish poems about cities in this period that perhaps even evoke and elevate an idea of Jewish urban space. One such set of urban poems that provides a revealing context for Joffe's work may be found in the *landsmanschaft* journals written in New York in the interwar period. Though not as highly regarded as their more canonical Yiddish contemporaries, these poems provide a fascinating window into the experience of immigrants as they move out of Europe and into New York's urban landscape. The poems about Vilna, Lodz, and other cosmopolitan centers of Jewish life were characterized by what Rebecca Kobrin calls the "shtetlization" of the Eastern European city; these city centers were in fact reimagined as intimate, and *shtetl*-like, a process Kobrin associates with both the writers' sense of the catastrophe and ruin in Europe, coupled with the alienating modernity of New York's streets.[53] Ultimately, Joffe's *poema* bears the same kind of relation to canonical Tel-Aviv poetry, to the symbolist, universal city of Shlonsky and Alterman that the *landsmanschaft* poems have toward the great, lyrical urban voices of American Yiddish modernism. In both instances, and within the larger parameters of Jewish literary history, these sub-canonical genres provide a fascinating counterpoint to those normative genres and themes of Jewish literary expression.

Another context for Yoffe's *poema* is the tradition of travel writing in Yiddish literature. Joffe's poem does not give us the kind of seasoned traveler familiar to us from Yiddish fiction, a figure caught in the ironic tension between movement and stasis; instead we find a poetic speaker in the grip of the abject wonder of the newly arrived, whose naiveté and optimism is shattered by the poem's conclusion. Historically speaking, Yiddish literature in Europe has often created an imagined sense of Jewish space. As Dan Miron has shown in his work on the *shtetl*, and Leah Garrett more recently in her book on Yiddish travel narratives—Jewish characters inhabited and moved through these imagined Jewish spaces in increasingly modern fashion, always inevitably looking back at the terrain of the homeland left behind. Tel-Aviv may also be understood as an imagined Jewish space to be moved toward, and through, and even over (in the case of the *geist*), and this movement (especially the aerial view, one might argue) is expressly related to Jewish cultural and political autonomy.

* * *

Tel-Aviv in these years is more than an imagined city; especially in the 1930s, when *Tel-Aviv: Poema* appears, a visceral part of Tel-Aviv's reality, as well as that of the surrounding Yishuv, is violent. It may not be surprising to note the absence of local violence in Yoffe's *poema*. Hanan Hever has written precisely of such a lacuna in Hebrew symbolist verse of the period; he argues that the space of the sea in early modern Hebrew culture offered a seemingly neutral terrain, whose smoothness represented an unconflicted, pastoral domain—everything the actual land was not.[54] It could be that the extensive use of the aerial perspective in Yoffe's *poema* is an example of this discourse of displacement, related both to the local landscape, and to the violence in Europe, the violence at home.

Finally, it seems appropriate that such a book would be published in Buenos Aires, itself a contested urban space, where the relation between territory, language, and ideology was a topic of debate among Jewish writers. In contemporaneous Yiddish and Spanish writing in Buenos Aires, not the city but the *pampa,* the countryside—home of Gerchunoff's famous "cowboys" was considered the site of Jewish renewal. Here, too, we find the same type of disqualification of urban experience that characterized the production of literature in the Yishuv. Moreover, the very existence of *Tel-Aviv: Poema* disrupts conceptual boundaries, severing the tie between geography, nation, and language that is so crucial in the Yishuv in the 1930s.[55] Substantively, the *poema* as a whole moves beyond the physical and imaginary borders of Tel-Aviv, creating a visceral, lateral connection between Jewish writings about urban life in ostensibly disparate settings. In spite of the poem's express claim for Tel-Aviv's achievement as an urban center and its arguments for the distinctiveness of a *yidishe shtot*, there is a palpable sense that the experience of *goles* remains alive and well, for better or for worse, in the hearts and minds of the city's inhabitants. Yiddish is a reminder of Tel-Aviv's failure to be truly new, of its ultimate psychological dependence on some other space, that place which it thought it had left behind.

## NOTES

The second epigraph comes from Sh. Fraylach, *Eretzyisroel in 1937: A reyze iber shtet, kolonyes un kfutsos* [Eretz-Israel in 1937: A journey through colonies and collective settlements] (Buenos Aires, 1938), 47.

1. Z. Segalowicz, *Mayne Zibn Yor in Tel-Aviv* (Buenos Aires, 1949), 23.

2. There is no mention of the book in either *Di Tsukunft* (New York) or *Literarisher Bleter* (Warsaw), two major journals of the period. There is no mention of either Joffe or his work in the Yiddish "little magazines" published in Palestine in the 1920s and 1930s. The title is included in a list of Yiddish publications by the Committee for the Twenty-fifth Jubilee of *Di Prese, Literatur in Argentina 1944* (Buenos Aires, 1944), 932.

3. I am grateful to Robbie Pekarer for his anecdotal account of seeing copies of Joffe's book in Jewish libraries in Argentina and elsewhere in Latin America.

4. With the notable exception of Shlomo Skulski's *Ashira lach Tel-Aviv: aluma shel sonetot* [Tel-Aviv Sonnets] (Tel-Aviv, 1947). For a general discussion see Dan Miron, *Reysheeta shel shirat Tel-Aviv* [The Beginnings of Tel-Aviv Poetry] in *Irve-Utopia: A collection of material in honor of Tel-Aviv–Jaffa's 80th Anniversary*, ed. Haim Luski (Tel-Aviv, 1989), 184–207 [Hebrew], and my comments below. Portions of Natan Alterman's *Kochavim Ba-chuts* (1938) constitute a *poema*, of sorts, devoted to Tel-Aviv. See below the connection between Joffe's work and Alterman's *feuilletons* from the 1930s.

5. Barbara Mann, "Literary Mappings of the Jewish City: Other Languages, Other Terrains," *Prooftexts* 26.1–2 (2006): 1–5.

6. Nurit Govrin, *Literary Geography: Lands and Landmarks in the Map of Hebrew Literature* (Jerusalem, 1998) [Hebrew].

7. Svetlana Boym, "Estrangement as Lifestyle: Shklovsky and Brodsky," in *Exile and Creativity: Signposts, Travelers, Outsiders, Backward Glances*, ed. Susan Suleiman (Durham, NC, 1998), 241. On this phenomenon in Hebrew writing see Barbara Mann, *A Place in History: Modernism, Tel-Aviv, and the Creation of Jewish Urban Space* (Stanford, 2006).

8. For a thought-provoking illumination of this tension in modern Jewish writing see Sidra Ezrahi, *Booking Passage: Homecoming and Exile in the Modern Jewish Imagination* (Berkeley, CA, 2000).

9. Avraham Shlonsky, *Shirim II* (Tel-Aviv, 1971), 73 [Hebrew].

10. Ginsburg's brother Shimon also authored a long poem about a city, "New York—Poema," in 1937.

11. Pesach Ginsburg, "Sand Metropolis," *Hashiloach* 44 (1925): 62–68, 131–142. All citations are from this version.

12. Ibid., 66.

13. Ibid., 132.

14. Ibid., 133.

15. Ibid., 134.

16. Ibid., 142.

17. Shlonsky, *Shirim II*, 226–236.

18. Hanan Hever, *Pitom mare hamilchama: leuimyut ve'alimut bashirat shenot ha'arbayim* [Nationalism and Violence in Hebrew Symbolist Poetry] (Tel-Aviv, 2001); and Yochai Oppenheimer, *The Right to Say No: Political Poetry in Israel* (Jerusalem, 2003) [Hebrew].

19. The *poema*'s opening evokes Ezekiel's vision of Jerusalem and the Temple, which begins with a visitation from a divine messenger, a "man who shone like copper" (Ez. 40:3).

20. Yael Chaver, *What Must be Forgotten: The Survival of Yiddish in Zionist Palestine* (Syracuse, 2004), 67.

21. Mann, *A Place in History*, 149–153.

22. Chaver, *What Must be Forgotten*, 120.

23. Papiernikov, *Shtamen: Bleter fun literarishe un kritik* [Roots: An anthology of literature and criticism] (Tel-Aviv, 1938), 4. [*Royt—/ iz dos kleyd/ fun mayn muze . . .* ] [Red is the clothing of my muse].

24. Y. Ch. Biletzki, *Mikoyach der nayer hebreisher literature* [The power of the new Hebrew poetry] *Shtamen* (Tel-Aviv, 1938): 18–19.

25. Ibid., 19.

26. For a broad and provocative discussion of these themes in Hebrew literary culture, see Michael Gluzman, *The Politics of Canonicity: Lines of Resistance in Modernist Hebrew Poetry* (Stanford, 2003).

27. Julie A. Buckler, *Mapping St. Petersburg: Imperial Text and Cityshape* (Princeton, 2005), 65.

28. Ibid., chapters 1–2, esp. pp. 64–88. For example (p. 78), "Beginning in the 1830s, Petersburg's main boulevard, Nevsky Prospect, came to exemplify the growing eclectic trend in architecture and was represented in literature according to the same aesthetic principles."

29. Alexander S. Pushkin, "The Bronze Horseman," in *The Ardis Anthology of Russian Romanticism,* ed. Christine Rydel (Ann Arbor, 1984), 151.

30. Mark LeVine, *Overthrowing History: Jaffa, Tel-Aviv, and the Struggle for Palestine* (Berkeley, 2005).

31. Pushkin, "The Bronze Horseman," 151.

32. Ibid., 152.

33. Chana Kronfeld, *On the Margins of Modernism: Decentering Literary Dynamics* (Berkeley, 1996).

34. According to Dan Miron, Alterman's *feuilleton Hazon hagmalim* [Vision of the camels] was also a parody of Avraham Shlonsky's work; see "The Beginnings of Hebrew Poetry in Tel-Aviv," 200 [Hebrew]. On the sense of history in Alterman's journalistic prose see Mann, *A Place in History,* 90–94.

35. Dror Eydar, *Alterman-Baudelaire: Paris–Tel-Aviv—Urbanyiut vemitus bashirey pirchey haro'a vekochavim bachutz* [Urbanism and myth in Baudelaire and Alterman] (Jerusalem, 2003).

36. Yuri Lotman, *Universe of the Mind: A Semiotic Theory of Culture* (Blooming-ton, IN, 1990).

37. Ibid., 192.

38. Ibid., 192.

39. Joffe, *Tel-Aviv: Poema,* 9.

40. Ibid., 14.

41. Ibid., 19.

42. Ibid., 22.

43. Ibid., 26–27.

44. Hersh-David Nomberg, *Erets-yisroel: Anyduken un bilder* (Warsaw, 1925), 15.

45. Ibid., 12–13.

46. The balcony is featured in another part of the *poema,* where it also represents the city's relative liberalism and open qualities, 39.

47. The girl's emergent multilingualism recalls a well-known set piece from one of the earliest works of Hebrew prose fiction written in Palestine, Y. Ch. Brenner's 1909 novella, *Nerves,* a work generally characterized by linguistic instability. Toward the end of the story, a young woman walks the streets of the unnamed "colony" and gracefully sings a combination of Yiddish, Hebrew, and Arabic.

48. I am grateful to Julian Levinson for this point, and for drawing the connection between Joffe's work and the depiction of landscape and social class in the Yiddish *poema Kentucky* (1925), where black dialect is rendered in Hebrew script.

49. Ibid., 49.

50. Ibid., 55.

51. Ibid., 55–59.

52. Alterman was already making this connection in some of his work. See Hever, *Pitom mare hamilchama.*

53. Rebecca Kobrin, "The Shtetl by the Highway: The East European City in New York's Landmanschaft Press, 1921–1939," *Prooftexts* 26 (2006): 107–137.

54. Hever, *The Zionist Sea: Symbolism, and Nationalism in Modern Hebrew Poetry* (Jerusalem, 2007), 20–21 [Hebrew].

55. Edna Aizenberg, *Parricide on the Pampa: A New Study and Translation of Alberto Gerchunoff's* Los gauchos judios (Madrid, 2000).

# TWELVE

# A Poet and a City in Search of a Myth: On Shlomo Skulsky's Tel-Aviv Poems

*Aminadav Dykman*

Poems about cities are among the oldest known to us. We have lines about the city of Erekh in the Babylonian *Gilgamesh* epic; and, what is the *Iliad* if not (among other things) the story of the fall of a city? One need not mention the poetic passages about Jerusalem in the book of Psalms. Different city-myths are delicately woven into the odes of Pindar, and Ovid has left us a most vivid and dramatic poetic version of the founding of Rome.[1] Major cities, such as Paris or Moscow, have large bodies of poetry incorporated into their literary history.[2] Poems about cities are not limited to cities with a long history. In the vast corpus of city-poems in various languages there are poems that deal with young or newly founded cities. An example is Vladimir Mayakovsky's hymn to the city and workers of Kuznetsk, written for the expansion and renaming of that Siberian coal-mining center in 1929:

> [ ... ] In four
>
> years
>
> a garden-city
> will be here!
> [ ... ]
> I know—
>
> The city *will* be
>
> I know—
>
> The garden *will* flourish,
>
> Since there are
>
> Such people
>
> In the Land
>
> Of the Soviets![3]

In the hundred years that elapsed since its foundation, Tel-Aviv has produced a fair body of poetry. Some of the leading poets of the Hebrew language wrote about Tel-Aviv during different periods, among them such towering figures as Natan Alterman, Avraham Shlonsky, and Leah Goldberg, or, in more recent times, David Avidan, Nathan Zach, and Meir Wiseltier. Dan Miron has described and analyzed the bulk of this body of poetry in his seminal study.[4] Yet many lesser-known, but not less intriguing poetic texts that deal with Tel-Aviv still await proper study.

This essay focuses on Shlomo Skulsky's 1947 collection of poems *Let Me Sing to You Tel-Aviv*. To the general reader Skulsky means little, if anything. Students of Hebrew literature may remember him as a gifted translator of poetry, and a prolific writer for children. Older Israelis, especially those linked to the Revisionist political movement, may remember him as the author of several celebrated poems of the genre generally known as "songs of the underground movements," the Irgun and Lehi.

Born in a small Polish town in 1912, Skulsky studied at the Academy for Hebrew teachers in Wilno, and took up a career as a schoolteacher. For several years he was the editor-in-chief of the Hebrew-language children's magazine *My Country*. Not much is known about his life under the Nazi occupation in Poland. However, from the scant information given in the preface to his collection of poems, and from what can be deduced from the poems themselves, we learn that he fled to the Soviet Union, spent some time in the Gulag as "a prisoner of Zion," and later joined the anti-Nazi partisans. In 1941 he managed to reach Palestine, where he was arrested by the British police and interned in the infamous camp at Atlit. A fervent supporter of the Revisionists, he soon joined the Tezel underground, and was active in the party's youth movement Betar. Having earned a BA in humanities from the Hebrew University of Jerusalem, Skulsky again worked as a schoolteacher in various institutions in Ramat-Gan and Tel-Aviv. Alongside his pedagogic career, he continually worked as a translator, writer, and literary editor (for more than a decade he edited the literary supplement of *Herut,* the organ of the Revisionist movement, until its demise in 1966). His main occupation was in the field of children's books; according to one source, he published over a hundred, both original and in translation.[5] Shlomo Skulsky died in Tel-Aviv in 1982.

## "Ashirah Lakh Tel-Aviv"

During his lifetime, Skulsky published only two collections of original poems, and two other books of poetry in translation. Both translated volumes were from the works of the Polish national poet Adam Mickiewicz: the dramatic poem *Konrad Wallenrod*,[6] and the epic poem *Grazyna*.[7] Skulsky's first collection of original poems, titled *From Among the Pieces,* an intended allusion to the "covenant of the pieces" of Genesis 15, was published in Tel-Aviv in 1942.[8]

His second book of poems was published five years later. *Let Me Sing unto You, Tel-Aviv* is a collection of sonnets, each of which deals with a different facet of the city, or a theme directly related to it. Skulsky gave his book the subtitle "A Sheaf of Sonnets." This generic definition bears affinity to the better-known form of "sonnet-wreath" (or *corona*), a form that was introduced into Hebrew poetry by the poet Shaul Tchernichowsky, who also gave it its Hebrew appellation, *kelil-sonetot.*

In view of Skulsky's Polish cultural background, and his more than occasional acquaintance with the poetry of Mickiewicz, it is reasonable to assume that the initial idea of casting his poetic thoughts about Tel-Aviv in the form of a collection of sonnets was inspired by the latter's famous cycle of *Crimean Sonnets* (1826). Mickiewicz's cycle was probably in the mind of Tchernichowsky, who also wrote a cycle of Crimean sonnets in the 1920s. However, Skulsky's endeavor was more ambitious: instead of a cycle of fifteen sonnets (as in a *corona*, or in Tchernichowsky's cycle), or eighteen sonnets (as in Mickiewicz's cycle), *Let Me Sing unto You, Tel-Aviv* consists of seventy-two sonnets, which makes it in fact, a mini-*canzoniere*,[9] whose heroine is not some Petrarcan flesh and blood Laura, but the abstract feminine figure of the city of Tel-Aviv.

At the head of his book Skulsky placed an epigraph from Ezekiel (36:10), which leaves no doubt as to his general conception of Tel-Aviv. The verse in question runs thus: "and I will multiply men upon you, all the house of Israel, even all of it: and the cities shall be inhabited, and the wastes shall be builded." This quote directly relates to the one incorporated into the city's official emblem, "again I will build thee, and thou shalt be built." All seventy-two sonnets were written in the same pattern: *abababababcdcdcd.* Skulsky divided his book into five sections, each bearing a title: "In Your Paths," "Your Dwellings," "Your Feast-days," "In Exultation," and "Your Future Fate."

The opening sonnet (which, like the closing sonnet, stands out of the main collection) is titled "I Love You." The function of this sonnet is clear: apart from serving as a prologue, it also defines the entire book as a continuous love poem, which is precisely what a *canzoniere* should be. The opening quartet offers a precise definition of the essence of the city:

> You are dear to me, Tel-Aviv, my lovely city, / Hebrew town, you are indeed dear to me! / My vision, rescued-and-brought to the land of our fathers, / that was poured in concrete upon the barefootedness of sands.

He combines the words *ha'ir ha'ivrit,* "the Hebrew town." It is common knowledge that this appellation was the kernel of the foundational myth of Tel-Aviv.[10] The entire city is described as a materialization of a "vision poured in concrete,"[11] upon bare sands; this too belongs to the same foundational myth. In the following quatrain, up to the sonnet's end, Skulsky starts weaving a new myth for Tel-Aviv:

> City, one forgives you your wandering, in a dance, / the wind blowing in your dress, / [looking] like a capricious girl, — / Ah, but I know your soul:—in it, a fire is burning, / coals, carved from my Holy City [...] // for you are the daughter of old-age [*bat-zekunim*] of your mother, Jerusalem.

Skulsky here reacts to a well-known aspect of Tel-Aviv's reputation, namely, its being a "frivolous," even hedonistic town.

As Maoz Azaryahu has shown, written expressions of this attitude can be traced back to 1915.[12] Skulsky, however, offers his reader an "explanation" of this frivolity—Tel-Aviv is all jumpy because she is young, burning with the fire implanted in her by her mother, Jerusalem. A possible literary source for this myth involving a mother-daughter personification of two cities (one old, the other newly founded) can be found in Alexander Pushkin's poem "The Bronze Horseman" (1836). In Pushkin's poem the relationship is indeed somewhat different, but the "deep structure" is the same:

> A hundred years have passed, and the young city,
> [...] splendidly has risen.
> [...] and before the younger
> Capital, ancient Moscow has grown pale,
> Like a widow in purple before the new empress[13]

A strong image from Pushkin's "Bronze Horseman" may also be behind the mythical picture depicted in the opening sonnet of the first section, "A Street and a Square." The first quatrain of this sonnet informs the reader he is about to hear a wondrous local legend, "woven on the spindle of [passing] days [ . . . ] ever since 1909." The city itself tells the story of Meir Dizengoff's wedding. Actual geographic locations (Dizengoff St. and Dizengoff Circle) are turned into mythical material:

> My groom extended his arm to his bride, gave her a gift, / put a sacramental ring [on her finger], and said "you are hereby . . ." // . . . "and his arm turned into a street / and the ring turned into a crowning square — / and the Dizengoff couple was thus married in me forever . . .

This "legend," with its almost primitive element of metamorphosis, is actually an artificial etiological myth in the best Ovidian tradition. It "explains" why Dizengoff St. is straight, and why the square is round. At the closing line of the sonnet, the straightness of the street is given yet another semiotic value: "and his arm commands: Grow, City, for you are yet small!" The founding father of the city is metamorphosed into the city itself. His "gesture" reminds one of Pushkin's lines concerning the posture of the statue of Peter the Great, the bronze horseman himself:

> What thought
> Was on his brow, what strength was hidden in him!
> And in that steed what fire! Where do you gallop,
> Proud steed, and where will you Plant your hoofs?
> O mighty master of fate! Was it not thus,
> Towering over the precipice's brink,
> You reared Russian with your iron curb?[14]

The only difference is that Pushkin's genius leaves the question of the symbolic steed's course open, while in Skulsky's modest sonnet there is no enticing ambiguity.

### Poetic Topography

In the first two sections of his book, Skulsky turns his attention to specific sites in Tel-Aviv. Read as a sequence, his sonnets are designed to represent a panorama of the city. Many of the sonnets revolve around familiar landmarks: Rothschild Boulevard, the sea shore, the seven sycamore trees, the Yarkon River, the Mahlul shanty town, London Square, the Tel-Aviv port (the first four sonnets form an itinerary along the beach), the Town Hall, Magen David Square, Meir (Dizengoff) Park ("Gan Meir"), the Yemenite quarter, the house where Ahad Ha'am lived, Habimah Theatre, the zoo, the town funeral hall on Mazeh St., the maternity ward on Balfour St., and, finally, the Tel-Aviv cemetery on Trumpeldor St.[15]

These two sections are obviously arranged as a tour of the city, and as a kind of itinerary of life, from birth to death. These two itineraries are interwoven, and have different protagonists: the city itself, and its generalized dweller.

Skulsky published his book in 1947, which by that point in time already had a well-established tradition of Tel-Aviv poetry, whose undisputed leader was Natan Alterman.[16] Following one of the most common poetic moves in this tradition, which was also brought to its peak by Alterman, Skulsky depicted his Tel-Aviv as a living organism, whose different parts (or limbs), be it streets or shop windows, are all endowed with a life of their own. The same is true for the actual living entities that populate this organism, the citizens of Tel-Aviv themselves. The organism in question has but one aim: to grow ever larger. This notion is overtly expressed in the last sonnet of the opening section of the book. Its title is an unequivocal imperative: "Grow!"[17] The tercets read:

> Harness my city, asphalt reins, / hands, rush the houses to the race! / City, drop the rein that binds you, the Yarkon [River]; / westward, unto the sea, and let the water recess! / push eastwards, southwards and to the north—and may you grow, / and fill all space as you fill my heart with joy.

Many of the sonnets of *Let Me Sing unto You, Tel-Aviv* read like mere exercises in rhetoric, cast in sonnet form. Many of the themes treated by Skulsky were also quite common in the corpus of Tel-Aviv poetry. The description of the wind as the desert's revenge for the city's domination over the sands, "Hamsin" (p. 48), or the quasi-futuristic depiction of Allenby St. as a gigantic conveyor belt that revolves between two squares "Allenby, My Machine" (p. 14), or the sonnet "Sons of Tel-Aviv" (p. 67), which ends with the trite rhetorical question: "Are there such people in any other town?"

However, in some of Skulsky's sonnets one finds a thought, a formulation, or a point of view that is innovative. Let us briefly examine two such cases. In a sonnet titled, simply, "Houses" (p. 29), Skulsky offers a symbolic (and also political) interpretation of Tel-Aviv's overall architectural view. The upright new houses, he wrote, all standing apart remind one of those upstanding wealthy Jews who, in traditional synagogues, used to claim a privileged place near the eastern wall. The description ends with a rhetorical question: "Is there any Hebrew house which is that proud?" In the old country, continues the poet, the houses stood in a different manner: clinging together, crowded against each other. The "meaning" of the new architectural order is expounded in the closing tercet:

> And even though the brotherhood [of those houses] is not common among you, / my feelings, [o you] "upstanding ones," burn for you — / for the brotherhood of slaves—[is the] toy of Fear.

Tel-Aviv's multilingual environment and the "language war" for the exclusive supremacy of Hebrew are well known. The celebrated poet Zalman Shneur (1887–1959) wrote an acid description of the linguistic situation in Tel-Aviv of the 1940s:

> In Yiddish, Russian, or Polish / a man greets his friend innocently. / "Who is speaking a foreign language? . . Hush . . . Shhh!? Hebrew, and Hebrew only!"[18] / shouts the voice of the oppressing "Battalion." / This is a voice from heaven, and no one can change it,— / in Tel-Aviv.

Skulsky was clearly on the side of Hebrew (and Hebrew only). When describing London Square, "Next to London Square" (p. 21), he does not forget to "forgive" the city for the sin of giving the square a foreign name. He elaborates on this theme of the good fight against foreign names in an interesting sonnet titled "Straight and Crooked [Ways]" (p. 84). The streets of Tel-Aviv, he writes, are like an open book. Each morning stroll is also a reading of the book of Chronicles. The names of heroes, martyrs, and men of genius excite feelings. Each street and square is a lit commemorative candle. However, "Sometimes I stand astounded, and ask: / What is this foreign name in your midst? / it clings to the past of the Jewish people like a skin-disease."

However, in another sonnet, "Melodies of My Street" (p. 19), Skulsky turns the multilingual reality of Tel-Aviv into a charming image:

> Not the call of the cock, another voice wakens me, / the call "maransi, maransi!" [Arabic: "oranges, oranges!"], which coughs the Arab; / the sun

just started to shine through the cracks of the shutters, and I hear / the melody of the greengrocer: "vegetables, grapes!" [ . . . ] The shouts of your vendors [sc. Tel-Aviv] became my clock, which urges me / to welcome a new day and leave my bed.

The following shouts, at different hours of the day, are in Yiddish and Hebrew: "old stuff!" at noon, "white clothes!" in the afternoon, and "lots of news!" at dusk.[19]

## "No Legends Were [Ever] Created in You"

As one progresses through the last two sections of *Let Me Sing unto You, Tel-Aviv,* Skulsky's overall vision of the city becomes clearer. In his excellent paper on the "Eretz-Israel" genre in Hebrew poetry, Shlomo Har'el successfully demonstrates how poets of the First and Second Aliya were constantly subordinating what they actually saw before their eyes (i.e., concrete details of scenery they had viewed) to abstract visions charged with historical past.[20] Examples of this phenomenon are legion. Shmuel Bass (1899–1949), in his sonnet about a nocturnal pilgrimage to "Gush Halav,"[21] describes the fog-covered Mt. Atsmon in one line: the other thirteen lines deal with what was not actually there—a spiritual vision of the armies of the celebrated first-century rebel John of Giskala.

The problem with Tel-Aviv was that it had no glorious historical past or magnificent architecture. The poet Yitzhak Katzenelson (1886–1944) highlights this "non-mythical" quality in the nursery-rhyme-like poem he wrote to honor the city in 1934,[22] "[In this city] there are no golden castles, there is no / royal palace, no king; but who is comparable in beauty? / Who is comparable in splendor?" What Tel-Aviv lacks in mythical beauty is compensated for in human warmth:

> This white city—good people / live in those whitewashed houses; / when a man meets a man in the street — / [it is] a friend who meets a friend. // It is warm [in this city], one feels good, as in a mother's womb, / stones laugh out of the walls[23] — / can you name this city? / Tel-Aviv is that city's name.

Skulsky was well aware of this problematic quality of Tel-Aviv. He treated it in a separate sonnet, whose title is self-explanatory: "No Legends Were [Ever] Created in You" (p. 92):

No legends were [ever] created within you, [o] city, / the mouths of elders
did not embroider a veil of secrets for your head; / there is no grand-
mother laden with years who tells / of ghosts, of horrors, of pogroms and
blood . . . // No downfall and destruction to spread illness in your foundations, / the horrors of the past do not lay heavy upon you; / Daughter of the
desert! You grew up in freedom, a poetess, / you are all legend, you are an
undreamt dream . . . // When I hear your voice from under the pier,— / it
sounds [to me] not the roar of my ancient heroes, / as do the rocks of the
City of David, when my heart listens [to] her voice . . . // It is not the story
of my zealots that had left its mark on you . . . / But your proud brow tells
me": I shall be courageous, / I will astound [sc. everybody] with a legend
about new mighty men! . . .

The idea that Tel-Aviv was a "freeborn" city, free of the heavy burden
of Jewish history, was certainly not new. Nor was the notion that this is
the main difference between this city and Jerusalem. However, Skulsky
does offer an innovative "solution" for the problem of a non-existent
mythical past: simply, Tel-Aviv's mythical aspect is to reside not in its
past, but in its future. Tel-Aviv, according to him, is predestined to become a mythical city. The same idea is behind his semiotic interpretation
of the city's emblem (in the sonnet "City Hall," p. 31):

Every city in the world chooses for its symbol / the heroic memory which
throbs in it in a commendable manner, / a witness of the splendor of its
emblem, a true witness, a crown of [its] past; // you chose a shield for
your emblem, fixed a lighthouse in the middle, / your lit tower shall be
the crown of your future.

The first stage in this mythical existence of the future seems to be
Tel-Aviv's replacement of Jerusalem. In a sonnet titled "A Hebrew City"
(p. 82), Skulsky depicts Tel-Aviv as a city within which "lies the star of
David," where "synagogues pray with their domes Jewish prayers, silent
supplications," as opposed to Jerusalem, where the sky is "wounded with
the tops of minarets and their crescents." Maybe, wrote Skulsky, a day
will come when God will bring to Tel-Aviv, as he will to Jerusalem, the
might of David, announcing its coming not with gunfire from mosques,
or the din of church-bells, "but with the sound of the Jewish shofar, the
shofar of the messiah." The final sonnet in *Let Me Sing unto You, Tel-Aviv*
develops this theme in full:

I know that you too, like your mother Jerusalem / are waiting for your miraculous groom to appear — / She, your mother, stretches her hands to him from her rocks, / you, her daughter, are waiting for him, pining— // he shall come, as dawn [comes] on the edge of the horizon, / you will mount your roofs to welcome him, / he will come . . . in all your beauty you will cast down your eyes before him, / lifting your veil for the kiss of your beloved one. //—mounted on a white she-ass, girdled with azure wreaths, / he will appear, don you with a marital crown, / consecrate your marriage to him with a sacramental ring. // Then your mother will come closer, feel him, smell [his wreaths?] / a tear of joy will tremble between her eyelashes: / yes, my daughter, here he is! Your messiah king has come!"

In view of Skulsky's fervent support of the Revisionist movement, and considering the date of the composition of his book, there can be no doubt as to the interpretation of this sonnet. The coming of the messiah is simply the end of British rule over Palestine. In another sonnet, titled "An Organ With No Strings" (p. 76), Skulsky writes: "the voices of megaphones on top of every antenna / will break the news of your liberation to the wide world: 'Listen to the voice of redeemed Tel-Aviv!'." The pairing of words "redeemed Tel-Aviv" was usually reserved for "redeemed Jerusalem." There is every reason to believe that in his political poetic vision Skulsky was following the footsteps of Uri-Zvi Greenberg. Greenberg, the undisputed bard of the Revisionists, made ample use of the symbol of the messiah in his lofty political poems of the 1930s and 1940s. As the case may be, Skulsky's poetic "proposal" to substitute Tel-Aviv for Jerusalem in the context of political redemption can certainly be seen as a surprising innovation. What, then, is the overall vision of Tel-Aviv as it emerges from this *canzoniere*? A new Jewish town's destiny will replace both Jaffa, as "queen of the seas,"[24] and Jerusalem as well, a city whose destiny is to become mythical, though it has no mythical past.

### "I Remember Your Youth: A Tiny Neighborhood"

Skulsky came to Palestine in 1941, having lost his family in the Holocaust, and having been imprisoned in a Soviet Gulag. This autobiographical aspect of his poetic persona is reflected in a few sonnets of *Let Me Sing unto You, Tel-Aviv*. Yet at the same time Skulsky deliberately assumes another persona, that of a pioneer, one of the first builders of his beloved city. This is particularly evident in the sonnet "Your First Street" (p. 4), which deserves to be translated in full:

> I remember your youth: a tiny neighborhood, / small as an olive, humble as the Sabbath; / yet you have a gate, and a chain — / no one shall cross your doorstep—here you alone dominate! // A diligence—your vehicle, squeaking, barely advancing, / crawling [through] "Nablus Road" towards Jaffa, slowly . . . / Devastation hurling sand-storms over you, / Shmuel Hager's broom fights it alone. // The first "boulevard," the soda shack, / Dr. Hisin swaying on his donkey each day, / the first water-cistern, which filled it [i.e., the city] with bubbling light of life. // You were still small, yet cast a longing eye / over *abed-al-nabu* hill, over the crooked "Sea Path," / and commanded the sea to extend at your feet.[25]

Skulsky is personalizing memories that could not be his own. The scenes and places he depicts go back to the period between 1910 and 1929, decades before he actually came to live in Tel-Aviv. Yet he seems to be suggesting that a true son of this city must have such memories, in the spirit of the Passover Haggadah: "in every generation, let one consider himself as if he came out of Egypt personally."

There is no point in pretending that *Let Me Sing unto You, Tel-Aviv* is a forgotten masterpiece written by an unduly neglected poet of genius. Rather, it is a mediocre, at times a feeble, collection of sonnets; nevertheless, it is most interesting, both for its unusual form and for its almost unique vision of Tel-Aviv as a mythical city *par excellence*.

## NOTES

1. Cf. Ovid, *Fasti*.

2. Pierre Citron's monumental two-volume study *La Poésie de Paris dans la literature française de Rousseau a Baudelaire* (Paris, 1961). For Moscow, see E. G. Basova and S. G. Kondratenko's anthology *Stikhi o Moskve* (Moscow, 1997) [Russian].

3. Full Russian text, Vladimir Vladimirovich Mayakovsky, *Polnoe sobranie sochinenii* (Moscow, 1958) 10:128–213.

4. Dan Miron, *Founding Mothers, Step Sisters: The Emergence of the First Hebrew Poetesses and Other Essays* (Tel-Aviv, 1991), 181–245 [Hebrew].

5. Cf. G. Kressel, *Lexicon of Hebrew Literature in Recent Generations* (Tel-Aviv, 1967), 2:537 [Hebrew].

6. Adam Mickiewicz, *Konrad Valenrod*, trans. into Hebrew by Shlomo Skulsky (Jerusalem, 1944) [Hebrew].

7. Adam Mickiewicz, *Grazhina*, trans. into Hebrew by Skulsky, Tversky (Tel-Aviv, 1950).

8. So dated by Kressel; Kressel, *Lexicon of Hebrew Literature in Recent Generations*, 536. The book itself is not dated.

9. *Canzoniere* [Song Book] is the name of Francesco Petrarca's book of poems (also called *Rime sparse* [Scattered Verses]). Of the book's 336 poems, more than 300 are sonnets. In later times it became customary to dub any large collection of sonnets (which are not arranged as a *corona*) a *canzoniere*.

10. Maoz Azaryahu, *Tel-Aviv: Mythography of a City* (Syracuse, 2006).

11. The Hebrew text may have an additional pun to it. Skulsky here uses the verb *mulat*: in classical Hebrew this would mean no more than "was rescued." However, it is also possible to read the verb as a derivation of the noun *melet,* which in Modern Hebrew signifies "concrete, cement." The verb here would thus mean both "was rescued" and "was [cast in] concrete."

12. Azaryahu, *Tel-Aviv,* 69.

13. D. M. Thomas's translation. See Alexander Pushkin, *The Bronze Horseman and Other Poems,* trans. by D. M. Thomas (London, 1982), 247–248.

14. Ibid., 256.

15. On Rothschild Boulevard and the Trumpledor cemetery see Barbara Mann, *A Place in History: Modernism, Tel-Aviv, and the Creation of Jewish Urban Space* (Stanford, CA, 2006).

16. Dan Miron, *Essays on Literature and Society* (Tel-Aviv, 1991), 264–265.

17. Skulsky, *Let Me Sing unto You, Tel-Aviv* (Tel-Aviv, 1947), 22.

18. Shneur's *pointe* requires an explanation. His poem is written in Ashkenazi Hebrew (trochaic tetrameters). The improbable vocalization of the word *ivrit* [Hebrew language] signals that this exclamation is pronounced in Sephardic Hebrew. This is to be expected, since the members of "The Battalion for the Defence of The Hebrew Language" were opposed to not only Yiddish and all other foreign languages, but also to Ashkenazi pronunciation of Hebrew.

19. The first exclamation, which can still be heard in Tel-Aviv (yet in an abbreviated form—"*alte zachn*" only), belongs to the petty merchants who used to buy used household items of all sorts. I found no explanation for the second exclamation. The last exclamation obviously belongs to vendors of evening newspapers.

20. Shlomo Har'el, "The Eretz-Israeli *Genre* in Poetry," in *Turning Points in Hebrew Literature in Relation to other Literatures,* ed. Ziva Shamir and Avner Holtzman (Tel-Aviv, 1983), 201–212 [Hebrew].

21. For the text of this sonnet, see *Selected New Hebrew Poetry,* ed. Asher Barash (Jerusalem, 1930), 454 [Hebrew].

22. "Tel-Aviv" was published in the *Bulletin of Tel-Aviv Municipality* (Tel-Aviv, 1933–34): 2.81 [Hebrew]. The editors added an announcement: "The poet Yitzhak Katzenelson, whose poem is hereby printed, is currently visiting Eretz-Israel."

23. Obviously an intended reversal of the celebrated verse in Habakkuk 2:11: "for the stone shall cry out of the wall."

24. See the sonnet "The Sorceress and the Charming One," 83. The messiah, who appeared at the end of the previous sonnet, will hear the song of Tel-Aviv and will enter the city, turning his back on Jaffa.

25. I was unable to identify Shmuel Hager. "Nablus Road" led from Jaffa to Saronah and Nablus. "The Sea Path" was the road later named after General Allenby (1918). The first soda shack appeared in 1926, at the crossing of Herzl St. and Rothschild Boulevard.

# THIRTEEN

# Decay and Death: Urban Topoi in Literary Depictions of Tel-Aviv

*Rachel S. Harris*

"This city doesn't deserve to exist. This is just a misunderstanding."

The founding and growth of Tel-Aviv reverberated with the ideology of Jewish national revival and the quest to build a modern Jewish city different than both the Jewish *shtetl* in East Europe and the cities of the Levant. The Tel-Aviv creation narrative focused positively on the constructive energies of urban pioneers engaged in building the first Hebrew city.[1]

Although criticism of Tel-Aviv, mainly from the Labor Zionist establishment (which preferred an agricultural ideal), existed from the very beginning of the city's construction, forbidding descriptions of the urban landscape were rarer in fiction and poetry. It was not until the 1970s—late in comparison to portrayals of the city evident in Europe—that writers adopted negative universal urban topoi, widespread in European and American literature, to depict Tel-Aviv. Imagery representing the urban environment as a place of alienation, decay, disillusionment, and failure, with its attendant sexual, financial, and moral corruption, has been adopted and adapted in Israeli fiction. Writers increasingly depict Tel-Aviv society as decadent and corrupt; the city is portrayed as a monster; while the *flâneur* protagonist is shown to be isolated and alone. The city is depicted frequently with dark, forbidding streets, and a seedy underworld dense with corruption and prostitution.[2]

Given the powerful Zionist rhetoric of Tel-Aviv in its foundational phase, in adopting modernist urban tropes in literary depictions of Tel-Aviv, authors were engaged in challenging the traditional Zionist narrative of Tel-Aviv, even suggesting that the city did not stand up to its reputation as a thriving metropolis or that Tel-Aviv betrayed the Zionist ideals that underlay its founding. In this essay, I consider four literary works that share the centrality of Tel-Aviv in the narrative and the suicide of one or more protagonists: Ya'akov Shabtai, *Past Continuous* (1977), Binyamin Tammuz, *Requiem for Na'aman* (1978, 1992), Yehudit Katzir, *Closing the Sea* (1990), and Etgar Keret, *Kneller's Happy Campers* (2000).

In these texts, the dark portrayal of Tel-Aviv indicates the realization of the mythological city first imagined in literary form. Tel-Aviv's success lies in its normalization and its similarity to other modern cities. Literary depictions of negative urban tropes challenge the city's mythological foundations but reinforce the claim that Tel-Aviv is indeed a city like any other. By emulating Western models, the real city echoes the universal urban experience. Nevertheless, even in the later literature of the 1990s and 2000s, it is clear that Hebrew fiction acknowledges the distinctly local characteristics of Tel-Aviv. In adopting urban literary topoi to convey Tel-Aviv, Israeli writers present a new city while simultaneously reinforcing an old idea: Tel-Aviv is a hybrid between East and West, myth and reality.

## Nostalgia for the Lost City of Tel-Aviv

Set in Tel-Aviv in the 1970s, Shabtai's *Past Continuous* describes three discontented middle-aged friends (Goldman, Israel, and Caesar) and the founding generation of their parents. The novel opens with the death of Goldman's father, and the information that Goldman commits suicide exactly nine months later. As a result, all the events in the novel are presented within the framework of death.

In a form of escapism, *Past Continuous* reflects the nostalgic attitude that had taken hold in the 1930s in the longing for the "small and intimate neighborhood where everyone knew everyone else."[3] By constructing "a monolithic and naive panoramic picture with sand dunes, white buildings, blue sea, and sky," Shabtai reinforced a myth echoing the "messianic and utopian spirit that ha[d] pervaded the entire Zionist project."[4] Thus Shabtai tapped into both the reality of the 1970s and the idealized attitude toward Tel-Aviv's early years.

Shabtai's immortalization of Tel-Aviv juxtaposes the image of the decaying city of the 1970s with a nostalgia-laden perception of Tel-Aviv's foundational era during the protagonist Goldman's youth. Through Goldman, Shabtai presents the longing for a childhood landscape that has now been vanquished: "The empty lots and gardens and parks and little woods and virgin fields . . . had now disappeared and given way to streets lined with apartment complexes and offices and commercial and industrial areas."[5] This depiction corresponds to the "Nostalgic sentimentality [that] was prevalent mainly among old-time residents, for whom the disappearing cityscapes were associated with the geography of childhood."[6] The novel's popularity and canonical status derive from Shabtai's encapsulation of the Labor-oriented elite's fears during a period when the decline of the political and cultural hegemony of the Labor movement became increasingly manifest.

The novel's nostalgic longing represents this particular moment in Tel-Aviv history and contrasts sharply with the city's earlier political narrative that celebrated urban development. In 1951 a monument to commemorate Tel-Aviv's founders "told the story of Tel-Aviv as one of the transformation of a sandy wilderness into a blossoming, modern city."[7] Yet in Shabtai's novel the personification of the city as a "crazy creature" expanding over the "vineyards and the melon patches" distresses the character Baruch Chaim. Unable to keep up "with all the new houses and roads and factories," Baruch Chaim represents a challenge to Tel-Aviv's "build and be built" mythology—a triumphant construction narrative made official in the city's motto. Shabtai inverts this narrative in *Past Continuous,* suggesting that the building of Tel-Aviv had a destructive effect on the local landscape. Moreover, the story documents a sense of estrangement from the city: "[H]is pride was mixed with a feeling of distress because the city was slipping away from him and making him feel like a stranger."[8]

This ambivalence toward the city's formation also utilizes the traditional topos of alienation within the urban landscape. As Goldman witnesses the process of deterioration and destruction in the city, he conflates the annihilation of the old landscape with the influx of a new population: "The town, which in the course of a few years had been filled with tens of thousands of new people, who in Goldman's eyes were invading outsiders turned him into a stranger in his own city."[9] Georg Simmel observed the alienating effect of the thronging metropolis, where strangers lived side by side.[10] However, for Goldman the strangers are newcomers and invaders: his alienation evinces a sense of loss of familiarity with "his city."

By portraying a space filled with strangers as well as longing for the sands of the nostalgic past, Shabtai contests the notion of the success of building something new and wholesome in Tel-Aviv, a city that would be "[S]omething clean, beautiful and healthy." It seemed wrong—"anti-Zionist"—to exchange the conditions of a European ghetto for a Middle Eastern one.[11]

Shabtai's novel confronts this vision of a modern city through the character Grandma Clara's despair. After having dragged Grandpa David from the Diaspora because of her involvement with groups promoting a "Love of Zion," she is soon disheartened to discover the discrepancy between her dreams and reality.

> [A]mong the square white houses and glaring wastes of sand which got into her shoes, and sometimes even into her food, in the harsh light of the sun, in the dusty, fly-filled heat, she felt alien and deceived, and many years had to pass for this feeling to fade a little and lose its sharpness, but in the meantime she expressed her disappointment in a stream of Yiddish and Polish and Russian curses and a flood of abuse and angry, indignant complaints.[12]

In this dystopian representation of the city under construction, Tel-Aviv was an exhausting, ugly, and chaotic place. The sand in Grandma Clara's shoes, the symbol of the desert and the Orient, indicates that the city had not become the European metropolis that it was intended to be. Simultaneously, the use of Yiddish, Polish, and Russian curses signifies Tel-Aviv's failure to escape the burdens of European ghetto life. For Goldman, the sand's reappearance is both nostalgic and a challenge to the narrative of its banishment in the emergent metropolis. Instead, the city is being consumed by the sands which cannot be held at bay.

## Tel-Aviv—The Monster City

Despite early appearances, the city's encroachment over nature in Baruch Haim's depictions, and the encroachment of the sands over the city in Grandma Clara's observations, highlight the city's constant battle with the hostile landscape. Ultimately Tel-Aviv becomes a ravenous force consuming everything in its path, leaving destruction in its wake. This depiction of the city as a destructive monster is a trope commonly found in Modernist art and literature. Examples include Baudelaire's images of the city as a whore in *Les Fleurs du Mal,* the Moloch Machine in Fritz Lang's 1927 landmark Modernist film *Metropolis,* and the tension of John Huston's 1950 film noir classic *The Asphalt Jungle.*[13] The "symbolic speech of the city as 'moloch,' 'whore,' 'labyrinth,' or 'asphalt jungle',", according to Klaus Scherpe: "tries to master the complexity of the modern metropolis in an atavistic manner, by reducing it to elementary formulas."[14] This effect is achieved by describing the city as a terrifying creature; as Raymond Williams has shown, the city becomes "a destructive animal, a monster, utterly beyond the individual human scale."[15]

Yehudit Katzir's 1990 novella *Closing the Sea* about Ilana, a school teacher from Haifa who visits Tel-Aviv for the day, develops this primordial imagery in her bestial representations of Dizengoff Center. Ilana's emotional crisis and subsequent suicide occur following her visit to Tel-Aviv and the failure of her plans to see a childhood friend and experience the promised delights of the city.

Katzir's depiction of the destructive quality of Tel-Aviv also ties into tropes commonly employed by her contemporaries. Katzir belongs to a new generation of authors, including Etgar Keret and Gadi Taub, who describe Israel in tropes reminiscent of American literature.[16] Published during the 1990s, these writers have been nicknamed the "thin language" generation for their representation of contemporary life in Israel using the vernacular. Katzir represents a trend of Americanizing Hebrew literature which, according to Miri Kubovy, includes "an increasing number of American themes, characters, landscapes, and experiences [ ... ] usually [presented] in contrast to Israeli reality."[17]

Katzir denotes aspects of American consumerism in her depiction of Tel-Aviv's Dizengoff Center, Israel's first mall. Dizengoff Center's manifestation as a "great white beast" reveals a conception of Tel-Aviv's savage nature.[18] Katzir's use of Dizengoff Center engages with Israelis' nuanced perceptions of Tel-Aviv's success in the 1980s and 1990s. At first, Ilana celebrates the Center's external appearance; once inside, however, Ilana's experience is one of terror and horror. She buys an expensive and inappropriate dress from a macabre shop assistant, and then in a moment of hysteria is unable to find the shop again when she decides to return the dress. Finally she finds the shop but is unable to return the item. A series of ghoulish scenes reinforce the mall's sinister nature. In the bathroom stall Ilana finds graffiti describing a lurid sexual act, with her name and a telephone number attached. She feels assaulted and violated by this message on the wall. There is no respite from the horrors of the beast. Instead of finding a relaxing café, she is consigned to the neon-lit food court, and to a drink that fails to quench her thirst. In the meantime, she listens to widows discuss their husbands' lives and deaths in grisly detail.

Eventually this experience of Dizengoff Center as beast overwhelms Ilana. What began as awe and praise for the American-style shopping mall turns to dread as Ilana becomes alarmed and confused by the chaos:

> She didn't know which side of the beast she was on now, the front legs or the hind legs, but her own legs hurt, and her stomach was cramped and her head was spinning and her eyes needed to be shut.[19]

Ilana's nervous breakdown is triggered by the overwhelming dynamism of the city and her visceral response to the shopping center's monstrosity. Through the monstrous depiction of Dizengoff Center, Katzir suggests that Tel-Aviv's corruption is evidenced in its materialistic consumerism and disregard for the welfare of others.

Katzir's contrast between the external image of the shopping mall and the horrors found within echoes Grandma Clara's disappointment that Tel-Aviv has failed to escape the Levant and to fulfill the promises of its founders to build a modern European city. Clara's contact with the flies and sand disgusts her; a sensory experience evident in both novels. Tel-Aviv's squalid and visceral reality assaults Ilana's senses of smell, touch, sight, hearing, and taste from her very first moments in the city:

> The bus reached the Central Bus Station and opened its doors with a hiss of relief. Ilana got out, and the hot heavy air enveloped her in a sticky embrace, with the smells of urine and nutshells and frying oil and the shouts of fruit vendors and people selling cassettes, and noises too ornate, like the Oriental sweets she had never learned to like. At the base of the dirty green columns sat blind old men or amputees.[20]

The city is dirty and the air suffocating. The violent smells and the shouts of vendors over a background noise of *Mizrahi* music, represented by the selling of cassettes, indicate the Levantine character of the city. The image of the amputees sitting against the pillars evokes both European *shtetl* life and Arab cities. This depiction challenges the Tel-Aviv mythology represented in early posters, photographs, and Nahum Gutman's drawings of cool boulevards on which elegantly attired men and women promenade.[21] Instead, the city now resembles the early twentieth-century Jaffa that Tel-Aviv had tried to escape.

### Buildings and Death: Physical Decay

Central to Shabtai's novel is the city's decay. In describing the urban landscape, he suggests the buildings are monuments to European architecture that had once "attempted to imitate the architectural beauties and splendors of Europe, in the style of Paris or Vienna or Berlin, or even of castles and palaces." Instead, the city's putrefaction is seen in the buildings' collapse: "All these buildings no longer had any future because they were old and ill adapted to modern tastes and lifestyles . . ."[22]

The narrative of Tel-Aviv as "the white city" with new, modern buildings contrasts with the decay of the city—through the image of death. Death takes two forms: that of the city and that of individuals. Death is represented in the city by its cemeteries. Shabtai's novel and Amos Gitai's 1995 film adaptation *Devarim* open with a surreal hunt through the city's graveyards to find Goldman's father's funeral. Unable to meet up with the mourners at the cemetery, Israel and Casesar return to Goldman's apartment, which metaphorically extends the site of death to include the whole city. The juxtaposition of tombstones against the city's high-rise buildings in Gitai's film symbolizes "the feeling that nothing has really been achieved."[23] The search through the cemeteries and among the tombstones parallels Goldman's own aimless wandering through the city. Goldman roves among the white Bauhaus buildings of Tel-Aviv lamenting the loss of his childhood world—a place of Zionist commitment to building a new society, of hope and innocence. In this *flânerie*, the cemetery becomes a metonymy of the city: "This is already not my city, and she will never be. This is just rubbish [ . . . ] this city doesn't deserve to exist. This is just a misunderstanding. [ . . . ] This is just nothingness. This is a graveyard."[24]

Nathan Zach and Lev Hakak have each argued that the death of individuals has permeated Israeli fiction since the 1970s. This preoccupation "with madness, suicide, murder, alienation—in sum, with the dreadful aspects of life" represents the disparity between the hopes and dreams of Zionism and the reality of the state in its early years.[25] Writing about Tel-Aviv has used the suicide of individuals (along with other forms of death) to convey disillusionment with the city.

Katzir's protagonist Ilana dies after a day in Tel-Aviv, and at least twenty-four characters die in Shabtai's novel. Death saturates the text, as illustrated by Zipporah, Goldman's aunt. She visits the graves of the many characters who die in the course of the narrative: "Until in the end the dead enmeshed her life in so dense a web that one day, in an hour of repose, she said humorously to Uncle Lazar, that with so many dead people and so many visits to graveyards it sometimes seemed to her that she herself was already dead."[26] In each of the novels explored in this essay at least one central character dies by suicide. In stark contrast to the optimistic, future-oriented "build and be built" ideal, both the city and the individual are doomed.

The images of Tel-Aviv as a necropolis are even more menacing in literature of the 1990s. In *Closing the Sea* Katzir even suggests that the city is killing its inhabitants by sucking the life out of them.

> [Ilana] tried to admire the fountain that spins and plays music, [ ... ] but her eyes were drawn instead to the old people sitting on the hard cement benches around it. The sun hung over them in the steamy air like a round lemon drop sucking whatever sap they still had left.[27]

Etgar Keret intensifies the atmosphere of death in his fantastical novella *Kneller's Happy Campers,* published in 2000. This darker, more sinister view depicts the city as an endless nightmare in which all of the characters are already dead, having committed suicide and are now living in Tel-Aviv—a symbolic hell, an inescapable place of death.

Keret's Tel-Aviv unites specific local indicators with aspects of a universal metropolis. Just as Katzir describes Dizengoff Center as a mall "just like in America," so too, in Keret's depiction of Tel-Aviv, the city has lost its distinct character as a Hebrew or Jewish city.[28] He compares the city to Frankfurt, thereby denying the distinctly Hebrew aspect of Tel-Aviv which early Zionist ideology had celebrated as its essential feature. Haim, the protagonist in Keret's novel, works in a pizza parlor that is part of a chain. Haim's flat mate is a German who also works at the pizzeria. His flat mate's observation that the area reminds him of his home merely compounds the effect; Tel-Aviv seems just like Frankfurt. The definitive criticism of Tel-Aviv comes when Haim remarks that Frankfurt too must be "a hole."[29]

Haim and his friend Ari conclude that now that they are dead, Tel-Aviv is barely inferior to the afterlife: "This place is just like where I came from, only a bit worse."[30] Keret's novella was written two decades after Shabtai's novel, which opens with a description of Goldman's father's death and Goldman's death nine months later narrated by Caesar. Keret opens his novella similarly: "Two days after I committed suicide," but it is now the protagonist who is narrating—there is no one else left alive to tell the story. Keret expands upon the image, constructed by Shabtai, of Tel-Aviv as a cemetery.[31] In this dystopia the city is no longer just a symbolic graveyard, the last resting place of ideological dreams; it is the afterlife. Tel-Aviv becomes the figurative punishment meted out to people who have taken their own lives. In this allegory of Tel-Aviv, Keret is suggesting that the "Hebrew city" has become a place of the living dead.

## Tel-Aviv as a Place of Corruption

The city's physical decay is also a metaphor for the decay of human beings through moral, sexual, and financial corruption. Even in the early years, literary depictions of Tel-Aviv contested the claims that the city would foster Zionist ideals of national revival. S. Y. Agnon's novel *Only Yesterday* (1945) illustrates the disillusionment of the immigrants of the Second Aliya who perceived the city to be a betrayal of Zionist ideology. Agnon's anti-hero Yitzhak Kumer is unable to work the land due to competition from the cheaper and more efficient Arab laborers. Offered the opportunity to find alternative work in the city or flee to Jerusalem, Yitzhak abandons secular socialist Zionism and returns to a religious world.

Benjamin Tammuz was a significant figure within the Israeli literary and cultural establishment, and in his novel *Requiem for Na'aman* (1978, republished 1992), he articulates the same questioning attitude toward the city that Agnon had demonstrated. Tammuz traces the lives of four generations of the Abramson family from the first Zionist immigrants to Palestine at the end of the late nineteenth century to the generations

of the 1960s and early 1970s. Reacting to Tel-Aviv's petit-bourgeois nature, the idealist Elyakum asks: "Think for yourselves and answer me:
was it worth it to come to swamps and malaria and murders, in order
to be lawyers and to work in a bank?"[32] Both Agnon and Tammuz echo
critical attitudes toward the bourgeois vision underlying Tel-Aviv. This
criticism had already appeared in the 1920s, when Tel-Aviv's increasingly
petit-bourgeois character was seen as an anathema to the Zionist belief
in the redemptive power of rural, cooperative settlement.

Though celebrated as a bourgeois city, Labor Zionism was also an
important aspect of 1930s and 1940s Tel-Aviv. Notably, the workers'
housing represented an attempt to "implement a collective or communal
ideal in the construction of residential neighborhoods."[33] In the spirit of
the Bauhaus school, architects designed buildings to "encourage a sense
of community that would foster working-class solidarity and nurture the
kind of individuals who would grow into and participate in proletarian
societies."[34] Nevertheless, within forty years of this construction period,
Shabtai wrote about what he perceived to be the failure to realize these
urban socialist ambitions. In *Past Continuous,* Goldman's father and
his friend Leviathan, horrified by Tel-Aviv's development, attempt to
found a new urban-collective city. They spend two years drawing up the
charter, "which embraced all aspects of individual, family and social life;
took into account all the rights and obligations of the members and all
the problems and deviations which might confront them."[35]

However, the lack of commitment to the project results in its ultimate failure. Through this allegory Shabtai contends that Goldman's
generation abandoned their Zionist ideals (and for Shabtai this meant
a socialist Zionist framework) and as a result, Tel-Aviv failed to live up
to their vision of the city. A second allegorical representation of Tel-
Aviv appears in Goldman's translation of Prevlova, a fantastical world.
This allegory of the city as a malevolent place is found after Goldman's
suicide, and consequently, Goldman's death is associated with the city's
horrors. Prevlova's inhabitants are rootless hordes, challenging Tel-
Aviv's self-image as a Jewish homeland that offers an alternative and
even an end to diasporic wanderings. The bodies in this fantastical land
live for a single day, but expand to hideous proportions, fed by the decadence of the city, finally dying and rotting. "The creatures that remain
floating on the surface of the water are boiled by the midday sun and

serve as nourishment for the approaching hordes of nomads."[36] Decay is
not just the state of the landscape, but the condition of the individual.
As a comment on Tel-Aviv, Shabtai suggests through this story that each
successive generation leaves behind nothing of substance or meaning.
Goldman's suicide is an expression of this betrayal of values and failure
to realize the urban socialist vision.

The urban dwellers in post-1970 literature occupy themselves in a
variety of ways, through sexual pleasures, business, and consumerism,
but these are shown to be corrupt forces that are inherently destructive.
Sexual corruption is a central metaphor of Tel-Aviv's decline. In each
of these novels, sexual depravity compromises the ideological vision of
a new Jewish future with its wholesome overtones. In *Closing the Sea,*
Ilana is confronted by images of naked breasts on the magazine covers
at the kiosk in the bus station and the sexually suggestive messages in
the Dizengoff Center bathroom. On her return journey from the city a
religious man sits next to her in the shared taxi, covers his knees with
his coat and, while feeling Ilana's thigh, proceeds to masturbate. On
arriving home Ilana undresses, wishing to wash away the physical and
symbolic pollutions of Tel-Aviv. She cannot be cleansed and, lying in
the bath, she drowns.

Licentiousness and sexual immorality exemplify Tel-Aviv's corruption, in accord with Raymond Williams's view of the city as a place of
waste and profligacy represented through promiscuity, prostitution, and
pornography.[37] Through Caesar, images of bizarre, sordid, or depraved
pornography pervade Shabtai's novel. The many literary depictions of
sex and prostitution symbolize the betrayal of Tel-Aviv's Zionist ideals
in two ways. Firstly, the reality cannot match the expectations of fantasy,
and so in turn, the characters increasingly become sexually depraved.
Secondly, the liaisons do not lead to offspring. Even when Israel's girl-
friend is pregnant he rejects her and she moves to Jerusalem, suggesting
Tel-Aviv cannot sustain new life.

Prostitution is a ubiquitous symbol of the urban environment. Rich-
ardson, Fielding, and other eighteenth-century British novelists were
quick to use this image, and it was not until a century later that prostitution featured in French literature.[38] In English literature, prostitution
depicted a changing fate for women (as with Fanny Burney's *Evelina*)
from which they could rise and return to society, or sink into obscurity

or death. It was not until the late nineteenth century, with the rise of Modernism, that the prostitute became a vehicle for representing "male fantasies about female sexuality," a depiction that served "to focus male ambivalence about desire, money, class, and the body."[39] In Tel-Aviv fiction, suicide and prostitution are paralleled, becoming dominant images of the corruption of the city. Shabtai's use of prostitution reflects the demise of the puritanical and idealistic ethos that characterized the early pioneering phase of the Tel-Aviv Zionist narrative.

Goldman's constant pursuit of prostitutes is frequently humiliating. In his first encounter the woman takes his money but "all she let him do was embrace her a little and touch her breasts through her dress and kiss her once or twice."[40] On another occasion, Goldman "once received a beating on account of a prostitute." Goldman's sexual relationship with Paula, the hostess of a nightclub, also suggests prostitution. Many of his sexual acts with Paula are conducted in public among other middle-aged men "who had come to find a little release and a little happiness in the company of the hostesses."[41] Goldman's encounters with Paula are squalid and transitory, as is the social situation in which the hostesses operate. Goldman's experience with Paula is unfulfilling despite his hopes that such an act of sexual debauchery will fulfill his desires and his fantasies. "After it was over he was left with nothing but the sense of shame and sin, and a feeling of disappointment, because none of it bore any resemblance to the wild sexual fantasies which he cultivated in his imagination."[42]

As a child, Goldman saw his neighbor, the prostitute Kaminskaya, whom he lusted after, commit suicide. Her sexual promise is unattainable because he is too young at first, and then because she dies. Like the Tel-Aviv dream, she is forever out of reach. Unlike his father, he is attracted rather than repelled by prostitutes, indicating the moral breakdown between generations. Goldman's father violently opposes prostitution, which he considers to be a sign of moral decay. Furthermore, Goldman's ambivalent attitude contrasts with his father's attitude suggesting that the current generation is no longer morally virtuous, and has failed the founding generation of Tel-Aviv.

Arguments advocating prostitution echo arguments advocating suicide in Shabtai's novel. Goldman rationalizes his reason for the former, simultaneously giving arguments that are used for the latter. The naiveté of Goldman's argument is at once evident, yet he uses prostitution only as a way of illustrating his more important argument about the lack of culpability for suicide. The pursuit of prostitutes, like his subsequent suicide, reveals his disdain for the morality of the collective. In prostitution, sexual acts no longer have a procreative purpose. Therefore, it is associated with suicide, which indicates the material death of the city and of its ideals. Sexual depravity and the ambiguous moral attitudes toward it prefigure the popular conceptions of Tel-Aviv in the 1980s and 1990s as a "sin city," where transgression of moral conventions is rendered positive, signifying the city's success.[43]

The pursuits of sexual and financial excess in Shabtai's novel are also paralleled. Caesar feeds Goldman's sexual fantasies with his own licentious behavior. His attitude toward sexual relations is merely an extension of his parents', Zena and Erwin's, coupling of sexual and financial excess. Their overindulgence in all things obscures their hatred for one another. Erwin assumes his wife has forgotten his adulterous betrayal because of her decadent purchases. However, her shopping expeditions barely satisfy her, and her new acquisitions often remain packed in their bags. This notion of consumerist decadence characterized Tel-Aviv throughout its history, with Dizengoff St. "associated with pleasure, entertainment, fun, and consumption."[44] However, even Tel-Aviv acquired new dimensions of debauchery and dissolution with the rise of a nouveau riche middle class in the 1960s and 1970s.

Tammuz's *Requiem for Na'aman* explores the image of hyper-consumption in his depiction of a generation committed to the good life made possible by an emergent affluent society that was not committed to the puritanical, pioneering ethos. In this novel, the fashionable homes of the upper classes in Tel-Aviv become monuments to consumerism. In a deeply satirical portrayal of wealth, he ridicules the compulsive acquisitions of this class, and those who could not afford full integration into the world of status and social connection, and therefore choose their own systems of imitation in order to compete in this hierarchy.

> In all the best houses one could find special clay pots, archaeological, bearing the signature of a Minister of Israel; he who knew the Minister personally received such potsherds as a gift; and he who was not so fortunate paid the full price, in shops in New York, when he was on a graduate trip there.[45]

In describing the archaeological artifacts of Israel, which become symbols of social status, Tammuz suggests the dislocation between a genuine interest in the history of the national homeland and a desire to climb the social ladder. Furthermore, the items are purchased in New York. The owners have not excavated these treasures from the Land of Israel, because they do not work the land and are removed from it physically and ideologically. Yet Tammuz's description of this social class still ties consumerism to unique aspects of local Canaanite or Palestine archaeology.[46] The items belong to the Land of Israel and hence status is still measured by an ideological connection. However, in Shabtai's novel, even this final link to Zionism is severed. The artifacts mentioned in *Past Continuous* are African masks, or items from Asia, China, and the Far East, demonstrating the disconnection between national ideals and the tastes of Tel-Aviv society.

In Shabtai's novel, financial corruption in the city is also a mark of moral decay, symbolized by Max Spillman. Max lives in an unnecessarily lavish accommodation, "a five-room apartment in one of the expensive new buildings," contrasting the modest socialist housing values employed in Tel-Aviv's Bauhaus period.[47] Spillman, who owns a gas station, has been convicted of corruption: he diluted petrol with paraffin and tampered with the indicators on the pumps; yet even after being tried, convicted, and fined, he feels no remorse because he neither believes the crime is serious nor that he will be punished for it. Even his customers do not consider his actions to be "an unpardonable sin, but at the very most as an unfortunate slip which should be forgotten as soon as possible and which was no reason for upsetting their relationship with him." Spillman represents Tel-Aviv's moral corruption: "Even the devil has run away and left them in the hands of a rabble of animals like Max Spillman and all kinds of mad dogs who called themselves Jews."[48]

Tammuz similarly describes the financial duplicity of fashionable Tel-Aviv society during the relatively affluent and politically stable 1960s and 1970s, when traditional ideals of selfless service eroded, giving way to cynicism and the pursuit of personal gains. For example, such individuals "take something from the party coffer, or exert pressure on contractors and accept what are called bribes."[49] The new elite behaved in fraudulent ways by letting their self-interest triumph over moral obligations to the collective: "People who all their lives only gave and gave and gave to the nation, to the State and to the party, why should they not enjoy a little bit for themselves in their old age, in Switzerland?" Not only do they steal for personal gain, they abandon the entire Zionist project in moving to Europe. Tammuz's equation of ideological and financial corruption indicates the demise of the Zionist foundational ethos.[50]

Tammuz and Shabtai's representations of Tel-Aviv anticipate the celebration of sin and hedonism that particularly has characterized the public discourse of Tel-Aviv since the late 1980s. Though Tel-Aviv's vibrant nightlife was part of the city's reputation since the 1930s, by 1989, "The Nonstop City" had become its official slogan.[51] But Katzir's representation of 1980s Tel-Aviv demonstrates, through Ilana's experience, the nonstop city gone out of control. Ilana hopes to shop for a fashionable dress that she will be able to wear later that evening for her meeting with her childhood friend Tami. She plans to sit in a café and stroll along the seashore. Coerced into buying a prohibitively expensive dress, that is unattractive and entirely unsuitable for her lifestyle, she is then unable to afford lunch in a café. She opts to eat unsatisfying fast food while perched on plastic chairs. The failure to satisfy her thirst is made worse by the oppressive heat, forcing her to acknowledge the impossibility of roaming through Tel-Aviv in order to reach the seafront as she had dreamed, and so she aborts this plan. Finally, her friend fails to appear for the planned meeting and when she does arrive cannot stay; instead she drives Ilana to the Central Bus Station for her return journey to Haifa.

## The Tel-Aviv *Flâneur*

In Shabtai's novel, the anti-hero Goldman appears always as "a man walking, as if alone, in its streets."[52] This depiction is part of a literary tradition in which significant, isolated objects and iconic images are used to indicate the "separated subjectivity of the observer."[53] Goldman exemplifies a pattern of isolation and sense of alienation in the city evident in other characters in the novel, such as Baruch Haim. Shabtai casts Goldman as the traditional European *flâneur* (the stroller). Coined by Walter Benjamin in his analysis of Baudelaire's nineteenth-century poetry of Paris, and Edgar Allen Poe's story *The Man of the Crowd* (1840), this figure is an urban explorer wandering through the city, analyzing the landscape as he promenades without purpose, resisting incorporation into the milieu, forever standing on the edge of a crowd, isolated and alone. Goldman's endless *flânerie* (stroll) that forms the spine of Shabtai's novel denotes the loneliness of the protagonist, even suggesting imminent death.

Goldman wanders through the city in a trance and begins a dialogue with the streets. He considers Yarkon St. despicable and frightening, its associations with prostitution engendering feelings of terror and shame. Instead of representing the ideal of the wholesome new society, Shabtai represents the street as a place of decay and immorality that at once attracts and repels Goldman. He formulates theoretical arguments to justify his increasingly corrupt conduct: "The only morality acceptable to him as a non-believer did not repudiate prostitution, or adultery."[54] Instead of religion, which he refers to as conventional morality, he prefers to adopt "humanistic" morality based on reason, but with no limitations on social conduct. Hence Goldman can justify all behavior, even when it is ultimately unfulfilling. The only boundaries are those represented by the walls and buildings of the city. "The girls standing with their little handbags on the corners or in the doorways of the gloomy old buildings [...] most of which were in darkness so that they looked as if nobody lived in them and all they contained were broken bits of furniture and dust and cobwebs and evil spirits."[55] These signs of moral and physical decay are at once inviting and repellent. For Goldman this negative aspect of Tel-Aviv suggests that the entire city is abandoned. Tel-Aviv has become a ghost town, haunted by evil spirits assuming the form of living people, or the specter of things past. Goldman as *flâneur* is tortured by the ugliness of the city, which serves as a metaphor for the state of his soul.

Only individuals without the ties of family or community can operate in this Tel-Aviv. The city's curse lies in its ability to feed every caprice while ensuring that city dwellers are always missing something else. There is no satisfaction in any pleasure, since every decision closes off other options. Cities intensify the human condition of missed opportunities, choices, and inaccessibility. "Every glimpsed interior, every passerby, every figure in a distant window, every row of doors, every map itself is both an invitation and a rebuff."[56] The fear that something may be missed becomes the final paralyzing terror for the characters of Shabtai's novel. As a result, they grope at random, trying to fill and fulfill their lives.

## Destruction of "Tel-Avivness," Creation of "a City"

In Keret's recent novella, Haim thinks that life is meaningless and point-less, that "nothing matters."[57] Haim eventually gains wisdom, under-stands life's significance, and chooses action rather than the passivity of the living dead. His previous powerlessness and obsession with ques-tions about the purpose of remaining alive are transformed when he learns that the act of living is the answer. At the story's close Haim believes he has changed his pattern. He likes and thinks about a woman named Lihah, which is contrasted with his previous "dreaming" about a woman named Ergah, his infatuation with whom had led to his suicide. "I don't dream about her at all, but I think about her a lot."[58] Haim is transformed by choosing life, as suggested by his name, which means "life." Taking Lihah's advice, he makes a conscious effort to do things differently, to try to live life by the principles that she suggests like, "do-ing things just slightly wrong so that you know you are living."[59] Keret's novella is heir to a literary tradition that rejects the ideological tenets which first formed Tel-Aviv. From the beginning of the twentieth cen-tury, the city had been reimagined in literary terms that later proved to correspond to new perceptions of Tel-Aviv in reality.

Though its ideological modes changed throughout the century, fic-tion continued to question Tel-Aviv's ability to fulfill the founders' vi-sions. Even as the city abandons its heritage as the first Hebrew city by becoming a city like any other in Keret's novella, the sense of Tel-Aviv's ultimate success is reinforced. For, as the writers examined here have shown, by using images of the *flâneur,* sexual decadence, and corruption, Tel-Aviv's universal aspects as a metropolis are celebrated.

Although earlier visions of socialism had collapsed, the nature of Tel-Aviv as an international city just like any other, a burgeoning me-tropolis that fulfilled the "build and be built" philosophy underlying its construction and growth, is manifested in the city's very existence. Nevertheless, even at the dawn of the twenty-first century, Keret does not entirely abandon the particularistic aspects of the city either; he also highlights those characteristics unique to the city's geographical locus. The sea, the streets, and even the characters reflect a modern Is-raeliness. The juxtaposition of celebrating and criticizing these local re-gional markers characterizes newer cities, like Tel-Aviv, that stand in the shadows of the great metropolises such as Paris, London, or New York: "The underlying idea being that a sense of provincialism and a thirst for recognition are often two sides of the same coin."[60] Keret's protagonist Haim is a metonym for the city, for in just surviving Haim and Tel-Aviv fulfill their purpose, while Haim is also a symbol of the Tel-Aviv inhabitant whose life is on one hand modern and urban, and on the other constrained by the particular situation in Israel.

Keret's novella argues that neither Haim nor Tel-Aviv is the living dead. Instead, both appear to do things "just slightly wrong" and in doing so demonstrate their existence. The city more than deserves to exist—it does exist! It is this literary vision of the city that balances recognizable universal urban topoi and specific local identity symbols. Motifs of decay and death dominate depictions of Tel-Aviv, thereby highlighting the disparity between the early urban pioneers' dream and the modern reality, yet—as its literary imagery shows—Tel-Aviv as a modern metropolis signifies the city's ultimate success.

## NOTES

The epigraph comes from Ya'akov Shabtai, *Past Continuous* (Tel-Aviv, 1977), 285 [Hebrew]. Citations are from the Dalya Bilu translation: Ya'akov Shabtai, *Past Continuous,* 1st English ed. (Philadelphia, 1985). If not otherwise indicated, all translations are my own.

1. Recent scholarship on Tel-Aviv has analyzed the significance of ideological images and names in the construction of the city's narrative: Maoz Azaryahu, *Tel-Aviv: Mythography of a City* (Syracuse, 2007); Barbara Mann, *A Place in History: Modernism, Tel-Aviv, and the Creation of Jewish Urban Space* (Stanford, CA, 2006); S. Ilan Troen, *Imagining Zion: Dreams, Designs, and Realities in a Century of Jewish Settlement* (New Haven, 2003); Eric Zakim, *To Build and Be Built: Landscape, Literature, and the Construction of Zionist Identity* (Philadelphia, 2007).

2. Francis Carco and Ford Madox Ford, *Perversity* (Chicago, 1928); Jean Rhys, *Good Morning, Midnight* (New York, 1939). *Perversity,* translated by Rhys, is the story of a prostitute and her pimp cavorting in the Paris underworld watched by the girl's voyeuristic brother, and is characteristic of modernist representations of urban sexual depravity.

3. Azaryahu, *Tel-Aviv,* 94–95.

4. Hanna Soker-Schwager and Dalya Bilu, "A Godless City: Shabtai's Tel-Aviv and the Secular Zionist Project," *Prooftexts* 26.1–26.2 (2006): 240–281, 241–242.

5. Shabtai, *Past Continuous,* 75.

6. Azaryahu, *Tel-Aviv,* 100.

7. Ibid., 95.

8. Shabtai, *Past Continuous,* 183.

9. Ibid.

10. Commentating on Edgar Allen Poe's *The Man of the Crowd,* Walter Benjamin explores the sinister elements of the city as a place of anonymous thronging masses. The passersby can only be differentiated by their wardrobes—a trope present in much of urban literature. Examples are found in the works of Dickens, Sartre, Defoe, Baudelaire, Camus, and Paul Auster, among others.

11. Troen, *Imagining Zion,* 90.

12. Shabtai, *Past Continuous,* 135.

13. David Harvey, *Paris, Capital of Modernity* (Paris, 2003), 265.

14. Klaus R. Scherpe and Mitch Cohen, "Modern and Postmodern Transformations of the Metropolitan Narrative," *New German Critique* 55 (1992): 72–85, 74.

15. Raymond Williams, *The Country and the City* (London, 1973), 159.

16. Miri Kubovy, "*Inniut* and *Kooliut:* Trends in Israeli Narrative Literature, 1995–1999," *Israel Studies* 5.1 (2000): 244–265.

17. Ibid., 244.

18. Yehudit Katzir, *Closing the Sea* (New York, 1992), 125 [Hebrew]; *Uncle Peretz Takes Off* (Tel-Aviv, 1973) and in *Past Continuous* (New York, 1985). Shabtai also considered the Dizengoff Center's presence a symbol of the monstrous and alienating metropole as it annihilated the Nordia neighborhood that had been "home to a substantial part of the Shabtai family." Hanna Soker-Schwager, "A Godless City," 255.

19. Katzir, *Closing the Sea,* 125.

20. Ibid., 118.

21. Avraham Soskin's work was featured through a retrospective exhibition at the Tel-Aviv Museum of Art (2003); Annarita Lamberti, "Preserving the Recent and Most Recent Memories of Tel-Aviv" (ESF-LiU Conference, "Cities and Media: Cultural Perspectives on Urban Identities in a Mediatized World," Vadstena, Sweden, 25–29 October 2006); Mann, *A Place in History.*

22. Shabtai, *Past Continuous,* 268.

23. Yael Munk, "False Nostalgia and Cultural Amnesia: The City of Tel-Aviv in Israeli Cinema of the 1990s," *Shofar* 24.4 (2006): 130–143, 140.

24. Shabtai, *Past Continuous,* 375.

25. Nathan Zach, *On Romance in Hebrew Literature and other Topics* (Jerusalem, 1983) [Hebrew]; Lev Hakak, *Equivocal Dreams: Studies in Modern Hebrew Literature* (Hoboken, NJ, 1993).

26. Shabtai, *Past Continuous,* 346.

27. Katzir, *Closing the Sea,* 126.

28. Ibid.

29. Etgar Keret, *Kneller's Happy Campers* (Tel-Aviv, 1998), 48 [Hebrew].

30. Ibid., 72.

31. Ibid., 47.

32. Benjamin Tammuz, *Requiem for Na'aman* (Tel-Aviv, 1978), 62 [Hebrew].

33. Mann, *A Place in History,* 165.

34. Troen, *Imaging Zion,* 107.

35. Shabtai, *Past Continuous,* 55.

36. Ibid., 383.

37. Williams, *The Country and the City,* 143.

38. Nils Johan Ringdal, *A World History of Prostitution* (New York, 2004), 280.

39. Charles Bernheimer, "1880: Prostitution in the Novel," in *A New History of French Literature*, ed. Dennis Hollier (Boston, 1994), 780. Honoré de Balzac, Gustave Flaubert, Emile Zola, and Joris Karl Huysmans evoke the allure of the prostitute and the tension between the desire to possess the female body, and the fear of doing so.

40. Shabtai, *Past Continuous,* 165.

41. Ibid., 163.

42. Ibid., 164.

43. Azaryahu, "Nonstop City," in *Tel-Aviv: Mythography of a City.*

44. Ibid., 106.

45. Tammuz, *Requiem for Na'aman,* 189.

46. Michael Feige and Zvi Shiloni, eds., *Archaeology and Nationalism in Eretz-Israel* (Sde-Boker, 2008) [Hebrew].

47. Shabtai, *Past Continuous,* 194.

48. Ibid., 195.

49. Tammuz, *Requiem for Na'aman,* 193–194.

50. Uri Ram, "Postnationalist Pasts: The Case of Israel," *Social Science History* 22.4 (1998): 526.

51. Azaryahu, "Nonstop City."

52. Williams, *The Country and the City,* 233.

53. Ibid., 246.

54. Shabtai, *Past Continuous,* 75.

55. Ibid., 214.

56. Hana Wirth-Nesher, *City Codes: Reading the Modern Urban Novel* (Cambridge, UK, 1996), 67.

57. Keret, *Kneller's Happy Campers,* 51.

58. Ibid.

59. Ibid.

60. Maoz Azaryahu, "Tel-Aviv: Center, Periphery and the Cultural Geographies of an Aspiring Metropolis," *Social & Cultural Geography* 9.3 (2008): 303–318, 304.

# FOURTEEN

# Art and the City:
# The Case of Tel-Aviv

*Dalia Manor*

It has been suggested that the date now commonly accepted for the founding of Tel-Aviv was selected primarily thanks to the photograph by Avraham Soskin (1881–1963) that documented the moment.[1] This "moment of birth," usually identified as the land lottery held by the members of Ahuzat Bayit Society on 11 April 1909, was no more historic than any other possible event: the founding of the Society itself in 1906, naming the new neighborhood Tel-Aviv in 1910, the recognition of its township status in 1921, not to mention the founding of earlier Jewish neighborhoods outside Jaffa in the 1880s. Moreover, serious doubts have been raised as to the link between this photograph and the actual land lottery ceremony. As Haim Feirberg has convincingly argued, the picture probably depicts a different gathering altogether that took place a couple of months earlier.[2] Soskin, who first published the photograph around 1926 in a small album of his Tel-Aviv photographs, gave it a somewhat vague title, "The meeting founding Tel-Aviv 1908."[3]

Various explanations can be offered for why an insignificant event, a rather technical procedure like the land lottery, came to represent the mythic moment of the birth of the city. However, there is no doubt that Soskin's picture—whatever its real subject—contributed to the defining of this moment as historic. What the photograph shows and, of no less significance, what it does not show, is responsible a great deal for the city's founding myth: a large group of men and women seen from the back, unidentified individually, their dark European outfits conspicuous against the background of the white sand dunes that surround them. The composition edited out Jaffa, the primarily Arab town, as well as the nearby Jewish neighborhood of Neve Tzedek, and various agricultural features.

When identified as the beginning of Tel-Aviv, and juxtaposed with pictures of the same place on later dates, as Soskin did in his album of Tel-Aviv views, the image becomes a pure manifestation of an important idea about Tel-Aviv: that it was formed *ex nihilo,* the city that sprang from the sands.[4] The weight that this photograph has accumulated over the years in the story of Tel-Aviv demonstrates above all the role it has played in creating the myth in the first place: the sheer visualization of the idea of a modern, Western city that rises in the midst of an uninhabited empty place, a city without a past.

Several art works that portray Tel-Aviv convey similar sentiments regarding its mythic foundation: first and foremost, those made by Nahum Gutman that enhanced the myth of Tel-Aviv's innocent birth. In discussing art that depicts the city of Tel-Aviv, however, it is worth noting at the outset that images of Tel-Aviv in art are scarce, at least until the 1980s. Visual images of the city have been produced over the years mainly by professional photographers who worked for national institutions, and later on by independent and press photographers.[5] In painting, on the other hand, Tel-Aviv has been rarely depicted, a fact that is not always acknowledged. The relative paucity of material has not prevented the theme of "Tel-Aviv in art" to become the subject of exhibitions, articles, and artistic albums usually published on the occasion of the city's anniversaries.[6]

Four artists in particular came to be identified with art about Tel-Aviv: Reuven Rubin (1893–1974) and Nahum Gutman (1898–1980) in the 1920s and 1930s—a key period in the formation of the Tel-Aviv myth; Yosef Zaritsky (1891–1985) in the 1930s and 1940s; and Raffi Lavie (1937–2007) in the 1960s and 1970s. All are highly ranked in the canon of Israeli art, and their association with Tel-Aviv has certainly contributed to maintaining this status. In recent decades the so-called Tel-Aviv period in these artists' repertoires, especially the first two, is often highlighted on the occasion of the city's anniversary, focusing on the mutual link of artist and city, i.e., the exhibition *Rubin's Tel-Aviv: A Salute to Tel-Aviv*

האספה המיסדת של תל־אביב 1908.
The meeting founding Tel-Aviv 1908                    Gründung von Tel-Aviv 1908

*on the Occasion of its 75th Anniversary* held at the Rubin Museum in Tel-Aviv in 1984 or *Gutman's Tel-Aviv* held in 1999 at the Nahum Gutman Museum in Tel-Aviv on the occasion of the city's ninetieth anniversary. That Gutman and Rubin are considered to be *the* artists of Tel-Aviv is due to the tendency of historians of the city to single out these two artists. Thus they overemphasize the position of Rubin and Gutman within the wider context of Israeli art and the artistic activity in Tel-Aviv throughout its century.[7]

In fact, "most painters did not paint Tel-Aviv; they painted from Tel-Aviv," according to Ziona Tagger, one of the prominent artists of that generation.[8] During the 1920s, when Tel-Aviv developed rapidly to become the major city of the Yishuv and subsequently the center of artistic activity, it was rarely painted by its artists. Gutman, Rubin, Tagger, and other artists of the time turned their eyes to Jaffa, Jerusalem, Safed, and the Galilee, preferring ancient cities, Arab villages, and exotic views of the country. Tel-Aviv, like most of the Zionist projects in Palestine at the time, was by and large ignored by its local artists.[9] This omission was

תל־אביב — 1926.

Tel-Aviv 1926

Tel-Aviv 1926

not due to lack of knowledge or appreciation. On the contrary, artists like Rubin were proud of their city, its modern architecture and other new facilities, especially when compared to Jerusalem. "I could not live in Jerusalem," Rubin said at the time to the French writer Edmond Fleg. "Jerusalem is a museum; in order to live I need Tel-Aviv."[10]

Nonetheless, Tel-Aviv was far less attractive to him as a subject for painting, as was evidently seen in a recent large-scale exhibition held at the Tel-Aviv Museum of Art and dedicated to Rubin's painting during his first decade in Palestine.[11] Of over 120 paintings in the show, only five depict sections of Tel-Aviv, and a few more show parts of the city in the background of the main subject. The rest of the paintings depict scenes in Jaffa and the Arab surroundings of Tel-Aviv, views of Old Jerusalem and other parts of the country.

While Rubin continued to paint Jerusalem and the Galilee through-out his career, his Tel-Aviv paintings were limited to the first five or six years after his settlement in Palestine in 1923. His paintings of the 1920s are highly stylized in terms of spatial arrangement and color scheme;

Fig. 14.2. Reuven Rubin, *Tel Aviv*, c. 1923–1924, oil on canvas,
55×75.5 cm. Sacks-Abramov Collection, Tel Aviv-Jerusalem.
*Courtesy of Rubin Museum Foundation.*

like all works of art, they are generated by the artist's imagination and
the artistic conventions of his time rather than being a "true" representation of reality. Yet Rubin is credited as the most significant artist to
document Tel-Aviv in its formative years, "the new city that had begun
as a little neighborhood and turned into a metropolis."[12]

Of the handful of paintings of Tel-Aviv that Rubin produced in those
years, one in particular, now simply titled *Tel-Aviv*, seems to be responsible for the magnifying of the artist's perceived role as chronicler of
Tel-Aviv.

The painting is a medium-size canvas dominated by yellowish colors, showing an aerial view of a group of small houses with red roofs
and blue doors and windows. The top edge of the canvas shows the blue
sea with three small boats. This naïve-like style of painting is typical of
Rubin in this period. Like Soskin's photograph, the exact subject matter
of the painting and its date are not certain, but this has not interfered
with its interpretation. The painting, writes Shlomo Shva,

seems to tell us all that Tel-Aviv was in those days—a few scattered houses dotted among the endless sand dunes, standing randomly, without protection, and yet challenging logic as they express the renewed Jewish effort to take their destiny in their own hands and to establish a homeland in Palestine.[13]

Nevertheless, Tel-Aviv in 1923 or 1924, when Rubin painted this picture, was far more developed than what is offered in this description, with over 1,000 houses and a population of over 20,000.[14]

In 1955 the catalogue of Rubin's exhibition at the Tel-Aviv Museum attributed the 1912 date to this painting.[15] Whether this was simply a misprint, it seems that Rubin did not bother to correct it later. The date, corresponding to Rubin's first stay in Palestine as a Bezalel student in Jerusalem, started circulating in various publications, including his 1966 retrospective exhibition catalogue, a monograph published in New York in the 1970s, books about Israeli art, and it is still used in texts about Tel-Aviv.[16] That Rubin hardly painted during his period at Bezalel, the fact that the style of his earlier known paintings was utterly different, and that the first houses of Ahuzat Bayit beared no resemblance to what is seen in this picture, did not prevent authors from describing the painting as visual evidence of the first houses in Tel-Aviv. Dr. Haim Gamzu, the director of the Tel-Aviv Museum, wrote in 1966 that Rubin's picture of Tel-Aviv, which back in 1912 "consisted but of a score of tiny houses and a dozen tents . . . has remained one of its most authentic 'portraits', one of the first childhood likeness of our town—today a large city . . ."[17] While the erroneous date of the painting was later rejected in favor of 1922 (said to be the year of Rubin's settlement in Palestine), the interpretation of the painting's subject as "a settlement defending itself against the sand and the wide-open spaces"[18] has remained unchanged.

Rubin, who in 1922 was still traveling in Europe and afterward was active in Bucharest where he held an exhibition early in 1923, came to Palestine in April 1923.[19] In November 1924 he opened an exhibition in Bucharest showing fifty-seven oil paintings from 1923–1924. It followed his first exhibition in Palestine held in March 1924 at the Citadel—Tower of David—in Jerusalem, which later travelled to Tel-Aviv. Of the paintings in the Bucharest exhibition checklist, one is vaguely titled *A View in Tel-Aviv*. Two others refer to Neve Sha'anan, a neighborhood to the south of Tel-Aviv that was not yet part of the town; one is titled *The Sea*

*Shore* and two others are titled *A Yemenite Neighborhood in Tel-Aviv* and *An Arab Neighborhood in Tel-Aviv (sic)*.[20]

Although Rubin's paintings were not naturalistic or straightforward documentation, they were nonetheless based on reality. A section of the landscape shown in the painting *Tel-Aviv,* with similar small houses and tents, is seen as a view through the window in another painting by Rubin.[21] If Rubin's painting was responding to a real location (I believe it was), what was the place he painted? By comparing photographs and other sources, this can be identified as the newly built Nordia neighborhood, the first neighborhood named after Max Nordau, consisting of small houses, one or two rooms each. Built in a short span of time around 1923 on land previously purchased by the Jewish National Fund (JNF), the neighborhood was founded to accommodate the influx of immigrants and Jewish refugees from Jaffa.[22]

The neighborhood soon disappeared within the rapidly developing city and was forgotten.[23] The fate of this neighborhood further obscured the subject of this painting and led to the later confusion of dates. Whether or not this attribution can be substantiated any further, it is certain that the painting does *not* depict the first houses of Tel-Aviv. The myth of Tel-Aviv is stronger than any scholarly attribution, and so is the desire to visualize this myth in pictures. The painting in the latest exhibition of Rubin's work at the Tel-Aviv Museum is correctly dated 1923, but the catalogue describes it by way of retelling the myth of Tel-Aviv:

> Houses born *ex nihilo,* appearing out of the sand dunes without any pre-conceived order or sign of "human intervention." There is no strategy of urban planning here. "An invisible hand" has set down these toy houses in the "sand box" by the sea. . . . there is nothing but a stretch of golden, primeval sand, on which no man has yet set foot. Every city has its moment of birth.[24]

If the myth of Tel-Aviv that sprang as a natural wonder out of the golden sands seems to be enforced in Rubin's painting, Gutman's case is the opposite: his paintings and drawings had contributed significantly to the myth of "little Tel-Aviv." Gutman, who returned to Palestine in late 1925 from his stay in Europe, joined his colleagues in painting Jaffa and other ancient towns and villages. Only in the 1930s, in a retrospective and rather nostalgic view, did he start producing the drawings of

ציור לד ; נחום גוטמן : »עיני ראוך, תל-אביב, בילדותך« (השומרים בלילות).

Fig. 14.3. Nahum Gutman, illustration from *Tel-Aviv Book,* ed. Alter Druyanov,
1936: titled "My Eyes Saw You, Tel-Aviv in your Childhood (The Night Watch)."
*Gutman family, Courtesy of the Gutman Museum of Art.*

Ahuzat Bayit that later became part of the iconic images of the city.
Eight drawings by Gutman, titled as a personal testimony, *My Eyes Saw
You, Tel-Aviv in Your Childhood,* were included along with other visual
material in the first book on the history of Tel-Aviv, the 1936 book edited
by Alter Druyanov.[25]

Typical of these drawings is the image of the vast expanse of sand in
the midst of which a handful of houses are planted along the main street
that ends with the grand Herzliya School that dwarfs everything else.

The sun during the day and the moon at night are practically smiling, promising a benign natural environment, while Jaffa is seen as a
silhouette, far away in the distance, totally detached from the little settlement in the middle of nowhere. The vast empty space between Jaffa and
Tel-Aviv visualized in these drawings, in opposition to the situation on
the ground, has been interpreted lately as if Gutman foresaw the dis-

traction of Manshiya, a quarter of Jaffa that spread northward along the seashore and was gradually destroyed after being conquered in 1948.[26] Gutman of course was well aware of Jaffa, Manshiya, and Neve Tzedek, which he often depicted in paintings and drawings during the 1920s, 1930s, and later. However, he totally separated the Arab and the Jewish communities in his art, like most artists of his generation.[27]

The nostalgic yearning for the "good old days" of Tel-Aviv, already evident in the 1930s, received a significant impetus with Gutman's book *A Small Town with Few People* (1959) on the occasion of the city's Jubilee celebrations.[28] The book, consisting of illustrated memoirs and stories from Ahuzat Bayit, was published in several editions over the years, thus disseminating among generations of young readers the image of Tel-Aviv as an innocent and isolated settlement built on the empty dunes. Concurrently, Gutman began adapting the small illustrations for use in a monumental public setting in which the story of the city was portrayed: a 25-m-long wood-panel mural titled *Early Days* was painted for the Jubilee exhibition of 1959.[29] This was the first in a series of public art pieces that Gutman created throughout the 1960s and 1970s and depicted the story of Tel-Aviv.[30] These mosaic murals are located at historical sites, such as the former site of the Herzliya School, today the Shalom Tower, or near the first municipality of Tel-Aviv in Bialik Square, and serve as monumental storyboards that convey the myth of the city to its inhabitants. As public art they also function as actual sites recommended for visitors as part of the city's historical sightseeing tours.[31]

Gutman not only helped establish the visual image of the myth of Tel-Aviv in the public imagination, but he himself became a prominent part of this story: the story of his boyhood in little Tel-Aviv is repeatedly told among the stories of the city's personae; the Gutman Museum (opened in 1998) in Neve Tzedek is promoting various educational projects on the artist and the city; and several guided walks in Tel-Aviv follow Gutman's life and stories as part of their theme.

The prominent artists of the 1920s were not too keen on depicting Tel-Aviv, especially when compared to more exotic and ancient places in the country. Occasionally Tel-Aviv was painted in those years, but these works are little known today. Arie Lubin (1897–1980) is known to have made numerous drawings and watercolors of Tel-Aviv, especially of the modern buildings of the city.[32] Most of these works have remained as yet unexplored and mostly unseen in public. At the annual exhibitions of the Jewish Artists Association, the major platform during the 1920s for artists in the Yishuv to show their work, a marginal number of images of Tel-Aviv were displayed, generally by lesser known artists.[33] An interesting exception that deserves further study is the several paintings of Tel-Aviv of the 1920s by Ludwig Blum (1891–1974), an artist who is mainly identified with images of Jerusalem, and whose status has been somewhat marginal in the Israeli art canon. Blum's fairly realistic depictions show the city as a compact town, unlike the empty sand dunes seen in those paintings that became part of the canon of Israeli art. His detailed representation of Tel-Aviv buildings and rooftops was quite unusual among contemporary pictures of the city.[34]

By the 1930s more images of Tel-Aviv were painted, several by Haim Gliksberg (1904–1970).[35] It is often argued that artists in Palestine at the time fell under the spell of Paris, or more accurately, the Jewish School of Paris. This is the explanation given to the sudden change to a darker color scheme, the thick impasto texture, and expressive brush strokes. Moreover, the Paris influence is credited with the relative interest in the cityscape motif, mainly that of the boulevard, the first and only one in Tel-Aviv at the time, Rothschild Boulevard.[36] A number of views of the Boulevard were painted by Gliksberg and others, such as Avraham Naton and Yehezkel Streichman, who later became better known as abstract artists and members of the New Horizons group. A few views of Bograshov St. with deep perspective and trees on both sides reflect a similar spirit.[37] What is peculiar is that one of the most typical themes in Paris life and art, the café, did not make its way to the canvases of Tel-Aviv in spite of the widespread presence of lively cafés in the city in those days.[38] Artists focused on the little kiosk on Rothschild Boulevard. One wonders if this choice does not resonate with the mood of nostalgia for "little Tel-Aviv," which was already evident in the public discourse of the period, in which the famous kiosks had always occupied an important role.[39]

For those artists who did paint the city the kiosk was hardly a major theme in their art. An interesting exception is the large body of works produced by Yosef Zaritsky during the 1930s and 1940s. Moving from Jerusalem to Tel-Aviv in 1930 Zaritsky built his house on Mapu St. (called then Hagalil, marking the northern edge of Tel-Aviv) on the corner of

Ben Yehuda St. There he created hundreds of watercolors dedicated to a single section of the landscape seen from his window and from the roof of his house.[40] Standing on the rooftop, Zaritsky turned his eyes eastward, toward Ramat Gan, the nearby town, and painted the view of its hills in the background, the Tel-Aviv rooftops in the middle-ground, and the radio antenna or the roof railing in the foreground. When Zaritsky turned his back on the sea, as it is often pointed out, it was by no means a cultural or a political statement but purely an aesthetic choice.

The Mediterranean Sea as seen from Zaritsky's location—on top of a four-story house, some 300 m from the sea shore—is merely a flat bright surface under the dazzling, often colorless sky; not as visually interesting as the opposite side that shows a much more varied view. Tel-Aviv is certainly partly seen in these watercolors, yet it is almost difficult to identify them specifically as paintings of Tel-Aviv.

In the history of Israeli art no other single location is depicted so often and in such a variety of ways, argues Shlomo Shva; and still, these are not paintings of a "real" place, he claims, but rather the artist's imagined version of the place.[41] Tel-Aviv itself was not Zaristky's primary subject; rather, it was the act of painting—as indicated by the figure of a painter on the roof seen in some works. This tendency to move away from realism was manifested not only in Zaritsky's subject matter, but style. In the 1950s his style evolved closer to full abstraction, through the process of turning visual impressions of space, light, and objects into a grid of lines and abstracted elements.

It was not the modern city of Tel-Aviv that Zaritsky was after but rather a pretext for his project as a modern painter aspiring to liberate art from narrative and figurative elements. Zaritsky was not even particularly attached to the city, as he wittily declared in 1980, "Fifty years I am in Tel-Aviv but until today I feel myself Jerusalemite."[42] It is curious therefore that he has been linked to one of the growing myths of Tel-Aviv, that of the "White City."[43] His close contacts with architects and the "architectural" syntax of his paintings were presented in an exhibition held at the Tel-Aviv University Gallery, as a link between Zaritsky's paintings and the 1930s International Style architecture of Tel-Aviv.[44] The modern language of art and architecture is presented as a common ground for a comparative exercise. In this case, however, Zaritsky, whose house stood on the edge of the newly planned city of the following decades, is described as an artist who "gave expression to the changes and the rapid development of the city . . . he observed the beginnings of the incursive encounter between the urban space and the amorphous nature that he represented by the virgin landscape in the background . . ."[45]

Not only are his paintings said to represent urban development and the civilizing, conquering of nature, he is also presented as one of the city's founding fathers, "one who took part in the society that built the White City."[46] Zartisky, who was always cautious regarding the use of national rhetoric in artistic discourse, and whose critics have always preferred to analyze in formalist terms, is now embraced not only by the modernist myth of Tel-Aviv but also by the heroic stories of its foundation. "Zaritsky's Tel-Aviv," writes Mordechai Omer, director of the Tel-Aviv University Gallery, "was a new Hebrew city that has risen and been built on the sands of the Mediterranean shore."[47] From a retrospective distance the different visions of Tel-Aviv produced by Gutman, Rubin, and Zaritsky blend together into similar ideals and myths.

Zaritsky's major influence on Israeli art from the late 1940s to the early 1960s was in leading the abstract trend. As abstraction became the dominant style, images of the city have virtually disappeared. This, of course, was not exceptional. Images of Paris, Berlin, and New York in art were more common during the first decades of the twentieth century than later. In the 1960s, the return of daily life both as subject matter and in materials, following the influence of American Pop Art and European Nouveau Realism, brought the city back into art. At times the street itself invaded art, while new artistic methods, in turn, influenced the city.

A "happening" held on a Tel-Aviv street in 1970 resulted in one of the most iconic images in Israeli art: *Tel-Aviv + Pollution* by Michael Druks. The artist (b. 1940) was invited by avant-garde filmmaker Jacques Katmor to create a televised event. He then organized a rather violent attack on a cylindrical street billboard: its thick skin, the result of some ten to fifteen years of weekly pasted advertisements, was cut with an axe and peeled off before the eyes of the passersby and the television cameras.[48] *Tel-Aviv + Pollution,* an "assisted readymade,"[49] as the artist calls it, one of the remnants of the skinned billboard, alludes to the city skyline with its blackened edges. Moreover, it offers an unromantic image of the city, a record of an accumulating present. It presents a systematic display of the film and entertainment stars of the moment and advertisements of

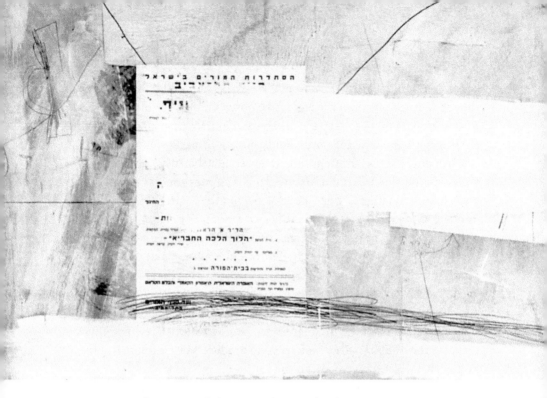

Fig. 14.4. Raffi Lavie, untitled, 1976, acrylic, pencil and
collage on plywood, 80×120 cm. Private collection.

special events, covered and buried under new layers, like archaeological
remains of the public sphere. Bygone glamour, street publicity, and the
smog and pollution of the city are trapped together. Evident of the il-
lusory quality of the present, this is an utterly prosaic image of the city,
devoid of myth or pathos.

In Israeli art criticism of recent decades the artist Raffi Lavie is often identified with Tel-Aviv. Like Druks, he also used advertisements
and billboard announcements in his collages. These are usually textual
notices and very often they advertise concerts, literary events, lectures,
and public debates on art in Tel-Aviv, a city of high culture.

For Lavie, as a young artist growing up in Ramat Gan, Tel-Aviv
was undoubtedly the wonder city of art and culture, where he absorbed
his artistic influences at museum exhibitions and where he acquired
art history knowledge at public lectures.[50] Lavie was mainly an abstract
painter, but, as part of his experiments in collage, he created assemblages
of images usually taken from magazines and calendars, a practice not

unusual in art of the time. It is interesting to note that no image of Tel-Aviv features in these works. He mostly used images of European landscapes or in some cases views of Ramat Gan, where he lived until moving to Tel-Aviv in the summer of 1973.[51] Lavie is considered *the* Tel-Avivian artist not due to images of the city he created but rather due to a stylistic analogy suggested between the city and his art:

> Tel-Aviv, whitewashed (peeling off), the city with a bewildering amalgam of styles, a metropolis of glaring white light and ever-shifting, volatile beats, is all there in Raffi Lavie's work. . . . Tel-Aviv belongs to that realm of the "other aesthetics"—for which Raffi Lavie strives.[52]

This idea, which was later developed by curator Sara Breitberg-Semel into an aesthetic concept of Israeli art, was first introduced by Lavie himself when describing his art as "Tel-Avivian." In an interview on the topic "What does it mean to be an Israeli artist?" Lavie was adamant that had he been born with the same character in a different country his painting "would be completely different."

> Not only am I a "sabra" but a Tel-Avivian. My painting is explicitly Israeli. . . . I am not a sociologist. I only know how I feel, and I feel that I am a Tel-Avivian . . . A typical Tel-Avivian. I have always lived with my face to the sea. This is me—the clarity of my colors, the dazzling of the light, the nuances of pinks, grays, and white. These are no doubt Tel-Aviv, though I have only realized this lately, in retrospect.[53]

Whereas Lavie never painted Tel-Aviv he nonetheless claimed a visual link existed between the look of the city, its light and climate, and his own choice of colors and style of paintings. To an extent he follows Zaritsky, who had often proclaimed the influence of the light and the climate of the country on his painting.[54]

A magnified version of this idea was at the heart of a large-scale group exhibition held at the Tel-Aviv Museum in 1986 titled *The Want of Matter—A Quality in Israeli Art*. The idea that a certain local aesthetic idiom can be discerned in contemporary Israeli art in relation to the Tel-Aviv environment was extended to other artists, many of whom were Lavie's former pupils. The idea referred not only to aspects of color and composition but to the use of materials and the very attitude to materiality, especially the preference for meager and plain materials. An important aspect of this theory that is not always taken into account is the unmistakable identification of Tel-Aviv with Israeliness. A group of artists the curator calls The "Tel-Avivians" are defined as Israeli-born artists

> who absorbed their primary concepts of landscape and climate, society, culture and art, here in Israel. . . . one can say that they belong to that sheltered inner circle comprised of the descendants of the Labor movement's members. They were part of the youth or the kibbutz movement, the very core of the country's 'elite' . . . An understanding of the artists' social origins is important to a discussion of the Tel-Aviv group in light of the tremendous impact of social Zionist values on the ideal of the nation. . . . These values . . . created the accepted norms of behavior, dress, and preferred forms of expression. The meagerness of material as an expression of spiritual content is the legacy of social Zionism.[55]

In view of this analysis it is not surprising that the list of so-called Tel-Avivian artists in this exhibition include those who were born on a kibbutz or are kibbutz members, those who did not grow up in Tel-Aviv or even do not live there. The identification of the Eretz-Israel of the Labor movement with the city of Tel-Aviv as proposed in this theory is not exclusively an aesthetic observation, and may be seen as a response to the changing political climate. Maoz Azaryahu notes that after 1977, when the Labor party lost its hegemony, Tel-Aviv came to represent the last refuge of "normal" and "sane" Israeliness; an Israeliness that is identified with the political left, with secularism, liberalism, and Western values in general; a sort of "enlightened" Israel (which nevertheless carries an air of elitism and exclusivity).[56] Above all, it is Jerusalem which is rejected, along with everything associated with it.[57] In the art field as elsewhere in Israeli culture, the rivalry between the two cities helped define their specific identities, particularly that of Tel-Aviv.[58]

In order to characterize the Tel-Avivian aspects in the art of Lavie, Breitberg-Semel contrasts it with Jerusalem, a city of monuments and heavyweight history. Tel-Aviv, she writes, "is a city without focus (no Western Wall, no city walls, no Augusta Victoria), just like his paintings."[59] The focus in Jerusalem is not an urban one but a conceptual one. Whereas Tel-Aviv, as the poet Meir Wieseltier put it, is "a city without a concept."[60] It is a city with no special dimension other than just being a city of people, argue Zali Gurevich and Gideon Aran in their essay on the locale in Israeli identity. As such, they add, Tel-Aviv unlike Jerusalem can offer a clear-cut response to the perpetual question of Israeli identity:

> it is free of confusion, it is all "Israeli," it is all "ours." In contemporary Israeli culture it signifies the liberation from struggle over the place; the turning away from the non-Israeli within the Israeli; from Judaism on the one hand, and from the local Arabs on the other hand.[61]

This characterization is precisely the pure, simple, and secular Tel-Aviv presented by *The Want of Matter*: "For the 'Tel-Aviv child' there is no 'religion', no 'nation', no 'land', there is only the concrete city. There is no ideology, but true vitality."[62] The nostalgic tone evoked in representations of Tel-Aviv in art, whether intended by artists or imposed on them by later interpreters, is to an extent also the case of the concept of *The Want of Matter*.

When the exhibition was shown in 1986, the shabby elderly city, discussed in forgiving affection in the exhibition text, was already on the verge of a face-lift, if not a real change of character. In 1984 another exhibition held at the TAM invigorated a gradually growing public awareness toward the conservation of the city's architectural heritage. Curated by architecture historian Michael Levin, *White City: The Architecture of the International Style in Israel: A Profile of a Period* was not specifically about Tel-Aviv; rather it focused on the various characteristics of modern architecture and their implementation in pre-state Israel, the major influences on this trend and its manifestations in various buildings around the country. Nonetheless, Tel-Aviv's modern architecture was at the center of this study and, in retrospect, the exhibition is seen as the beginning of a process that culminated twenty years later in the declaration by UNESCO of "White City of Tel-Aviv—The Modern Movement" as a World Heritage Site.[63] Of the various results of this process there was the transformation of the worn out city into a fresh and modern city, returning it both visually and conceptually to its ideal youth. At the same time, another rejuvenation development was apparent in the old center of the city: the emergence of an alternative youth culture in and around Shenkin St. during the 1980s.[64] By that time the Tel-Aviv of Lavie and *The Want of Matter* already belonged to the past.

One of the youngest participants in *The Want of Matter* exhibition and perhaps the least identified with its concept was David Reeb (b. 1952), one of the important emerging artists of the 1980s. This was the time when figurative painting was reintroduced to contemporary art internationally as well as in Israel, as part of a so-called "return to painting" trend. Reeb was one of the prominent artists of the new painting trend, and early on he became known for his political paintings that involved images of the Israeli army in war and in the occupation, often based on photographs. The catalogue of *The Want of Matter*, in line with its overall aesthetic theory, referred mainly to the "intentionally poor" pictorial elements in Reeb's works in terms of a flattening approach to matter and to the figure.[65] The highly charged political content of the paintings is not discussed. Along with his political works Reeb has always painted "traditional" themes from direct observation, such as plants and vases with flowers or landscapes, including Tel-Aviv views. In fact, Reeb is fairly exceptional in having regularly painted Tel-Aviv since the 1980s, continuing to do so today.[66] Tel-Aviv roofs, blocks of apartments, and tree tops viewed from Reeb's rooftop in the old center of Tel-Aviv, not far from Shenkin St., are typical of his early paintings on the subject in the late 1980s: old, charmless, and often dirty houses, densely painted in a realistic manner, devoid of sentimentality or nostalgia, and without poeticizing the scruffy and neglected look.

Reeb likes this view of flat roofs with the solar hot water tanks and forest of TV antennae. "Your own place is always beautiful," he remarks, revealing not a possessive attitude but a natural feeling of belonging to the place; he also states, matter-of-factly: "Since I am here, I paint what is here."[67] Unlike Zaritsky, who looked from his rooftop toward the horizon, to the hills of Ramat Gan as a starting point for his paintings, Reeb is interested in his immediate surroundings. As an artist the formal arrangement of the view on the surface of the painting is highly significant for him, yet no less meaningful is the fact that this view is part of his living environment. His factual, realistic approach is a noteworthy departure from the mythic images of the city during the 1920s and 1930s. In a sense Reeb is the first artist to make Tel-Aviv, the real place, an important element in his oeuvre.

At the time, Reeb painted only on paper and produced a series consisting of several sheets, sometimes divided into separate scenes. Here he was interested in juxtaposing two manners of painting—one based on direct observation of outdoor scenes and the other based on pho-

Fig. 14.5. David Reeb, *Tel-Aviv—Gaza,* 1988, acrylic on paper, 6 parts,
100×70 cm each. Collection David Tartakover, Tel-Aviv.

tographs he found in newspapers; one in color and one in black and
white; and two types of subject matter—one is familiar: lovely views
from his balcony in Melchett St., and one that is recognizable only from
the media—Gaza City of the first Intifada. What is so powerful in this
forthright juxtaposition of the two cities, beyond the painter's experi-
mentation, is that it exposes the vast, unbridgeable, ever-growing distance between them: Tel-Aviv is colorful and lit up, even if the colors
are fading in places, while Gaza is gloomy and colorless; Tel-Aviv is
erect and decorated with greenery, whereas Gaza's houses have turned
to rubble by the military; Tel-Aviv is serene while Gaza is full of violent
motion; Tel-Aviv images show no people, while Gaza's population is on
display: large families, Israeli soldiers, and Palestinian fighters. If Tel-

Aviv is frequently compared to Jerusalem, or to great world cities such as Paris and New York, or as would be expected, to Jaffa, the paralleling with Gaza offers an entirely different perspective: it directly associates Tel-Aviv with the occupation.

This connection is rarely seen in Israeli art[68] and little discussed elsewhere in the public sphere. While Tel-Aviv is free and as safe for the artist, as it is for his viewers, it can no longer pretend to be the innocent settlement on the pure sands or the modern clean "white city," detached from the Israeli-Palestinian conflict and the violent reality of the region. Unlike the nostalgic patina that many Tel-Aviv images accumulate, this became more poignant over the years. In the twenty years since it was painted, Tel-Aviv has developed and flourished while Gaza has slowly been destroyed.

* * *

Throughout most of its century Tel-Aviv has played only a limited role in the work of its artists. Being Israel's center of artistic activity and its most important city made little difference to its function as a subject for art. Why is that so? The simple explanation is that the city as such was not attractive to many of its artists. Painter Yosef Kossonogi admitted: "Usually we sought after nature in town, not the urban town. . . I mainly painted the Yarkon stream, the sycamore trees, or Jaffa when it still had fishermen."[69] On a similar note, referring to the abundance of landscape painting at the time, art critic and curator Yigal Zalmona claimed that "The need to express the experience of primality naturally led the artists of the 1920s to paint landscape rather than urban scenes."[70] In essence, these statements assume that urban cityscapes and industrial developments would intrinsically be unappealing to the modern artists of Jewish Palestine either for aesthetic reasons or due to ideological preference for countryside views.[71] This choice is by no means self-evident. Not only was the rise of modern art closely linked to the development of the metropolis and the rise of the bourgeoisie, first and foremost in nineteenth-century Paris, but artists there, most notably the Impressionists, were keen on depicting various aspects of city life, the sheer manifestation of modernity.[72] Likewise, American artists of the first decades of the twentieth century found the fast-growing city of New York both stimulating as the expression of the new and the modern, and representing the American spirit.[73]

For avant-garde movements such as Italian Futurism and Russian Constructivism, the urban environment and modern technologies were not only an aesthetic inspiration but also the core of their cultural and social ideologies. Of course, the city was not always romanticized; hostility and anti-urban attitude were also present in early twentieth-century art, particularly in German Expressionism. Various art trends in Europe and North America responded to the city as a reflection of the modern condition and as *the* universal representation of modernity. In view of that, the reluctance of Israeli artists to respond to Tel-Aviv as a modern city may be related to the general ambivalence toward the city and urban life in the Yishuv.[74] The preference for countryside scenes in the 1920s owes no less to the influence of French art of the time, particularly the conservative and nationalist oriented tendencies that professed a "return" to traditional pre-modern values.[75]

However, another question should be asked here: why would artists be *expected* to depict Tel-Aviv at all? Artists are not documentarians, and modern artists in particular were averse to the idea of imitating the visible world. In addition, artists in the Yishuv have not felt obliged to represent the Zionist enterprise developing around them.[76] This was the role of photographers. In those days photography was not yet considered art and artists used to distinguish themselves from photographers and refer to photography as the opposite of art. To copy nature "with photographic realism," said the painter Israel Paldi, was the opposite of what an artist should aspire to, since it involves appealing "exclusively to the senses, to awaken no higher response than mere recognition." What an art work should be, according to Paldi, was "not impression taken directly from nature, but the synthesis in the mind of the artists of many observations."[77]

The visual image of Tel-Aviv as a growing urban center, with its modern architecture, busy street traffic, public institutions, shops and markets, and various forms of entertainment was distributed primarily through photographs and films. Like Soskin in his 1926 album of Tel-Aviv views, many of the photographers and filmmakers of the following decades focused on the modernity of Tel-Aviv and emphasized its resemblance to a western metropolis. As discussed above, paintings of Tel-Aviv seem to have had another role; to reiterate the myths of the pure and naïve city that sprung from the sands, or the modernist, progressive, and international White City, or yet another image, that of the secular, open-minded locus for the authentic free-spirited *sabra* and the manifestation of Israeli identity. The way critics and historians have been receptive to the stories and myths of Tel-Aviv in analyzing its art is above all a testimony to the ongoing appealing power of these myths.

* * *

Since the 1980s there have been some changes in the relationship between Tel-Aviv and Israeli art. The rise of fine art photography in the 1980s by young photographers who brought recent international influences meant a new focus on un-heroic, mundane, and marginal sights of Israeli life. In Tel-Aviv, Barry Frydlender revisited the Cassit Café, one of the mythic establishments of the city that had passed its prime, and was now occupied by bygone celebrities. In Frydlender's images those are often blurred as his lens focuses on the elderly waiter. Looking at the overlooked has since been the interest of many Israeli photographers, and capturing Tel-Aviv backyards was one aspect of this trend. Yet the city as a subject, as shown in a recent exhibition organized to mark the one hundredth anniversary at the Tel-Aviv Museum, is not the preoccupation of contemporary photographers. Instead, many of them opt for the intimate experience and for quite isolated spaces. In a way, this large exhibition of forty-three artists demonstrates the absence of the city from its art.[78]

The rapid change in the Tel-Aviv skyline since the 1990s was noticed by photographers as well as by painters. A small number of artists who have developed an American-influenced realism have started painting broad vistas and cityscapes of Tel-Aviv.[79] The growing number of high rises and office towers that poke the skyline allow artists to paint the city from above in marvelous panoramic scenes previously reserved mainly for Jerusalem—a distanced generalized viewpoint, an adoring gaze that combines the light and sky above with the real and symbolic city below. From the height of the newly built luxury apartment towers and the glass skyscrapers Tel-Aviv looks magnificent: silently gleaming in the pinkish soft light of the sky and the sea.

On the other hand, lower Tel-Aviv, the mundane, gray, and gritty city, especially the ambiguous area on the southern margins of the historic city, between Jaffa and Tel-Aviv, attracted the attention of several artists who live or work in the area.[80] In the history of Tel-Aviv art the very fact that artists have searched for their subject within their vicinity is exceptional; all the more so, when the view is of a haphazard collection of workshops, rooftops, cranes, and building sites, gray industrial buildings, disorderly parked cars or gloomy pedestrians among buses' fumes—no picturesque scenes.

The interaction of artists with this area is the result of significant process in its own right: spreading from the old Central Bus Station area through the Florentin neighborhood and the industrial district south of Salame Road, this is probably the largest concentration of Israeli artists' studios. Neglected for decades by the city authorities and ignored by historians and chroniclers of Tel-Aviv, this buffer zone on the hyphen between Tel-Aviv and Jaffa has undergone dramatic change in the last decade. Still in the midst of a gentrification process, the area offers a strange mixture: dilapidated houses next to garages that have turned into designer furniture stores; sex services and drug dealers next to fashionable cafés and art galleries; real-estate enterprises renovating apartment blocks next to old carpentry workshops and car service garages; graffiti covered walls and piles of garbage next to new elegant housing projects. Art and artists are visibly part of this process. Like in other cities, artists went to the area to look for cheap rent and large spaces for their studios.

Various enterprises followed suit, among them the opening of private galleries, from a tiny cooperative artists' gallery opened in 2005 in Florentin to the relocation in 2009 of an established gallery from its glitzy, long-held place on Dizengoff St. to an industrial space next to workshops and artists' studios. Two public galleries also exist in the area, the gallery at the Artists' Studios in Florentin, operating since 1990 (opened in 1988 as a municipal project), and the exhibition space as a branch of Bezalel Academy of Arts and Design opened in 2001 in an industrial building on Salame Road for the academy's MFA program. In between, there are more galleries and alternative art spaces opening every year in this area.

In its centenary year, the map of galleries in Tel-Aviv connects the different quarters of the city: from the location of the first galleries on and around Gordon St. off Dizengoff St., the hub of the city in the 1960s and 1970s, to the currently booming Rothschild Boulevard area and its fairly new galleries, down to Neve Tzedek—a bustling, prosperous, over-designed, renovated, touristy "old city"—or to the yet undeveloped former central bus station, and further south to the Florentin area. Actual art maps are sometimes printed on the occasion of art events organized by the city culture department: the annual summer "white night" cele-bration marking the White City's recognition (since 2003), and the "lov-ing art" night of the art season opening in the fall (since 2002). While the city of Tel-Aviv only occasionally features in the work of its artists, the art and its institutions certainly play a role in the story of the city, from its founding myth to the present-day festivals.

## NOTES

1. Sharon Rothbard, *White City, Black City* (Tel-Aviv 2005), 84 [Hebrew].

2. Haim Feirberg, "Lottery for Plots of Ahuzat Bayit: The Creation of an Urban Myth," *Israel* 4 (2003): 83–107. See also Yaacov Shavit and Gideon Biger, *The History of Tel-Aviv*, vol. 1 (Tel-Aviv, 2001), 70–71 [both in Hebrew].

3. Abraham Soskin, *Album of Tel-Aviv Views* (Tel-Aviv, ca. 1926). Feirberg ("Lot-tery for Plots of Ahuzat Bayit," 102) argues that Soskin identified wrongly, although in good faith, the photograph as showing a founding event in the history of Tel-Aviv and that he made other mistakes in titles and dates.

4. Barbara E. Mann, *A Place in History: Modernism, Tel-Aviv, and the Creation of Jewish Urban Space* (Stanford, 2006), 74. The notion of Tel-Aviv as emerging from the empty sands and bringing civilization to the wilderness was spread during the 1920s and 1930s. See Maoz Azaryahu, *Tel-Aviv—The Real City* (Sde-Boker, 2005), 55–61 [Hebrew].

5. Batia Carmiel, *Tel-Aviv in Photographs: The First Decade, 1909–1918* (Tel-Aviv, 1990), 10–15; Hana Kofler, *Tsalmania in Tel-Aviv: Rudi Weissenstein (1910–1992)—Tel-Aviv 1930s–1960s* (Tel-Aviv, 2002) [both in Hebrew].

6. For a detailed survey of the subject, see Shlomo Shva, "The Painted Tel-Aviv," in *Tel-Aviv in its Beginning, 1909–1934*, ed. Mordechai Naor (Jerusalem, 1984), 107–121. See also *Tel-Aviv: 75 Years of Art*, ed. Yona Fisher (Givatayim, 1984); Carmela Rubin, cur., *Tel-Aviv at 80* (Tel-Aviv, 1989) [all in Hebrew].

7. Mann, *A Place in History*, 77, 79–88, 134–141; Joachim Schlör, *Tel-Aviv: From Dream to City* (London, 1999), 25–28; Mark Levine, *Overthrowing Geography: Jaffa, Tel-Aviv, and the Struggle for Palestine, 1880–1948* (Berkeley, Los Angeles, London, 2005), 154–155, 333 n16; Yaacov Shavit and Gideon Biger, *The History of Tel-Aviv*, vol. 2 (Tel-Aviv, 2007), 264–265, and vol. 4 (Tel-Aviv, 2002), 194–195 [Hebrew].

8. Quoted in a catalogue of the exhibition *Tel-Aviv: Little Metropolis* held in May 1979 at the Givon Gallery in Tel-Aviv on the occasion of the seventieth an-niversary of the city. Not paginated; text retrieved from the electronic resource of Israeli Art.

9. Dalia Manor, *Art in Zion: The Genesis of Modern National Art in Jewish Palestine* (London, 2005), 113–133.

10. Quoted by Edmond Fleg, *The Land of Promise* (London, 1933), 130–131, and Manor, *Art in Zion,* 121.

11. Carmela Rubin, *Dreamland: Reuven Rubin and His Encounter with the Land of Israel in His Paintings of the 1920s and 1930s* (Tel-Aviv, 2006) [Hebrew].

12. Carmela Rubin, *Rubin's Tel-Aviv* (Tel-Aviv, 1984) [Hebrew]; Schlör, *Tel-Aviv,* 27–28.

13. Shlomo Shva, "Tel-Aviv on Canvas," in *Tel-Aviv: A Salute to Tel-Aviv on the Occasion of its 80th Anniversary,* ed. Carmela Rubin (Tel-Aviv, 1989).

14. Between the summer of 1922 and the summer of 1924, Tel-Aviv (united with its adjacent neighborhoods) grew from 1,007 to 1,936 houses (excluding barracks and tents) and its population grew from 12,862 to 21,610. Shavit and Biger, *Tel-Aviv,* 1, 93; Ilan Shchori, *The Dream Turned into Metropolis* (Tel-Aviv, 1990), 400; Dan Giladi, *Jewish Palestine during the Fourth Aliya (1924–1929): Economic and Social Aspects* (Tel-Aviv, 1973), 54–55 [both in Hebrew].

15. *Rubin: Retrospective Exposition: 40 Years of Painting in Israel* (Tel-Aviv, 1955) [Hebrew]. Several other paintings are wrongly dated in this catalogue, among them *The Madonna of the Homeless* of 1922 (Rubin Museum), dated 1917–1918.

16. *Rubin: Retrospective Exhibition* (The Israel Museum, Jerusalem and The Tel-Aviv Museum, Helena Rubinstein Pavilion, 1966); Sarah Wilkinson, *Reuven Rubin* (New York, 1974) 30; Dorith LeVite and Gideon Ofrat, *The Story of Art in Israel,* ed. Benjamin Tammuz (Tel-Aviv, 1980), 34, here titled *The Beginning of Tel-Aviv;* Dan Yahav, *Tel-Aviv-Jaffa: Dream's City* (Tel-Aviv, 2005), 313 [Hebrew].

17. Haim Gamzu, introduction to *Rubin: Retrospective Exhibition,* n.p.

18. Shva, "The Painted Tel-Aviv," 110.

19. Rubin's Romanian passport, issued on 20 February 1923, shows an exit from Romania on 17 April and entry to Palestine on 24 April on a visitor's visa (later extended). See also Manor, *Art in Zion,* 217, n. 3. The Rubin Museum official publications, the catalogue of the permanent collection (2nd edition 2003), and the museum website (April 2009) adhere, however, to 1922 as the year of Rubin's settlement in Palestine and the date of the painting *Tel-Aviv.*

20. Câminul Artelor, *Regina Maria,* in *Expozitia Rubin* (Bucharest, 1924). RMA. A painting titled *Landscape near Tel-Aviv* was exhibited at the Jerusalem exhibition in March 1924 of 56 oil paintings. It may be the same one that was exhibited in Bucharest, but it is hard to tell whether it relates to the painting now titled *Tel-Aviv.*

21. *Open Window (Potted Plant on the Window Sill),* 1923, oil on canvas, 65×50.5 cm, collection of Phoenix Insurance Co.

22. Gideon Biger, "Nordia—The Neighborhood that Vanished," *Ariel* 48–49 (1987): 144–146 [Hebrew]; Shavit and Biger, *Tel-Aviv,* 1, 218–219; Yahav, *Tel-Aviv-Jaffa* 474–476.

23. The name "Nordia" was preserved until the 1970s as a name of a nearby group of shacks built on a plot belonging to an Arab landowner, Hinawi, the site of Dizengoff Center. See Tamar Berger, *Dionysus in the Center* (Tel-Aviv, 1998) [Hebrew].

24. Nitza Drori-Peremen, "The Young Man and the Sea," in Carmela Rubin, *Dreamland,* 205.

25. Gutman's first illustrations of Tel-Aviv were published in the theatre journal *Bamah* of 1933–1934. The *Tel-Aviv Book,* initially planned for publication on the occa-

sion of the twenty-fifth anniversary of Tel-Aviv (1934) included various visual docu-
mentations such as photographs and maps. Gutman's drawing had a similar function
in the book. See Edna Moshenson, "From Jaffa to Tel-Aviv: Small Town with Few
People," in *Nahum Gutman,* ed. Edna Moshenson (Tel-Aviv, 1984), 52–53 [Hebrew].

26. Rotbard, *White City, Black City,* 134.

27. This is also true in the case of Rubin who had rarely joined the figures of an
Arab and a Jew on the same canvas, mainly for symbolic reasons. See Manor, *Art in
Zion,* 97, 161–162. Another interesting exception is Rubin's now-titled *Hassan Bek
Mosque* of 1923 (oil on canvas, 50×70 cm, private collection). It shows Manshiya with
the Mosque on one side, and on the other side a group of tents—perhaps the temporary Allenby Camp for newcomers—with a relatively small empty space of dunes
between them.

28. Azaryahu, *Tel-Aviv—The Real City,* 112.

29. Doron Lurie, "The Lost Panels Mystery: The Making, Disappearance, Discov-
ery and Conservation of *Early Day* by Nahum Gutman," *Proza* 95–96 (1987): 65–68
[Hebrew]. On the Jubilee exhibition, see Maoz Azaryahu, "Tel-Aviv Birthdays: Anniversary Celebrations of the First Hebrew City 1929–1959," *Israel Studies* 14.3 (2009).

30. For Gutman murals see *City of Sand and Sea,* ed. Nahum Gutman, and added
text: Shlomo Shva (Ramat Gan, 1979) [Hebrew].

31. The mosaic at the Shalom Tower was recommended as a starting point of a
"Guided Stroll from Ahuzat Bayit to Little Tel-Aviv," in *Tel-Aviv in its Beginning,
1909–1934,* ed. Mordechai Naor, 196. The mosaics in Shalom Tower and Bialik Square
feature in the Orange Route of Little Tel-Aviv, one of four sign-posted routes devised
for visitors in the city. Available from: http://www.tel-aviv.gov.il/Hebrew/Tourism/
Tours/Orange.asp. Accessed 16 April 2009. These tours are intended primarily for
the Israeli Hebrew-reading public. See also http://www.tel-aviv.gov.il/English/home
.asp. In February 2008 Gutman's mosaic sculpture in Bialik Square was removed in
advance of the renovation of the Square and the old municipality building. It was
claimed that the structure hid the view of the municipality façade. The mosaics are
to be relocated as part of a developing project on no. 1 Rothschild Boulevard on the
border of Neve Tzedek and Ahuzat Bayit. The White Route, one of three new sign-
posted walking routes of Tel-Aviv inaugurated in 2009, starts here. http://tayarut
.index.co.il/siteFiles/1/33/339783.asp. Accessed 1 September 2010.

32. Shva, "The Painted Tel-Aviv," 112–113; see *Tel-Aviv at 80* (two drawings of 1926).

33. The 1924 exhibition checklist includes 161 paintings, including *Tel-Aviv* by
V. Wechtel and *The Beach in Tel-Aviv,* by Zuckerman. A painting by Israel Paldi, titled
*A Neighborhood by the Sea Shore,* may refer to Tel-Aviv: *3rd Annual Exhibition at the
Citadel Jerusalem,* 14 April–15 May (Jerusalem, [1924]). This proportion was typical
of later annual exhibitions. See Manor, *Art in Zion,* 188, appendix A.

34. A number of previously unseen paintings of Tel Aviv by Ludwig Blum were
displayed in an exhibition of the artist's work organized by the author in Beit Hat-
futsot Museum in Tel-Aviv, September–December 2009. See Dalia Manor, *The Real
and the Ideal: The Painting of Ludwig Blum* (Tel-Aviv, 2009).

35. According to Bella Kalev, the artist's daughter (conversation with the author,
10 March 2009), Gliksberg produced twenty-nine paintings of Tel-Aviv since moving
there from Jerusalem in 1928. He was mainly attracted to old Tel-Aviv street corners,
i.e., Ahad Ha'am St. and Hashahar St., Iddelson St., the kiosk on Rothschild Boule-

vard, Bialik House courtyard, and several views in Neve Tzedek. Gliksberg, however, is better known as a portrait painter. He also made numerous drawings related to Bialik. For a few of his Tel-Aviv views see Aya Lurie, *Treasured in the Heart: Haim Gliksberg's Portraits* (Tel-Aviv, 2005), 23, 123, 129, 134, 136, 137.

36. Haim Gamzu, *Painting and Sculpture in Israel* (Tel-Aviv, 1951), 19–23; Gideon Ofrat, *One Hundred Years of Art in Israel* (Boulder, CO, 1998), 65–66.

37. For illustrations see *Tel-Aviv at 80.*

38. Anat Helman, *Urban Culture in 1920s and 1930s Tel-Aviv* (Haifa, 2007), 158ff; Batia Carmiel, ed., *Coffeehouses in Tel-Aviv, 1920–1980* (Tel-Aviv, 2007) [both in Hebrew].

39. The first kiosk for selling soft drinks only, a 2×2-m wooden hexagon designed by Joseph Barsky, the designer of Herzliya High School, was built in 1910 following a decision by the neighborhood's committee. Two more kiosks were built in the next decade and many more during the 1920s. Source: http://tel-aviv.millenium.org.il/NR/exeres/2F96A27D-EDE6-433C-94DC-2FCC59611662,frameless.htm. Accessed 12 April 2009. A photograph of the kiosk by Soskin was published in his *Album of Tel-Aviv Views,* and has remained one of the mythological features of Tel-Aviv as a "first." The kiosks in the paintings of the 1930s are probably kiosks that were built later.

40. Mordechai Omer, *Zaritsky: A Retrospective* (Tel-Aviv, 1984), 54 [Hebrew].

41. Shva, "The Painted Tel-Aviv," 118; Omer, *Zaritsky,* 54–56 [Hebrew].

42. Quoted in Omer, *Zaritsky,* 38.

43. On the myth of the White City, see Azaryahu, *The Real City,* 227–248; Rotbard, *White City, Black City,* 11–88.

44. Irit Sadan, *Buildings and Vision from a Bird's Eye View: Tel-Aviv in the Paintings of Zaritsky, 1930–1945* (Tel-Aviv, 2000) [Hebrew].

45. Ibid., 33.

46. Ibid., 5.

47. Mordechai Omer, foreword to *Buildings and Vision from a Bird's Eye View,* 3.

48. Conversation with the artist, 26 August 2008. For still photographs from the short film see Galia Bar Or, *Michael Druks: Travels in Druksland* (Ein Harod, 2007), 27.

49. "Readymade" is a term coined by Marcel Duchamp referring to an object that is already made (usually an industrially manufactured one) and found, rather than produced by the artist. "Assisted" readymade denotes an involvement of the artist in constructing or altering the object.

50. David Ginton, *Raffi: The Early Paintings, 1957–1961* (Tel-Aviv, 1993), 83 [Hebrew]. Lavie was an enthusiastic connoisseur of classical music, and in his youth he had aspired to a career in music. In a conversation with music critic Hanoch Ron, he was asked whether by the inclusion in his work of a poster announcing a concert at the Tel-Aviv Museum he was "remembering the concerts that used to be held there years ago." Typically, Lavie rejected the idea, claiming that he was only interested in the "color and paper quality and a very special print"; in *Raffi Lavie: A Selection of Paintings,* cur. Sara Breitberg (Tel-Aviv, 1980), 29.

51. Between 1973 and 1975 Lavie tried his hand at photographs of non-specific views in the vicinity of his home, into which he had planted sticky notes with written words. This one-off little-known experiment and a few Super 8 films shot from the balcony of his apartment at Yonah Hanavi St. are the only direct representations of Tel-Aviv in his art.

52. Sara Breitberg, "The 'Aesthetics' of Raffi Lavie," in *Raffi Lavie: A Selection of Paintings*, 35.

53. Ruth Debel, "What Does it Mean to be an Israeli Artist?" *Art News* 77 (1978): 55.

54. Omer, *Zartisky*, 33.

55. Sara Breitberg-Semel, *The Want of Matter—A Quality in Israeli Art* (Tel-Aviv, 1986), 185.

56. Azaryahu, *The Real City*, 164.

57. Ibid., 267.

58. In an earlier exhibition Breitberg-Semel had defined the rivalry between the two cities as a competition between two Schools: Bezalel in Jerusalem and the Midrasha (Art Teachers Training College, in effect outside Tel-Aviv) where Lavie was the most influential figure. She argues for a clear superiority of the Midrasha with regard to the treatment of foreign influences. Sara Breitberg-Semel, *A Turning Point: 12 Israeli Artists* (Tel-Aviv, 1981) 35. Gideon Ofrat offers the rivalry prism to discuss Israeli artistic activity of the 1970s and 1980s in the chapter "Two Cities with Two Epistemologies, 1970–1985," in *One Hundred Years of Art in Israel*, 257–300. The split between Tel-Aviv and Jerusalem goes back to Ofrat's writing of the 1930s. Accordingly, he splits the decade into two chapters in the book—one to each city and its trends.

59. Breitberg-Semel, *The Want of Matter*, 182.

60. A line from Wieseltier's poem on Tel-Aviv, "I Have Sympathy," from his book *Something Optimistic—The Making of Poems* (Tel-Aviv, 1976) [Hebrew]. The poem became popular upon being put to music in 1980. The Hebrew term *conseptzia* (used in the poem) denotes a well-established idea that in some cases has proven to be utterly wrong and dangerous, especially with regard to national security, i.e., the 1973 Yom Kippur War.

61. Zali Gurevitch and Gideon Aran, "On the Place (an Israeli Anthropology)," *Alpayim* 4 (1991): 43 [Hebrew].

62. Breitberg-Semel, *The Want of Matter*, 182.

63. This is the official title of the site for conservation. See http://whc.unesco.org/en/list/1096. Accessed 11 April 2009. There are more world heritage sites in Israel but this is the only one of the twentieth century. On the influence of the *White City* exhibition, see Azaryahu, *The Real City*, 239–241; Rotbard, *White City, Black City*, 21–22.

64. Azaryahu, *The Real City*, 192–223.

65. Breitberg-Semel, *The Want of Matter*, 170.

66. Cf. *Two Pigeons*, 2004; *Bird on Rooftop*, 2004, at http://www.davidreeb.com/view.php?1&id=243. Reeb also paints powerful institutions in Tel-Aviv such as banks, the Habima Theatre, and the Tel-Aviv Art Museum, which is across the road from the *kirya* with its major IDF base. See *Kirya*, 2008, at http://www.davidreeb.com/view.php?1&id=432. Accessed 12 April 2009.

67. Conversation with the author, 12 April 2009.

68. A series of photographs by Guy Raz of lifeguard towers in Tel-Aviv beach and in Gaza beach (1999–2002) focus on the similarity in construction and function of this beach feature and the notion of "the same sea," but also exposes, in a deeper look, the difference between the two sites.

69. Quoted in *Tel-Aviv: Little Metropolis*.

70. Yigal Zalmona, *Landscapes in Israel Art* (Jerusalem, 1984), 12 [Hebrew]. Shva similarly suggests a kind of emotional/aesthetic split experienced by artists who em-

braced the new developments in the country but were visually attracted to the old and the Oriental. Shva, "The Painted Tel-Aviv," 110.

71. For a further discussion of the relations between landscape and national ideology, see Dalia Manor, "Imagined Homeland: Landscape Painting in Palestine in the 1920s," *Nations and Nationalism* 9.4 (2003): 533–554.

72. T. J. Clark, esp. "The View from Notre-Dame," in *The Painting of Modern Life: Paris in the Art of Manet and his Followers* (New York, 1985), 23–78.

73. Wanda M. Corn, *The Great American Thing: Modern Art and National Identity, 1915–1935* (Berkley and Los Angeles, 1999). New York continued to be an inspiration for artists as a subject, site, or material, particularly for artists of the 1970s. Hayden Herrera, "Manhattan Seven," *Art in America* 65.4 (1977): 50–63.

74. Azaryahu, *The Real City*, 37–53.

75. The issue of French influence is discussed in Manor, *Art in Zion*, 176–181.

76. The artists' failure to reflect the pioneering ethos and "Hebrew labor" was noticed and accepted with criticism. See Manor, *Art in Zion*, 169.

77. William Schack, "Israel Paldi," *The Menorah Journal* 14 (1928): 161; "Our Painters," *The New Palestine* 14.14 (1928): 426. Ludwig Blum's documentary and "photographic" depictions were perhaps one of the reasons why his art was not accepted in the modernist canon of Israeli art.

78. Nili Goren, *2009: Tel-Aviv Time* (Tel-Aviv, 2009).

79. This tendency was prominent in the exhibition curated by the director of the Tel-Aviv Museum of Art, Mordechai Omer, *90th Anniversary of Tel-Aviv–Yafo: Contemporary Cityscapes, Israeli and American Artists* (Tel-Aviv, 1999).

80. An exhibition dedicated to art in and about this marginal area was exhibited at the Tel-Aviv Artists' Studios Gallery in Florentin in November–December 2008. Dalia Manor, *Salame/Herzl: Views from Tel-Aviv South* (Tel-Aviv, 2008).

# PART THREE

# Planning and Architecture

# FIFTEEN

# The 1925 Master Plan for Tel-Aviv by Patrick Geddes

*Volker M. Welter*

Politics and History are interwoven, but are not commensurate.
—*Lord Acton*

Reflections on the city of Tel-Aviv are often framed by discussions of modernity, especially the Jewish experience of modernity.[1] The origin of the city was the Jewish suburb of Ahuzat Bayit that was founded outside Jaffa in 1909, and changed its name to Tel-Aviv a year later. The city's many buildings of the 1930s and 1940s in the styles of Le Corbusier, the Bauhaus, and other versions of European modernist architecture suggest that Tel-Aviv is the realization of architectural modernism's dream of an ideal city erected on a clean slate. The stories of Tel-Aviv's origin on sand dunes, vineyards, and orange groves seem to support this characterization. Superficially, Tel-Aviv's urban fabric indeed indicates a modern city with few, if any, historical roots. Yet from its inception, the city was part of the Zionist project of resettling the land of the forefathers, an endeavor that sought to re-establish roots in the ancient homeland.

The Tel-Aviv that took shape from the mid-1920s onward grew according to an urban master plan by the Scottish city designer Sir Patrick Geddes (1854–1932). In 1925 Geddes visited Palestine for the third time, on the occasion of the inauguration of the Hebrew University in Jerusalem. He had already visited the country in 1919 and 1920, upon being appointed official planner of the Hebrew University along with his son-in-law architect Sir Frank Mears (1880–1953) in 1919. After the celebrations on 1 April 1925, Geddes traveled to Tel-Aviv where he spent the next two months working on the master plan for a large-scale extension of the first, modern Hebrew city. During its gradual implementation in the decades following 1925, his master plan underwent changes and adaptations, but the basic layout of large blocks created by north-south and east-west cross streets intersected by narrower access lanes was adhered to. Geddes appears to have succeeded where many other modern urban planners failed: his ideal city of the future became reality.

Patrick Geddes's 1925 master plan was both a contribution to Tel-Aviv's modern appearance and to its foundations in history. This essay approaches Geddes's Tel-Aviv by asking what ideas about the modern city the Scottish natural scientist—who had meandered from biology via sociology into town planning—had to offer that fascinated Zionists like Israel Zangwill (1864–1926), Montague David Eder (1865–1936), and Haim Weizmann (1874–1952). The attraction of Geddes rested on his two-pronged approach to the city. By the late 1910s, he had consolidated his ideas about cities and their planning into a synergistic concept of large-scale regional planning. Geddes called this conceptual model a valley region or valley section. The goal was to integrate urban and rural ways of life into a regional civilization or region-city.[2] This was potentially of interest to the larger Zionist project.

While the region-city was Geddes's vision for the city of the future, it was nevertheless rooted in history, because it was the latest stage of a long historical development. To paraphrase the title of Geddes's best-known book, *Cities in Evolution,*[3] cities evolved out of history and were not created with a single stroke or by, indeed, a revolution. With this evolutionary approach to cities and regional planning, Geddes could address the needs of the Zionist movement with regard to both the foundation of a modern Hebrew society in Palestine and the linking of this to Jewish history.

The first part of the essay will look at Geddes's early contacts with various Zionists in 1919 that led to a Scotsman becoming one of the first planners to work for the Zionists in Palestine. It will also set out Geddes's regional vision for both a resettled Jewish Palestine and the city of Tel-Aviv. The second part will focus on the main characteristics of the plan for Tel-Aviv. The third section will argue that Geddes embedded in the plan manifold links with the histories of both Jaffa and of cities in general. Thus the plan questions whether Tel-Aviv really was a city without precedent, as many Zionists have argued and some scholars continue to state. Throughout the essay, possible sources for Geddes's plan will be introduced that include a new suburb Geddes had planned for the city of Balrampur, India, in 1917, and the plan of Edinburgh, the city that had stimulated Geddes's interest in urban issues while he lived there in the late nineteenth century. It was also in Edinburgh, incidentally, that a prominent Zionist and Geddes met for the first time.

### "Here . . . You Have . . . a Small Region . . . with Growing Towns of Their Own"[4]

Contacts between Zionists and Geddes can be traced back to the decades flanking 1900. In 1895, Geddes was visited by Zangwill who had traveled to Edinburgh to learn about Geddes's fin de siècle journal, *The Evergreen: A Northern Seasonal,* and ended up admiring his urban renewal work in the city.[5] Zangwill's cousin, David Eder, a doctor, Fabian socialist, and the first Freudian psychoanalyst to practice in Britain, contacted Geddes in 1908 with regard to a lecture the latter was about to deliver to the Fabian Society.[6] These interchanges centered upon social and urban reform and a reconciliation of modern life with nature—ideas that were referenced in various ways when the Zionist organization had to decide whether to employ Geddes.

After his visit, Zangwill wrote that *The Evergreen* was modeled on a journal that the Scottish poet Allan Ramsay had published in 1724 in order "to stimulate a return to local and national tradition and living Nature."[7] As Zangwill observed, Geddes pursued a similar goal with his social reform and urban renewal activities. Town planning was a question of balancing human activities and societies with the natural environment. Accordingly, modern-day planning had to begin with both the larger region and the natural environment as the basis of all human activity. Eder asked Geddes to lecture on eugenics to the biology group of the Fabian society. He agreed, but gave the lecture a distinct twist by speaking about the return of the Greek gods and muses to the city as symbols of a renewed harmony between humanity and the environment. It was his striving toward a "marriage of life and modern thought"[8] that had attracted both Zangwill and Eder to his thoughts and work.

A few months after the Balfour Declaration, Geddes renewed the contacts with Zangwill by writing to him from Indore, India, on 1 April 1918. He recalled their meetings in Edinburgh and, at an unknown date, "again at [Joseph and Mary] Fels's house." He reminded Zangwill of his urban renewal work in Scotland and elsewhere before turning, in his idiosyncratic writing style, to his real concern:

> As you know, I am interested in many things; but above all in the cleansing and mending—with something of renewal—of the old cities;—(+ I fancy I was captive in Babylon, + thence back for the rebuilding of Jerusalem's wall + towers! with Nehemiah + his men, at about as early an age as yourself—so fully are we Scots also children of the O[ld]. T[estament]!) . . . So here I come to my question:—Will you—the Zionists—buy me, with my more conservative method, at Jerusalem? For the clean-up at least—and the 'Preliminary Report'?[9]

Zangwill forwarded this somewhat audacious letter to Jerusalem where his cousin worked at the Relief & Reconstruction Department of the Zionist Commission. Eder replied to Geddes on 16 July 1918:

> I need scarcely tell you how I would rejoice to see you here, engaged in reconstructing our ancient city. We want modern fulfillments [sic] with ancient methods. I know yours [sic] is the kind of apprenticeship that would make you most useful here.[10]

Geddes's opportunity came in 1919 when the Zionist Commission assembled a group of experts to report on such issues as, for example, architecture and planning, agriculture, sanitation, engineering, and lighting.[11] Eder specifically recommended Geddes for two reasons. First, Geddes's approach to cities and planning encompassed a concern for both the past and the future. Second, Geddes's emphasis on the interdisciplinary character of planning touched upon different concerns of modern society and life:

> Prof. Geddes knows how to maintain what is traditional and beautiful of the past whilst combining it with all the necessary requirements in a way of sanitation and hygiene and modern requirements. Town planning requires someone who can combine with knowledge engineering,

sanitation, gardening, building with the spirit of reverence for the past, and Prof. Geddes is the only man, who by his past work, is able to fulfill all these requirements.[12]

Soon after this recommendation, negotiations between Geddes and officials of the Zionist movement in London began regarding the design of the Hebrew University in Jerusalem. These included a meeting with Weizmann, a fellow natural scientist. Like Eder, other Zionists gained a favorable impression of Geddes, emphasizing, for example, his "total lack of prejudice, as are but seldom met with."[13] In the case of Weizmann, the mutual admiration went so far that the Zionist leader considered sending his son to Montpellier, France, in 1926, where Geddes had been setting up a private university since 1924 that included plans for a Zionist college to accommodate future Zionist students from Palestine and Europe.[14] Shortly after his interview with Weizmann, Geddes received the commission for the university. He departed for Palestine in early September 1919 and stayed until late November when he returned to his teaching duties at Bombay University.

Already during the negotiation phase Geddes discussed with Weizmann a distinctly wider scope for his work in Palestine than just the Hebrew University:

> I might start almost at once, and take such course through Palestine as you may desire, thus securing e.g., Haifa, Jaffa, and other districts on ways to and from Jerusalem; with their towns and settlements; and giving such reports and advise as may be possible.[15]

Other Zionists, for example the German-born Arthur Ruppin (1876–1943), noted that "the problems before us deal with rural and urban settlement." Accordingly, Ruppin requested Geddes's opinion on rural projects in Dagania, Kinneret, Kerak (near Kinneret), and Tiberias.[16] To Ruppin's list, the agricultural engineer Jacob Ettinger (1872–1945) added, with Kfar Saba and Tel Adas, two more rural locations.[17]

All projects for which Geddes's advice had been requested and on which he worked during his trips to Palestine are listed in Table 15.1.[18] In addition to the Zionist commissions, Geddes convinced the British Military Administration to let him write reports on Jerusalem and Haifa. By the end of the summer of 1920, he had completed work on all projects

**Table 15.1. Comparison of Advice Requested from Geddes and Reports Written by Geddes (Respectively Related Activities)**

| Advice/planning reports requested | Reports & related activities by Patrick Geddes |
|---|---|
| Palestine: Agricultural survey/vegetation mapping | 'Terrace Culture in Palestine' [analytical drawing] |
| | 'Report on Aforestation' |
| Jerusalem City | 'Jerusalem: Actual and Possible 1919' |
| | [Geddes apparently wrote a second Jerusalem report in 1920] |
| Jerusalem Hebrew University | 'The Proposed Hebrew University of Jerusalem', 1919 |
| | 'Proposed Science Building adjacent to Gray Hill House' |
| Jerusalem: Jaffa Road village | 'Report on Town Plan for Kiryat-Anavim (Dilb), near Jerusalem' |
| Jerusalem: New Synagogue | Conceptual drawings exist [1920] |
| Jerusalem: Wailing Wall | 'Proposed Improvements of Approaches to Wailing Wall' November 1919 |
| Haifa City | 'Garden Village South of Polytechnicum' 1920 |
| | 'Town Planning in Haifa. A Report to the Governor by PG' 1920 |
| | 'Carmel Top Estates 1920' 1920 |
| | 'Zionist Commission's Carmel Estate' 1920 |
| Tel-Aviv City | 'Town Planning Report—Jaffa and Tel-Aviv' 1925 |
| Tel-Aviv synagogue | 'Report on Plans for Synagogue' 1920 |
| Talpioth | Geddes commented on proposals for Talpioth |

| Advice/planning reports requested | Reports & related activities by Patrick Geddes |
| --- | --- |
| Tiberias | 'The Hot Springs of Tiberias' 1920 |
| | 'Tiberias and Neighbourhood' 1920 |
| Planning Colonies: Existing and prospective | 'Minor Towns and Rural Development' |
| Kinnereth-Kerak and/or Kinnereth | Preliminary work on Kinnereth was apparently done by Geddes |
| Daganiah | Geddes visited Daganiah and Migdal |
| Kfar Saba, and Tel Adas | Geddes & Salant, Ahuzat Bayit (Kiryat Samuel), 1920 |
| | 'Notes on Town Planning Ordinance' 1920 |
| | Birket Mamilla, scheme by Becker & Salant, signed by Geddes |
| | Cities and Town Planning Exhibition |
| | 24 September 1920, to 10 October 1920, Boys' Hebrew School No. 1 |

initially agreed upon. Accordingly, the 1925 master plan for Tel-Aviv was a continuation of a mosaic of planning initiatives that contributed toward reviving the ancient region of Palestine: "Zionism stands for regional reconstruction, for better combination of town and country accordingly; so hence the opportunity of Tel-Aviv."[19]

Geddes's appreciation of Palestine was influenced by his realization that the Zionist projects were most likely the last opportunity for him to realize a conurbation as an example of contemporary planning. With that term he referred to a new, regional type of urbanized territory that was based on the valley section and integrated villages, towns, and large cities—both old and new. It was Geddes's contribution to the much discussed redefinitions of town and country as both had undergone rapid change from the nineteenth century onwards. His Zionist endeavors envisioned Palestine as such a contemporary conurbation.

## Planning the New Tel-Aviv, the First Modern Hebrew City

Even before his 1925 visit, Geddes had been asked several times to comment on Tel-Aviv and adjacent areas. In 1919 Ettinger and Ruppin requested Geddes's advice regarding a "garden-city on the ground of the orangery Kappus" to the south of Tel-Aviv.[20] A year later, time pressures prevented Geddes from commenting on an enlargement of Tel-Aviv and Jaffa.[21] He certainly would have liked to, for on his way back to Bombay he mused about the missed "opportunity . . . of at least a day or two in Jaffa, to arrange notes + plans further."[22] However, in the same year Geddes commented on designs for a new synagogue in Tel-Aviv.[23] Thus, when he began to plan the enlargement, Geddes was familiar with aspects of Tel-Aviv, adjacent neighborhoods, and Jaffa. In turn, he was also known to public figures in Tel-Aviv. In 1925, when the city fathers pondered again the extension of the town, Mayor Dizengoff, Samuel Tolkowsky, author of a history of Jaffa,[24] and other local dignitaries decided to "take the advice of Professor Geddes on general matters of Jaffa and Tel-Aviv Town Planning, Harbour [sic] Building, Railway Station question etc."[25]

Fig. 15.1. (*facing*) Plan of Tel-Aviv, c. 1926, from *Der Städtebau*, no. 2, 1929, 49.

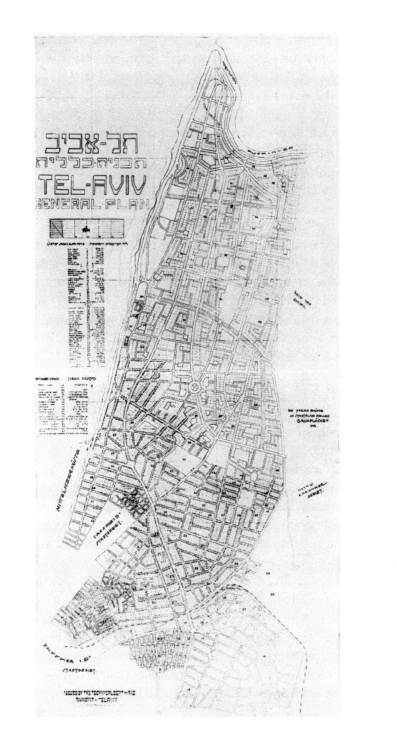

תל-אביב
תכנית-כללית
# TEL-AVIV
## GENERAL PLAN

ISSUED BY THE TECHNICAL DEPT. OF THE
TOWNSHIP OF TEL-AVIV

Geddes's master plan covered the terrain between the Auja River, today's Yarkon River, in the north, today's Bograshov St. in the southeast,
and Mapu St. in the southwest; roughly up to where Tel-Aviv had grown
by 1925. The eastern border is today's Ibn Gvirol St., while the beach
forms the western limit (Fig. 15.1). At least four major features characterize the master plan. First, a hierarchical grid of streets forms large
blocks. Second, small-scale domestic dwellings serve as the standard
building type. Third, each block and dwellings within it were to be arranged around central open spaces. Fourth, a concentration of cultural
institutions in the area of today's Habima Theatre with nearby Dizengoff
Circle as the "Central City feature."[26]

First, the grid is constituted by four types of streets and forms the
basic division of the land.[27] Several major streets traverse the extension from south to north beginning at the ocean with today's Yarkon
St. and ending farthest east with Ibn Gvirol St. These major streets are
intersected by a series of widely spaced, east-west oriented, secondary roads. A third class of streets comprises tree-lined boulevards that
include Sderot Keren Hakayemet (since 1974 Sderot Ben-Gurion) and
Sderot Nordau. Finally, a network of minor streets—Geddes called them
"Home-Ways"[28]—penetrates the interior of the large blocks.

These "large city blocks"[29] were primarily intended for domestic dwellings, the second characteristic of the plan. The municipality
stipulated 560 square meters as the individual lot size.[30] The standard
building was to be a detached, occasionally semi-detached, house with a
maximum of two stories and flat roof, with perhaps a partial sun room;
Geddes argued that "mass public opinion" supported such homes[31] (Fig.
15.2). Dwellings were planned in double rows along the perimeter of each
block. The outer rows were directly accessible from the streets. Access
to the inner rows was via the minor streets that ran through each block
and thereby circumscribed the central open space. He rejected culs-de-
sac, then popular among town planners as a means of achieving smaller
communities within a larger city. Instead, he overlaid the regular grid
with irregular minor streets.[32] These networks of functionally differentiated streets prevented, so Geddes claimed, unnecessary conversions of
land into streets and helped to assure that about half of all dwellings were
located in the silence of the interior of each block.[33]

Fig. 15.2. Garden entrance, 10, Zlatopolski Street, a modest edifice
that follows the specifications for homes set out by Geddes
(photograph: Volker M. Welter).

Fig. 15.3. A "rose and vine" lane in Zlatopolski Street as envisioned by Geddes giving access to plots that do not directly border the central open space (photograph: Volker M. Welter).

The main grid generated oblong large blocks that stretch from north to south. This orientation maximized the number of lots for dwellings with one main façade which faced west to capture cool ocean breezes. The block pattern begins on either side of Gordon St., but is particularly well articulated beyond Sderot Keren Hakayemet, the next cross street to the north. Up to this boulevard, pre-1925 Tel-Aviv and the Geddesian urban layout intersect, whereas further north Geddes's ideas were un-hindered by any existing urban fabric. Landmarks like, for example, the village of Sommeil at the eastern edge of both the master plan and today's Arlozoroff St., and an Arab cemetery overlooking the ocean at the western end of the same street, were incorporated into Geddes's plan but left otherwise untouched.

The third characteristic was the interior central spaces in each block to be used "to enlarge the house plots . . . [or] to provide space for gar-den, play-ground, tennis court . . . ; indeed all these are [sic] as far as possible."[34] The inner rows of dwellings directly accessed these mutual spaces from the home-ways. The inhabitants of the outer rows of houses used narrow "rose and vine lanes"[35] between neighboring plots (Fig. 15.3). All private gardens and yards, the lanes, and the various streets Ged-des described as extensively greened spaces were filled with fruit trees, mulberry trees, vegetables, flowers, and decorative plants: "The model and ideal before us is that of the Garden Village. But this no longer as merely suburban; but as coming into town; and even into the very heart of the city block."[36] The spatial image Geddes evokes here refers back to an urban block typical in medieval English cathedral cities that had been lost under the ever-denser urban fabric from the late Middle Ages onwards.

In *Cities in Evolution,* Geddes identifies similarities between mod-ern garden cities and the land division in early thirteenth-century ca-thedral cities as illustrated, for example, in a reconstruction drawing of Salisbury, England, by Sir Frank Mears[37] (Fig. 15.4). These blocks offered low-density dwellings in huge gardens that, inversely, raised a possible issue of affordability—a comparable difficulty Geddes and his colleague Henry Vaughan Lanchester (1863–1953), a British architect and town planner, encountered when they both worked in India in 1915. Lanchester criticized new government regulations that would "get rid

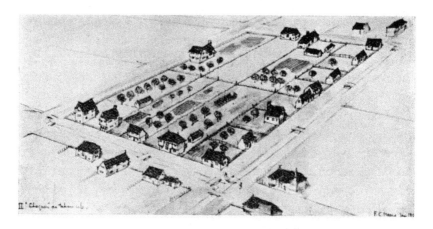

Fig. 15.4. Reconstruction drawing of residential blocks in thirteenth-century Salisbury, England, from Patrick Geddes, *Cities in Evolution* (London, 1915).

of the sweepers lane"—small alleys leading into blocks—but at the price of both a "dull and insipid effect" and lot sizes that would disadvantage poor citizens.[38] Lanchester's alternative was a bone-shaped, oblong block with dwellings along the perimeter. While the lots at the shorter ends faced main streets, those at the longer sides were pushed inside toward the center. Accordingly, between two such blocks a small garden space was created, rather than a narrow lane. Thus among the sources of Geddes's Tel-Aviv plan we find block patterns from English cathedral cities as improved by colonial planning in British India.

The copious gardens had a second function relating to traditional land uses. In the 1890s, Geddes had begun to garden vacant plots in Edinburgh's overcrowded old town. Besides increasing the efficient use of urban land and beautifying the city, Geddes claimed that the practice revived traditional land uses as the gardens were located on ancient cultivation terraces that had once structured the slopes of castle rock. Later, in the same spaces, the city walls that rose would slowly suffocate the old town. In the Tel-Aviv report Geddes points out that "Many Tel-Aviv people, like other townsfolk, are accustomed to enjoy the active bustle of street life and are often little accustomed to the quieter joys of a garden quarter." He continues: "But all townsfolk are open to garden pleasures too,"[39] thus the more than generous supply of gardens was an educational endeavor. In addition, Geddes introduces an economic argument by stating that the centrally located gardens, leisure grounds, and playgrounds were cheaper to build and to maintain than streets.

Finally, the many garden spaces led Geddes to identify the new Tel-Aviv as "a transition place and a link between the over-crowded cities of Europe and the renewal of Agricultural Palestine."[40] By connecting negative aspects of European urban life with positive ones of agricultural life in Palestine, Geddes tapped into the argument among some Zionists that the exiled Jewish people had become a people of cities—or even worse *Luftmenschle*—rather than remaining a people of the land. The latter had to be regained for a successful resettlement of Eretz Israel. The provision of private dwellings in lavishly gardened surroundings was Geddes's solution to what had remained a theoretical Zionist argument, as only a small number of Jewish immigrants ever moved into agricultural settlements.[41] The role for Tel-Aviv as the mediator between town and country also dovetailed with Geddes's region-city as a merger of urban and rural ways of life.

The fourth main characteristic of the master plan is the spatial concentration of cultural institutions. This group and its location were of utmost importance to Geddes because to sustain, for example, theaters, museums, opera, and educational institutions distinguished a city from a mere town:

> Every city of the past that has adequately risen to the conception of the Culture-Institutions seen and felt as appropriate to the expression of its ideals . . . has chosen for these purposes the very noblest site within its area.[42]

The site had to be large enough to allow the institutions to be built in close proximity in order to "prevent mutual forgetfulness."[43] Moreover, the former should be elevated to ensure that the latter would visually dominate the city as a Greek Acropolis of old.[44] Geddes's idea anticipated Expressionist "city crown" concepts as they emerged in Germany at the end of the First World War and were exported to Palestine by Zionist architects like Richard Kauffmann (1887–1958) and Fritz Kornberg (1889–1944). Yet older historical roots of the idea can be found in the British debate about the modern city. Already in 1847, Benjamin Disraeli had demanded that the rapidly expanding British capital urgently needed a new "head" composed of public buildings.[45] When the architect Oskar Kaufmann (1873–1956) designed in 1934 a civic forum around his proposal for the Habima Theatre, he called the entire complex *Rosh Tel-Aviv,* or the "Head of Tel-Aviv."[46] The same words are used to name the area around today's theatre in the 1937 plan of Tel-Aviv.[47]

When Geddes began to plan Tel-Aviv, the city had already decided to build a theatre and music venue at the junction of Sderot Rothschild and Sderot Ben-Zion. Geddes agreed with this choice as it was topographically the highest site in Tel-Aviv, although it was at the northeastern most edge of the existing city. This off-center location diminished the ability of the cultural acropolis to unite the new town with the old one, comparable, for example, to the centrally located grouping of cultural institutions, mainly museums and galleries, between both old and new Edinburgh.

However, according to Geddes, every city required a central city feature, for example, a square that would stitch together the newer and older parts. In his 1917 report on the Indian town of Balrampur, Geddes planned a new suburb to the south as "a small but real New Town." It was developed around a "central star of roads" that functioned as both bazaar and business area. From there a major road led into the residential area[48] (Fig. 15.5). The square was also the first urban space the new town citizens would enter when approaching from the existing town. Geddes tried to capture this important symbolic function with a hexagon shape drawn at the center of the square.

Earlier, in 1911, Geddes had temporarily installed what he called a chapel of the city in one of the galleries of Edinburgh's cultural acropolis. The central feature of this chapel was a hexagon as a symbol of the synthesis of art, sciences, history, and life that only the modern city could achieve. Crystalline shapes like hexagons and octagons were the most condensed symbols of the city Geddes used. As such, these forms appear in many of his plans including the ones for the suburb of Balrampur and for Tel-Aviv.[49] The similarities between the latter two plans are striking.

Like its smaller Indian predecessor, the new Tel-Aviv originated from a central square—Zina Dizengoff Circle—surrounded by a star of streets. In both plans the squares are located closest to the old town

III. NEW SUBURB.

N

Scale of Feet.

PARK

Bridge

School

SUWAON        SUWAON

Zinco, July, 1917.—No.471-4-350

Fig. 15.5. Plan for a new suburb in Balrampur, India, 1917, from Patrick Geddes, *Town Planning in Balrampur* (Lucknow, 1917).

with long streets traversing the adjacent new residential areas. The latter show comparable blocks with narrow access lanes, although the pattern is both more developed and visible in the case of Tel-Aviv. While in Balrampur the main square's form approximates a circle, its Tel-Aviv counterpart was conceived as a "Hexagon Place."[50] Along its sides, Geddes envisioned four-story, architecturally unified buildings with shops and offices on the first two to three floors with apartments above. The square was to be part of the business and shopping district of Tel-Aviv. At its center, Geddes proposed a band stand. Moreover, the hexagon square was supposed to function as the symbolic link that would tie the new Tel-Aviv to the old one and, by implication, to Jaffa as the origin of all neighborhoods within the conurbation Jaffa–Tel-Aviv.

At the same time this most condensed city symbol illustrates in an exemplary manner the gap between Geddes's arcane but highly developed thoughts and his preference for simple, if not simplistic, symbolic forms. That the hexagon contained all his ideas about the city was obvious to Geddes and to those initiated into his perspective. His old acquaintances Zangwill and Eder may have belonged to this select group, which included, perhaps, Weizmann and Dizengoff; yet it almost certainly did not include the architect Genia Averbuch (1909–1977),[51] who won a competition for Dizengoff Circle in 1934 with a modernist design. Her streamlined circle missed the opportunity to lastingly inscribe into urban fabric a crystal-shaped square, the one symbol most important to Geddes.

## From Jaffa to Tel-Aviv—The Evolution of a Conurbation

It is remarkable how little Geddes aimed to sharply separate the new Tel-Aviv from both the older Tel-Aviv and Jaffa. This approach differed from that of many contemporary planners who took great care to keep their cities of tomorrow untainted by those of both the present and the past. For example, in 1898, Ebenezer Howard (1850–1928) conceived the garden city in opposition to large metropolises like London. The latter was to be demolished and rebuilt along garden city lines. In the 1920s, Le Corbusier (1887–1965) depicted the new city as a radical alternative of tower blocks in a park-like setting that would replace existing cities like Paris.

Geddes proceeded differently. He closely knit together the new Tel-Aviv with the original neighborhood of Ahuzat Bayit (later Tel-Aviv), the ancient city of Jaffa, and the latter's outlying neighborhoods. For Geddes, existing cities were not just the background against which new cities would stand out in splendid isolation, nor were they mere residues of earlier historic periods. Rather, old cities were the foundation from which every new city sprang. This included cases where the latter was to be located on what was perceived as virgin, undeveloped, or never before urbanized territory. Fittingly, Tel-Aviv's extension was to be built on sand dunes, orange groves, and vineyards, all slated to disappear. Locations like these were easily misunderstood as the proverbial clean slate for the modern planner's urban visions. Yet Geddes contested that presumption:

> Hence our modern town, even when yesterday but prairie, was no mere vacant site, but was at once enriched and encumbered by the surviving traditions of the past; so that even its new buildings are for the most part but vacant shells of past art, of which now only the student cares to trace the objective annals, much less penetrate to the inner history.[52]

Accordingly, the task of the planner—the student of cities—was to seek out those links with the past that situated a new city within the development of both a specific city and the history of cities as a general phenomenon of human culture. The assumption that cities existed through cycles of history was informed by Geddes's professional knowledge of theories of evolution. Moreover, his perception of the city rested primarily on past traditions and historic periods as encapsulated in the "vacant shells" of buildings old and new. This evolutionary understanding of a city greatly emphasized the importance of the urban fabric for the continuation of both city and history over that of the memories of particular groups of inhabitants. Moreover, new citizens, or temporary inhabitants such as a planner, could participate in the history of a city by studying or occupying past buildings.

Ideas like these deeply informed Geddes's Tel-Aviv plan. The new Tel-Aviv continued the growth of Jewish neighborhoods northward and away from Jaffa, one of the oldest cities in the world. This trend had begun when the Jewish neighborhoods Neve Tzedek and Neve Shalom were founded in 1887 and 1890, respectively.[53] Yet already much earlier

Jaffa itself had expanded beyond its old boundaries, for example with the Manshiya quarter to the north whose roots stretched back to Egyptian soldiers settling there in the 1830s.[54]

Despite the fact that the new Tel-Aviv was to be created even further north of Jaffa, Geddes considered both towns as parts of the same regional entity.[55] His report is titled *Town-Planning Report—Jaffa and Tel-Aviv*.[56] The first chapter begins with a discussion of such planning issues as, for example, port amelioration, locations for industry and businesses, and traffic connections that were beneficial for Jaffa, and, by implication, for Tel-Aviv.[57] The report was an attempt to consolidate the conurbation Jaffa–Tel-Aviv that had begun to emerge in the mid-nineteenth century.[58]

Geddes's geographical imagination did not stop with Jaffa–Tel-Aviv. The report recommended the purchase of land beyond the Yarkon River in expectation of future urban growth and in order to counterbalance land speculation in the area planned by Geddes. Moreover, it anticipated the need to eventually extend suburban railways from Jaffa–Tel-Aviv to Herzliya, even further north, and to other Arab and Jewish neighborhoods and settlements in the area.[59] On an even larger scale, Geddes envisioned Tel-Aviv to be part of a health-based regional economy that would link it with Tiberias and Jerusalem by way of medical sanatoriums: "No reputation of Israel is better (or less interfered with the Anti-Semites) than the medical."[60] Thus Geddes's regional approach to the city also determined the planning of the new Tel-Aviv with regard to its role within a reconstructed Palestine.

A second connection, literally in this case, between the newest and the oldest parts of the conurbation Jaffa–Tel-Aviv were the major streets Geddes provided. Some of the routes of the north-south streets, especially those close to the ocean, but also east-west streets, for example Arlozoroff St., were not solely based on Geddes's intuition. Instead, they broadly continued directions of existing streets that, for example, originated in Jaffa, old Tel-Aviv, or other neighborhoods nearby. In one of his Indian town planning reports Geddes explained that "existing roads . . . are the past product of practical life . . . , and observation and common sense alike show them to be in the right directions."[61] Often these directions only needed to be continued in order to ensure that an extension like Tel-Aviv's would dovetail with the urban fabric of existing towns and neighborhoods, and hence their economic, social, and cultural life.

A third new-old relationship is embedded in Geddes's evolutionary reading of the varying patterns of the land division that were observable in the neighborhoods around Jaffa. This urban growth illustrated a "gradual (and almost subconscious) change from bad planning in the south, and to better planning toward northward."[62] South did not refer to Jaffa proper, it must be emphasized, but to the Jewish neighborhoods of Neve Tzedek and Neve Shalom, "the continuance of the old Menshieh quarter with its many small streets, crowded together, and as close as small plotting can admit." This footprint resulted in the waste and inefficiency of "mean and dusty thoroughfares" while too little land allowed for dwellings oriented east to west.[63] By comparison, old Tel-Aviv was better designed with "an orderly plan, with its homes, its Town House and Boulevard."[64] Geddes was especially impressed by the formality of Herzl St. that led straight to the front of the gymnasium building at the end of the street.

Other neighborhoods illustrated further improvements. For example, to the north and west of the Manshiya quarter, the chessboard pattern continued but with larger blocks, even if still with too many east-west streets. This changed only north of Allenby St. where the frequency of those streets was reduced. An example of good urban design was the short cul-de-sac Simta Plonit at the beginning of King George St. Admirable was the small dwellings' isolation from dust and noise and that there existed "no walls or high fences separating the houses from the road, so that all gardens combine into a single group [with] mutual co-operation in economy, with increased beauty and pleasure."[65] Finally, the blocks south and north of Bograshov St. in the Nordia neighborhood were praised for their north-south alignment that guaranteed east-west exposure for a maximum of building lots.

Thus the urban fabric illustrated the evolution of modern urban design from its dense beginnings outside Jaffa to later developments with patterns more generous and more responsive to geographical and climatic conditions. Jaffa was integrated into this history as the point of origin of the conurbation that Geddes was about to expand. The introductory paragraph of his report stated that regardless of its "ethnic distinctiveness and the civic individuality of Tel-Aviv, as Township, its

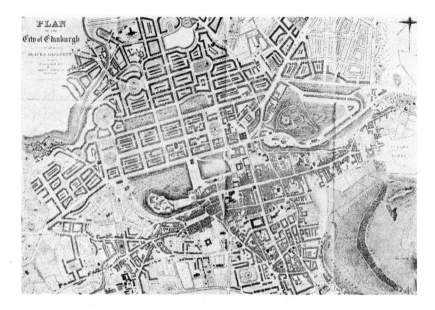

Fig. 15.6. Plan of the city of Edinburgh with the new town to the north, c. early
nineteenth century, from Patrick Geddes, *Cities in Evolution* (London, 1915).

geographic, social, and even fundamental economic situation is determined by its position as Northern Jaffa" and "The old town, the modern
Township, must increasingly work and grow together."[66] The identification of Jaffa with the "old town" did not amount to its dismissal as
a filthy old town.[67] Rather, Geddes confined his evolutionary readings
to an analysis of neighborhoods built from about the early nineteenth
century onwards. Hence it was his critique of modern town planning
and building practices that was mirrored in the contrast between "new
town" and "old town."

Geddes used the latter two terms as generic ones; a usage he often
indicated by their capitalization.[68] Both also harked back to his time in
Edinburgh, a city that is characterized by an urban-geographical division into an Old Town, located majestically on Castle Rock, and a New
Town, an elegant eighteenth-century expansion to the north (Fig. 15.6).
The plan of the former is somewhat irregular, determined by the terrain
and the dense build-up. The plan of the latter consists of a geometrical

grid, regular urban blocks, public gardens (though accessible only to adjacent property owners), and a network of smaller service lanes that cut through the interior of the blocks.

In addition to this basic division, Edinburgh's urban fabric featured physical remnants of almost every period of the city's history. Periods that had left little trace—like the Middle Ages—Geddes aimed to recreate with his urban renewal initiatives in Edinburgh's Old Town that Zangwill had encountered in 1895. The more periods of a city's history that were present in the urban fabric, the better the opportunities for the citizens to recapitulate their city's growth. Following contemporary theories of evolution, Geddes thought this to be necessary before a new cycle of urban growth could be added to any town.[69]

In broad strokes then, Edinburgh's spatial division informed the design for the expansion of Tel-Aviv. While the latter mimicked Edinburgh's New Town, Jaffa recalled the Old Town. Tel-Aviv's new town, however, improved upon the one in Edinburgh, which was dominated by the rigid geometry of its grid. Geddes's intention was not to achieve balanced formality between the masses of urban blocks and the open spaces of the streets. Instead, as he explained with regard to the open spaces at the center of the residential blocks in the new suburb for Balrampur:

> [T]ownsfolk are really still very largely villagers. In the street or the lane they are not really at home: their true place . . . is in the Village Square. For this social life, both of old and young, such squares and open spaces . . . make up Village Centers which are second to none I know of in the world, whether of East or West.[70]

Thus the residential blocks with their central open spaces in the plans for both Balrampur and Tel-Aviv attempted to inscribe into the modern extensions the humanistic assumption that people share a universal way of life across ethnic, religious, and other divisions.

Edinburgh also inspired Geddes's evolutionary reading of the urban fabric of the neighborhoods around Jaffa. Comparable to the interweaving of Edinburgh's history into the urban fabric, the modern conurbation Jaffa–Tel-Aviv had a similar resource at its disposal. Starting from Jaffa as the point of origin, the surrounding neighborhoods depicted the evolution of both the city's growth and modern town planning. Accordingly, the new Tel-Aviv was not an attempt to overcome either old Tel-Aviv or Jaffa. Instead, Geddes saw the relation as mutually beneficial. The new town extended the older ones into the future according to the most recent principles of urban planning. In contrast, the older towns anchored their youngest sibling in history the very moment the planner, the mediator between the old and the new, began to trace the lines of his master plan on a sheet of paper or, in the case of Tel-Aviv, into the sand of the dunes, vineyards, and orange groves.

* * *

Was Tel-Aviv built according to Geddes's master plan? With regard to the characteristics discussed in this essay the answer is: "Yes, but. . . ." The street pattern and division of the land into larger blocks were implemented, even though the number of central spaces within the blocks was curtailed. Some of the dwellings followed Geddes's suggestions. Yet, once the influx of European refugees had begun, large areas of the city were filled with taller apartment buildings on a larger footprint. The cultural institutions of the city of Tel-Aviv are concentrated in the area Geddes had recommended, but they are not as numerous or in the exact locations as described. In short, enough of the master plan has been realized, especially of the basic characteristics, to allow one to identify Tel-Aviv as one of Geddes's most important realized commissions.

Recently, a political-historical study of Jaffa and Tel-Aviv claimed that Geddes's "plan was never implemented" because Geddes considered the new Tel-Aviv to be part of a greater Jaffa and was thus complimented out of town, so to speak, by his Jewish clients.[71] Equally, architectural historians tend to overlook the master plan as it does not fit the image of Tel-Aviv as a city created by architectural modernism. Yet Geddes's commissions in Palestine, and more specifically in Tel-Aviv, were more multifaceted than these criticisms allow for.

Politically, Geddes's commission and work mirrored in many ways the more than complicated situation of Palestine under the British Mandate. Geddes was commissioned by the Jewish municipality to design the new Tel-Aviv, yet he conceived of it as a development of a larger conurbation that would include Jaffa with its historically mixed population. He was not part of the British Mandate administration, yet used his connections with his fellow countrymen to advance his aims as city designer. Although this did not put him at odds with his Zionist clients, it equally did not guarantee any support by the Arab population, or indeed sympathy from the British administration.

Architecturally, both Geddes's master plan and his theory of the city were affirmative of the modern city as long as it would not replace the city of the past but extend it. Yet the perception of Tel-Aviv has usually been dominated by its modernist architecture, since that became the dominant style from the 1930s onwards. This is typically understood as signifying the modernity of Tel-Aviv, both as the first Hebrew city and as one of the earliest large-scale modernist cities; in either case, a city without any ties to the past. While this myth dovetails nicely with the one that architectural modernism overcame for good both historicism and history, Geddes's master plan spoils the immaculate image of Tel-Aviv as the White City of Modernism created *ex nihilo.*

Geddes's work is a reminder that what makes history rarely proceeds according to the simple binaries laid out by historians. To paraphrase Lord Acton's remark, quoted at the beginning of this essay, architecture, city planning, and politics are related but not commensurate. Thus historians should be wary of simply reading one for the other.

I would like to acknowledge kind permissions by the Trustees of the National Library of Scotland (NLS), Edinburgh; Strathclyde University Archives (SUA), Glasgow; and the Central Zionist Archives (CZA), Jerusalem, to quote from papers in their custody.

## NOTES

The epigraph is cited in Samuel Tolkowsky, *The Gateway of Palestine: A History of Jaffa* (London, 1924), title page.

1. For example, Joachim Schlör, *Tel-Aviv, Vom Traum zur Stad. Reise durch, Kultur und Geschichte* (Gerlingen, 1996) (*Tel Aviv, From Dream to City,* trans. Helen Atkins [London,1999]); Mark LeVine, *Overthrowing Geography: Jaffa, Tel-Aviv, and the Struggle for Palestine 1880–1948* (Berkeley, CA, 2005); Barbara Mann, *A Place in History: Modernism, Tel-Aviv, and the Creation of Jewish Urban Space* (Stanford, 2006); Maoz Azaryahu, *Tel-Aviv: Mythography of a City* (Syracuse, NY, 2007).

2. Volker M. Welter, "Geddes' Vision of the Region as a City—Palestine as a 'Polis,'" in *Social Utopias of the Twenties: Bauhaus, Kibbutz, and the Dream of the New Man,* ed. Jeannine Fiedler (Wuppertal, 1995), 72–79; Volker M. Welter, *Biopolis—Patrick Geddes and the City of Life* (Cambridge, MA, 2002), ch. 3.

3. Patrick Geddes, *Cities in Evolution, An Introduction to the Town Planning Movement and to the Study of Civics* (London, 1915).

4. Patrick Geddes, "Talks from the Outlook Tower, The Fifth Talk: Our City of Thought," in *Patrick Geddes: Spokesman for Man and the Environment,* ed. Marshall Stalley (New Brunswick, 1972), 349–364.

5. *The Evergreen: A Northern Seasonal,* 1 (1895–1896).

6. David Eder, *London, to Patrick Geddes,* 24 April 1908, SUA, T-GED 9/831.

7. "Edinburgh," in Israel Zangwill, *Without Prejudice* (London, 1896), 289–293. The essay was reprinted as "Geddes and Edinburgh," in *The Interpreter Geddes: The Man and His Gospel,* Amelia Defries (London, 1927), 313–317.

8. Israel Zangwill, "The Apostle of Eutopia," in *The Interpreter Geddes,* 30.

9. Geddes to Zangwill, 1 April 1918, CZA, A120/326, my additions. Geddes was a friend of Joseph (1853–1914) and Mary (1863–1953) Fels, who had lived in England since 1901.

10. Eder to Geddes, 16 July 1918, NLS, MS 10546, 20.

11. Mr. Robinson, "Memorandum on Sending of Experts to Palestine," 6 May 1919, CZA, Z4/1721.

12. [Signature illegible], for Acting Chairman of the Zionist Commission, to Inner Actions Committee, 15 May 1919, NLS, MS 10598, 34–35.

13. Dr. Sonne to Mr. Simon, 12 August 1919, CZA. Z4/1721, quoted in note 4 of Gideon Biger, "A Scotsman in the First Hebrew City: Patrick Geddes and the 1926 Town Plan for Tel-Aviv," *Scottish Geographical Magazine* 108 (1992): 1, 4–8.

14. Haim Weizmann to Vera Weizmann, 7 and 10 July 1926, *The Letters and Papers of Chaim Weizmann,* ed. Pinhas Ofer (New Brunswick, n.d.) 13A: letters 43 and 51. The plan fell through when Weizmann learned that Geddes would not personally be in Montpellier that summer.

15. Geddes to Weizmann, 24 July 1919, Weizmann Archive, Rehovot, File 522, a typed version in CZA, Z4/1721.

16. Ruppin to Palestine Office, Jaffa, 5 September 1919, CZA, Z4/2790; Arthur Ruppin, *Tagebücher, Briefe, Erinnerungen* (Diaries, Letters, Memories), ed. Schlomo Krolik (Königstein, 1985), 304.

17. J[acob] Ettinger to Patrick Geddes, 30 September 1919, NLS, MS 10546, 94–95.

18. Patrick Geddes and Frank Mears, "Memorandum on Future Arrangements between Zionist Commission and Professor Geddes and Colleagues for Town Planning and Architectural Work," [n.d.], CZA, Z4/10.202. Most likely identical with a memorandum that Geddes mentioned in a letter to Weizmann from 4 November 1919 (Geddes to Weizmann, NLZ, MS 10516, 25). The table relies in parts on references to Palestine reports by Geddes cited in Peter Green, "Patrick Geddes," PhD diss., University of Strathclyde, 1970. Some reports are no longer in the Geddes archives at University of Strathclyde. Possibly they were among materials lost by the archives in 1966. Philip Boardman, *The Worlds of Patrick Geddes: Biologist, Town Planner, Re-Educator, Peace-Warrior* (London, 1978), 431.

19. Geddes, *Town-Planning Report—Jaffa–Tel-Aviv* (unpub. typescript, Tel-Aviv, 1925), 44 (hereafter referred to as Geddes, *Tel-Aviv*).

20. Ettinger, Zionist Commission, Palestine Office, Agriculture and Colonisation Department to Geddes, 30 September 1919, NLS, MS 10546, folio 94–95. For Kappus, see Jakob Eisler, *Der Deutsche Beitrag zum Aufstieg Jaffas 1850–1914. Zur Geschichte*

*Palästinas im 19. Jahrhundert* (Wiesbaden, 1997), 95; and LeVine, *Overthrowing Geography,* 64.

21. Geddes to the mayor of Tel-Aviv, 20 October 1920; TAHA, file 1–168.

22. Ibid., 8 November 1920.

23. Geddes, *Report on Plans for Synagogue* (Tel-Aviv, n.d.) ["Jerusalem October 1920" (handwritten addition on last page)].

24. See note 1.

25. Siegfried Hoofien to Geo[rge] Halpern, Jewish Colonial Trust, London, 29 April 1925, CZA L51/171.

26. Geddes, *Tel-Aviv,* 23.

27. Classification of the roads borrowed from Sabaï Anouk Ramedhan-Levi, "Réalisation des Propositions de Patrick Geddes pour Tel-Aviv, 1925: Permanences, Détournements, Ruptures" (master's thesis, École d'Architecture de Paris-Belleville, 2001), 35–40.

28. Geddes, *Tel-Aviv* 19.

29. Ibid.

30. Ibid., 11.

31. Ibid., 14.

32. For the history of the block pattern see Neal I. Payton, "The Machine in the Garden City: Modern Architecture and Traditional Urbanism in Tel-Aviv," *Planning Perspectives* 10 (1995): 359–381; Rachel Kallus, "Patrick Geddes and the Evolution of a Housing Type in Tel-Aviv," *Planning Perspectives* 12 (1997): 281–320.

33. Geddes, *Tel-Aviv,* 16.

34. Ibid., 19. However, when Tel-Aviv was built, many of the open spaces were actually subdivided for dwellings, thus reducing the total amount of open space in the core of Tel-Aviv.

35. Ibid., 20.

36. Ibid., 19.

37. Geddes, *Cities in Evolution,* 6–7.

38. Lanchester to Geddes, 2 December 1915, NLS, MS 10569, 41–42 (41 recto, 42).

39. Geddes, *Tel-Aviv,* 16.

40. Ibid.

41. Tom Segev, *One Palestine, Complete: Jews and Arabs under the British Mandate* (New York, 2001), 249–261.

42. Geddes, *Tel-Aviv,* 56.

43. Ibid.

44. Ibid., 57.

45. Benjamin Disraeli, *Tancred or the New Crusade* (London, 1847), 112. See Volker M. Welter, "From *locus genii* to Heart of the City—Embracing the Spirit of the City," in *Modernism and the Spirit of the City,* ed. Iain Boyd Whyte (London, 2003), 35–56.

46. *YITA* 6–7 (1934), 283 [Hebrew]; and *Bamah* 3 (1934): 9–11 [Hebrew]. For Kaufmann see Antje Hansen, *Oskar Kaufmann—Ein Theaterarchitekt zwischen Tradition und Moderne* (Oskar Kaufmann—A Theatre Architect between Tradition and Modernism) (Berlin, 2001).

47. Zev Vilnay, *Steimatzky's Palestine Guide* (London, 1937), appendix: Plan of Tel-Aviv.

48. Geddes, *Town Planning in Balrampur. A Report to the Hon'ble the Maharaja Bahadur* (London, 1917), 30–34.

49. Welter, *Biopolis*, 215–221.

50. Geddes, *Tel-Aviv*, 23. Geddes reported a hexagonal-shaped square. The title sketch and some maps of Tel-Aviv indicate an octagonal-shaped square.

51. Edina Meyer-Maril, "Jewish Women Architects in Palestine 1920–1948," in *Jewish Women: A Comprehensive Historic Encyclopedia* (Jerusalem, 2006).

52. Geddes, "Civics: As Applied Sociology Part II," in *The Ideal City*, ed. Helen Meller (Leicester, 1979), 159.

53. LeVine, *Overthrowing Geography*, 76.

54. Ruth Kark, *Jaffa: A City in Evolution, 1799–1917* (Jerusalem, 1990), 110–111.

55. LeVine claims that the regional perception of Jaffa that recognized outlying neighborhoods and agricultural sites as essential parts of the city was an Ottoman-Islamic idea, as opposed to a late-nineteenth-century European one (*Overthrowing Geography*, 57). This ignores the debate among nineteenth-century European geographers such as the French communitarian and friend of Geddes, Elisée Réclus, who debated the expansion of historic cities into regions as a consequence of economic and political changes since the late Middle Ages. Through, for example, Gustav Landauer, Franz Oppenheimer, and Martin Buber, this debate was influential on the Zionist debate of how best to resettle Palestine.

56. Geddes, *Tel-Aviv*, 1.

57. Ibid., 1–11.

58. LeVine, *Overthrowing Geography*, 51–59.

59. Geddes, *Tel-Aviv*, 15.

60. Geddes to Eder, 2 May 1925, CZA L12/39. The sanatorium quarter was proposed for roughly the site of today's Independence Park and the adjacent Hilton Hotel (Geddes, *Tel-Aviv*, 29–32).

61. Geddes, *Town Planning in Lahore. A Report to the Municipal Council* (Lahore, 1917), 7.

62. Geddes, *Tel-Aviv*, 17.

63. Ibid.

64. Ibid.

65. Ibid., 18.

66. Ibid., 1.

67. LeVine claims that this was the standard attitude of Europeans toward Jaffa (*Overthrowing Geography*, 57).

68. Geddes, *Tel-Aviv*, 17.

69. Welter, *Biopolis*, 131–132.

70. Geddes, *Balrampur*, 33.

71. LeVine, *Overthrowing Geography*, 171.

# SIXTEEN

# Preserving Urban Heritage:
# From Old Jaffa to Modern Tel-Aviv

*Nurit Alfasi and Roy Fabian*

The city of Tel-Aviv–Jaffa is Israel's metropolitan core and a dominant cultural center. Tel-Aviv–Jaffa is extraordinary in that it is among the few Israeli cities that incorporate preservation of the built environment as a principle in city planning and, in doing so, promote and institute successful preservation initiatives of large urban areas. In effect, Tel-Aviv is at the forefront of local governments regarding the preservation activities it promotes. The city was the first in Israel to institute a local preservation policy regarding the conservation of Old Jaffa during the 1950s and early 1960s. In the 1990s, Tel-Aviv garnered local and international acknowledgement of the value of its modern architecture, culminating in UNESCO's nomination of the "White City" in 2003 as a World Heritage Site. Old Jaffa and the White City are exceptional sites in the Israeli urban landscape, as their preservation is managed by the local government as part of the local development policy. Although many other Israeli cities have archeological and historic sites, few operate comprehensive preservation programs and even fewer succeed in integrating the historic districts into the living city. Moreover, it seems that Tel-Aviv is extending its preservation policy to new sites, as indicated by the recent conservation of the German colony of Sarona and the Ottoman train station in Jaffa.

A closer look reveals, however, that the adoption of a preservation policy followed periods of inner debates and political struggles within the municipal government. Furthermore, each time the preservation issue arose, primary administrators tended to reject it and fought for the adoption of a non-limiting development policy. As a counterforce, however, informal groups of actors from within and without the municipal administration influenced the powerful urban officials and enforced the adoption of a preservation policy by the municipality. In contrast to civil movements that pressure elected officials by raising public opinion, this essay shows how informal groups influence the urban administration and promote their ideology, viewpoint, and interests. We claim that such informal groups are a common mechanism in the local urban arena. In effect, the preservation of Jaffa in the early 1960s, as well as the preservation of the White City forty years later, occurred due to the performance of such informal alliances between private citizens and individuals from within the local government.

This essay focuses on the contribution of *ideological developers* to the preservation of Old Jaffa and the White City. The term "ideological developer" describes a developer whose motivation is ideological as opposed to financial. The informal organizations that the ideological developer forms are termed *circumstantial coalitions*. The research exposes the unstable nature of these arrangements and highlights the differences and similarities in their emergence and operation. Thus, in addition to investigating the history of preservation in Tel-Aviv, we attempt to contribute to the study of urban politics in general and to the discourse regarding *the process of governance* in particular.[1]

Our research sheds light on the way individuals acquire power and influence at the urban level. Especially, we explore the way they transform their views into governing policies and manage to aim, plan, and act. We claim that these informal actors make a fundamental contribution to policymaking in local governments, as the selected cases of preservation in Tel-Aviv demonstrate.

This essay begins with a brief introduction to urban regime and the role of governing coalitions at the local level and then turns to the case studies of preservation in Tel-Aviv: the preservation of Old Jaffa and the White City. In both cases we stress the crucial role of informal supporters and the circumstantial coalitions they establish with officials and politicians in order to promote their ideas. Finally, we elaborate on the operation of the circumstantial coalitions and examine their strategies.

## Regime Theory and the Case of Tel-Aviv

Regime theories, associated with the works of Clarence Stone and Stephen Elkin, deal with the political powers that operate at the urban
level.[2] In the American city, business groups and local government administration are mutually dependent, and the interaction between them
is necessary for managing the local level. Governing capacities in U.S.
cities derive from formal as well as informal networks and are relatively
stable and enduring in nature.[3] Similar studies conducted in the UK,
however, found that the central government is highly influential at the
local level.[4] Thus urban regeneration partnerships in the UK are traditionally based on local authorities collaborating with civil bodies rather
than with the private sector, and focus on redistributive functions rather
than financial gain.[5]

The backdrop to local governance in Israel is closer to that of the UK
rather than the business-dominated atmosphere in American cities. As
governmental agencies operate in a centralized manner, land ownership
is basically nationalized, and the state activates tight financial control
over municipal administration. Local government in Israel is limited
both in its ability to set strategies and to deploy policy tools. Thus long-
term alliances between the private and municipal public sectors are not
so common. This is also the case with Tel-Aviv: compared with other
local governments in Israel, Tel-Aviv is relatively independent—both
financially and with respect to policymaking on various issues.[6] The
mayor of Tel-Aviv heads the "Forum of the 15," an organization including the fifteen richest cities in Israel, which are not financially supported
by Ministry of Interior. In addition, although the Israel Land Authority
(hereafter: ILA) owns about ninety-five percent of the state's land, it is
the owner of only 44.4 percent of Tel-Aviv's area, while the municipality owns another 24.8 percent of the city's area. Nevertheless, due to the
relations of central and local governments in Israel, the city is not free to
ally with market forces and form stable, long-term cooperation, as cities
in the United States often do.

Urban policymaking in Tel-Aviv–Jaffa involves small but influential pressure groups that gain access to urban administration and affect
local strategy. Similar to local partnerships in the UK, the coalitions

formed in Tel-Aviv are driven by interests that are not purely lucrative. Small groups of ideological developers (IDs) impact the formation of Tel-Aviv's preservation policy. The IDs are strongly committed individuals who leverage human and social capital to establish a circumstantial coalition with members from the municipal administration. With the intensive leadership of the IDs, the coalition works systematically to facilitate policy tools and pursue an operative preservation policy. This essay elaborates on the operation of the circumstantial coalition that brought about the conservation of Old Jaffa in the 1960s. It then compares it with the operation of the White City circumstantial coalition more than thirty years later, and discusses the impact such small groups of devotees have on local policymaking.

## The Preservation of Old Jaffa

### DEMOLISHING THE OLD FABRIC

Current-day Old Jaffa retains little physical evidence of its past as the urban center from which metropolitan Tel-Aviv developed. The remains of Jaffa are now an urban reserve. The narrow alleyways bear new names after signs of the Zodiac and the old living quarters serve as art galleries and restaurants. It seems as if Old Jaffa is naturally integrated into the urban lifecycle.

The interest in preserving Old Jaffa started only after the systematic demolition of the place had begun, in September 1949. Old Jaffa was vacated by its original residents following the 1948 war, and then seized by the state to be handled by the Custodian of Absentees' Property (hereafter: CAP) and the ILA. The City of Tel-Aviv was given the responsibility to manage the quotidian issues of Jaffa, its southern neighbor. In the following months Tel-Aviv took possession of sections of Jaffa until eventually, on 24 April 1950, Jaffa was annexed to Tel-Aviv, and some parts of it allocated to Bat-Yam and Holon. This responsibility, however, was a challenging task. The houses of Jaffa were rundown as a result of the 1948 war and neglect, and lack of infrastructure in general. The municipality of Tel-Aviv established the Jaffa Administration—a municipal department designated to deal with the various aspects of living in Jaffa.

The formal bodies involved in Jaffa—the municipality of Tel-Aviv, the ILA, and the CAP—appointed an engineers' commission to study the state of the buildings in the Old City of Jaffa. The official concern was that the damaged residences were a hazard.[7] However, there were other tacit incentives for the destruction of the old fabric. General contempt and animosity toward Arab cities was related to the deep adherence to rational-modern ideas of urbanism. In addition, the municipality of Tel-Aviv had a lot to gain from the demolition of Old Jaffa. Tearing down Old Jaffa would provide the municipality with greater control over a highly accessible piece of land located on the shoreline and bordering the city. Arnon Golan, who studies the handling of other Arab cities in those years, reports similar deliberations that took place in governmental as well as local agencies.[8] In addition, the great housing shortage for the Jewish population, the "public security" argument, and the desire to prevent the return of former residents drove decision-makers into adopting the demolition policy, as with the demolition plan of Manshiya, Jaffa's suburb, and the actual destruction of the Old City of Haifa[9] as well as Tiberias's Old Quarter.

Thus a written report by the Engineers' Commission in August 1949 includes a clear recommendation to demolish *the entire* Old City. The commission warned of unstable buildings, which would collapse if demolition procedure did not start immediately. The report did not refer to the cultural or aesthetic value of the area and referred briefly to several holy places—mosques and monasteries. The report was adopted by the city engineer. Moreover, it seems that officials from the municipality, the land owner (ILA), and the governmental agency in charge (CAP), agreed that Old Jaffa had to be demolished.[10] Indeed, as soon as the country was no longer at war, the demolition was initiated and continued until late 1950. The destruction started with buildings close to the coastline and progressed toward the city core. The urban fabric of Old Jaffa was doomed to a quick destruction.

### CIRCUMSTANTIAL COALITIONS AND THE PRESERVATION FRONT

The protest against the demolition of Old Jaffa was, at first, weak and ineffective. The group that struggled during the next decade to preserve

Jaffa was comprised of three individuals with respected professional status yet diminutive political influence and indirect access to power. The first was Samuel Yevin—archeologist and head of the Antiquities Department in the prime minister's office. The second was Eliezer Brutzcus—engineer, urban planner, and head of the Research and Survey Division in the Planning Department. The third was Marcel Janco—architect, painter, and leading member of the Association of Painters and Sculptors in Israel. Janco was born in Romania in 1895 and moved to Palestine in 1941. He was a member of the avant-garde Dada art movement, and in 1953 he initiated the artists' colony in Ein Hod, near Haifa. He worked as an architect for various governmental planning agencies in Israel, including Tel-Aviv. Yair Paz has mapped out the action taken by these three individuals in an effort to save the Old City of Jaffa from demolition.[11] Their strategy utilizes networks within the public sector to promote a preservation agenda. Thus they successfully created and operated what we coin "circumstantial coalitions."

Although these three activists functioned as part of a group, in effect each was acting individually, driven by his own interest in the preservation efforts. Samuel Yevin was the first to learn of the decision to demolish Old Jaffa. Yevin realized that even though the demolition of Jaffa contradicted local planning rules,[12] legal and procedural arguments alone could not halt the demolition.[13] Therefore, he pleaded for the cultural importance of Old Jaffa and the need to safeguard the city's holy places, including the first synagogue of Jaffa as well as several churches and mosques. Yevin wrote an urgent letter to the CAP, where he raised issue with the unprofessional attitude of the engineers' commission that surveyed Jaffa. He then offered to set up a bigger commission, including officials from various governmental ministries, such as the Ministry of Religious Affairs and the Ministry of Health, in addition to planners from the District Planning and Building Commission.[14] In addition, Yevin contacted administrators from these agencies, trying to create an opposition to the official municipal policy. Apparently, Yevin recruited Eliezer Brutzcus, who shared his view that demolishing Old Jaffa was more a knee-jerk reaction than any enlightened planning policy. By the end of September 1949, Brutzcus wrote a long letter to the CAP and pleaded against the destruction of the city.

## THE FIGHT AGAINST THE DEMOLITION

The two administrators, Yevin and Brutzcus, continued to collaborate in promoting a preservation agenda for nearly a decade. While Yevin's strategy was to stress the importance of Jaffa's religious monuments, Brutzcus aspired to preserve the old fabric in its entirety due to its unique aesthetics.[15] Paz reports the pressure that Yevin and Brutzcus exerted on officials, mainly governmental administrators, in their demand to stop the destructive operation and reconsider the future of Jaffa.[16] Resulting from Yevin and Brutzcus's claims, an additional commission was assembled to reevaluate and finalize the debate regarding the Old City of Jaffa. This time the commission was headed by the Ministry of Labor. It included architects (Marcel Janco thus joined the preservation front) and representatives from the Ministry of Religious Affairs, the Antiquities Department (including Yevin himself), and the Planning Department. The commission's aim was to examine whether buildings designated for demolition could be rehabilitated.[17] In the first two reports the commission handed to the Minister of Labor, in September and October 1949, the commission continued to recommend preserving only the listed buildings, in addition to cleaning the Old City, which was piled with heaps of trash. Brutzcus, however, insisted on preserving the city on a larger scale. He met with the commission in an attempt to promote his idea, and wrote to the tourism consultant in the prime minister's office. "Preserving a few scattered houses and leaving them among the ruins is a worthless action. The essence of such projects of preservation is keeping the atmosphere of the Old City," he wrote.[18] Dr. Altman, the consultant, was indeed impressed by Brutzcus's arguments and became a supporter of the preservation idea.[19] Thus only in its final report, dated 28 November 1949, did the commission find that seventy-two percent of the houses marked for demolition could be restored.

A circumstantial coalition of administrators from various governmental agencies that rejected the Tel-Aviv municipality's intention to demolish Old Jaffa was assembled by the end of 1949. It included members from the prime minister's office, the Antiquities Department, and officials from the Planning Department. The city of Tel-Aviv expressed a clear interest in the demolition of Jaffa, now part of Tel-Aviv. For example, as the destruction slowed down by the end of 1949, due to the massive influx of new immigrants to the old houses and the general housing shortage, the city engineer wrote to the CAP. He warned that further collapse of buildings was imminent and stressed, "It is strongly advised to demolish all the houses of the Old City once and for all."[20]

THE FIGHT FOR PRESERVATION

The most pertinent idea—of rehabilitating Jaffa by means of developing it into an artists' colony—came up in the discussions and negotiations that took place throughout 1950, alongside the continuing destruction— although with less intensity—of the Old City. The promoter of this initiative was Marcel Janco, who was fascinated by the vernacular Middle Eastern architecture and its sensitivity to climate and topographical conditions. He envisioned the old fabric of Jaffa as a backdrop to fertile artistic activity and tried to promote his vision both within and outside the municipal administration, with the help of the circumstantial coalition. Janco managed to interest the National Association of Architects, the Association of Painters and Sculptors, in particular the painter Reuven Rubin, and to influence the Preservation Commission—a ministerial commission constructed December 1950 which aimed to study the monuments and the architectural heritage of Jaffa and to assure the protection of buildings of religious, archeological, historical, and artistic significance.[21]

In December 1950, Marcel Janco and the painter Reuven Rubin appeared before a newly established Preservation Commission. The two artists appealed to retain the Old City and develop it into an artists' colony. Janco said, "The modern city, Tel-Aviv, is not pretty. As a matter of fact, it is ugly. There is one beautiful corner; please, do not ruin it."[22] He also reported that several artists had already settled in the chosen blocks and located their residences as well as studios there. By the end of this meeting, Janco managed to receive shaky approval to preserve small building blocks and alleyways in the southwestern section of the Old City, and designate them as artists' residences. The CAP was determined to raze the city. As a result of their pressure and after a few more houses collapsed during the winter of 1950–51, a separate governmental commission was set up to investigate the difficulty involved in evacuating the rickety buildings. As this commission reassessed the need to pull down most of the buildings, a ministers' commission was set to deal with the evacuation of the city and its demolition. Janco, Yevin, and Brutzcus carried out a bitter fight against the continued destruction with the help of the preservation supporters, writing letters and applying pressure to administrators from various governmental ministries. The circumstantial alliances they created with officials bore fruit. Minister of Education Zalman Shazar visited the site and was impressed by the beauty of the place; Cabinet Secretary Ze'ev Sherf expressed his surprise at the demolition; the Association of Painters and Sculptors wrote to the CAP and other officials and protested against the continuous disregard of cultural assets;[23] Brutzcus delivered a detailed map of Old Jaffa, pointing out buildings worthy of preservation, to the Ministry of Interior.[24] Mounting political pressure began to show results, and Mayor Rokach met with Janco and Rubin in an effort to reassess the municipality's policy with respect to the extent of the preservation and the artist colony idea.

By the end of 1950 the demolition of houses in Old Jaffa declined until in early 1951, it finally stopped. Apparently, evacuation of residents was postponed as there was almost no alternative housing available.[25] From the municipality's point of view, Old Jaffa remained a problematic asset: the state of the buildings was poor and dangerous[26] and massive invasion occurred to buildings that were evacuated.[27] However, the coalition still worked to preserve Old Jaffa's remains. Janco collaborated with the Association of Architects and Engineers and continued his efforts. In March 1951, the association wrote to the minister of education and promised to conduct a detailed survey of Old Jaffa and to prepare a plan for a "cultural district," once the decision to construct an artists' colony was made.[28] The detailed map attached to this letter, pointing out the exact buildings fit for painters and architects, was most likely created by Janco. Indeed, Janco and other artists were invited to the meetings of the Preservation Commission.[29] However, progress was slow. In November 1952, the artists' association readdressed the authorities and reminded them of the obligations to preserve the two blocks, evacuate their inhabitants, and designate the area for artists. They complained that besides retaining the buildings, nothing had been achieved thus far. However, in 1953, Marcel Janco established an artists' village in Ein Hod, on the ruins of the Arab village Ein Chud, and in effect left Jaffa's preservation front.

## CONSTRUCTING THE ADMINISTERED
### TOOLS FOR PRESERVATION

Aaron Horwitz, an American urban planner, was commissioned to plan Tel-Aviv–Jaffa's future development. The demand for preservation and the existence of the Preservation Commission paid off, as the 1954 Tel-Aviv Master Plan he proposed related to a small preserved district dedicated to art and tourism in Old Jaffa. Now that demolition stopped and a decision to create the artists' colony was made, it was only a matter of implementation. Again, a circumstantial coalition was enlisted for support. Yevin and Brutzcus continued to pressure the local authority and tried to create administrative and financial means for the preservation to take place. Letters were sent to the municipality from Office of Interior and Office of Commerce and Industry (Division of Tourism) demanding preservation of the Old City. This ritual continued throughout the 1950s. In the meantime, the buildings continued to deteriorate and some even collapsed. Only two blocks remained that could be preserved, and the IDs aimed at constructing the administered tools for the task. Gradually, it became evident that government officials needed to collaborate with the municipality for the preservation of the remaining two blocks. In July 1958 the director of the office of the prime minister, Teddy Kollek, visited the site in an attempt to promote its rehabilitation. Together with the deputy mayor, Kollek surveyed Jaffa's remains, and agreed that money should be allocated to the development of the site.[30] Six months later a full partnership between the Israeli government and the Tel-Aviv–Jaffa Municipality was signed, to establish a company that would administer the site defined as the Old City of Jaffa.[31]

In September 1960, the Company for the Development of Ancient Jaffa was created as a public firm, with equal ownership of Tel-Aviv–Jaffa Municipality and the Government.[32] Its aims were to develop the Old City into a cultural and entertainment center, while protecting its religious and archeological sites.[33] Funding for initial investments in the first years came from the two public owners. The land was leased to the Company for the Development of Ancient Jaffa by the ILA for a period of five years for one Israeli Lira per year.[34] The company managed roughly 112 dunams, which were defined as the limits of the Old City of Jaffa. By the early 1970s, the Old City was rehabilitated and its buildings rented to local artists and various businesses.

The preservation of the Old City of Jaffa thus exemplifies the methodology utilized by the IDs. Moreover, it provides an opportunity to trace their influence in local decision making. In the case of Old Jaffa, the advocates first struggled to stop the demolition that took place from 1949 to early 1951. They recruited governmental officials, suggested setting up new commissions, and provided relevant information, in an attempt to influence policy decisions. Once the demolition stopped, the circumstantial coalition shifted their efforts to preservation. Again, pressures were exerted, new information and ideas presented, and organizational efforts deployed. The establishment of the Preservation Commission was an important achievement of the IDs; it provided the framework for the artists' colony initiative, which was adopted into Horowitz's master plan. The construction of the Company for the Development of Ancient Jaffa resulted largely from the persistent effort to keep Jaffa on the agenda and reinforce its value and potential contribution to urban culture.

## Circumstantial Coalitions and the
## Preservation of the White City

From the end of the 1990s through the beginning of the 2000s, the preservation of the White City was finalized under circumstances quite similar to the preservation of Old Jaffa. In this case as well, a small group of activists pressured decision-makers and high officials through associations with administrators that created an unofficial preservation front. This time, the IDs included two preservation supporters that did not hold official positions. The two were sculptor Dani Karavan and architecture historian Dr. Michael (Micha) Levin. Although the IDs had no formal political power, officials and politicians granted them frequent audience, including Shlomo Lahat, the mayor of Tel-Aviv during 1974–1993. Karavan was personally acquainted with Mayor Lahat, and Levin was the director of the Tel-Aviv Museum of Art from 1986 to 1990. Levin also later served as Mayor Lahat's consultant until 1993. While the IDs managed to bring the preservation of the White City to fruition, they were disappointed by the partial adoption of their vision. In the following section, a brief review is given of the structure of forces and coalitions that operated in Tel-Aviv in the 1980s and 1990s with respect to the preservation of modern architecture. The role of circumstantial coalitions—temporary alliances of activists, administrators, and politicians—in urban policymaking in general and with respect to preserving the built heritage in particular is then discussed.

## THE WHITE CITY: A CONCISE BACKGROUND

The White City of Tel-Aviv is an area that was built in the 1930s and 1940s by Jewish architects that immigrated to Palestine from Europe and introduced the modern architectural techniques they had practiced there. As the city rapidly expanded in this period, this modern architectural style, also referred to as International Style, became dominant in the city center.[35] This well-defined building style, so different from the Oriental Style of Old Jaffa as well as the Eclectic Style of Tel-Aviv's earlier days, is also associated with the Bauhaus School. Each building is unique, yet they all share the same appearance: three to four stories high, with clear horizontal emphasis, light plaster walls, flat roofs, and windowed staircases.[36]

The buildings aged rapidly due to poor building materials. The smooth plaster peeled, the lime brick walls cracked, and the metal banisters corroded. Within a short while, the modern architecture of the city center appeared ugly and dull. In addition, as the city continued to expand, the city center underwent a transition, turning a residential district into a busy financial center. Throughout the 1960s and 1970s, residential apartments were usurped by small businesses and light industries, which exacerbated the deterioration of the buildings and infrastructure. As families left this area, schools and community centers became disused. The population of the city center grew older and poorer. The nearby metropolitan Central Business District expanded into the area that now suffered from heavy traffic and pollution.

By the mid-1970s, district-planning authorities prepared a metropolitan outline plan, which suggested developing secondary employment centers that would relieve the pressure on the metropolitan CBD. In addition, the plan called for reinstating residences in central Tel-Aviv and restoring its communal atmosphere.[37] Derived from this initiative, the municipality of Tel-Aviv together with the Ministry of Housing prepared a detailed plan for the center of Tel-Aviv, called the Lev Ha'ir (heart of the city) plan. The plan, created in 1981 by architect Adam Mazor, proposed the development of various tools for the physical and social revival of the city, including reorganization of traffic flows and parking permission, up-zoning of residential lots, and prohibiting the diffusion of businesses into residential buildings. The idea of preserving buildings from Tel-Aviv's early days was introduced as part of these tools. However, since the planners were unaware of the cultural significance of the local International Style buildings, they linked the preservation idea with buildings of the Eclectic Style. In addition, since they were interested in commencing urban renewal rather than preservation per se, they suggested that buildings that undergo preservation be supplemented with one to three floors.[38] Soon, this attitude was challenged by a small group of devotees of the Modern, International Style, that—like the supporters of Old Jaffa—carried on a stubborn, persistent struggle for the preservation of this urban heritage.

## THE CIRCUMSTANTIAL COALITIONS OF
## MODERN HERITAGE PRESERVATION

In 1980, both Karavan and Levin became aware of the contribution of the Bauhaus School to the architecture of Tel-Aviv, and in particular to the uniqueness of Tel-Aviv as having one of the largest collections of Bauhaus buildings in the world.[39] It seems a traveling exhibition hosted by the Tel-Aviv Museum of Art concerning the architecture of the Bauhaus School was the catalyst of this awareness. Although the exhibition did not link Bauhaus architecture to Tel-Aviv, the two understood the impact of the Bauhaus School on Tel-Aviv's architecture and, at the same time, recognized that the buildings designed in this style were in abhorrent condition. Inspired by this exhibition, Michael Levin initiated voluntary research regarding the impact of Bauhaus architecture in Israel, and a few years later, in 1984, served as the curator of an exhibition titled "White City" at the Tel-Aviv Museum of Art.[40] Several years later, in 1988, Dani Karavan presented Kikar Levana[41] (white square)— a large sculpture located in a park overlooking the city of Tel-Aviv.[42] Levin's exhibition and Karavan's sculpture represent the origin of the "White City" metaphor with respect to Tel-Aviv's International Style, as noted by Azaryahu.[43] In addition, they are evidence of the IDs' commitment to exposing the importance and beauty of Tel-Aviv's modern architecture in general, and the preservation of the modern heritage in particular.

The city administration, including the city engineer and planners from the municipal planning department adopted the Lev Ha'ir plan and shared the plan's attitude toward preservation. Thus, in line with the plan, the Planning Department adopted a list of about 300 buildings in the city center, most of them belonging to the Eclectic Style, and designated them for preservation. In addition, the Planning Department accepted the fact that preservation was a tool for attracting development to the area and aspired to increase the residential units in the Lev Ha'ir district by twenty-five percent, mainly by adding stories to preserved buildings.[44]

Since their attempt to collaborate with Lev Ha'ir's planners did not work out, Karavan and Levin searched for other potential alliances that could transform the official policy. In the interim, the editors of *Ha'ir,* a popular local weekly, initiated an urban preservation campaign. In the early 1990s, in light of the Lev Ha'ir plan, the magazine invited architects to design a plan for the preservation of city center buildings. Eighteen houses on Ha'Gilboa St., a small street in the center district, were raffled among eighteen architects. Architectural plans and models were presented in a public exhibition, called *Ha'Gilboa Street: A Case Study.* However, the buildings were originally three to four stories high and the directive to the architects was to add one to two stories to each building. Changing the buildings' outline was a fundamental point of contention between Karavan and the magazine's editors. For example, during a symposium that accompanied the exhibition, Karavan, who was in the audience, exclaimed: "We are facing a terrible disaster. We have a precious asset and we are about to ruin it."[45] Clearly, Karavan and Levin did not find assistance from *Ha'ir*'s editors or among the architects of the Ha'Gilboa buildings.

Their access to influential figures within the municipality, as well as the impact of Levin's exhibition, provided the preservation supporters with an alternative route of action. They gained the support of the city museum's director and the Tel-Aviv Fund's director, as well as the interest and acknowledgment of the city engineer. In addition, they managed to utilize Karavan's personal acquaintance with the mayor of Tel-Aviv. In line with their suggestion, the Local Council passed a resolution stating that the city would purchase five buildings in the Bauhaus Style and use them as showcases of the preservation effort. Implementation of this decision was delayed, however, and the IDs continued to pressure high officials. This circumstance led them to create a most efficient coalition, which was an association with the Tel-Aviv Development Fund (TADF), a municipal firm under the auspices of the municipality. TADF's director, who became a preservation supporter, agreed to finance the work of an architect who would choose the buildings that best exemplify the International Style. As an outside body, TADF proved to be more flexible than the municipality in hiring personnel. Karavan and Levin recommended architect Nitza Szmuk and were highly involved in her work. Szmuk supported the aims of the preservation front and, within a short while, was busy conducting a comprehensive survey of the International Style architecture in Tel-Aviv.[46]

Despite the supportive atmosphere Karavan and Levin created with the city engineer, the municipal Planning Department was not keen to cooperate with the preservation architect of the TADF. Tacit struggles as well as open clashes took place in 1990. Karavan and Levin demanded that the survey results of more than 1,300 structures of the International Style be recognized and utilized by the Planning Department. This demand was controversial, as officials from the Planning Department found it hard to accept such an extensive database, prepared and conducted by outsiders.[47] However, at the beginning of 1991, the amendment to the National Law of Planning and Building was accepted, ordering local planning authorities to include a preservation committee, to prepare a conservation plan and to set guidelines for a preservation appendix.[48] Szmuk, the preservation architect, was asked to help and was given a small workplace in the Planning Department and the assistance of a graphic designer. She was still employed by the TADF but gradually became part of the daily work of the department. The survey she had completed was the basis of the municipal conservation plan that the department initiated, and city planners consulted her whenever inhabitants and developers appealed with changes to buildings that were on her list. Since early 1993, Szmuk was employed by the municipality and TADF and, by 1994, she became a full municipal worker.

The peak of integration between the IDs and the municipality was symbolized by the White City celebration, conducted by the municipality in 1994. The city engineer was actively involved in organizing the event and the city was a cosponsor, with UNESCO. The extended event included an exhibition of the International Style contribution to Tel-Aviv architecture,[49] based on Levin's exhibition from a decade ago, as well as a signpost campaign around the city that pointed out significant Bauhaus buildings, a photographic exhibition related to the Bauhaus movement in Tel-Aviv Museum of Art, and more.

However, the preservation front did not settle for local recognition of the importance of modern architecture and sought ways to force the local authority to preserve the buildings belonging to the International Style. Apparently, they encouraged the departing mayor to invite UNESCO's Director-General, Federico Mayor, to attend the primary event of the White City celebration.[50] With the mayor's blessing, they initiated efforts to gain UNESCO's inscription of Tel-Aviv as a World Heritage Site, which they hoped could obligate the city to strictly preserve the urban fabric.

Obtaining the nomination from UNESCO involved much effort. As before, it required a devoted and coordinated involvement of the preservation front. In 1994, Israel did not yet adhere to the World Heritage Convention, whose formal ratification occurred in October 1999, and was not committed to protect built heritage. Moreover, the new city engineer suspected that the limitations to the further planning and development of the White City resulting from such a nomination would exceed its possible advantages. These limits were precisely what found favor with the IDs. Once Israel adhered to the World Heritage Convention, the White City was included in the proposed list of preserved sites, necessary for the UNESCO nomination. Then, they pressured the mayor and city engineer to support the short listing of the White City.[51] Thus Karavan and Levin continued to guide the nomination process that finally took place in June 2003, with the same stubborn commitment and pressure. To this day, the IDs continue to serve as the preservation gatekeepers. For example, at the beginning of 2007, Karavan is highly involved in a struggle against the municipality of Tel-Aviv, which is striving to change the structure of Heichal Hatarbut, the large performing arts center located in the buffer zone of the White City. To this end,

Karavan is utilizing his personal leverage in the art world and recruits artists and architects worldwide to support his agenda.

* * *

The growing interest in questions of urban governance and local policymaking highlight the impact of organized civil groups as well as a businesslike interest in local policymaking. Our research regarding the processes that led to the preservation of Old Jaffa and the White City reveals the central role assumed by informal groups at municipal and national levels. In both cases, small groups of individuals managed to influence official bodies to adopt a preservation policy very much in contrast to the original policy. In the case of the White City, the CCs worked to impact municipal officials, whereas in the case of Old Jaffa, they also pressed various national agencies. By persistent, coordinated action, with the help of influential partners, and by utilizing their own professional and personal status, these small groups of individuals changed the urban landscape in line with their own values, and contributed substantially to the richness of the urban fabric.

In the Israeli context, the preservation of urban heritage in Tel-Aviv may be considered an outstanding example of municipal commitment to urban heritage. Therefore, processes that took place behind the scenes of the municipal administration are extremely significant. The recurring mechanism discussed demonstrates the crucial role of IDs in the crystallization of local preservation policy in two distinct cases. The impact of IDs was important despite the fundamental differences between Old Jaffa and the White City, and the time periods in which the policies took shape. While the preservation of Old Jaffa required the effort of administrative agencies, the preservation of the White City poses a much more demanding challenge—regulating the development of a lively city. Nevertheless, despite the different historical circumstances, the involvement of the local authority in the preservation was influenced by the efforts of a group of supporters. Thus, in terms of urban development, these supporters not only initiated the preservation efforts but also contributed professional knowledge to its implementation.

The research reveals the nature of the coalitions that operate behind the scenes and that impact decision-making in the municipality of Tel-Aviv. Small groups of individuals with specific professional knowledge

and acknowledged personal capital join forces with other influential actors and create effective coalitions. The activists in the hard core of the
coalitions, the IDs, lack formal organization and function. They do not
operate on behalf of an economic or civil body and do not promote the interests of a defined public. Thus they form conditional and circumstantial
alliances: the makeup of the coalitions change in relation to the current
status and needs, in line with occasional opportunities and events. The
small group that promoted the preservation of Old Jaffa included governmental officials and national public figures, resulting from occasional
acquaintances of Yevin, Brutzcus, and Janco. However, it also stemmed
from the existing political structure, in which the state was the owner of
the land and buildings while the city was given an operational responsibility. The coalitions to preserve the White City were composed of local
officials. As the IDs wished to influence the mayor and the Planning
Department, their efforts were directed toward the urban administration.
Unlike the Old Jaffa case, the governmental level was irrelevant here.

The struggle for the preservation of urban heritage is a rather elitist
issue. This was the case in the 1950s, when Old Jaffa faced the invasion
of newcomers to deserted houses, as was the case in the 1980s and 1990s,
when urban groups struggled to allocate public goods. Thus the IDs could
not promote their issue via organized civil groups and NGOs, nor did they
attempt to raise massive public opinion to support their views. Instead,
the circumstantial coalitions were the tool they utilized to impact decision
makers. In both cases, the coalitions operated intensely for a relatively
long time period. Nevertheless, they did not manage to completely realize their vision. Old Jaffa was largely demolished, and only part of it was
preserved. With respect to the White City, the Planning Department did
not fully adopt the claim that preservation does permit additional construction and various amendments to modern buildings. Still, these two
cases demonstrate the important role assumed by non-economic cultural
interests on policymaking and its implementation in Tel-Aviv–Jaffa.

## NOTES

1. Eran Vigoda, "From Responsiveness to Collaboration: Governance, Citizens,
and the Next Generation of Public Administration," *Public Administration Review*
62.5 (2002): 527–540.

2. Clarence N. Stone, *Regime Politics* (Lawrence, KS, 1989); Stephen L. Elkin, *City and Regime in the American Republic* (Chicago, 1987).

3. Clarence N. Stone, "Urban Regimes and the Capacity to Govern: a Political-Economy Approach," *Journal of Urban Affairs* 15.1 (1993): 1–28.

4. For example: Alan DiGaetano and John S. Klemanski, "Urban Regimes in Comparative Perspective: The Politics of Urban Development in Britain," *Urban Affairs Review* 29.1 (1993): 54–83; "Urban Regime Capacity: A Comparison of Birmingham, England, and Detroit, Michigan," *Journal of Urban Affairs* 15.4 (1993): 367–384; Alan DiGaetano and Elizabeth Storm, "Comparative Urban Governance: An Integrated Approach," *Urban Affairs Review* 38.3 (2003): 356–395.

5. Jonathan S. Davies, *Partnerships and Regimes: The Politics of Regeneration Partnerships in the UK* (Adlershot, 2001); "Urban Regime Theory: A Normative Empirical Critique," *Journal of Urban Affairs* 24.1 (2002): 1–17; "Partnerships Versus Regimes: Why Regime Theory Cannot Explain Urban Coalitions in the UK," *Journal of Urban Affairs* 25.3 (2003): 253–269.

6. Nurit Alfasi and Tovi Fenster, "A Tale of Two Cities: Jerusalem and Tel-Aviv in an Age of Globalization," *Cities* 22.5 (2005): 351–363.

7. During the winter of 1949/1950, several houses collapsed due to exceptional snowfall. On 16 April 1950, eighteen people died and another twenty-eight were injured when a building near the Old City of Jaffa collapsed.

8. Arnon Golan, "The Politics of Wartime Demolition and Human Landscape Transformation," *War in History* 9.4 (2002): 431–445.

9. Tamir Goren, *Fall of Arab Haifa in 1948* (Sde-Boker, 2006) [Hebrew].

10. By the end of August 1950, a second engineers' commission inspected the Old City and reached the same conclusion. The commission considered three alternative solutions: rehabilitating the site, evacuating the residents and fencing off the area, or demolishing it, and ruled out the first two.

11. Yair Paz, "Preserving Architectural Heritage in Deserted Neighborhoods after the War of Independence," *Cathedra* 88 (1998): 95–134 [Hebrew].

12. *The Official Gazette of the Government of Palestine,* No. 1375, 24 November 1944, declares large parts of Jaffa as antiquities, according to Antiquities Ordinance No. 51 of 1929. The demolition of Jaffa, thus, was prohibited by law.

13. Paz, "Preserving Architectural Heritage."

14. Yevin to Mr. H. Reizel, the CAP, Israel State Archive (ISA), 43, 2747/GL-8, 19 September 1949.

15. Brutzcus to the CAP, SA, div. 43, 2747/GL-8, 24 October 1949.

16. Paz, "Preserving Architectural Heritage," 110–114.

17. Final report of "The Committee for Monuments in Ancient Jaffa," Tel-Aviv Historical Archive (henceforth: TAHA), 15/114, 28 November 1949.

18. Brutzcus to Dr. Altman, SA, div. 43, 2747/GL-8, 25 October 1949.

19. Paz, "Preserving Architectural Heritage."

20. Tel-Aviv City Engineer to the CAP, TAHA, 15/114, 6 January 1950.

21. Protocol of meeting: The Committee for Preservation of Structures of Historic, Architectonic, and Religious Values in Ancient Jaffa, SA, div. 43, 2211/G-3, 21 December 1950.

22. Ibid., 28 December 1950.

23. National Association of Architects to Mr. Porath, the CAP, SA, div. 43, 2211/G-3, 28 February; National Association of Architects to the art subdivision in the Ministry of Education, SA, div. 43, 2211/G-3, 19 March 1951.

24. Brutzcus to Mr. M. Cahana, the Ministry of Interiors, SA, div. 43, 2211/G-3, 21 January 1951.

25. Golan, "The Politics of Wartime Demolition"; Paz, "Preserving Architectural Heritage."

26. Mayor Rokach to Mr. D. Gefen, the regional office in Jaffa, SA, div. 43, 2211/G-3, 2 February 1951. The letter reports on distressful housing conditions in Old Jaffa, including the lack of running water, sewage solutions, and electricity.

27. A. Ben-Dor, the Antiquities Department to M. Porath, the CAP, SA, div. 43, 2211/G-3, 27 June 1951. The letter deals with safeguarding evacuated buildings in Old Jaffa from invaders.

28. S. Shaag, the Association of Architects and Engineers to the Minister of Education, SA, div. 43, 2211/G-3, 19 March 1951.

29. Minutes of The Committee for Preservation of Structures of Historic, Architectonic, and Religious Values in Ancient Jaffa, SA, div. 43, 2211/G-3, 28 December 1950 and 11 April 1951.

30. Minutes of meeting between Deputy Mayor Shechterman and Teddy Kollek of the Office of the Prime Minister, TAHA, 15-167, 3 July 1958. A principal agreement is mentioned regarding the construction of a company for the development of Jaffa.

31. Minutes of meeting between Deputy Mayor Shechterman, Teddy Kollek, Mr. Yanai of the Office of Tourism, and Architect Tanai, TAHA, 15-167, 8 January 1959. The agreement called for financial investments by all parties.

32. Protocols of the Company for the Development of Ancient Jaffa, TAHA, 28/454, 8 September 1960. Twenty-five percent of the company was maintained by the Governmental Company for Tourism, and another twenty-five percent was handed over to the Company for the Development of Tourism.

33. Report, Survey of Municipal Companies, TAHA, 28/454, December 1963.

34. Protocols of the Company for the Development of Ancient Jaffa, TAHA, 28/454, 20 October 1960. The protocol mentions that following a five-year trial period the area will be leased for a longer period of time.

35. Yaacov Shavit and Gideon Biger, *The History of Tel-Aviv,* vol. 1 (Tel-Aviv, 2001) [Hebrew]; Irit Amit-Cohen, "Synergy Between Urban Planning, Conservation of the Cultural Built Heritage, and Functional Changes in the Old Urban Center: The Case of Tel-Aviv," *Land Use Policy* 22 (2005): 291–300; Maoz Azaryahu, *Tel-Aviv: Mythography of a City* (Syracuse, 2006).

36. Abba Elhanani, *The Struggle for the Independence of Israeli Architecture in the Twentieth Century* (Tel-Aviv, 1998) [Hebrew]; Nitza Szmuk, *Houses of Sand,* (Tel-Aviv, 1994) [Hebrew]; Amit-Cohen, "Synergy Between Urban Planning."

37. Shavit and Biger, *The History of Tel-Aviv;* Niki Davidov, interview, Tel-Aviv–Jaffa, 6 January 2004.

38. Davidov, ibid.; Tzofia Santo, interview, Tel-Aviv–Jaffa, 8 April 2004.

39. Michael Levin, interview, Tel-Aviv–Jaffa, 25 August 2003.

40. The exhibition was part of the seventy-fifth anniversary of Tel-Aviv and the first to link the small houses of Tel-Aviv to the cultural heritage of modernism.

41. The sculpture is presented on the artist's website: www.danikaravan.com.

42. Karavan grew up in the center of Tel-Aviv. His father was the municipal gardener. He learned to appreciate the unique built environment and felt committed to the place.

43. Azaryahu, *Tel-Aviv: Mythography of a City.*

44. Davidov, interview, 6 January 2004; Santo, interview, 8 April 2004.

45. The exhibition and symposium were presented in the magazine: Esther Zandberg, "Ha'Gilboa Street: A Case Study," *Ha'ir,* 5 May 1990, 12–21.

46. Levin, interview, 25 August 2003; Nitza Szmuk, interview, Tel-Aviv–Jaffa, 26 August 2003; Dani Karavan, interview, Tel-Aviv–Jaffa, 17 August 2006.

47. Levin, ibid.; Szmuk, *Houses of Sand;* Santo, interview, 8 April 2004; Karavan, interview, 17 August 2006.

48. Amendment number 31, regulation proposal 2045, 12.3.1991, and Amit-Cohen, "Synergy Between Urban Planning," 292.

49. The exhibition organizers chose to name the event "The Bauhaus Exhibition" for marketing reasons.

50. Karavan, interview, 17 August 2006.

51. Levin, interview, 25 August 2003; Szmuk, *Houses of Sand;* Karavan, ibid.

# SEVENTEEN

# Balconies of Tel-Aviv: Cultural History and Urban Politics

## Carolin Aronis

> If we compare the house to the human body, we could say
> that the windows are the eyes of the house, the bases are
> the legs of the buildings, the balcony is its smile, and the
> façade is the spirit, the soul of this human creation.
> —*Meir Dizengoff, 1934*

Tel-Aviv for many years had been dubbed "a city of balconies." In its urban fantasy balconies are smiles, an expression of the beauty and openness of the city, but in day-to-day reality they are almost considered an eyesore. The balconies of Tel-Aviv have an important role in the social life of the city and they are a crucial part of its history and culture. Located between private and public, balconies simultaneously belong to both arenas. Accordingly, they invite conflict and struggle over their look and functions, and they constantly redefine, as well as express, the relationships between residents and the urban public sphere.

This essay explores different aspects of urban politics and the cultural history of balconies. In particular, it sheds light on façade balconies in Tel-Aviv as sites of dispute between residents and authorities. Through a socio-cultural and architectural perspective, I present the historical changes of style and use of balconies as sites of contention in the city. The conclusions deal with the crucial role of balconies in Tel-Aviv in creating connections between private and public spheres, and establishing values of leisure, privacy, identity, boundary, and place. Until now, there has been no academic research on balconies as cultural and political artifacts, especially in Tel-Aviv.

Fig. 17.1. The painter Reuven Rubin and his future wife on a Tel-Aviv balcony. "Les Fiancées," 1929, oil on canvas (Reuven Rubin Museum).

The most common images of the balcony are those represented in mythological tales, usually involving a romantic situation such as when a prince climbs up to a balcony on a girl's braid, a suitor serenading his beloved at night, or Romeo who sends Juliet messages of passion through her balcony. Another famous image is the leader addressing his or her people from a balcony overlooking a square. In many works of art the balcony is represented as a unique place in the urban landscape, where residents can be in touch with the public sphere, or as a hanging garden, which decorates the grisly streets of the city.

In addition to the aesthetic aspects, which can be seen clearly in architectural plans, the balcony also has a *liminal* character. As a three-dimensional aperture of the apartment into the street and bounded by rails, it usually protrudes from the exterior walls of buildings, and can be considered a physical threshold of both public and private arenas. "Betwixt and between," it is an intermediary zone.[1] It is a place that liberates the resident from the claustrophobia of the apartment, while at the same time it keeps at bay any agoraphobic sensations from the bustling street.[2] This middle space is a locus of detachment from and attachment

Fig. 17.2. Common balconies in Tel-Aviv, the same balcony in three different appearances. 50, Arlozorov Street (photo by Stanley Waterman, 2008).

to both the apartment and the street, and assembles a unique mixture of "front stage" and "back stage," to use Erving Goffman's metaphors.[3] Private and public are intertwined on the balcony and confound the notions of what is supposed to be open to the public, and what is a private, personal matter.

Especially in hot climates, such as Tel-Aviv's, the balcony creates openness and ventilation. However, the physical surface of the balcony is free from any defined use, and thus, it invites many kinds of temporal uses. Besides being a place for communication between home and street, the balcony serves as a place of leisure—for resting, observing neighbors, and playing cards, as well as a place of work—for drying laundry, shaking rugs, or simply as a storage space for all sorts of useless items. Since physically the balcony seems to be an incompletely constructed room, some people feel a necessity to close their balcony, to create a "full" room from it. A closed balcony frequently serves as an office, a small room for children, or as an extension of the living room.

All these well illustrate the "virgin" character of the balcony, which can always be redefined, reconstituted, re-established, and used in new ways. The "freedom" of this space enables its multi-functional use, and as will be shown later, lures residents to appropriate it for their own benefit.

The urban balcony has a broad history, but here I deal solely with its existence in Tel-Aviv and its relations to the developing city. The analysis is based on the methodology of *Material Culture*, looking at the Tel-Aviv balcony as an urban artifact, which is an object that exemplifies the social norms and cultural values of any given society or culture.[4] The research is based on a wide range of socio-cultural and architectural sources, including old city plans and plans of the development of private buildings, letters of request and complaint from residents to the authorities over time, interviews with residents, and exhibits of balconies in photographs and artistic productions.

## The Tel-Aviv Balcony: Space Dynamics

I present here the ways in which the Tel-Aviv balcony has changed over the years, as a space dynamic that highlights the constant tension between residents, authorities, architects, and builders. I stress the relations between the private and the public by considering the structure of the balcony, its uses, and the creation of communication or detachment between the two sides.

The delineation of historical periods in this context may be somewhat arbitrary; however, it provides a useful framework through which to understand the process of change. In addition, it is important to note that each style of balcony is *added* to styles that existed earlier; the earlier ones continue to exist and the new do not replace them. Thus, apart from the first period, the newer styles of balconies are invariably found alongside earlier ones, supplementing them.

### 1909–1920S

Tel-Aviv was founded in 1909 as a "garden city," a neighborhood of Jaffa with a suburban character. It was only in 1921 that it was declared a

Fig. 17.3. Front balcony as a bridge between the house and the street.
18, Sirkin Street. Unknown photographer, 1920s. (Ram Goffna
Collection, Tel-Aviv Historical Archive).

township. These early years are characterized by the establishment of
regulations for the parceling of land, building rights, and fair allocation
of resources.

*The Suburban Balcony:* The first balconies formed part of the
neighborhood's private houses.[5] Until the early 1920s these houses were
planned according to European Mediterranean models, with no commitment to any local architectural tradition. The construction was spa-
cious, and the houses were surrounded by broad gardens. In front of
most homes, which were mostly single story, there was a broad balcony,
raised about a meter above the ground. One or two stairwells led from
the street to the balcony and from it to the house. The balcony thus
served as a main entrance, or as a *bridge,* a space connecting the street
and the house (see Fig. 17.3).[6]

*The First Laws:* The neighborhood committee's first regulations
obliged the residents to maintain a space of at least 2 m from the façade.

It was forbidden to build the front balcony or the house in line with the street; a "setback"—a neutral buffer zone between the building and the street—was obligatory. Features such as the setback served to protect the residents' privacy and to improve their control over events in the street.[7] However, as letters of complaint to the committee indicate, some residents had built their balconies closer to the street than permitted.[8] It is not clear if this positioning expressed a desire to protrude more into public space, but those who built their homes near the street were accused of preventing the balconies of other homes from receiving the cool breeze, the sun's rays, and the view.

One of the firmest rules during that period concerned building rights. For the sake of protecting the broad gardens around the houses and as part of the suburban character of the neighborhood, it was prohibited to build on more than thirty-three percent of the lot. Covered balconies were considered part of these building rights. However, it was permitted to build additional uncovered balconies on another seven percent of the lot. Building was permitted on only forty percent of the area, and close to twenty percent of that consisted of uncovered balconies. These regulations, maintained obsessively by the committee, led to the construction of small houses consisting of two to three rooms with large uncovered balconies.[9]

In practice, these regulations enabled the construction of more than a single balcony per house. For example, from time to time an additional balcony was built to the rear of the house, mostly as an extension of the kitchen functions, but these rear balconies did not lessen the importance and centrality of the large front balcony. While the rear balcony was used for work and activities such as cooking and laundry, the front balcony allowed for pleasure, relaxation, entertaining, and communication with the street. For example, one city resident, Ziona Rabau, writes about mothers who used to sit on the front balcony on Herzl Street on Saturday nights, relaxing and conversing with one another from one balcony to the next.[10]

*Requests for Balcony Closure:* Surprisingly, the balcony did not content residents. As early as 1911, there were requests for balcony closure, in order to transform it into a closed space, disconnecting it physically from events in the street, as well as noise, the weather, dirt, and the like.[11] The front balcony was often seen as a real room that could be used as part of the apartment. Some residents wanted to extend their restricted living quarters and others wanted to protect themselves from the heavy heat, flies, and mosquitoes in the summer, and from the cold wind and rain that entered the house in the winter. Closure, for many, was a genuine need.

Up to the end of the 1920s, residents would request permission to transform the balcony into a standard room with brick walls. For instance, in a letter of 1924, a resident submitted a request to close their balcony facing Herzl Street, since ". . . it cannot be used as a balcony anymore as this whole part faces the constantly bustling street."[12]

The committee consistently refused to grant such requests and sometimes the head of the committee (the future mayor) was personally involved in the response. Those residents desperate to close their balconies did so without a permit, incurring penalties, demolition warrants, and prosecution.[13] If the authorities were unable to trace the lawbreakers on their own, there were neighbors who acted as informers and demanded to do justice to the "sinners."[14]

As a result of not being permitted to close the balconies with solid materials, there were requests from residents in the 1920s (and later in the 1930s) to enclose their balconies with windows, so as to provide them with a relatively open look. However, these requests were also rejected.[15]

The rationale behind the arguments of the residents, neighbors, committee, or municipality alike was generally connected with the look of the street. Beyond individual needs, many residents argued that closure would beautify the appearance of the street, whereas neighbors opposing such requests as well as the committee/municipality argued that closure would be to the street's detriment. Clearly, the aesthetic look of Tel-Aviv was very important to all parties, and balconies played an extremely important role in this.[16]

*The Hanging Balcony:* The Third Aliya (1919–1923) and the Fourth (1924–1928) added tens of thousands of residents to Tel-Aviv, which had, by that time, been granted autonomy from Jaffa and declared a township. This population increase changed people's perception of earlier plans for the neighborhood. Buildings with two or three stories began to appear and some of the private houses added a floor or two.[17] The balconies were designed as part of the luxurious building style of those years (the

Fig. 17.4.
Hanging balconies
in Lilienblum
Street, built in the
1920s (photo by
Carolin Aronis,
2006).

Eclectic Style) and were built on the upper floor, protruding from the front and sealed by a decorative rail that did not obstruct the view of the outside or the inside. A person sitting on the balcony was fully visible to the public eye (see Fig. 17.4).

The hanging balconies changed the physical relations between the house and the street. For the first time, the street did not face the balcony but extended underneath it. This was the first step in detaching the balcony from the ground, creating a more distant and elevated view of the street. The painter Reuven Rubin represented this view in his 1928 painting, *Yona Hanavi Street in Tel-Aviv*, in which the street is glimpsed by a person standing on the balcony. This position toward the street also gives a sense of power and control.[18]

*A Change in Regulations:* In 1926 important regulations for new buildings were promulgated in the "Town Building Scheme."[19] For the first time it was stated explicitly that 6.6 percent of all construction should include balconies. If in earlier years the regulations had only *promoted* the construction of balconies, it became a demand in 1926.

Another interesting regulation permitted the design of three-story buildings in certain locations of the city on a much larger area, obviating the need for ground-floor balconies. This regulation highlighted the inappropriateness of building balconies so close to the street and corresponded with a considerable increase in the requests by residents to close balconies in those years; it also indicated a way the municipality coped with this problem.

1930S–1950S

An economic crisis at the end of the 1920s and the Fifth Aliya (1929–1939) resulted in more construction and the adoption of more thrifty styles.[20] Modernistic styles and the construction of project (block) buildings (*Shikunim*) started to gain in popularity.

*The Functional Submerged Balcony:* The balcony that characterized the period, mainly the 1940s and 1950s, was designed in the Functional Building Style (Art Deco). This "clean" and simple architectural style featured straight lines and no decoration. This was also the beginning of a more modern style in Tel-Aviv, dubbed the International Style.[21] Although the intention was to pare costs, the building of balconies continued. They included a high sealed rail, sometimes with an upper shadowing apron. In contrast to the hanging balcony of the 1920s, which protruded from the walls of the building to the street, all these balconies became submerged within the structure, an integral part of the building (see Fig. 17.5).

Among other things, it is possible that this style catered to the 1925 recommendations (adopted in 1929) of the Scottish urban planner Patrick Geddes. He remarked that northern European architectural styles, which had characterized most of the buildings, were inappropriate for the Middle East climate. He regarded the large windows typical of northern Europe as superfluous and requiring closure by shutters, which reduced the amount of ventilation. Thus Geddes recommended that "Commonsense adaptation of this bright light and hot climate requires reduction of sunward window-space accordingly."[22] It is unclear if the local planners, especially the architects, took explicit note of the recommendation, but

Fig. 17.5. Large shady International Style balconies. 24, Yosef Israels Street
(photographer: Stanley Waterman, 2008).

the International Style in the following years did include small, narrow
ventilation strips facing out. Large and shady balconies contributed to
the increase of a cooling breeze.

Toward the middle of the twentieth century the connection between
the street and the balconies was further diminished. People sitting on
their balconies experienced better ventilation than before but were also
less visible and less exposed to the street environment. The balcony had
begun to be more domestic than communal or public.

*The Project (block) Balcony:* The project (block) building style (*Shi-kunim*) was developed in Tel-Aviv of the 1930s.[23] These were groups of
buildings built by public organizations or small private groups on the
ideological basis of cooperative building. In the 1940s and 1950s such
neighborhoods kept emerging, particularly on the periphery of Tel-Aviv.
After the 1950s, many projects were built in a uniform style.[24] They were
standard and monotonous-looking buildings with simple balconies,
mainly half-submerged, and surrounded by a simple iron rail. Since

Fig. 17.6a.
Project buildings
(*Shikunim*) in La
Guardia Street
(photographer: Willy
Follender, 1954).

Fig. 17.6b.
Family on the balcony.
Ben-Zion Boulevard
(photographer:
Ephraim Erde, 1950s).

it was common practice in those years to build one balcony vertically above the next, they were covered but exposed to sun and heat. Most often, the block residents had identical and facing balconies, which were very close to each other.

As the apartments were usually very small (two to three rooms), the balconies functioned as an important addition. Interviews with residents, along with period pictures and songs, reveal that the balconies were not only employed for dissipating the heavy heat but also as an extension of the living room and kitchen: for entertainment, for meals, and as a pleasant place for resting. Some residents explained that the balcony was a refuge and haven from the tiny and stressful apartment.[25] For these reasons, the use of the balcony was especially intensive in those years.

*Balcony Facing Balcony:* Due to the enhanced use of balconies and the proximity of buildings, residents were forced into intensive social relationships. The sight of neighbors' balconies was so common that a famous Tel-Aviv song from 1961, called "*Mirpasot*" (Balconies), included the refrain: "balcony facing balcony . . . this is a city of balconies." The song deals with the various things that take place on balconies or in apartments to the rear and which are visible to a person standing on their balcony: a baby being placed in a playpen, a woman arranging her hairdo, a man playing the cello, a babysitter studying for an exam.[26]

Nitza Carmi, who lived at 22 Pinsker Street as a girl in those years, remembers that the houses were so close to one another that most of the conversations with her friends took place on the balconies. Moreover, she explained: "There was no privacy at all. Everyone used to peek at and eavesdrop on the other. When our guests ate lunch on the balcony, the neighbor's son would follow every detail. Once, during the meal, he asked without any embarrassment, if we were planning to eat compote (dessert)."[27]

In fact, by the 1930s, there was a depiction in *Hapoel Hatzair* of Tel-Aviv as a "city-street." The street could be seen from the apartments and "people on the street can look straight into the rooms and at the people sitting and talking on them. There is no boundary between home and street, neither architecturally nor psychologically."[28]

The balcony of those years can be compared to a small child, innocent yet impolite, who, unintentionally and without malice, reveals

personal and embarrassing details about her parents. The balcony presented the residents with a significant threat of the "front stage face," as
Goffman defines it.[29] The private world, the "back stage," was exposed to
all and damaged a person's public image. This consequence of exposure
forced both planners and residents to be creative in finding ways to cope.

*Regulation Changes:* In light of Tel-Aviv's tremendous population
increase and subsequent crowding problem, the municipality's Technical Department promulgated new regulations regarding balconies in
1934. It became obligatory to maintain at least three meters between one
balcony and another and the height of a balcony from the sidewalk also
had to be at least three meters.[30] The planners tried to find solutions to
the proximity of spaces by determining partitioning distances around
the balconies, but in practice this distance did not make a significant
change.

*Covering with Fabrics:* Applications requesting that balconies be
closed, usually with windows, kept arriving at the municipality but met
with little approval. As a consequence, residents found sophisticated
ways to separate the balcony from the street, such as stretching fabrics on
top of it. In the 1930s and 1940s and even into the 1950s residents started
to cover their balconies with curtains and fabrics. A more expensive solution was the *markitza,* a small round roof made of a fabric that could
be folded. Covering with a fabric was considered to be less hermetic an
enclosure than bricks and windows and was easy to remove; from a legal
standpoint, no offence was committed. When residents desired privacy,
or to shut out the sun, they stretched the fabrics on top. However, this
did not enable the balcony to be used as a room, especially in winter.

## 1960S–1980S

As a result of the widespread and sophisticated practices of residents,
these years were marked by a partial surrender of the authorities and
the builders to the will of the residents. During this period the balcony
was wholly appropriated into the domestic space and its connection to
the street declined.

*Patent Inventions:* The residents did not make do with fabrics only.
As balconies were close to one another, the apartments small, and the
street busy, residents were tempted to close the balcony in such a way

that allowed it to be a real living space, separated from the outside. Consequently, residents invented different practices of closure, which could be regarded as temporary and lawful, but still useful and convenient.

In 1957 the *trisol* was invented. This was a system of asbestos shutters, which was regarded as an original Israeli invention. It was made of vertical strips whose angle could be changed. The *trisol* made it possible to break the sun's rays without blocking the wind, while also making it possible to close the shutters completely.[31]

In 1959 the *trizaz* was invented. Similar to the *trisol* system, it included the additional option of drawing the shutters to either side of the balcony, revealing most of the front to the street, creating a multifunctional system. In no time at all, it became possible to turn the balcony into a relatively sealed room, or return it to its open position. The *trizaz* offices and factory were located in Tel-Aviv and were awarded a solo exhibition in the city's Constructor's House. They received publicity from the Israeli professional magazine *Engineering and Architecture,* important evidence that this was not some clandestine practice on the part of the residents, but one that was also overtly adopted by the builders and architects.[32]

One of the popular songs of the 1960s was "The Patent Invention Song."[33] This song celebrates "the Jewish brain" as it generates many different kinds of inventions. Despite the scorn which those terrible inventions encountered in the song, the unique creativity of those times is clearly portrayed. One invention that receives a disdainful description is the *trizaz.* The song mocks the happiness accorded the purchaser of such sophisticated shutters, which "break the ultra-violet rays." It also sneers at the possibility of drawing the unstable shutters to such an extent that they run, fly, and fall completely off their tracks.

In 1961 plastic shutters on an aluminum frame were invented.[34] These were stable and very convenient to use. In many respects, these three shutter systems were each a kind of rigid and sophisticated curtain, and replaced the fabrics of the previous period. They were also relatively inexpensive and affordable.

*Obsessive Closure of Balconies:* In light of the various options, the 1960s and 1970s were characterized by an obsessive propensity for balcony closure with shutters. Whether these were project balconies or balconies of the International Style, most Tel-Aviv balconies were closed

Fig. 17.7.
Balconies closed by
plastic shutters. On
the top left, "Trizaz."
Yochanan Hasandlar
Street (photo by
Willy Follender,
1970s).

in these years. Moreover, more than an existential need for space and privacy, the closure derived from social pressure, one interviewee claiming, "There were no discussions at home about our balcony closure. My parents closed it only because all our neighbors did."[35] Several interviewees explained that although their balcony was closed, they did not use it as a room or an additional living quarter.

Nevertheless, the closure boosted the character of the balcony as a multi-functional space in the apartment. The ability to open and close the space added a variety of possible purposes; for example, a table on the balcony could at different times be used for entertaining guests, for family meals, and for doing homework, sewing, and other chores.[36] The entire space was used in different ways during the course of the day.

*Abolishing the Communication Function:* The ability to interact with people by means of the balcony was a central feature for many years. Until the closure of the balcony, it was used as a special *communication medium* between apartment and street. Closure physically and symbolically highlights this lost function. Various communication technologies that began to emerge in Israel at the end of the 1960s replaced the balcony as the link between the private and the public.

Until this period there were no *intercom systems* in buildings, so people used the balcony to call one another. Calling and whistling to and from the street were acceptable then. Children called their friends to come down to play and several hours later their mothers called them from the balcony to come home.[37]

Without a telephone, residents used the balconies as a means of communication with friends who lived in adjacent buildings. They came out to the balcony to see if there was light in a friend's house, a sign that she was home and could be visited.[38] A popular children's game of those times was a kind of primitive telephone in which the children would stretch a rope between two balconies and attach a can to each side in order to talk and listen to each other.[39]

The absence of an elevator meant that the balcony was used for transferring objects to and from the street. Residents used the balcony for throwing things to the street, such as keys that had been forgotten, or to lift heavy objects from below. Heavy bags with provisions or the morning newspaper were raised by means of a rope and, at times, that rope was used in the opposite direction for lowering garbage bags.[40]

However, the balcony was not only used as a medium of interpersonal interaction but also as a means for mass media. Television entered homes only at the end of the 1960s and 1970s. Until then, the balcony functioned as an alternative theater. People would sit on the balcony and watch people on the street or on the neighboring balconies. Television, apparently the preferred visual entertainment, drew the tenants inside and encouraged them to leave the balcony.

The arrival of these technologies stimulated the trend of closing the balcony and diminishing its use as a communication space. However, following closure, the balcony sometimes turned into a study or a room

Fig. 17.8.
(Right to left):
Confined
balconies and
"sun balconies,"
Nehardea Street
(photo by Stanley
Waterman, 2008).

for teenagers. Interestingly, and ironically, it is in these "half-rooms" that one can usually find a computer—"a window to the wider world." Hence, by means of the Internet, this space still allows for communication with the outside world.

*The Invasion of Air Conditioning:* Another technology that had considerable effect on the use of the balcony was the introduction of domestic air conditioners.[41] In the 1970s and 1980s air conditioning began to be installed in apartments, and the balcony was no longer needed to provide a pleasant breeze during the summer months. When air conditioning was on, it was even essential to close the shutters, resulting in an almost absolute detachment from the street.

*Confined Balconies:* The balconies of the 1970s and 1980s reflected this closure trend. As the balcony was expected to be closed anyway in those years, a trend began to build from the outset with shutters at the front, two side walls, and a ceiling. Thus, the balcony was "swallowed up" inside the apartment. Its presence in the public space disappeared as it became confined to the private space. As a consequence, the fronts of buildings became flat (see Fig. 17.8).[42]

Two large glass doors and sometimes a bulge in the ceiling or wall marked the boundary between the living room and the balcony. The balcony was still at the front of the apartment, yet was invisible from the outside unless the shutters were open. Many residents removed the glass doors and extended the living room at the expense of the balcony. Others created a study or a children's room from the balcony, as noted above.

Such balconies expressed the total incorporation of the balcony within the apartment. More than ever before, the balcony became a useful space in the context of the domestic sphere, but most of its former uses diminished greatly.

*A Legal Permit for Balcony Closure:* A special zoning regulation (Town-Building Scheme *Mem*) was promulgated in 1978 and, dealing with building rights and enlargement, explicitly permitted balcony closure. This regulation set down conditions concerning manners of closure, but did not prohibit closure itself. It is apparent that the municipality, having failed to stamp out balcony closure, chose to enable it in ways that would ensure the aesthetic appearance of the urban landscape.

Builders were obliged to close the balconies themselves, in a uniform manner, before residents took possession of their apartments. In addition, open balconies in existing buildings could be granted a closure permit on condition that the city engineer authorized the application. Moreover, residents had to undertake that the closure would simultaneously involve the entire front of the building. The municipality had partially surrendered to the demand for balcony closure, but had tried to be realistic in having control over the aesthetics of the outcome.

## THE 1990S AND THE TWENTY-FIRST CENTURY

Architects and builders in this period are less obligated to a specific location or style of building. However, these years have been characterized by a trend to revive the concept of the traditional balcony.

*The Comeback of the Balcony?* Surprisingly, and in contrast to the confinement of balconies to the interior of apartments in the previous period, there has been a considerable comeback of protruding balconies in recent years.[43] This is a kind of experiment, undertaken by builders to revive the good old days and return some romantic flair to the city. New buildings are being built with balconies that look as though they have been glued to the front. They are bound by a thin metal rail or greenish or transparent glass that gives them a fragile and airy look, fully exposing the people sitting on them to the street. These balconies are usually referred to by builders as "sun balconies." Even though the sun is not always there, this name is a demonstration of the will or need to bring back the "sun" and the exterior to the balcony (see Fig. 17.8).

In order to make it more difficult for residents to close these balconies, the new regulations define a space of at least six meters above each balcony, a feature that caused the construction of "skipping balconies."[44] These balconies allow neighbors to have a little more privacy and provide an opportunity to build a more legitimate *sukka* (a booth constructed to celebrate *Sukkot,* the festival of Tabernacles). However, the residents are still exposed to the street, and few Tel-Aviv residents observe *Sukkot* strictly, due to the predominantly secular nature of the city.

The balconies in these buildings are the complete antithesis of the concealed balconies of the previous period. These new balconies are placed in the public space and belong to that arena more than to the apartment. The new structure of the balcony and the new regulations do not facilitate the appropriation of the balcony into the private space. Based on tours of the streets and interviews with residents, it seems that they tend to make very little use of the balcony, if any. Some flowerpots testify to life in the apartment behind the balcony, but the residents are seldom present on it.

Despite attempts by planners and builders, the new balcony no longer serves as a means of connecting the private to the public, but only as a reminder of the balcony as it once existed. Moreover, since today's buildings are so much taller, the balconies are naturally high up too, reaching the horizon rather than the street. Consequently, residents, when they do use the balcony, find themselves casting a distant glance at the street below, no longer intimately connected to it.

*Preserving the Balconies:* The trend to reinstate balconies in the urban landscape appears at the same time as the demand to reopen balconies that had been closed in structures that are bound for preservation.
In 1996, guidelines were issued for the rehabilitation of structures and
sites to be preserved in Tel-Aviv with the aim of looking after local heritage assets.[45] The process of preservation includes renovating the building to resemble how it looked at the time it was built. The municipality,
which offers assistance in the preservation process, requires opening the
closed front balconies and preserving their original style.

This procedure, which has already been conducted on several old
buildings in the city, has exposed the balconies anew, particularly those
of the 1930s and 1940s. These balconies, with fresh paint and openness,
are reminders of the splendor of the early balconies. The preserved balconies are unique islands in the city, nostalgic flashes that preserve and
enliven the myth of the open and communal Tel-Aviv balcony.

*Open Deserted Balconies and Closed Shutters:* A small number of
balconies in Tel-Aviv remained open throughout the years despite the
general historical trend toward closure, in addition to the new construction of "sun balconies" and the opening of balconies in buildings destined for preservation. However, walking the city streets and interview-
ing residents reveal that tenants scarcely use the balconies; these spaces
are largely deserted. Likewise, in the closed balconies, the shutters are
generally drawn, the gaps only slightly open allowing penetration of air.
The exposure of residents from to the street is highly diminished.

It is obvious that Tel-Aviv's residents are adamant about setting a
clear boundary between the "front stage" and the "back stage." Not only
do they do this in order to separate their private worlds and that of the
public, but also to exercise control over their lives. It would appear that
they wish to be the ones to determine when this boundary is traversed
and how penetrable it is.

* * *

The Tel-Aviv balcony, as seen from this historical survey, plays a
significant role in the social and cultural life of the city. The balcony was,
and still is, an object of desire and a locus of creativity as well as concern
to different parties: residents, authorities, architects, and builders. The
authorities have tried to keep the balconies open and through them to

preserve the aesthetics of the city and the openness of the street. The residents have usually preferred to close the balconies when in need of privacy, protection from the tumult of street, and for additional living space. Captured between these opposing needs, architects and builders have tried to please both sides, while maintaining the quality and the look of the buildings. Hence, different styles of balconies have been created over the years.

By focusing on the balcony's position between private and public, this study describes the "movement" of the balcony from the street into the home and then back outside. From the early years of Tel-Aviv the balcony has transformed from a harmonic liminal zone between private and public to the purely private space of the 1970s and 1980s. Moreover, the introduction of new communication technologies and air conditioning since the late 1960s made some of the balcony's traditional functions, such as ventilation, leisure, and face-to-face communication with those in the vicinity, obsolete. Thus over the years it has been slowly disconnected from the street, on both the vertical and horizontal planes.

In the last two decades the open balcony has returned to the cityscape, although it has not reassumed the functions it had in earlier periods in the city's history. The popular Tel-Avivian image of residents resting on their balconies, eating watermelon, peering at their neighbors, or talking to someone on the street have become rare sights in recent years. Tel-Aviv has become, with the passing of the years, a city of closed, confined, and deserted balconies. It seems that since the 1920s, Tel-Avivians have grown to prefer a more individualistic domestic space. With urbanization, the balcony lost its communal significance, and increasingly the authorities were compelled to yield to residents' desires to close the balcony and to transform it into a private space.

The Tel-Aviv balcony embodies the paradox that prevails between the city's myth and its daily reality. The city's fictitious openness, as expressed in its 1960s dubbing as "a city of balconies," was not valid then, just as surely as it is not valid today. The balcony's "smile," in the metaphor used by Dizengoff, has changed to a mocking smile. However, nowadays the preserved open balconies of Tel-Aviv continue to affirm the old myth, whereas those that are closed are interpreted as a violation of the "true" character of the city.

To a large extent, the relations between residents and authorities express a control and defiance relationship. The authorities' definition of the balcony as an open space instigated tactics of defiance. De Certeau's conceptions are fitting in this context: the residents have employed a range of daily tactics to cope with the authorities' strategic definitions and regulations.[46] The different uses of the balcony, the frequent altering of its purpose, and particularly its closure show how change occurred within the framework dictated. Moreover, it was the residents who drove these changes, enabling them to feel in control, and to determine the function of their own personal space.

Nevertheless, the tactics of defiance were exploited, even if unintentionally, to create a sense of home.[47] One of the stories of the renowned author and painter Nahum Gutman concerns the establishment of Tel-Aviv, which describes a family's arrival at its house in the neighborhood. The first step taken by the woman in order to transform the desolate house into a home was to place a geranium flowerpot on the rail of the front balcony.[48] It is apparent that there was a genuine need to decorate the balconies, fill them with objects, use them, and even close them, tear them down, and reconstruct them, in order to create a "place." The incompleteness of the balcony space and the lure of going through recurrent alterations and definitions fit in very well with the desire to build Tel-Aviv, as well as with the need to define identity and private ownership in the public sphere.

Thanks to Amit Pinchevski for introducing me to Urban Culture and to Maoz Azaryahu and Stanley Waterman for help. Thanks also to Esther Schely-Newman, Chaim Noy, Zohar Kampf, Tally Gross, Varda Wasserman, Amir Aba Cohen, Sarah Feingold, Daphna Razin, Nelli Verzervesky, Erez Reinherz, and the staff of Rubin Museum.

## NOTES

The epigraph is from Meir Dizengoff, *Construction and Industry Laws Book* (Tel-Aviv, 1934), III [Hebrew].

1. Victor Turner, "The Center Out-There: The Pilgrim's Goal," *History of Religion* 12 (1973): 191–230; Victor Turner and Edith Turner, *Image and Pilgrimage in Christian Culture: Anthropological Perspectives* (New York, 1978); Rob Shields, *Places on the Margin: Alternative Geographies of Modernity* (London, 1991).

2. Carmela Yaakobi-Volk claims such a feeling in reference to the Tel-Aviv roofs. "Double Exposure: The Tel-Aviv Roof," in *The Israeli City: Last Hebrew City?* ed. Oded Heilbronner and Michael Levin (Tel-Aviv, 2006), 159–166 [Hebrew].

3. Erving Goffman, *The Presentation of Self in Everyday Life* (New York, 1959).

4. E. McClung Fleming, "Artifact Study: A Proposed Model," in *Material Culture Studies in America,* ed. Thomas J. Schlereth (Nashville, 1982), 164–173; Jules David Prown, "The Truth of Material Culture: History or Fiction?" in *History From Things: Essays on Material Culture,* ed. Steven Luber and W. David Kingery (Washington, 1995), 1–19; Arjun Appadurai, ed., *The Social Life of Things* (Cambridge, 1986/2000).

5. Gideon Biger, "The Development of the Urban Area of Tel-Aviv in 1909–1934," in *The Beginnings of Tel-Aviv, 1909–1934,* ed. Mordechai Naor (Jerusalem, 1984), 42–61 [Hebrew]; Natan Harpaz, "From 'Dream Houses' to 'Box Houses': The Architectural Revolution of the 1930s in Tel-Aviv," in Naor, *The Beginnings of Tel-Aviv, 1909–1934,* 91–106; Nitza Metzger-Szmuk, *Dwelling on the Dunes* (Tel-Aviv, 1996), 19 [Hebrew].

6. See the discussion on bridges in Georg Simmel, "Bridge and Door," in *Rethinking Architecture,* ed. Neil Leach (London and New York, 1997), 65–70.

7. Susan J. Drucker and Gary Gumpert, "Public Space and Communication: The Zoning of Public Interaction," *Communication Theory* 4.1 (1991): 115–129.

8. A complaint letter to the committee, 1909, in the Tel-Aviv Historical Archive (hereafter: TAHA), 1-42.

9. For example, a decision by the committee not to allow to Ms. Baharav deviation for the permitted percents of the lot, 1911–1913, TAHA, 1-280.

10. Ziona Rabau, *In Tel-Aviv on the Sand Dunes* (Ramat Gan, 1973), 21 [Hebrew].

11. Request letters to the board, 1912, TAHA, 1-44; 1913–1914, TAHA, 280d.

12. A request letter, 1924, TAHA, 3-113a.

13. Protocols of the committee's meetings, 1914–16, TAHA, 1-281; and references to trials and destructions in letters, 1924–1925, TAHA, 3-113a; 3-113b.

14. Letters from neighbors of tenants who closed their balconies, TAHA, 3-113a; 3-113b; 3-112c.

15. Letters in 1924–1925, TAHA, 3-113a; 1936–1938, 1153.

16. Municipal announcements from the 1920s and 1930s called on residents to decorate their balconies in order to beautify the streets. Rechavam Ze'evi, ed., *City by Announcements: Jaffa and Tel-Aviv—1900–1935,* vol. 3 (Tel-Aviv, 1988) [Hebrew].

17. Biger, "The Development of the Urban Area of Tel-Aviv in 1909–1934"; Metzger-Szmuk, *Dwelling on the Dunes,* 19; Yaacov Shavit and Gideon Biger, *The History of Tel-Aviv,* vol. 2 (Tel-Aviv, 2007), 186 [Hebrew].

18. See Foucault's *Panopticism* for a relevant discussion about power and control. Michel Foucault, *Discipline and Punishment* (New York, 1977).

19. "Town Building Scheme," *Tel-Aviv Municipality News,* 15 May 1926, 18, TAHA, 3-112a.

20. Gideon Biger, "The Development of the Urban Area of Tel-Aviv in 1909–1934"; Ilan Shchori, *Construction in Tel-Aviv: The History of Building the First Hebrew City* (Herzliya, 1994) [Hebrew].

21. The definition of "International Style" was mainly based on the German Bauhaus School, established in 1919, and on the theory of the Parisian architect Le Corbusier, in the 1920s. See Metzger-Szmuk, *Dwelling on the Dunes,* 20–29.

22. Patrick Geddes, *Town-Planning Report: Jaffa and Tel-Aviv* (Tel-Aviv, 1925), 39.

23. About the *Shikunim* in Tel-Aviv, see Shchori, *Construction in Tel-Aviv*, 42–43, 45, 52.

24. Ibid., 39, 42–44.

25. For example, one of the interviewees, Daphna Razin, who has lived in Tel-Aviv since 1955, said, "When I wanted to be alone with my boyfriend, the only privacy we could get at home was, paradoxically, in the balcony, in front of neighbors' eyes" (23 June 2008).

26. Ayin Hillel (lyrics), Sasha Argov (music), Yossi Hizkyona (performance), "Mirpasot," *Yossi Hizkyona* (musical album) (Israphone, 1961) [Hebrew]. See also Eliyahu Cohen, *A City of Balconies: The Songs of Tel-Aviv 1909–1984* (Jerusalem and Tel-Aviv, 1985), 166 [Hebrew].

27. Interview with Nitza Carmi, 4 March 2008.

28. Shavit and Biger, *The History of Tel-Aviv*, 252.

29. Goffman, *The Presentation of Self in Everyday Life.*

30. *Construction and Industry Laws Book* (Tel-Aviv, 1934), 107–108 [Hebrew].

31. Zvi Efrat, *The Israeli Project: Building and Architecture, 1948–1973*, vol. 2 (Tel-Aviv, 2005), 869 [Hebrew].

32. *Engineering and Architecture* 17.1 (1959) [Hebrew].

33. Chaim Hefer (lyrics), Sasha Argov (music), Uri Zohar (performance), "*Shir Hapatentim*," published in the early 1960s, and again in 2001, "*Shirim Mishekvar Hayamim*" (Helikon, 2001) [Hebrew].

34. Efrat, *The Israeli Project: Building and Architecture, 1948–1973*, 870.

35. Interview with Nitza Carmi, 4 March 2008.

36. Interview with Zehava Grossman (7 February 2008), who as a teenager lived at 64 Bograshov St.

37. The song "*Panas Boded*," 1967, deals with nostalgic Tel-Aviv days when a mother called to her son in the street from the balcony. Haim Guri (lyrics), Sasha Argov (music), Hava Albertstein (performance), "*Panas Boded*" (*Perach Halilach*, CBS Records, 1967). Also from interviews with tenants.

38. Interview with Grossman, 7 February 2008.

39. For example, interviews with Aviva Gintzburg (9 February 2008) and her friend, Hana Dayagi (10 March 2008); both lived at 11 Geula St. from the early 1950s until 1972.

40. Interview with Hana Dayagi, Ibid.; and Elli Gintzburg, who lived at 259 Dizengoff St. from 1950 to 1971 (9 February 2008).

41. The first domestic air conditioners were made in Israel in the 1960s, but interviewees explained that due to their high cost they were not installed until the 1970s and 1980s. Hence, air conditioners were not the cause for closing balconies, but only strengthened this move.

42. Orit Yishai, "Return of the Balcony," *Masa Acher* 137 (2003): 36–38 [Hebrew]; Smadar Shefi, "Return of the Balcony," *Architecture of Israel* 12 (1992): 31–37 [Hebrew].

43. Udit L. Belkine, with Ayelet Prigat and Yotam Barlach, "The 'Religious' Staggered Balconies," *Architecture of Israel* 44.2 (2001): 24–33 [Hebrew]; Orit Yishai, ibid.

44. *Regulations for Planning and Construction: Regulations for Calculation Areas:* Article 4.5, 1992.

45. "Town Building Scheme," NH-2916, 1996/2003.

46. See the definitions of "strategic" and "tactics," in Michel de Certeau, *The Practice of Everyday Life* (London and Los Angeles, 1984/1997).

47. Zali Gurevitch and Gideon Aran, *"Al hamakom,"* *Alpayim* 4 (1991): 9–44 [Hebrew].

48. Nahum Gutman, *Small City with Few People* (Tel-Aviv, 1959/1977), 11–12 [Hebrew].

# EIGHTEEN

# The Architecture of the Hyphen: The Urban Unification of Jaffa and Tel-Aviv as National Metaphor

*Alona Nitzan-Shiftan*

In June 1967, Major General Motta Gur ecstatically declared, "The Temple Mount is in our hands"; a surge of messianic emotions swept Israeli Jews. Following the sudden victory over Jordan, the equally sudden possession of Jerusalem's holy sites symbolized for Israeli Jews a larger historical moment: the reunification of "the people of Israel" with their cherished biblical past. Moreover, they saw in recapturing the Old City a tangible affirmation of the unity between their newly founded state and their ancient Jewish nation, a union necessary to validate Israel's vision of itself as a stable nation-state. The decades that followed witnessed a monumental and laborious task to manifest the desired "reunification" in concrete and stone—to entwine an Oriental city with a modernist town into one urban entity. The success of the Zionist project seemed to be contingent on the ability to create one unified capital city whose built landscapes embodied both the depth of the past and the utopias of the future.

The euphoria that swept Israel in June of 1967, and made Jerusalem "our pride and our joy," has blurred our memory of an earlier, equally monumental attempt at such unification. As we shall see, the "dry run" of urban unification as a metaphor for national cohesion had already happened in Jaffa and Tel-Aviv in the early 1960s. Whereas Jerusalem is popularly known as "a city with a wall in its heart," the heart of Tel-Aviv, though not often acknowledged, is the hyphen it shares with Jaffa.[1] I argue that the walls of Jerusalem and the hyphen of Tel-Aviv–Yafo presented similar obstacles to the integration of these cities with their chosen past. The spatial unity of these modernist cities with a built heritage was meant to historically legitimize Jewish rule over mixed populations. Planners of both cities consequently marshaled considerable resources in order to overcome these obstacles.

The project of urban unification was so important because it metaphorically embodied Israel's larger nation-building project that offered Israeli Jews a biblical past, a progressive "national home," and an aspiration for a secure collective future. In Tel-Aviv, much effort was therefore focused on repairing the hyphen that disturbed the unification of the first Hebrew city with Ottoman Jaffa—the ultimate modern town with its reputed ancient counterpart. Spatially, this urban hyphen was located in Manshiya, a large and quite wealthy northern suburb of Jaffa. During the battles of 1948, Manshiya's Muslim majority fled their homes, which were heavily damaged and consequently settled by war refugees and later by Jewish immigrants. This predicament greatly interrupted national attempts to unify Jaffa and Tel-Aviv. Instead of expressing urban unity, Manshiya turned into an agitated urban hyphen trapped between the country's competing populations (see Fig. 18.1).

Through the lens of architectural and urban design, this essay examines a key moment in the history of Jaffa and Tel-Aviv, in which the hyphen between the two cities serves as a metaphor for the larger connection between nations and states. After Israel's independence, Prime Minister Ben-Gurion wanted Jaffa to complement Tel-Aviv's modernity with a visible past, with a sense of authenticity and connectivity to the land itself. In 1963 this aspiration took the form of an architectural competition for Manshiya. The proposed plans to turn this variegated and intimidating urban hyphen—an area of devastated houses and rich ethnic diversity—into an ordered and profitable business center reveal a monumental experiment in national visions of urban unification. As we explore this post-independence era, we also shed light on the decades before, when modernist Tel-Aviv was planned as the Jewish alternative to Arab Jaffa. Tel-Aviv's modernist past was used to represent a pacified national heritage, while the market identified Jaffa as both exotic and a source of thoroughly gentrified real estate.[2]

Fig. 18.1. Arial photograph of Manshiya, 1966.
Photographer: Willy Folander. *Source: TAHA.*

## A New Israel Hyphenating with the Old

In April of 1948 the Irgun (para-military organization) conquered Manshiya and evicted its remaining Palestinian residents. In May, the State
of Israel was founded.[3] The proximity of Tel-Aviv—the seat of Israel's
new government—to occupied Jaffa put into sharp relief the interde-
pendency between the narratives of a nation and the form of its cities.
After independence, Ben-Gurion realized that neither Socialism nor the
new motto of "Progress and Development" could satisfy the quest for
national cohesion. Both were foreign concepts to the majority of new
immigrants and alienated significant sections of the Yishuv. According
to Anita Shapira, a biblical-territorial approach was developed to fulfill
the political and cultural requirements of modern nationalism: concep-
tualizing a national community of Jews who ruled a sovereign state, and
shared a common (ancient) past, a concrete (historical) land, and collective destiny.[4] Mitchell Cohen suggests that this attainment completed the
reification of the Zionist Socialist movement, turning it into a national
movement unified around common symbols of nationhood.[5]

The key question was how to merge modern life with the imagined
biblical blueprint, how to establish Israel's ancient heritage as a matter
of fact, a given reality that had simply been lying dormant, waiting for
statehood, and moreover, how to translate this desire for a reassuring
past into a sense of belonging and local identity. Different cultural entities were entrusted with this task. Writers and artists, historians and
archeologists, educators and military commanders were encouraged and
inspired to use tradition as a modern resource in order to culturally
substantiate their newly founded state.[6] In our urban context, the task
was manifested in built form: how to resolve the contradiction between
Tel-Aviv as an emblem of the state's commitment to "progress and development" and Jaffa as a symbol of the nation's return to its biblical past.

In 1949, the government decided to annex Jaffa to Tel-Aviv. This was
a dramatic shift away from the former municipal policy which labored
to develop Tel-Aviv—the new northern Jewish suburb of Jaffa—into a
superior alternative to the established urbanity and reputed history of
Jaffa, the major economic center of the Arab population during the British Mandate. The official municipal border that the British drew in 1921

Fig. 18.2. Arie Sapojnikov, *Cover Illustration for Keren Hayesod* (Jerusalem, 1932).
Archive Collection of the Diaspora Research Center, Tel-Aviv University.
*Source: Batia Donner (curator),* To Live with the Dream *(Tel-Aviv, 1989), 26.*

between Jaffa and Tel-Aviv assumed urban and architectural form in the early 1930s. The emerging image of the "Jewish town" was thoroughly modern—simple, abstract, and efficient (see Fig. 18.2). Its "new architecture" of reinforced concrete consisted of simple rectangular volumes covered with smooth plaster and often painted white. This architecture was bare, compositionally asymmetrical, and decoratively minimalist, characterized by the abundant Mediterranean play of light and shadows. By the time of independence Tel-Aviv could already boast the largest concentration of modernist buildings worldwide; as we shall see, a half century later Tel-Aviv would return to this glorious legacy, in order to find a meaningful past, and an alternative to contemporary strife.[7]

Responsible for the shift were émigré architects and planners, who created an early bond between modern architecture and Zionism.[8] Modernism was so attractive for the Yishuv's leadership because it accorded with the triple negation advanced by Labor Zionism—of the Jewish Diaspora, the bourgeois culture, and the Orient.[9] It encouraged Europeans Jews, who emigrated to Mandate Palestine and were trained as architects either before or after emigration, to construct the site of the Jewish "national home"—Mandate Palestine and later Israel—as a tabula rasa, a place "free from past memories."[10] This "new architecture"—a general term that architects in the Yishuv used to refer to all trends of modern architecture (including international, organic, *neue sachlichkeit*, or "matter of fact")—perfectly matched the ideal of the New Jew: an independent, self-reliant Jew liberated from years of subordinated existence in the Diaspora. The New Jew and the new architecture shared a focus on the physiognomy of the body/the building/the town; on health and hygiene, arteries and circulation; on the necessity of bodies in the field, houses in the park, and of clean and healthy lungs as a cure for the body/ the city (see Figs. 18.3 and 18.4).

Scientific modernization was therefore the mode émigré architects chose in order to ensure the modern living that would distinguish them from native Palestinians. Julius Posener, for example, warned in 1937 that the Zionist working settlement could not rely on the Arab vernacular as a precedent because the planning of the settlement was conducted as an experiment based on scientific hypotheses, a utopian innovation of pure rationality.[11] Mayor Rokach and his City Engineer Yaakov Fishman extended this vision to the urban context of Tel-Aviv. "The science of Town

Fig. 18.3. "The Levant Fair Census of our Growth," poster of the
Seventh exhibition, 30 April to 30 May 1936. *Source: The Central
Zionist Archives, Jerusalem.*

Building," Rokach wrote in 1944, was "a *rebellion* against what existed in
the Middle Ages, when cities were limited in their size and surrounded
by Walls"; it was "a war against density and lack of hygiene."[12] As such,
Town Building was an efficient tool in his struggle for a unilateral di-
vorce from the urban image of Arab Jaffa and what it stood for under
British colonialism.

Fig. 18.4. Franz Krausz, *The Country of Our Future,* 1934, Gouache on paper,
100×70 cm, Collection of Michael Krausz, Tel-Aviv.  *Source: Doreet LeVitte
Harten and Yigal Zalmonah, eds.,* The New Hebrews: 100 Years of Art in Israel
*(Berlin, 2005), 313 [German].*

In this context it is not surprising that the decision to unify both cities was debatable. The tension it inspired surfaced as a spirited controversy over the name the unified city should take in order to convey an appropriate history. Should it be "Tel-Aviv" or "Jaffa" alone? Alternatively, if hyphenated, which would come first? According to Tom Segev,

> It was a highly patriotic debate. The public saw Jaffa as an Arab city, and after the state's establishment it was viewed as a backward city of immigrants. Tel-Avivians did not want its name. The justice minister, Pinchas Rosen, annoyed Ben-Gurion: "The whole world talks about Tel-Aviv and not about Yafo," he said, to which Ben-Gurion replied: "What does 'the whole world' matter to me? Yafo existed 4,000 years ago. From a historical standpoint it is important to emphasize that this is a Hebrew city and that it is now in our hands."[13]

How could Israeli Jews consider Arab Jaffa "a Hebrew city"? The sense this statement made for Israeli Jews is evidence of the laborious efforts of the new Israeli state, and their use of history and archeology to sustain the national narrative of biblical return.[14] A contemporary Mapai (the ruling Labor Party) publication, for example, reminded its readers of the "great and important pedigree" of Jaffa:

> Jaffa is one of the most ancient cities in our country and the world. Her name is mentioned in Egyptian inscriptions dating from 1970 BCE. And we learned, furthermore, that the trees of Lebanon destined for the Temple were unloaded in Jaffa's port. And in the days of the Maccabees, Jaffa was the port of Jerusalem, the capital city.[15]

Once Jaffa's significance to Jewish history was established, the biblical aura could also be used to encompass Tel-Aviv. Although "cedars of Lebanon were not unloaded" in Tel-Aviv, the pamphlet continues, "steel and iron beams and sacks of cement for construction of the walls of the Third Temple were unloaded there day and night for a whole generation—our generation."[16] The question was: what should this Third Temple look like? According to the minister of interior, the "nice merger" of Jaffa and Tel-Aviv, "one 4,000 years old and the other 40," symbolized no less than "the tie between a people and its land, . . . the project of revival, . . . our fight for independence and our triumph, . . . the consummation of our vision of gathering the exiles and returning the children to their own border."[17] Could *sachlich* modernism, or even

יזכור למנשיה

Fig. 18.5. Memorial to Manshiya, *Tvai* 4 (Tel-Aviv, 1967).

the larger scope of "the new architecture," express such a momentous symbolic merger?[18]

The restoration of Old Jaffa in the early 1960s and the exposed concrete towers that simultaneously mushroomed in Tel-Aviv evinced the difficulty of meshing the two cities' architectures. Considering this predicament, how should one treat the physical location of the hyphen between old Jaffa and new Tel-Aviv? This junction was Manshiya—a northern neighborhood of Jaffa that stretched along the shore like a finger pointing into the municipal area the British had prescribed for Tel-Aviv. In 1950, this previously Palestinian neighborhood came under the auspices of the Development Authority, a national branch of the new government that oversaw all issues of "absentees'" land usage and development; a hold on building activity at the site was established in early 1950 (see Figs. 18.1 and 18.5).

When Mordechai Namir took office as Tel-Aviv's mayor nine years later, he declared Manshiya's development a top priority.[19] A year later, the government and the Tel-Aviv Municipality (TAM) jointly founded *Ahuzot Hahof* Company Ltd., with the purpose of developing Manshiya;

the new company prepared a competition brief and a master plan for the site. Like Tel-Aviv City Engineer Aaron Horowitz's 1954 plan, and in the spirit of Yosef Almogi's initiative, following the 1959 *Wadi Salib* riots in Haifa, to demolish and redevelop areas considered slums, *Ahuzot Hahof* planned to destroy and clear the few Palestinian houses and shops that were left in the neighborhood. On 1 November 1962 it announced the competition, in collaboration with the Association of Architects and Engineers and with the international supervision of the IUA (International Union of Architects).[20]

According to the competition brief, *Ahuzot Hahof* aimed "to initiate a development plan that would turn the existing area into a typical urban center—'a City' that would serve the unified city of Tel-Aviv–Yafo and would facilitate their merger." Namir stated that, "once Manshiya is rebuilt, the two cities—young Tel-Aviv and ancient Jaffa—would be meshed and become one complete unit, a situation we aspire for, and one of the prime goals of our policy of municipal development."[21] In June 1963, architects submitted their proposals to develop the area Namir targeted—the piece of land stretching over 482 acres between Allenby Street, Eilat Street, and the Mediterranean, including Neve Tzedek and Kerem Hatemanim.[22] A total of 152 proposals were submitted. (This large number was eclipsed in 1986 when 175 entries were submitted for the competition to build the Supreme Court building.)

Three months later, the panel of eight judges announced two winners: first prize went to the German team of Fred Angerer and Alexander W. Branca, and second prize went to Jan Lubicz-Nycz. They also granted six other Honorary Mentions to entries of particularly admirable aspects. However, *Ahuzot Hahof* felt that none of these projects alone could address the enormous importance of Manshiya, and its role in defining this new hyphenated city. Therefore, in late 1963 the company commissioned Amnon Niv and Rafi Reifer,[23] a private firm of young *sabra* architects, to analyze all the entries and to suggest a proposal based on the combined merits found in each of the eight conceptual entries that won awards.

The result was a spatial analysis that supported the official agenda of creating a unifying center in the middle of *one* city,[24] which is split in the sketch to "City North" and "City South," leaving the names Yafo and the abbreviated Tel-Aviv (T-A) in parentheses. Instead of the habitual depiction of an orderly north vs. chaotic south, the graphic pattern is similar in both, as is the graphic area dedicated to each city. The sketch's tilted lines create a dynamic motion that urges south and north toward the existing break in the urban fabric, where the potential for a unified metropolitan center lies (see Fig. 18.6).

In their analysis of the existing situation, Niv and Reifer painted in opaque blue the existing CBD (Central Business District) and warned of its slippage eastward into residential quarters. Below this center they drew a thick black line that points to the severance of north and south along parameters related to quality of life, transportation, and urban functions. Between the existing CBD and the Mediterranean they encircled the large "publicly owned empty area" of Manshiya. This desired "emptiness," however, only existed because of urban renewal, that is, because of the projected evacuation of residents that settled in the devastated neighborhood after its Palestinian residents fled in 1948 and the appropriation of their property by the state as "absentees' assets."

Niv and Reifer's integrated proposition for the "empty area" reflected the contemporary confusion in modernist urban thinking. After World War II the reconstruction of devastated Europe and the rapid urban and financial growth in the United States created an acute demand for modern infrastructure that could sustain mass housing, commerce, industry, and rapid transit. As a result, monumental urban renewal projects mushroomed throughout the newly ordered world. By the late 1950s the impact of these mass-produced environments was overwhelming—huge, tall, and anonymous housing blocks were seen on the fringes of every city, and quarters that were declared slums were razed in favor of entrepreneurial mega-projects. The keen drive for progress gradually revealed its costs: the bulldozers that prepared "empty areas" for new, ordered, hygienic, and profitable environments also bulldozed the charm, the complexity, and the sense of community rooted in innumerable particular, non-generic neighborhoods around the world.[25]

For architects worldwide the new Israeli society, with its expedited rate of population growth and infrastructural development, offered a laboratory for urban experiments. Both the number of submissions and the reputation of judges such as Louis Kahn and Bruno Zevi indicate the international appeal of the competition. Jacob Berend (Jaap) Bakema, for

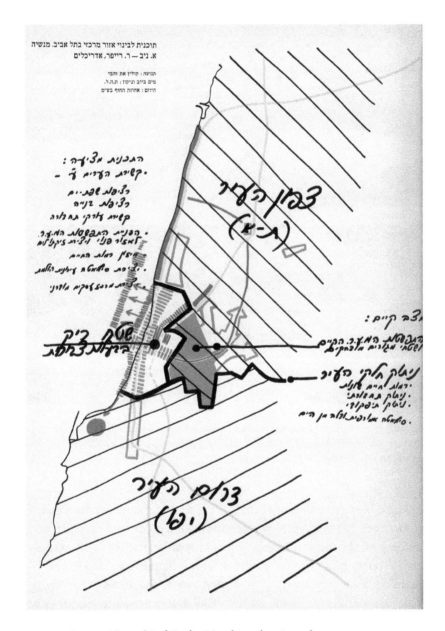

Fig. 18.6. Amnon Niv and Rafi Reifer, Manshiya planning scheme,
*Tvai* 4 (Tel Aviv, 1967).

Fig. 18.7. Jacob Berend (Jaap) Bakema and Johannes van den Broek, Manshiya Competition entry (no. 4), in *Team X Primer*, ed. Alison Smithson (Cambridge, MA, 1968).

example, was a member of Team X, a group that channeled the focus of modernism to issues such as place and identity, city and mobility, and concern for the social role and ethics of the architect. The "distinctively urban" entry he submitted together with Johannes van den Broek focused on a comprehensive civic center next to the area's urban shore, which would create a home for City Hall, the courts, and the area's financial activity (see Fig. 18.7).[26]

According to the judges, the attachment of this "fine urban space to a partially enclosed harbor" created "daring and dramatic movement."[27] On the municipal scale the architects advanced the central idea of Patrick Geddes's 1925 city plan—a belt of boulevards that connected the

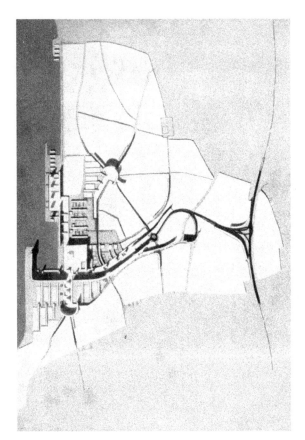

Fig. 18.8. Jacob Berend
(Jaap) Bakema and
Johannes van den
Broek, Manshiya
Competition entry
(no. 4), *Casabella* 293
(1964), 27.

city's social, civic, and cultural institutions—by stretching the abrupt
end of Rothschild Avenue toward the new CBD, overriding existing
neighborhoods. On the metropolitan scale they connected the project
to the Ayalon thruway, a major future highway. These two curved urban
conduits were reinforced by a long and tall mega-structural urban wall
that connected the existing CBD to the shore (see Figs. 18.8 and 18.9).

Following this scheme, Niv and Reifer also brought the two urban
movements together and joined them with a monumental linear space—
at once a road, an avenue, and a highway—ending in a civic square by
the sea. Yet although the judges considered Bakema and van den Broek's
"view of the city as a defined unit, wrapped by a wall with gates" to be
"attractive," Niv and Reifer were disturbed by the insufficient connec-

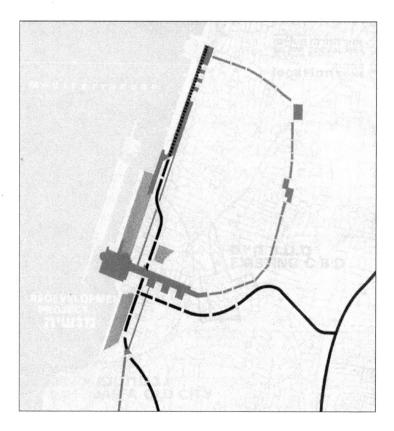

Fig. 18.9. Amnon Niv and Rafi Reifer, Manshiya Planning Scheme
—Location, *Tvai* 4 (Tel-Aviv, 1967).

Fig. 18.10. Nachum Zolotov, Adam Mazor, and Y. Amit,
Manshiya Competition entry (no. 41), *Casabella* 293 (1964), 36.

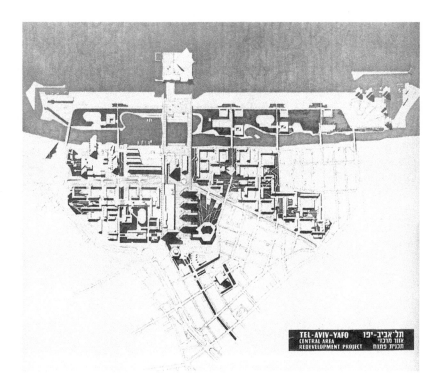

Fig. 18.11. Fred Angerer and Alexander W. Branca, Tel-Aviv–Yafo
Central Area Redevelopment Project, Manshiya Competition
entry (no. 6), *Casabella* 293 (1964), 32.

tion of the scheme with Jaffa. For this vital goal, they drew on Nachum
Zolotov, Adam Mazor, and Yehoshua Amit's proposal, which, according
to the judges, succeeded in keeping "the historic center of Jaffa (and its
connection to Tel-Aviv)," and highlighting its presence "in a pleasant
manner" (see Fig. 18.10). This achievement was a result of placing a deep
carved bay in south Manshiya, encircled by the hill of Old Jaffa to the
south and the linear shore development of Tel-Aviv to the north.

　　Niv and Reifer succeeded in devising such a bay between Old Jaffa
and the new CBD by extruding their civic square into the sea. This also
allowed them to implement the main virtue of the winning scheme,
which, according to its German creators Angerer and Branca, aimed
"to triple the seashore of Tel-Aviv" (see Fig. 18.11). The judges awarded
the German scheme first prize because it answered in a feasible way

Fig. 8.12a and 8.12b. (*above and facing*) Comments on winning entry,
*Maariv. Source: TAMA, 4/6043/2684*

what they considered to be Tel-Aviv's most urgent task—"improving and
deepening the seashore and creating a lagoon separated from the shore
yet connected to the new city center."[28] In this light Niv and Reifer's
integrated plan created four small bays, mirrored by the four bays of a
lengthy island to its west, stretching from the civic square northbound.

The accent on rebuilding the shore also reveals the difference between local and international priorities. The judging team, as well as the
two international entries they awarded prizes, considered "the sight and
sound and consciousness of the sea . . . vital to the city." It was highest on
their priority list because "the coastline itself is a historic phenomenon;
and to the human societies along its shores it gave in ancient times—and
does now—a feeling of eternity." The non-Israeli proposals, not surprisingly, sought to "increase by every possible mean" the virtues of "contact
with the sea, and enjoyment of it—both visually and physically."[29] By

contrast, for the local architects who promoted national and municipal values, Manshiya was primarily an urban hyphen responsible for the unity of north and south. In their view, the grand entry of the CBD to the sea was not as important as creating a continuous beach stretching from Jaffa to Tel-Aviv. For them, this continuous interface of the city with the Mediterranean was only one of many factors—including building mass, transportation, business, urban silhouette, and balanced quality of life—that had to ensure the urban unity and continuity of the merged cities.

While native architects were reserved about the winning German scheme because of its limited unifying force, the public was alarmed by an entirely different issue—in a country accommodating numerous Holocaust survivors, the notion of German winners was unpalatable. Tel-Aviv residents protested the results, pointing to the swastika they identified in the winning scheme as justification for their disdain[30] (see Fig. 18.12a). The mayor, for his part, was also reserved, for yet another reason. Before the envelopes identifying the winners were opened, Namir asked to switch the first and second prizes. He preferred Ian

Fig. 18.13. Jan Lubicz-Nycz, Manshiya Competition
entry (no. 98), *Casabella* 293 (1964), 33.

Lubicz-Nycz's scheme. The latter proposed, according to contemporary
newspapers, a set of "skyscrapers in the middle of the 'city'" that were
laid out like the "petals of a flower whose 'roots' are in the sea, taking the
shape of an island connected to the shore by means of one wide road"[31]
(see Fig. 18.13). The judges thought this proposal resolved "a problem of
civic design that faces every city in its central areas, where several uses
have to be combined in one structure and the structures themselves
grouped so as to give powerful expression to the city centre—in fact to
the spirit of the city itself."[32] What can we learn from this important yet
convoluted statement about the mega-structure trend, which, according
to its prime critic, Reyner Banham, would grow to be the central preoccupation of the 1960s?[33]

   Mega-structures promised to effortlessly contain mixed uses, to
be flexible, modular, and ever-increasing, to eclipse the limitation of
building in the air and on the water, and to be big enough to become
monumental centers of unmistakable character. Mayor Namir preferred
to override the architecture of both cities—Jaffa and Tel-Aviv—with a
monument that pushed modernism to its radical ends. Lubicz-Nycz's
proposal was built around a center strong enough to overcome the many
discrepancies between the incompatible cities Namir aimed to unite.
This scheme offered Namir a spectacular array of duplicable units, tow-

ers, and landfills. In 1963, the judges admitted, "the method suggested is untried," but they considered the project's daring vision experimental and "also inspiring."

In late 1963, when Niv and Reifer were commissioned to prepare the integrated master plan for implementation, aspirations were still high. In preparation for this plan, during 1961–1967 *Ahuzot Hahof* cleared 2,260 apartments and 166 businesses in Manshiya, compensated its residents, and bulldozed the surviving structures. In 1967, when this preparatory work was almost completed, Israel was facing a new reality.

## After 1967

As Manshiya was readied for its new unifying identity, Israel's army plunged into East Jerusalem. From the 1967 war a strong Israel emerged, swept with euphoria and self-righteousness and eager to possess a "unified capital." The rehearsal of unification, performed for the last eighteen years for the municipal audience of Tel-Aviv and Jaffa, was now ready for the real international gala: the unification of West Jerusalem—a modernist border town, with East Jerusalem, especially with its ancient Oriental core that was recently seized from Jordan.

In 1950, during the debate over the name Jaffa and Tel-Aviv should jointly take, many were afraid that naming the unified city Jaffa meant that "Jaffa would impose a conceptual occupation on Tel-Aviv after Tel-Aviv had imposed a military one on Jaffa."[34] Years later, these anxieties made a forceful comeback: in the great debate over the desired character of "united Jerusalem," the authors of the city's 1968 "master plan" advocated a modern, ordinary capital city, respecting yet separated from its sacred nucleus. Such bureaucratic logic was quickly overpowered by the demand of local and international protagonists to protect the unique holiness of Jerusalem and to emanate its aura onto the entire city.[35]

Jerusalem's unification was both quick and complicated, and its story is beyond the scope of this paper.[36] It is revealing, however, to point to some of the lessons Jerusalem's planners learned from Tel-Aviv–Yafo regarding urban hyphens. The hyphen between East and West Jerusalem was located in Mamilla, a quarter that grew out of the Old City like Manshiya grew out of Jaffa, and flourished during the same period. Stretching from the Jaffa Gate westward, this bustling multi-cultural

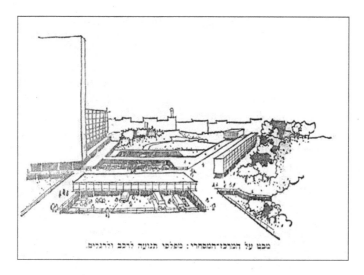

מבט על המרכז־המסחרי : מפלסי תנועה לרכב ולרגלים.

Fig. 18.14. Michael Kuhn, winning entry, East Jerusalem competition,
perspective, 1964; "'East Jerusalem,' a Symposium with Michael Kuhn,
Dan Etan, and Ram Karmi," *Ha'aretz*, 8 September 1967.

and multi-ethnic commercial center connected the traditional commerce of the Old City with the new markets of West Jerusalem. In 1948
Mamilla, like Manshiya, lost its vitality. For nineteen years the armi-
stice zone cut it from East Jerusalem, turning its eastern end into a
no-man's-land.[37]

Mamilla was destined to undergo major urban renewal even before the dramatic events of 1967. In 1965, architect Michal Kuhn won a
competition to shape its urban form as part of the eastern strip of West
Jerusalem (see Fig. 18.14). In 1967, when Mamilla regained its place as the
urban hyphen between the two unilaterally unified Jerusalems, architects and politicians decided that Kuhn's plan fell short of performing
the momentous task of unification. Kuhn's overt high modernism was
considered an obstacle, a rift rather than bridge between the modern and
ancient cities. A new competition was never announced. Mayor Teddy
Kollek was reluctant to delegate control to the architectural profession
during this fortuitous moment in Jerusalem's development, and follow-

Fig. 18.15. Moshe Safdie, Mamilla complex, perspectival rendering; reprinted from Moshe Safdie and Gilbert Weil, "Development and Construction of the Mamilla Project, Mamilla Planning & Design Team" (Jerusalem: Karta, Central Jerusalem Development, 1988), 87.

ing the experience in Manshiya, he preferred to avoid the potential predicament of German winners.

Joining forces, the state and the municipality founded Karta, which like *Ahuzot Hahof* in Tel-Aviv–Yafo, was entrusted with the urban renewal of Mamilla. Karta commissioned Moshe Safdie to design the entire quarter, while starting to evacuate the neighborhood of its residents—mostly Jewish immigrants from Arab countries. Safdie's proposal was as controversial as were the Manshiya plans, and similarly centered upon a futuristic mega-structure. The project he submitted in 1974 attracted severe criticism. Its size, infrastructure, and erasing power intimidated Jerusalemites and threatened to destine the project to oblivion and the site to eternal bareness. The lessons were learned. Inspired by developments in the new discipline of urban design, Safdie revised his project to address on the one hand the developmental appetite of politicians and entrepreneurs, and on the other hand the imaginary Jerusalem desired by the custodians of the city's unique image at home and overseas (see Fig. 18.15). Essentially a mega-structure, Mamilla now appears as a conglomeration of smaller environments: the David Village, the Hilton Hotel, the Akirov Quarter and mall, and the garden over the parking. Unlike the voided urban hyphen between Tel-Aviv and Jaffa, Mamilla in its current guise tightens (though not completely) the hyphen between East and West Jerusalem under the auspice of rampant capitalism.[38]

The eclipse of Mamilla over Manshiya as Israel's representational project meshing development and urban unification was symbolic of the immediate post-1967 years, when the prospect of a unified Jerusalem eclipsed the former centrality of Tel-Aviv. In the next decades, however, the consensus over Jerusalem's primacy was severely shaken, particularly with the onset of the first intifada (1987–1993)[39] and the vehement 1995 demonstration in Jerusalem that preceded Rabin's assassination. For many, Jerusalem of the Likud became "the core of the truth of Israel, the open abscess that exposes the illness that runs in the entire body."[40] Disillusioned, they embraced Tel-Aviv instead as a symbol of sanity, secularism, and healthy entrepreneurship.

During these conflicts of the 1980s and '90s, yet another paradox emerged in Israel's grappling for authentic identity. In the search to re-define a secure Israeli past, one distinct from the Jewish past that was now represented by Jerusalem, the longing for the architectural roots of "Israeliness" focused on modernism, which by definition is ahistorical. Tel-Aviv once again emerged as a promising site. Growing on fleeting dunes rather than on existential rocks, and planned according to a tabula rasa modernist ideology, Tel-Aviv was depicted as purely "modern" and thus disentangled ethnically from Palestine, and historically from the conflicted Orient.

The rediscovered modernist vernacular—which branded the terms the White City, the Bauhaus, or the International Style—was politicized as an emblem of "the modest" Zionist spirit that produced it,[41] and thus confirmed the hegemonic ideology that had formed the State of Israel. Despite this ideology's bias against the large city and its capitalist practices, it was this capitalism and its real estate engine that helped make Tel-Aviv, rather than Jerusalem, or the kibbutz, the focus of Israel's alternative architectural roots and the prime site of a more comforting architectural heritage. Eventually Tel-Aviv's ordinary modernist build-

Fig. 18.16. *The people of Tel Aviv are walking around with their heads held high. Now the whole world knows why!* Yehoshua/TBWA, "White City" Advertisement for TAM (May 2004).

ings seemed to eclipse the gravity of Jaffa's history and authenticity. This was recently confirmed when certain enclaves of "Bauhaus Tel-Aviv" were granted the desired status of a World Heritage Site (see Fig. 18.16). According to UNESCO it was the White City that held "outstanding universal value" because its émigré European architects "created an outstanding architectural ensemble of the Modern Movement in a new cultural context."[42]

The ensuing whitening of Tel-Aviv's peeling modernist buildings contributed to Tel-Aviv's reinvention of itself during the last two decades as a sane alternative to the conflict-ridden zone of Jerusalem; Tel-Aviv is hailed as a global metropolitan center, a city always on the move, a cultural and financial hub.[43] By the beginning of the third millennium local newspapers published a comprehensive campaign by committed residents who wanted to declare Tel-Aviv an independent state. The working hypothesis declared, "London is not England, New York is not America, Tel-Aviv is not Israel."[44] While the proposition to establish the State of Tel-Aviv was based on innovations such as local currency, the *Danro,* and a different time zone—European, of course—the imagined

Fig. 18.17. LONG LIVE THE STATE OF TEL-AVIV: At the end of
Israel's independence celebration a group of Tel Aviv residents wish
to separate the state and celebrate independence to the Dan Block.
No more financial discrimination, abusing laws and life according
to governmental-national priorities. The rebellion of the cheese
eaters and wine drinkers is launched. Dudu Geva and Eli Atiyas,
"Dudu Geva Is 'Duck'-ing Tel-Aviv's City Hall," from *Tekhi Medinat
Tel-Aviv* (Long Live the State of Tel-Aviv), *Ha'ir* (5 May 2003).

state could already boast its existing architecture as bearing the unique
mark of the "Bauhaus" or "International Style."

Entangled in the forces of globalization, the potential Tel-Aviv State
is positioned against the other pole of the political map—the notion of
a threat to Israel. Architecture conspicuously features on the agenda of
these opposing ideas. Supporters of the new state opted for a modernist
civic building—the TAM was adorned by Dudu Geva's duck character—
to illustrate their campaign. Opponents of the state's global image chose
an iconic commercial complex—the Azrieli Towers—to illustrate their
disdain (see Figs. 18.17 and 18.18). Neither considered the authenticity of
Jaffa pertinent to the symbolic capital of Tel-Aviv State.[45]

What happened to the famous hyphen? Niv and Reifer continued to
work on the "Town Planning Scheme" for nearly a decade. It was legally
approved in 1972 despite the fierce objections of Manshiya's residents and

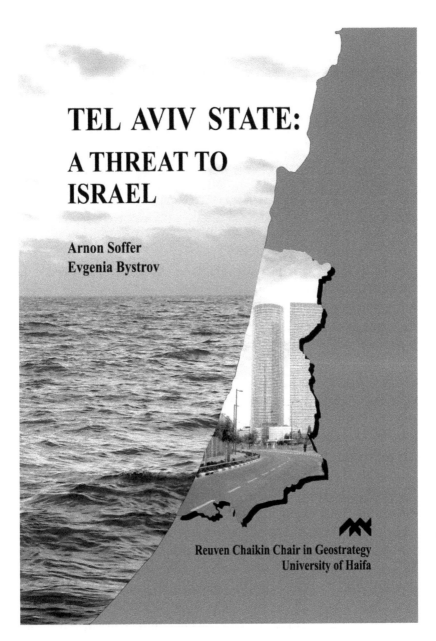

# TEL AVIV STATE:
## A THREAT TO ISRAEL

**Arnon Soffer**
**Evgenia Bystrov**

**Reuven Chaikin Chair in Geostrategy**
**University of Haifa**

Fig. 18.18. Arnon Soffer and Evgenia Bystrov,
*Tel-Aviv State: A Threat to Israel* (Haifa, 2006).

Fig. 18.19. Arial view
of Manshiya with
Hassan Bek mosque.
*Photo courtesy* http://
philip.greenspun.com

few of its planners.[46] In the years after, the area was lightly touched with
the spirit of a mega-project, and a few noticeable yet isolated high-rise office buildings were built. One of the centerpieces of their integrated plan,
the completion of the Geddes belt of Tel-Aviv's avenues that would bring
Rothschild Avenue to the new CBD, was killed by the spirited objections
of residents of neighborhoods such as Neve Tzedek, which the scheme
designated to be flattened. Similarly, the grand plans for the seashore
never materialized, and no artificial island was ever built to intensify the
seam between the city and the Mediterranean. The most conspicuous
feature of Manshiya is the Charles Clore Park designed by Hillel Omer
and opened to the public in 1973. The park was not a part of the original
competition but followed the guidelines of the 1954 Horowitz Master
Plan and succeeded in disguising the traces of Palestinian Manshiya.
Aside from Omer's park, little distinguishes Manshiya as anything but
a bland tract of land, except for two reminders of what was—before
1948—a lively neighborhood: the Hassan Bek mosque and the Irgun
Museum. Paradoxically, the latter inserts into a Palestinian building the
memory of the militant organization that destroyed the neighborhood
to which it belonged.[47]

Manshiya seems to be eternally "on hold." It is an urban scar that is
remarkable primarily because it refuses to succumb to the force of the
real estate market or to embody the prospect of high-rise business district
or highly priced seashore housing (see Fig. 18.19). Meanwhile, the city that
lies to the south of this tortured hyphen has lost both its intimidating

Fig. 18.20. "Occupied
Tel-Aviv," *Ha'ir*
centennial issue
(Tel-Aviv, 3 April
2009).

Palestinian identity and its authenticating biblical aura, the two con-
flicting Orientalisms that ruled the Jewish perception of Jaffa during
the 1950s. Yuppies slowly gentrified its urban fabric, preferring to incorporate Jaffa into their global Tel-Avivness as an enriching twist of
Oriental charm, rather than hyphenating with its people, history, and
built heritage.[48]

Tel-Aviv's centennial in 2009 provided an opportunity for soul-
searching reflection on the city and the wishful State of Tel-Aviv. According to the cover story of the centennial issue of *Ha'ir,* the local newspaper that invented much of Tel-Aviv's metropolitan legacy, as well as
its quest for independence, Tel-Aviv has painfully missed its window of
opportunity. The image of a tank overtaking Ibn Gvirol Avenue covers
the front page, while the image of soldiers dragging the city's corpse is
featured inside. A repeated logo of a red tank emphasizes the salient message: the State of Israel has occupied the State of Tel-Aviv (see Fig. 18.20).
The latter, "if there was ever such a thing, has passed away. It succumbed
to the rudeness and boorishness of the State of Israel."[49] Apparently, even
if the hyphen with Jaffa has been divested in the new millennium of its
intimidating Orientalism, the one Tel-Aviv shares with Jerusalem is not
as loose as "occupied" Tel-Aviv would like.

* * *

The analysis of urban unification—which I see as a spatial metaphor
for Israel's nation-building project—reveals the entanglement of political and architectural processes. The straightforward modernism of the
"new architecture" created for Tel-Aviv a progressive image separated

from, and contradictory to, Orientalist Jaffa. This image of modernity incarnated helped to distance Tel-Aviv from the hybrid zone of the territorial hyphen between itself and its culturally rich counterpart to the south. After 1948, Jaffa's hitherto negated Oriental urbanism was suddenly appealing because it perfectly fit the biblical imagination that was nurtured in nascent Israel. Apart from the financial and social aspects, the unification of Jaffa and Tel-Aviv symbolized the larger unification of the progressive Israeli state with the historical Jewish nation. At the time, the best way to tighten the space around this municipal/national hyphen was found in the concept of "urban renewal": the devastated buildings and social hybridity of Manshiya were to be razed, clearing space for a mega-structural urban hyphen tying the two places together.

In 1967, when the task of bulldozing Manshiya was almost completed, the focus on hyphenated urbanity as the embodiment of the hyphenated nation-state was transferred elsewhere. In June of that year the modernist capital town of West Jerusalem could finally hyphenate itself with the holy sites of East Jerusalem—"the foundational rock of our existence," as Benjamin Netanyahu would put it. The modernity of Israeli Jerusalem was suddenly considered an obstacle to the unity of the two Jerusalems. The mega-structure that Moshe Safdie suggested for Mamilla—the location of the urban hyphen linking East and West Jerusalem—had to be tapered down and re-Orientalized in order to fit the call.

Mamilla is currently at its final stages of construction, while Manshiya is mostly a green urban scar. The semi-emptiness of Manshiya stands for the process of severing the hyphen between nation and state. Tel-Aviv is now trying to resign from the laborious job of tightening the connection between its modernity and the antiquity of Jerusalem. The symbolic occupation of Tel-Aviv by Israel, the "scoop" of *Ha'ir* for the city's centennial, may serve as a reminder of the affinity between the two hyphens, urban and national, and its major cost—the occupation from which Tel-Aviv cannot escape.

## NOTES

1. I use the English name of the city Jaffa, unless I mention the official Hebrew name of the unified city—Tel-Aviv-Yafo (transliterated). The name "A City with a Hyphen in its Heart" appeared in an excellent documentary by Anat Zeltzer, Modi Bar-On, and Gabriel Bibliowicz; see: http://www.haaretz.com/hasen/spages/1087258. html (accessed: 20 August 2009).

2. A number of recent publications on Tel-Aviv–Yafo informed this study. For the emergence of Tel-Aviv–Yafo see Mark LeVine, *Overthrowing Geography, Re-Imagining Identities: A History of Jaffa and Tel-Aviv, 1880 to the Present (Israel, Palestine)* (Berkeley, 2005). For architectural studies of the seashore, see Yael Moria-Klein and Sigal Barnir, eds., *Back to the Sea*, Israeli Pavilion, 9th Architecture Biennale, Venice (Tel-Aviv, 2004). Recent Hebrew publications include Nathan Marom, *City of Concept: Planning Tel-Aviv* (Tel-Aviv, 2009); Maoz Azaryahu, "Cultural Historical Outline of the Tel-Aviv Seafront 1918–1948," *Horizons in Geography* 51 (2001): 95–112; Baruch A. Kipnis, ed., *Tel-Aviv Yafo: From a Garden Suburb to a World City, The First One Hundred Years* (Haifa, 2009); Haim Lusky, ed., *City and Utopia* (Tel-Aviv, 1989). For an ethnography of relations with Jaffa, see Daniel Monterescu, "The Symbolic History of the Hyphen: Urban Alterity between Jaffa and Tel-Aviv," *Zmanim* 106 (2009) [Hebrew].

3. Yaacov Shavit and Gideon Biger, *The History of Tel-Aviv*, vol. 2 (Tel-Aviv, 2007) [Hebrew].

4. For Ben-Gurion, the Bible, and Israeli identity, see Anita Shapira, *The Bible and Israeli Identity* (Jerusalem, 2005) [Hebrew]; Ze'ev Zahor, "Ben-Gurion's Mythopoetics," in *The Shaping of Israeli Identity: Myth, Memory, and Trauma*, ed. Robert S. Wistrich and David Ohana (London and Portland, 1995), 61–84.

5. Mitchell Cohen, *Zion and State: Nation, Class, and the Shaping of Modern Israel* (Oxford, New York, 1987).

6. On tradition as a modernist resource, see Nezar AlSayyad, *Consuming Tradition, Manufacturing Heritage: Global Norms and Urban Forms* (New York, 2000); Néstor García Canclini, *Hybrid Cultures: Strategies for Entering and Leaving Modernity* (Minneapolis, 2005).

7. Notes on the declaration and the preservation campaign: Alona Nitzan-Shiftan, "Whitened Houses," *Theory and Criticism* 16 (2000); Sharon Rotbard, *White City, Black City* (Tel-Aviv, 2005) [both in Hebrew].

8. Gilbert Herbert, "On the Fringes of the International Style," *Architecture SA,* September–October (1987): 36–43. Jeannine Fiedler, *Social Utopias of the Twenties: Bauhaus, Kibbutz, and the Dream of the New Man* (Wuppertal, 1995).

9. For the triple negation of the Zionist project see Alona Nitzan-Shiftan, "Contested Zionism—Alternative Modernism: Erich Mendelsohn and the Tel-Aviv Chug in Mandate Palestine," *Architectural History* 39 (1996), 147–180. Most national regimes rejected modern architecture as national expression in the interwar period. Exceptions can be found in regimes that based their ideology on projects of negation of the immediate past as explained below. See, for example, processes similar to the Zionist case in Kamalist Turkey, Sibel Bozdoğan, *Modernism and Nation-Building: Turkish Architectural Culture in the Early Republic* (Seattle, WA, 2001).

10. Julius Posener, "One Family Houses in Palestine," *Habinyan* 2 (Tel-Aviv, November 1937), 1–3 [Hebrew].

11. Julius Posener, "Villages in Palestine," *Habinyan* 3 (Tel-Aviv, 1938): 1–2. Posener disqualified the Palestinian vernacular, but admits into the canon Islamic architecture from far less intimidating geographies. See Nitzan-Shiftan, "Contested Zionism—Alternative Modernism."

12. Mayor Rokach to the colonial deputy of the Jaffa Region Governor, Tel-Aviv Historical Archives (TAHA), 4-4126, 24.09.1944, cited in Nathan Marom, *City of Concept: Planning Tel-Aviv* (Tel-Aviv, 2009), 121, emphasis in the original.

13. Tom Segev, *Ha'aretz,* 13 March 2009.

14. See Uri Ram, "Sociology: Between Essentialism and Invention," in *The Time of the 'Post': Nationalism and the Politics of Knowledge in Israel* (Tel-Aviv, 2006), 19–71 [Hebrew]; Neil Asher Silberman, *Between Past and Present: Archaeology, Ideology, and Nationalism in the Modern Middle East* (New York, 1989); Nadia Abu El-Haj, *Facts on the Ground: Archaeological Practice and Territorial Self-Fashioning in Israeli Society* (Chicago, 2001); Michael Feige and Zvi Shilony, eds., *Archeology, Religion and Nationalism in Israel* (Sde-Boker, 2008) [Hebrew].

15. Cited in Daniel Monterescu, "The Symbolic History of the Hyphen: Urban Alterity between Jaffa and Tel-Aviv," *Zmanim* 106 (2009): 81.

16. Ibid.

17. Ibid., 81–82.

18. Elsewhere I have examined the response of the architectural discipline to this challenge, and its attempt to invest émigré modernism with local identity inspired by the trends of "regionalism" and "brutalism." See Alona Nitzan-Shiftan, "Seizing Locality in Jerusalem," in *The End of Tradition,* ed. Nezar AlSayyad (London and New York, 2004), 231–255.

19. Tel-Aviv Municipality (TAM), *Year Book, 1963* (Tel-Aviv) [Hebrew].

20. TAM *Year Book, 1962* (Tel-Aviv) [Hebrew].

21. Namir cited in TAM *Year Book, 1962,* 259.

22. Ibid.

23. According to Niv (correspondence 2009), L. Mizraki was part of this partnership for a short period.

24. At first the TAM rejected the unification because of the extra municipal burden of servicing devastated areas. However, Mayor Namir, a Labor representative, was aligned with the government's policy and appreciated the economic benefit of developing cleared municipal areas.

25. See Jane Jacobs, *The Death and Life of Great American Cities* (New York, 1961); Sibyl Moholy-Nagy, *Matrix of Man: an Illustrated History of Urban Environment* (New York, 1968); *Native Genius in Anonymous Architecture* (New York, 1957); Hilary Ballon and Kenneth Jackson, eds., *Robert Moses and the Modern City: The Transformation of New York* (New York, 2007).

26. Alison Smithson, ed., *Team X Primer* (Cambridge, MA, 1968).

27. TAHA, Judges report, 2.09.1963, 4-6044-2687, 10.

28. Ibid., 9.

29. Ibid., 8.

30. TAHA, 4-6043-2684.

31. *Ma'ariv,* 4-6043-2684.

32. Ibid.

33. Reyner Banham, *The New Brutalism: Ethic or Aesthetic? Documents of Modern Architecture* (London, 1966).

34. Monterescu, "The Symbolic History of the Hyphen," 81.

35. The debate over the making of a "united Jerusalem" unraveled the tensions between two schools of modernism. The 1968 master plan for Jerusalem advocated a modern capital city serving its citizens. The Jerusalem Committee and its world-leading architects wanted to beautify Jerusalem in order to highlight its uniqueness. For the debate see Alona Nitzan-Shiftan, "Modernisms in Conflict: Architecture and

Cultural Politics in Post-1967 Jerusalem," in *Modernism and the Middle East: Architecture and Politics in the Twentieth Century,* ed. Sandy Isenstadt and Kishwar Rizvi (Seattle, London, 2008), 161–186.

36. Alona Nitzan-Shiftan, "Israelizing Jerusalem: The Encounter between Architectural and National Ideologies 1967–1977" (PhD diss., MIT, 2002), and forthcoming book.

37. See David Kroyanker, *Mamilla: Prosperity, Decay, and Renewal* (Jerusalem, 2009) [Hebrew].

38. On Mamilla in the context of post-1967 Jerusalem, see Alona Nitzan-Shiftan, "'United Jerusalem': A Testing Ground for the Discipline of Urban Design," in preparation.

39. Menachem Klein, "Jerusalem as an Israeli Problem," in *Mr. Prime Minister: Jerusalem-Problems and Solutions,* ed. Moshe Amirav (Jerusalem, 2005), 75 [Hebrew]; Menachem Klein, *Jerusalem: The Contested City* (London, 2001).

40. Dan Miron, *If There Is No Jerusalem: Essays on Hebrew Writing in A Cultural-Political Context* (Tel-Aviv, 1987), 234 [Hebrew].

41. Leaders from the Left and Right endorsed the style, but promoted it differently. For Shimon Peres, for example, who was the foreign affairs minister in the Labor government at the time of the 1994 celebrations, the style was the heritage of the Labor Zionism that founded the state. His opening speech at the 1994 conference is partially quoted in Daniel Monk, "Autonomy Agreements: Zionism, Modernism, and The Myth of a 'Bauhaus' Vernacular," in *AA Files* 28, (1994): 94–99. Roni Milo, Tel-Aviv's right-wing mayor, found in the International Style architectural heritage a foundation for tourism and a springboard for future economic development of a city with a strong tradition. See Milo's introduction to the celebrations of "Bauhaus in Tel-Aviv" in the accompanying brochure.

42. http://whc.unesco.org/en/list/1096 (accessed 12 September 2009).

43. Maoz Azaryahu, *Tel-Aviv—The Real City* (Sde-Boker, 2005), 143–192 [Hebrew].

44. Itamar Ben Can'an, "The State Walked Out on Me," *Ha'ir,* Centennial, 3 April 2009, 62 [Hebrew]. Can'an is the editor for cultural affairs of this influential local newspaper.

45. Uri Ram, *Jerusalem: The View From Tel-Aviv.* http://web.mit.edu/cis/jerusalem2050/Paper_Ram.pdf; Arnon Soffer and Evgenia Bystrov, *Tel-Aviv State: A Threat to Israel* (Haifa, 2006).

46. On the objections of Horwitz, Ben-Sira, Hashimshoni, and others see Marom, *City of Concept,* 311–318.

47. Tali Hatuka, *Revisionist Moments: Political Violence, Architecture, and Urban Space in Tel-Aviv* (Tel-Aviv, 2008), 89–152. [Hebrew], Zvi Elhyani, "Seafront Holdings," in *Back to the Sea,* ed. Yael Moria-Klain and Sigal Barnir, Israeli Pavilion, Ninth Architecture Biennale, Venice (Tel-Aviv, 2004), 104–116.

48. For the history and forms of Orientalizing Jaffa, see Monterescu, "The Symbolic History of the Hyphen"; Daniel Monterescu and Roy Fabian, "'The Golden Cage': On Gentrification and Globalization in the Luxurious Andromeda Gated Community in Jaffa," *Theory and Criticism* 23 (2003): 141–178 [Hebrew].

49. Ben Can'an, "The State Walked Out on Me."

# Afterword: Tel-Aviv between Province and Metropolis

## Maoz Azaryahu

> Be a tail to the lions rather than head to the foxes.
> —*Pirkei Avot 4:15*

Writing about Tel-Aviv in 1932, Poet Natan Alterman observed that

> Despite all indications, Tel-Aviv is not provincial; it is not provincial in the common meaning of the term. Tel-Aviv has many signs of provincialism—true indeed! Tel-Aviv is small—true indeed! But noise, multitudes, and great deeds do not make a town a metropolis ... Tel-Aviv is far from the "foci mundi" ... and nevertheless, it is a center, a double center, to the country, and especially to the people.[1]

The relationships between the city and the Israeli province on the one hand and specific world-renowned metropolitan centers such as Paris and New York on the other have figured prominently in the public discourse and cultural constitution of Tel-Aviv as an aspiring metropolis. The underlying issue was the dissonance between the apparent provincialism of the city and the persistent quest to become and be recognized as a city of distinction and fame.

In an essay in 1979, literary critic Yoram Bronovsky commented:

> Indeed, Alterman succeeded in capturing the uniqueness of Tel-Aviv in regard to the issue of the relations between center and province. Also today Tel-Aviv is not a provincial city even though it has "many signs of provincialism." ... However, it has the power and essence of the center.[2]

According to Bronovsky, it is not the measure of the city that determines whether it is a center. Athens is a large, yet rather provincial European city; Istanbul, despite her cosmopolitan tradition, has a provincial scent. In his judgment, "Tel-Aviv preserves a measure of agitation, of energy, which is characteristic of only a small number of cities in the world that are true foci of the center and according to them all other cities are defined as provincial."

Throughout its history, striving to make Tel-Aviv a great metropolis and addressing its provincialism commingled. The issue is one of scale. On a local (or Israeli) scale, the city qualified as a center, and from a Tel-Avivian perspective, the rest of the country, including Jerusalem, was considered periphery and deemed provincial. On a global scale, as commentators and local patriots were well aware, Tel-Aviv was on the margin when compared with the great metropolises such as Paris, London, or New York. These two scales converged in the local discourse of Tel-Aviv, evident in the ambiguity produced by the conflation of a sense of superiority and awareness of inferiority.

This essay expands on notions of what Yoram Bronovsky called "The uniqueness of Tel-Aviv in regard to the issue of the relations between center and province" that contributed to the cultural constitution of Tel-Aviv as an aspiring metropolis in successive phases of the city's history. Embedded into the city's official ideology and articulated in the terms and patterns of popular culture, such notions were formulated in metaphorical terms highlighting certain differences and hierarchies. Of special significance for this analysis is the issue of distinction, evident in attempts to make Tel-Aviv distinctive *from* the local, Israeli province, and at the same time distinguish it *as* a city on a par with metropolises such as Paris or New York or *as* a city that has a legitimate claim to fame on a global scale.

This analysis is divided into four parts, each dealing with a particular phase in the cultural history of Tel-Aviv. The first focuses on the "first Hebrew city" stage, which lasted from its foundation through the 1950s, when the notion of Tel-Aviv as a unique Zionist creation reigned supreme. The second part deals with the 1960s and the 1970s, when Dizengoff Street was a metonym of Tel-Aviv as a large and modern city. The third is devoted to the 1980s and the 1990s, when the celebration of Tel-Aviv as a "city that never sleeps" represented the hype around the notion of the city as a vibrant cosmopolis on a par with New York. The fourth addresses the "White City" as a contemporary expression of Tel-Aviv's distinction as formulated in terms of architectural heritage.

## Phase I: The First Hebrew City

Celebrating Tel-Aviv as the first Hebrew city cast its essence in the mold of her unique position within Jewish national revival. For Meir Dizengoff, the first mayor and an ardent promoter of the city, Tel-Aviv was "the seventh wonder of the world."[3] The praises poured on the city expressed a tremendous sense of pride over the achievement of building a new Jewish city. There were those who even maintained that Tel-Aviv was "a model and paragon, which the rest of the cities in the world should observe and emulate."[4]

Evaluation of the three urban centers of Jewish Palestine—Jerusalem, Tel-Aviv, and Haifa—belonged to the Zionist discourse of national revival. The comparative evaluation highlighted a notion of hierarchy and a symbolic rivalry over supremacy. In regard to Tel-Aviv it was said about Dizengoff that "[h]e did not care at all whether there are cities other than Tel-Aviv in the Land of Israel."[5] Dizengoff was committed to making Tel-Aviv "the center of the National Home."[6]

According to cliché, "Jerusalem is the city of the past, Haifa is the city of the future, and Tel-Aviv is the city of the present."[7] In 1924 Menachem Ussishkin, the president of the Jewish National Fund, noted that the advantage of Tel-Aviv was that she was "the most modern town" in the Land of Israel.[8] Ten years later he positioned the three cities in the "hierarchy of sentiment." In this hierarchy, Jerusalem occupied the first place, "And in this respect was beyond competition."[9] Tel-Aviv was in second place, since she was "a hundred percent Hebrew city." Haifa was in the third place.

As formulated by Ussishkin, the "hierarchy of sentiment" expressed the ideological commitment of a prominent Zionist leader. In 1933 poet Natan Alterman offered a different perspective. In his assessment Haifa, the city of heavy industry, would be the "crown" and would serve as "an older sister to the villages of the country and be a respected neighbor to the cities of the world."[10] In his prognosis, Tel-Aviv would keep a distance between itself and the rest of the country. He projected that the centrality of Tel-Aviv would not be articulated in the domain of economics and that it would not partake of "manual work." The city would rather play a major role in the country's "spiritual negotiation" with the world. Tel-Aviv would be a "capital of entertainment" for the country.

Poet Hava Pinhas-Cohen wrote, "The tension between Jerusalem and Tel-Aviv as symbolic entities . . . is the inner tension at the heart of Zionism. This is the dialectic of modern Jewish existence in the Land of Israel."[11] In the Zionist discourse of the period the two cities came to be associated with and representative of rival Zionist visions of national redemption. The tension was between the promise of a new beginning offered by Tel-Aviv and the insistence on historical continuity and commitment to Jewish tradition connected with Jerusalem. As poet Yehuda Karni observed in 1929, "The veteran patriots of our city say: Tel-Aviv will be our New Jerusalem."[12]

The image of Tel-Aviv as the cultural center of the Yishuv was reflected in the self-image of those residing in other Jewish settlements who saw themselves as provincial. In 1939 an essayist compared the residents of Tel-Aviv with those of Haifa.[13] According to his observation, the people of Haifa were "provincial, less vigilant and modern, simpler and slower, less ornately dressed and walking more confidently." The people of Tel-Aviv were "sociable and accessible, enthusiastic and carried away by capricious public opinion and its ever-changing heroes, its popular cafés and issues on the agenda." The people of Haifa, in contrast, were "humdrum and tedious, narrow-minded and lacking in social graces." Tel-Avivians had a reputation of being "arrogant."[14] In retrospect, poet David Avidan, who grew up in Tel-Aviv, wrote that "[t]he first Hebrew city endowed her natives with a sense of nobility."[15] He also maintained that the word "Tel-Avivian" "[a]lways had a special resonance, often negative and resentful."

In the eyes of its admirers, Tel-Aviv was "the seventh wonder of the world."[16] As "a gracious creation of the Zionist spirit,"[17] Tel-Aviv was unique, and in this capacity warranted special care and devotion. The distinction of Tel-Aviv, the sense that it was "unique,"[18] was related to her eminence as the "first Hebrew city" that arose from the sand dunes and in a short time became a large, modern city. In Dizengoff's vision, Tel-Aviv was destined to be "the center of the Mediterranean, one of the metropolitan cities of the world—Paris, London, New York, Tel-Aviv."[19]

Dizengoff believed in the power of a vision to shape reality, and his confidence in the future of "his" city was almost boundless. However, the notion that Tel-Aviv would become a world city like Paris, London, and New York was revealing. The analogy to big and famous cities, most prominently Paris, was a recurrent motif in the public discourse of the city.

The claim that Tel-Aviv was "a miniature Paris" expressed a sense of pride in the modern character of Tel-Aviv. Yet the association of Tel-Aviv with Paris also articulated a yearning to invest Tel-Aviv with the reputed greatness of the world-renowned metropolis. In 1932 journalist Uri Keisari observed that "There are people who believe that Tel-Aviv is Paris. No more and no less: Paris."[20] According to a report from 1934, when Tel-Aviv celebrated her silver jubilee, "Tel-Aviv is now a small Paris, and perhaps even more beautiful than Paris."[21]

Concurrently, the notion of Tel-Aviv as a city on par with Paris was indicative of provincialism, of an acute awareness of inferiority expressed in the striving to copy the prestigious model. Notably, not everyone shared this perspective. On the occasion of Tel-Aviv's silver jubilee in 1934, an editorial in the Labor-oriented newspaper *Davar* mocked the "ridiculous provincial snobbism evident in how people dress, in their habits, in restaurants, in coffee shops, in shops which are 'just like in Berlin,' 'just like in Paris'."[22] Uri Keisari, who ironically referred to the fact that some people considered Tel-Aviv on par with Paris, held the view that "She has something of her own. She is original. She is not a copy at all. The city is like a woman—herself and nothing more."[23]

### Phase II: Dizengoff Street

On the occasion of Tel-Aviv's golden jubilee in 1959 a commentator asserted that "There is nothing parochial or provincial about Tel-Aviv." He further claimed that Tel-Aviv had become a "cosmopolitan city."[24] When Tel-Aviv celebrated her golden jubilee in 1959 the vision of the Hebrew city had already become everyday reality. Its hegemonic position in Israeli culture was uncontested. At a stage where the mythic aura of the Zionist vision of the Hebrew city was waning and the ideological fervor that had accompanied its development was rapidly declining, the distinction of Tel-Aviv was not measured in terms of the realization of a Zionist vision but in terms of her characterization as the cultural center of national life and as a modern city connected to the "wide" world.

At this stage of its cultural history, the role of Tel-Aviv as an interface between the center—namely, the metropolitan centers of the West—and the periphery, namely, the rest of Israel, was manifested in the metaphors applied to characterize Dizengoff Street. In the 1950s Dizengoff Street became not only Tel-Aviv's central thoroughfare but also Israel's undisputed main street. The locale of Tel-Aviv's bohemia and the city's main commercial street, Dizengoff Street was identified with urban sophistication expressed in modern shops and leisure establishments. The combination of fancy shop windows and famous cafés infused Dizengoff Street with glamour and fame. Dizengoff Street was a major contribution to the reputation of Tel-Aviv as a dynamic and effervescent city.

In the local imagination, Dizengoff Street was perceived as the local extension of the big world. The street was referred to as "Fifth Avenue," "Tel-Aviv's Broadway," and "West End." "Fifth Avenue" alluded to the sophisticated shops that offered imported merchandise. "Broadway" and "West End" alluded to New York and London, respectively. These analogies underscored the leisure opportunities offered by theaters and coffee shops. Notably, these analogies also reflected the notion that the center consisted of New York and London.

These metaphoric references evinced a cultural reorientation. In the 1920s and the 1930s the city of reference was Paris. In the 1950s New York and London also became models for emulation. In what may be interpreted as an insinuation to Paris, journalist Shimon Samet defined Dizengoff Street as "the street of light."[25] Yet the popularity of "Broadway" and "Fifth Avenue" as analogies signified that from the perspective of Tel-Aviv, the center moved elsewhere.

As a prestigious shopping, leisure, and entertainment center, Dizengoff Street was unique in the cultural geography of Israel. Journalist Natan Dunewitz observed that "Dizengoff Street was more elegant than the peripheral neighborhoods."[26] Shimon Samet noted that "Residents of the province define it as a street that never sleeps."[27] Dizengoff Street represented the quest to be associated with the wide world by means of emulation and importation of patterns of popular culture. It was the place where new fashion was introduced into the Israeli scene. The trendy street was emblematic of the yearning to be in line with the centers of fashion abroad. Dizengoff Street, "Tel-Aviv's stately showcase," was also "a small window unto affluence and the wide world."[28] According to this framework of interpretation, Dizengoff Street concretized Ussishkin's notion from 1924 of Tel-Aviv as "a window onto Europe."

At the height of its fame Dizengoff Street served as an interface between the global center and the Israeli province. This position made clear the superiority of Tel-Aviv in relation to the rest of Israel, but also the peripheral position of the city in relation to the world cities that figured so prominently in the local imagination. As the ultimate link between "abroad" and a still-provincial Israel, importing the latest fashions and contemporary trends, Dizengoff Street always lagged behind London, Paris, or New York. Yet the main issue was of course that the rest of Israel lagged behind Dizengoff Street.

The awareness that Tel-Aviv belonged to a minor league of cities was expressed in the question posed by a journalist in 1972: "What could Tel-Aviv offer the denizens of the wide world? In what could it compete with the great metropolises of the world?"[29] The answer given was that what Tel-Aviv had to offer was effervescent nightlife, "something small, limited, but certainly original." In a situation where prestige was measured in comparison to the "great metropolises," originality and the distinction associated with it was held as an ideal. However, since in the case of Tel-Aviv originality did not translate into terms of reciprocal influence on the large metropolises, this alleged distinction actually represented awareness of the fact that the center of gravity was somewhere else, that Tel-Aviv was but a satellite in a larger configuration.

## Phase III: The City That Never Sleeps

In 1983 poet David Avidan had a different, much more laudatory assessment of Tel-Aviv's nightlife: "[Tel-Aviv] is the only city in the country that can be considered an equal member in the exclusive club of the best cities of the world, a small tiger, but a real tiger."[30] Notably, Tel-Aviv's nightlife distinguished the city as the unequivocal center in the local, Israeli framework—and also secured the city "membership" in a prestigious club of cities famed for their vibrant nightlife.

The 1980s and the 1990s witnessed a substantial upgrading of the position of Tel-Aviv as a center in the Israeli context and as an aspiring center in the periphery of the global context. This upgrading was associated with the notion of a "new Tel-Avivness," which was defined in terms of a unique urban experience. In 1989 the city was officially branded a "city that never sleeps." The popularity of this slogan reflected the aspiration to mold Tel-Aviv's image as a dynamic and effervescent city with characteristics of a world city.

The "new Tel-Avivness,"[31] according to poet David Avidan, emphasized awareness of "the centrality of Tel-Aviv in Israeli life" and in particular, in the nightlife opportunities the city had to offer. Common knowledge had it that "Tel-Aviv was the only city in Israel."[32]

Fueled by the energy of immigrants from the periphery coming to Tel-Aviv to realize the fantasy of the big city, Tel-Aviv offered opportunities that the provinces could not provide. Avidan noted that Tel-Avivness represented "awareness about the essential difference between Tel-Aviv and the rest of Israel and adherence to this difference . . ."[33] This awareness was evident in condescending attitudes toward the periphery, which virtually included everything that was not Tel-Aviv "proper." From a Tel-Avivian perspective, the residents of the periphery were "primitives representative of bad taste and ignorance. . . ."[34]

In the 1980s the symbolic rivalry between Tel-Aviv and Jerusalem was rekindled. At this stage, the rivalry and the characterization of the two cities in terms of a stark contrast was based on the assumption that the two cities represented two mutually exclusive options for representing Israel's cultural identity. From the perspective of Tel-Aviv's proponents, Tel-Aviv stood for an enlightened, liberal Israel, while Jerusalem represented a backward and fanatic Israel. In this context, Jerusalem was considered "the antithesis of the metropolis of the coastal plain . . . a disturbed, retarded place that is culturally out, the place of the obscure and unenlightened. . . ."[35]

The contempt toward Jerusalem reflected fear of a rival center. The comparison with world cities and the hierarchy of prestige positioned Tel-Aviv in the periphery of the big world. In 1985 journalist Doron Rosenblum wrote ironically about Tel-Aviv as a "Manhattanite, Parisian city."[36] The reference to Paris notwithstanding, in the 1980s New York represented the ultimate city of reference and a model to emulate: "New York is such a desired model."[37]

For the "new Tel-Avivians" Tel-Aviv was the local New York: "When I was young Tel-Aviv seemed to be like New York . . . But I grew up and realized that Tel-Aviv is New York."[38] The yearning for New York reflected an aspiration to belong to and be part of the big world. Journalist Ron Meiberg, a prominent marketer of American popular culture in his journalistic writing, admitted, "We all walk in Tel-Aviv and feel at heart that it is too small for us, that our natural place is in New York, London or Paris."[39] The feeling that real life takes place elsewhere is what motivates and constitutes the provincial predicament. The attempt to assimilate to the culture of the center is one kind of a response. Another is the attempt to mold the periphery in the likeness of the center.

The conscious attempt to mold Tel-Aviv in the likeness of New York was clearly evident in the "rebirth" of Sheinkin Street as the new bohemian center of Tel-Aviv in the 1980s. The popular notion of Sheinkin Street as a local version of Greenwich Village or Soho was associated with the attempt to bolster the image of Tel-Aviv as a city on par with New York or London. Dani Dothan, a cultural entrepreneur, later explained that his intention was to found in Sheinkin Street "a place of art galleries and cafés, of encounter and artistic fermentation, according to the Village model."[40] Journalist Yair Lapid explained, "Sheinkin consciously mimics similar streets in the world: The Greenwich Village in New York, Chelsea in London, the Latin Quarter in Paris."[41]

The association of Tel-Aviv with New York was expressed in the different nicknames given to Tel-Aviv. In an effort to liken Tel-Aviv to New York, Tel-Aviv was nicknamed the "Little Apple," namely, a smaller version of the Big Apple; Sheinkin Street, the local version of Greenwich Village, was nicknamed the "Tiny Apple."[42] According to journalist Thomas O'Dwyer, writing in *The Jerusalem Post,* the nickname the "Big Orange" was a pathetic expression that was reflective of provincial vanity.[43] The 1992 edition of the *Lonely Planet* tourist guide commented that "Unfortunately, the inhabitants of Tel-Aviv have a habit of comparing their city to New York: some call it even the Big Orange. . . ."[44] The relationship between Tel-Aviv and New York is the one-sided relationship between a cultural center and a periphery that considers the center as a model for emulation. The act of mimicking the center intends to fill the gap between the center and the periphery by "annexing" the periphery to the center. However, by necessity emulation and mimicking tend to emphasize the superiority of the center as the measure of what is culturally ideal.

## Phase IV: The White City

Besides the desire to imitate world cities, a thirst for recognition based on the belief that Tel-Aviv was unique prevailed. On the occasion of Tel-Aviv's golden jubilee in 1959 a commentator projected that "[Tel-Aviv] will serve as a magnet to visitors from abroad, for the history of Tel-Aviv and its development is very nearly unique—and certainly of far more than merely local concern."[45] In line with conventional rhetoric of an earlier period in the city's history, the argument was that as the first Hebrew city, Tel-Aviv was a unique phenomenon. However, when in the 1990s Tel-Aviv's claim to global fame re-emerged, it was in connection with the celebration of Tel-Aviv's International Style architecture of the 1930s and the 1940s, also known locally as Bauhaus, as a world-scale phenomenon.

Mostly designed by architects who had been trained in Europe, the Bauhaus buildings represented the architecture of the Modern Movement in Tel-Aviv. According to architectural historian Michael Levin

> From the perspective of sixty years, it is only recently that we have discovered that this often ridiculed Tel-Aviv . . . wrote an important chapter of early modern architecture of the twentieth century . . . : the phenomenon of an entire city in a distinguished style . . . was unique.[46]

Initially the concern of a small cultural elite, the notion that Tel-Aviv's International Style architecture could bolster the city's standing as a city of world fame and encourage tourism was recognized only later by the municipality. In 1994, an international conference titled *Bauhaus in Tel-Aviv* was held under the auspices of the Tel-Aviv Municipality and UNESCO. Publicist Doron Rosenblum noted with irony that Tel-Aviv was crowned the "world capital of Bauhaus."[47] The recognition of Tel-Aviv's architectural distinction by world-famous architects lent the city international prestige. In July 2003 this notion culminated in UNESCO announcing the listing of Tel-Aviv, or more precisely, "The White City of Tel-Aviv," as a World Heritage Site. From a Tel-Avivian perspective, UNESCO's acknowledgment of Tel-Aviv as a city of architectural distinction fulfilled a long standing desire to be recognized as a member of the prestigious club of world-famed cities.

On 7 June 2004 Tel-Aviv celebrated the first anniversary of its listing as a World Heritage Site in a plethora of public events. Notably, in an "invitation" letter sent to the citizens, Mayor Ron Huldai encouraged Tel-Avivians to attend the festive events sponsored by the municipality. The text praised the White City as having a "historical and unique urban texture." Notably, the mayor asserted that "With this the world has recognized the architectural and urban qualities of Tel-Aviv, including its buildings, boulevards and squares." The title of the public announcement made by the municipality in the Hebrew newspapers left no room for doubt about what the issue was about, "The Tel-Avivians raise their heads up . . . and now the whole world knows why!"

The reference to the world's recognition of the architectural distinction of Tel-Aviv made clear that the White City meant distinction and prestige on a world scale, at least for those interested in the history of modernist architecture as represented in the city's built landscape. The White City made Tel-Aviv an officially recognized member of a prestigious global club of architecturally distinguished cities. The White City invested Tel-Aviv with the prestige of the center.

* * *

The protagonist of a play about the early history of Tel-Aviv observed that "Tel-Aviv will never be a really big city. In Tel-Aviv they will always talk about the day when the city will become a really big city."[48] These lines seem to capture the "Tel-Aviv predicament," namely, the notion that being "a head to the foxes" was something to aspire to, and being "a tail to the lions" was not enough.

As a center in the periphery, Tel-Aviv unfolds between two extremes. On the one hand Tel-Aviv carries a sense of superiority based on the notion of the city as a cultural center that offers an alternative to Jerusalem and represents an extension of the civilized world in the local, Israeli province. In this dimension of its existence, Tel-Aviv was likened to Paris in the 1930s and described as a "giant, Manhattanite, Parisian city" in the 1980s.[49] On the other hand Tel-Aviv also carried a sense of inferiority based on an acute awareness that the city was on the cultural fringe of the wide world, that its existence on the periphery meant subordination to the center, where the really important things happened. In this dimension of its existence Tel-Aviv was depicted as "a tiny coastal town, in the grip of terror and plagued by heat waves, an ugly fishing village that forces its residents to dream: about some other place, another climate, different neighbors."[50] These opposing characterizations represented two complementary strategies to come to terms with Tel-Aviv as a place on the margin of the wider world.

In 1979 Yoram Bronovsky noted that ". . . Tel-Aviv is not a provincial city even though it has 'many signs of provincialism'."[51] Among the most persistent signs of provincialism was the notion that Tel-Aviv was or should be on par with world-renowned metropolises. This notion has pervaded the imagination of commentators, cultural entrepreneurs, and city officials. The cities of reference were the great European metropolises or, alternatively, New York. In the 1920s and the 1930s Paris was a source of inspiration. In the 1960s and the 1980s the cities of reference and deference were London and New York, respectively. Currently the message is "Forget Paris. We want to be like Berlin."[52] The cities of reference may change, but as Tel-Aviv enters the second century of its existence, the fascination with world-renowned metropolises and the desire "to be like" other cities of fame and distinction persist. It is an unavoidable paradox of provincialism that the conscious attempt to rise above provincialism is itself a powerful indication of provincialism.

## NOTES

All references are in Hebrew.

1. Natan Alterman, "Pictures—Hollywood and a City," *Ha'aretz,* 16 November 1932. Reprinted in Natan Alterman, *Little Tel-Aviv* (Tel-Aviv, 1979), 19.

2. Yoram Bronovsky, "On the Origins of Mythos Tel-Aviv," *Ha'aretz,* 31 August 1979.

3. M. K. "Touring the Land," *Ha'olam,* 17 May 1934, 302.

4. Shlomo Gorlik, "Like All Other Cities," *Ha'aretz,* 10 June 1934.

5. Aharon Ze'ev Ben-Yishai, "Meir Dizengoff—The Father of the City," in *Tel-Aviv,* ed. Yosef Aricha (Tel-Aviv, 1959), 155.

6. Ibid., 154.

7. Meir Berlin, "In the Name of the Future," *Yediot 'Iryat Tel-Aviv,* 1934, 262.

8. Menachem Ussishkin, "On the Future of Tel-Aviv," *Ha'aretz,* 7 July 1924.

9. Menachem Ussishkin, "Jerusalem, Tel-Aviv, and Haifa," *Ha'aretz,* 14 October 1934.

10. Natan Alterman, "Cities in the World," *Turim* 1.1 (1934): 20–21.

11. Hava Pinhas-Cohen, "The Tale of Two Cities," *Makor Rishon,* 11 June 1999.

12. Yehuda Karni, "Tel-Aviv Day," *Ha'aretz,* 2 May 1929.

13. P. Azai (Pinhas Lander), "Three Cities: Haifa," *9 Ba'erev,* 28 January 1938, 4.

14. M. K. "Touring the Land."

15. David Avidan, "The Nouveaux–Tel-Avivians," *Tel-Aviv,* 25 September 1992.

16. M. K., "Touring the Land."

17. *YITA,* 1934–1936, 393.

18. Alterman, "Pictures—Hollywood and a City."

19. Ben-Yishai, "Meir Dizengoff—The Father of the City," 154–155.

20. Uri Keisari, "Why I Love Tel-Aviv," *Kolnoa,* 29 January 1932, 6.

21. M. K., "Touring the Land," 302.

22. M. D. "Tel-Aviv's Silver Jubilee," *Davar,* 2 May 1934.

23. Keisari, "Why I Love Tel-Aviv," 7.

24. Walter Eytan, talk, *English Channel of the Voice of Israel,* 12 August 1959.

25. Shimon Samet, "Dizengoff St.—Tel-Aviv's Street of Light," *Ha'aretz,* 1 July 1958.

26. Natan Dunewitz, *Tel-Aviv: From Sands to City* (Jerusalem, 1959).

27. Samet, "Dizengoff St."

28. Yigal Sarna, "The Fiery Cake Has Cooled Off," *Yediot Ahronot* weekly supplement, 15 September 2000, 66.

29. *Ha'olam Ha'ze,* 10 January 1973.

30. David Avidan, *Tel-Aviv's Nights with David Avidan* (Tel-Aviv, 1983), 27.

31. Avidan, "The Nouveaux–Tel-Avivians," 15.

32. Gabi Nizan, "The New Tel-Avivness," *Politica* 23 (1988) 37–9.

33. David Avidan, "The City is Bigger than *Ha'ir,*" *Ha'ir,* 18 July 1986, 35.

34. Tamar Ben-Yosef, letter to the editor, *Ha'ir,* 14 November 1986, 13.

35. Eli Shay, "The Man with the Baskets," *Ha'aretz, Sfarim,* 28 February 2001, 14.

36. Doron Rosenblum, "The Expanding Jurisdiction of the Local Weekly," *Koteret Rashit,* 27 November 1985, 20.

37. Tami Gross, "All the Time He Travels around Himself," *Tel-Aviv,* 29 December 1989, 18.

38. Avi Shoshan, *Sin City* (documentary film, Israel's Channel 2), 1997.

39. Ron Meiberg, "The Golden Hills of Bristol," *Tarbut Ma'ariv,* 6 February 1998.

40. Tami Gross, "All the Time He Travels around Himself," 18.

41. Yair Lapid, "In Defense of Sheinkin," *Ma'ariv* weekend supplement, 28 May 1993, 58.

42. Asher Cohen and Asefa Peled, "Till Midnight," *Tel-Aviv,* 12 August 1989, 20.

43. Thomas O'Dwyer, "Big Orange Prize Puts the Big Orange on the Literary Map," *The Jerusalem Post,* 16 June 2000.

44. Neil Tilbury, *Lonely Planet Israel: A Travel Survival Kit* (Hawthorn, Australia, 1992).

45. Walter Eytan, *English Channel of the Voice of Israel,* 12 August 1959.

46. Michael Levin, "In Praise of the White City," *Ha'ir,* 20 May 1994, 31.

47. Rosenblum, "You Will Search for Cracks (the Neo-Realism of the Bauhaus in Tel-Aviv)," *Ha'aretz* weekend supplement, 27 May 1994, 12.

48. Avidan, *Tel-Aviv's Nights with David Avidan,* 21.

49. Rosenblum, "The Expanding Jurisdiction of the Local Weekly," 20.

50. Yakir Alkariv, "Sodom," *'Iton Tel-Aviv,* 29 June 2001, 64.

51. Bronovsky, "On the Origins of Mythos Tel-Aviv."

52. Amir Bogen, "The Monarch of Tel-Aviv," *YNET,* 1 March 2006.

# CONTRIBUTORS

NURIT ALFASI is senior lecturer in the Department of Geography and Environmental Development at Ben-Gurion University of the Negev.

MAOZ AZARYAHU is associate professor of Cultural Geography at the University of Haifa.

CAROLIN ARONIS is a PhD candidate in the Department of Communications at The Hebrew University of Jerusalem.

YORAM BAR-GAL is professor of Geography at the University of Haifa.

DEBORAH S. BERNSTEIN is professor of Sociology at the University of Haifa.

AMINADAV DYKMAN is senior lecturer in the Department of Hebrew Literature at The Hebrew University of Jerusalem.

ROY FABIAN is an architect and a PhD candidate in the Department of Geography at Bar-Ilan University.

RACHEL S. HARRIS is assistant professor of Hebrew and Comparative Literature at the University of Illinois at Urbana Champaign.

ANAT HELMAN is a lecturer in the Department of Jewish History at The Hebrew University of Jerusalem.

NAHUM KARLINSKY is a senior researcher and lecturer at the Ben-Gurion Research Institute and in the Department of Jewish History at Ben-Gurion University of the Negev.

BARBARA MANN is associate professor of Jewish Literature at the Jewish Theological Seminary in New York.

DALIA MANOR is a research associate in the SOAS Department of the Languages and Cultures of Near and Middle East at the University of London.

ALONA NITZAN-SHIFTAN is a senior lecturer in the Faculty of Architecture and Town Planning at the Technion.

ORIT ROZIN lectures in the Department of Jewish History at Tel-Aviv University.

TAMMY RAZI lectures in the Department of Communications at Sapir Academic College.

HIZKY SHOHAM is a lecturer in the interdisciplinary program for hermeneutics and culture studies at Bar-Ilan University.

YAACOV SHAVIT is professor of Jewish History at Tel-Aviv University.

ZOHAR SHAVIT is professor of Culture Research at Tel-Aviv University.

S. ILAN TROEN is the Stoll Family Chair in Israel Studies and director of the Schusterman Center for Israel Studies at Brandeis University.

VOLKER M. WELTER is professor of History of Art and Architecture at the University of California, Santa Barbara.

# INDEX